ALSO BY GEOFFREY C. WARD

Treasures of the Maharajahs

Before the Trumpet: Young Franklin Roosevelt, 1882–1905

A First-Class Temperament: The Emergence of FDR

The Civil War: An Illustrated History (with Ric and Ken Burns)

American Originals: The Private Worlds of Some Singular Men and Women

*Tiger-Wallahs: Encounters with the Men Who Tried to Save
the Greatest of the Great Cats* (with Diane Raines Ward)

Baseball: An Illustrated History (with Ken Burns)

*Closest Companion: The Unknown Story of the Intimate Friendship
between Franklin Roosevelt and Margaret Suckley*

The West: An Illustrated History

The Year of the Tiger (with Michael Nichols)

*Not for Ourselves Alone: The Story of Elizabeth Cady Stanton
and Susan B. Anthony* (with Ken Burns)

Jazz: A History of America's Music (with Ken Burns)

Mark Twain (with Dayton Duncan and Ken Burns)

Unforgivable Blackness: The Rise and Fall of Jack Johnson

The War: An Intimate Portrait of America, 1941–1945 (with Ken Burns)

A

DISPOSITION
TO BE RICH

A cartoonist for *Puck* assessed the chaos Ferdinand Ward had caused on Wall Street eight days after his fraudulent brokerage collapsed; in the foreground, Ward's ruined partner, General Ulysses S. Grant, clings to a spar from the Marine National Bank, the financial institution that went down with the firm.

A
DISPOSITION
TO BE RICH

HOW A SMALL-TOWN PASTOR'S SON

RUINED AN AMERICAN PRESIDENT,

BROUGHT ON A WALL STREET CRASH, AND MADE HIMSELF

THE BEST-HATED MAN IN THE UNITED STATES

Geoffrey C. Ward

ALFRED A. KNOPF · NEW YORK · 2012

THIS IS A BORZOI BOOK
PUBLISHED BY ALFRED A. KNOPF

Library of Congress Cataloging-in-Publication Data
Ward, Geoffrey C.
A disposition to be rich : how a small-town pastor's son ruined
an American president, brought on a Wall Street crash,
and made himself the best-hated man in the United States /
by Geoffrey C. Ward.—1st ed.
p.   cm.
"This is a Borzoi book"—T.p. verso.
Includes bibliographical references.
ISBN 978-0-679-44530-2
1. Ward, Ferdinand De Wilton, 1851–1925.   2. Capitalists and
financiers—United States—Biography.   3. Swindlers and
swindling—United States—Biography.   4. Financial crises—
United States—History—19th century.   5. Ponzi schemes—
New York (State)—New York—History—19th century.   6. Grant,
Ulysses S. (Ulysses Simpson), 1822–1885—Friends and
associates.   7. Children of clergy—New York (State)—
Biography.   8. Ward, F. De W. (Ferdinand De Wilton), 1812–
1891.   9. Rochester (N.Y.)—Biography.   10. New York (N.Y.)—
Biography.   I. Title.
CT275.W2752W37 2012
974.7'03092—dc23
[B]   2011035140

Jacket image: *The Wall Street Hell-Gate* by F. Graetz from *Puck*
magazine, May 14, 1884. Courtesy of the author.
Jacket design by Carol Devine Carson

Manufactured in the United States of America
First Edition

For my grandfather, Clarence Ward,
my father, F. Champion Ward—and
for my brother, Andrew, who might have
made a better story out of this material
but was kind enough not to try

Family is what counts.

Everything else is a side-show.

—F. CHAMPION WARD

If you cannot get rid of the family skeleton,

you may as well make it dance.

—GEORGE BERNARD SHAW

CONTENTS

A

DISPOSITION
TO BE RICH

Prologue

On the afternoon of August 8, 1885, the streets of Manhattan were given over to grief. Ulysses S. Grant had died five days earlier, after an agonizing fourteen-month struggle, first against financial ruin and then against throat cancer whose every hideous detail had been reported in the newspapers. Nearly a quarter of a million people had shuffled past the ex-president's bier at City Hall. Now, his coffin was to be borne north along Broadway to a specially prepared vault in Riverside Park at 122nd Street. No event—not even the funeral procession of Abraham Lincoln along the same street a little more than twenty years earlier—had drawn such crowds to the city. The two-year-old Brooklyn Bridge was closed to vehicles that morning so that Brooklynites could pour across the East River to join their fellow mourners in Manhattan. Passengers occupied each seat and stood in every aisle aboard the trains arriving at Grand Central and Pennsylvania stations; so many extra cars had been added to accommodate them that most trains had to be hauled by two locomotives. Ferries from New Jersey and Staten Island were packed, too, and the new elevated railway brought in some 600,000 more people from the city's outer regions.

One onlooker wrote that the entire length of Broadway—shops, offices, hotels, theaters, apartment buildings—was "one sweep of black," and even the tenement dwellers crowded along the side streets hung their windows with tiny flags and strips of inky ribbon. The vast black and silver hearse was drawn by twenty-four black-draped horses, each accompanied by a black groom dressed in black, and it was followed by a glittering military escort under the command of General Winfield Scott Hancock. Sixty thousand armed men took part in the slow-moving procession, which took five hours to pass. "Broadway moved like a river into which many tributaries poured," a spectator remembered. "There was one living mass choking the thoroughfare from where the dead lay in state to the grim gates at Riverside opened to receive him."[1]

Somewhere in that living mass stood a slender, alarmingly pale man wearing smoked glasses so that no one would recognize him. The disguise was probably a good idea. Until his arrest the previous spring, Ferdinand Ward had been Grant's business partner and apparently so skilled that older financiers had hailed him as the "Young Napoleon of Finance." But now, many held him directly responsible for the late general's impoverishment—and even, indirectly, for his death. As Ward himself later wrote, with the strange blend of pride and self-pity he always displayed when alluding to his crimes, he had made himself by the age of thirty-three "the best-hated man in the United States."[2] He had no right to be on the street that day, in fact; he had bribed his way out of the Ludlow Street Jail, where he was awaiting the trial for grand larceny that would soon send him to Sing Sing. In this, as in nearly everything else in his long life, he seems simply to have assumed that rules made for others need never apply to him.

Ferdinand Ward was my great-grandfather. I can't remember when I first began to hear stories about him. Nor can I remember who first mentioned him to me. It may have been my late father, who had met his grandfather just once while still a small child, and who remembered him only dimly, as an apparently amiable, impossibly thin old man with a drooping white moustache, rocking on the front porch of a frame house on Staten Island. To a landlocked Ohio boy like my father, the ferry ride across New York Harbor from the Battery had been more memorable than the aged stranger.

Perhaps it was my grandfather, Clarence Ward, who first spoke of his father to me. Though he was brought up by maternal relatives and had spent little time in Ferdinand's company, Clarence's bright blue eyes, even in his eighties, still mirrored fear and pain at the mention of his father's name. Little wonder: Ferdinand had hired a man to kidnap my grandfather when he was just ten years old, flooded him with blackmailing letters as a young man, threatened to see to it that he lost his first job, and, finally, took him to court—all to get his hands on the small legacy left to his son by his own late wife.

In any case, by the time I was twelve or thirteen, I knew at least the outlines of Ferdinand's story: pious parents, a Presbyterian minister and his wife, both former missionaries to India; an apparently tranquil boyhood in the lovely village of Geneseo, New York; a move to New York at twenty-one, followed by marriage to a wealthy young woman from Brooklyn Heights, and a swift rise on Wall Street that culminated in the 1880 formation of the firm of Grant & Ward, to include both the former president of the United States and James D. Fish, the president of a large Wall Street financial institution, the Marine National Bank. Four years of flush times followed: summer homes, blooded horses, purebred dogs, jewels from Tiffany, European artworks, lavish generosity to family and friends, the birth of a son.

Then, disaster: the collapse of first the Marine Bank, then the firm of Grant & Ward, and panic on Wall Street—all of it blamed on Ferdinand Ward. There was Ward's arrest and that of James Fish, and later two sensational trials that demonstrated that both men had deliberately set out to defraud investors, followed by seven years in prison during which Ferdinand's wife and both his parents died. Released in 1892, he devoted most of the thirty-three years left to him to harassing the son he barely knew while continuing to hatch schemes by which one person or another was to provide him with money on which to live, funds to which he always seems to have assumed he was somehow entitled. He never changed, never apologized, never explained.

I wanted to know more. Books didn't add much. They all focused, understandably enough, on Grant's tragedy: Ferdinand Ward appeared only as a stock villain, insinuating himself onstage just long enough to ruin the ex-president and his family, then disappearing behind prison walls.

But I couldn't help wondering how he had duped so many men who, as he himself liked to say, were old enough to be his father. What accounted for what his mother once called his fatal "disposition to be rich"?[3] How could he have been perpetually unrepentant, uninterested in anyone's troubles but his own, persuaded always that he, and not any of those whose money he misappropriated, was the aggrieved party?

My grandfather didn't much like to talk about his father, but I kept after him with a persistence that embarrasses me a little now. One day when I was visiting from college nearly fifty years ago he turned over to me a dusty cardboard carton filled with brittle papers tied into bundles with dirty twine. They were the contents of Ferdinand Ward's prison trunk, and had rested unread in the closet safe off my grandfather's study in Oberlin, Ohio, for more than half a century: scores of letters, still in their envelopes; faded photographs; court documents bound with red ribbon; tiny scraps of paper covered on both sides with near-microscopic writing.

They offered me the first real clues to what my great-grandfather was like. But they also raised as many questions as they answered, and brought me no closer to grasping what made him the man he came to be. He may have been a sociopath, born without a conscience or the ability to empathize, able only to imitate emotions genuinely felt by other people. He unquestionably was a narcissist; nothing ever seems to have mattered to him except himself. But the distinctive blend of self-righteousness and deceit, aggression and victimhood he displayed throughout his life turned out eerily to mirror the distorted personalities of the missionary parents who raised him. Trying to understand those intimate connections and to assess the impact of his depredations on those closest to him—his parents, his bewildered older brother and sister, his wife, and his only child—eventually led me to write the story of a family as well as the biography of a scoundrel. That story begins halfway around the world with half-hidden events that began to unfold fourteen years before Ferdinand Ward was born.

PART ONE

THE PURITAN

ONE

The Higher Calling

Shortly after dawn on March 20, 1837, at the end of a four-month voyage from Boston, the captain of the American merchant ship *Saracen* sighted the green Coromandel coast of South India and set his course northward along it, headed for the British port city of Madras.*

The *Saracen* was carrying three distinctive products from New England. Two were in great demand: bales of the rugged cotton twill then called "jeans," and more than one hundred tons of ice, cut from Massachusetts ponds into big blue-green blocks, then carefully packed into the *Saracen*'s hold, surrounded by layers of lumber, hay, sawdust, and tanbark to minimize melting over the course of the long voyage. For the British, suffering in the Indian heat, the regular arrival of American ice was a godsend. "The stoppage of the Bank of Bengal here could hardly exceed the excitement of a failure, during our hot weather, of the ice!" one Briton wrote. "And the arrival of our English mail is not more anxiously expected than that of an American Ice-ship, when supplies run low."[†]

---

* Modern Chennai.

[†] The "frozen-water trade" made the Boston entrepreneur Frederic Tudor America's first postrevolutionary millionaire. Thanks to him and his rivals, New England ice tinkled in glasses from Calcutta to the Caribbean, Sidney to South America. The *Sara-*

The third New England export aboard the *Saracen*—Puritanism—would find a less cordial welcome. The ship's sole passengers were six American missionaries and their wives as well as a physician and his wife dedicated to their care. They stood silently together on the quarterdeck, gazing at the distant shoreline. They had left friends and families and endured 118 days at sea in order to help bring their brand of Protestantism to the unconverted millions of the subcontinent, to create what one veteran missionary called "New England in India."* Timothy Dwight, the president of Yale and a founder of the American Board of Commissioners for Foreign Missions, under whose auspices they had embarked, had set their ambitious agenda: it was their charge, he wrote, to hasten the time "when the *Romish* cathedral, the mosque, and the pagoda, shall *not have one stone left upon another, which shall not be thrown down.*"[1]

For the little group on deck, prospects of hastening that time did not look immediately reassuring. Every landmark they saw that day underscored the enormity of the task they faced: a beachfront cluster of carved Hindu structures at Mahabalipuram had withstood the pounding surf for more than a thousand years; the gleaming white Cathedral of Saint Thomas, built by the Portuguese and said to mark the original tomb of the apostle, symbolized for the Americans not Christianity but "popery," more sinister even than the native "heathen" faith they had been sent to supplant; and when they at last came within sight of Fort St. George, the big coastal bastion from which Britons governed the vast Madras presidency, the carved *gopurams* of more Hindu temples and the scattered domes of Muslim mosques appeared above "Blacktown," the jumble of mud huts and whitewashed houses

---

cen was under charter by Tudor's first partner, Samuel Austin. The quote is from Gavin Weightman, *The Frozen-Water Trade: A True Story*, p. 200.

* Though they saw themselves as pioneers, Americans were actually latecomers to preaching Christianity in South India. Some Indian Christians hold that Saint Thomas himself lived and worked there in the first century. The Portuguese converted thousands of Tamil-speaking people to Roman Catholicism in Ceylon and South India during the sixteenth and seventeenth centuries. Danish Lutherans established a mission at Tranquebar in 1705. The London-based Anglican Society for the Propagation of Christian Knowledge (later the Society for the Propagation of the Gospel) had been on the ground for more than one hundred years when the *Saracen* company arrived, and missionaries from the nondenominational London Missionary Society had been at work in India since 1794. Still, the newcomers considered themselves the first bringers of the *true* Christian message.

that had grown up in the shadow of its walls. The missionaries' worst fears had been confirmed: the city was clearly the home of "errorists of every name and grade."[2]

Walls of foaming surf made it impossible for large vessels to get anywhere near the shore at Madras. So the captain of the *Saracen* lowered her sails two miles offshore and waited for orders from the harbormaster telling him where to drop anchor among the scores of merchant vessels and hundreds of smaller fishing boats already bobbing in the Madras Roads.

The Americans watched as two crudely fashioned catamarans—teak logs lashed together, each paddled by three kneeling men—struggled out toward them through the waves. Despite the still-bright late-afternoon sun, the missionaries were clad in black; their wives wore the long-sleeved dresses with full skirts and many petticoats thought suitable for the wives of clergymen back home. When the first catamaran reached the *Saracen* and its occupants clambered up the side to deliver anchoring instructions to the captain, the sight of them, dark skins shiny with sweat, naked but for loincloths and standing only a few feet away, drove several of the women and at least two of the men to their cabins to weep with shock and pray for strength.

"*These* are the Hindus, *these* the people among whom we came to dwell!" the Reverend Ferdinand De Wilton Ward remembered saying to his wife, Jane Shaw Ward, that evening as they settled into their berths to try to get at least a little sleep before going ashore the next morning.[3] Ward had celebrated his twenty-fourth birthday at sea; his wife was seven months older. Everything they had seen that day suggested that the gulf between New England and the ancient land to which they and their companions expected to devote the rest of their lives was wider than they'd imagined, the challenge of conversion greater than they'd dreamed. If the little band of missionaries was to have any impact on India at all, they would have to work together as one, Ward would write, bound up in "a united labor of love," with each member careful always to display consistent "patience and forbearance."[4]

But neither he nor his wife was prepared to remain united with anyone else for long. Neither was patient or forbearing, either. In the end it was not the immovability of India but the Wards' own intransigence and stubborn self-regard that would first drive the couple home in disgrace and then create the claustrophobic, embittered world that helped warp the personality of their younger son.

.   .   .

Rev. Ferdinand De Wilton Ward, the swindler's father and namesake, had been brought up to believe that his family, the Wards of Rochester, New York, were better than other people: more upright, more principled, more godly, and—perhaps as a reward for all that conspicuous virtue—bound to be more successful. Their prosperity and prominence, they believed, were inextricably linked with what Rev. Ward would call "their ancestral, heroic, puritan piety of which they were never, for an hour, ashamed."[5]

They had already prospered in Massachusetts and Connecticut for six generations by 1807, when Ferdinand's grandfather, Deacon Levi Ward, his Yale-educated father, Dr. Levi Ward Jr., their families, and several neighbors all left Haddam, Connecticut, together and joined the stream of New Englanders then headed for the "Genesee Woods," the dark unbroken forest that blanketed most of western New York. From the first, they considered themselves a cut above their fellow pioneers. Deacon Ward saw to it that his wife rode through the forest in a horse-drawn chaise with leather springs, the first such conveyance ever seen in the New York wilderness (or so his descendants later claimed). Once they reached and cleared the site that was first named "Wardville" and then became part of the village of Bergen, the deacon's eldest son, Dr. Levi Ward, built his family a frame house with cedar shingles rather than a log cabin, even though his new neighbors found it "somewhat aristocratic."[6]

Ferdinand De Wilton Ward was born in that house on July 9, 1812, the youngest of five boys and the second-to-youngest child in a family of thirteen children (eleven of whom would live to adulthood).[*] His earliest memories included the bright, beaded moccasins worn by the Indian hunters who emerged from the woods from time to time with game to barter, and the distant sound of howling wolves, heard as he lay shivering in bed.

His father was an unusually successful settler. By the time Ferdinand was born, Dr. Ward was running a provisions store, serving his

---

[*] The Wards were as prolific as they were successful. By the time Deacon Ward, the family patriarch, finally passed away at Bergen in 1839 at the age of ninety-two, twenty-two of his grandchildren and great-grandchildren had died, but three children, twenty-three grandchildren, and sixty-five great-grandchildren still survived—a total of ninety-one living descendants.

fifth consecutive term as town supervisor, overseeing mail delivery throughout the region, and acting as land agent for the State of Connecticut, charged with selling off some fifty thousand acres of cleared forest for farmland—and pocketing a handsome commission for every sale.

But he was not satisfied. In early 1818, when Ferdinand was five and his father was forty-six, his parents moved their large brood twenty miles or so to the east, to what was then called Rochesterville, on the Upper Falls of the Genesee River. Only seven hundred people lived there then, but the tumbling ninety-six-foot cataract at the village's heart was ideally suited for powering mills and workshops, and there was good reason to believe the tiny village would soon outdo all the surrounding settlements: the New York State legislature had decreed that the 363-mile Erie Canal, connecting Albany on the Hudson to Buffalo on Lake Erie, was to cross the Genesee at Rochester. Work was already under way. Once completed, the canal would link the American heartland for the first time to distant continents—and transform the thickly forested Genesee Valley into fields of ripening wheat for sale to the cities of the East.

Rochester was about to become the "Flour City"—the nation's first real boomtown—and Dr. Ward and all his offspring would profit handsomely from its startling growth. Ferdinand grew up in a world in which his father seemed to be everywhere at once, encouraging every new enterprise, urging his neighbors to ever-greater effort, summoning up a city from a forest. He helped lobby to make Rochester the seat of the brand-new Monroe County, opened stores, bought up big tracts of land, cornered the insurance business, helped establish the Rochester City Bank, the first New York financial institution ever chartered outside New York City, as well as the Rochester Savings Bank—and then served as president and director of each. He was a ruling elder of the First Presbyterian Church, helped establish the Female Charitable Society, the County Poor House, the Western House of Refuge, the Rochester Atheneum, the Rochester Society for the Promotion of Temperance. He was a life member of the American Colonization and American Tract Societies, too, and president of the Monroe County Bible Society, the very first in the country, whose goal it was to place a Bible in the hands of every citizen willing to accept one.

From the largest of the three handsome federal homes he built for himself and his family on North St. Paul Street, he would eventually parcel out his interests among his sons. William, the eldest—known as "Colonel" because he had briefly commanded the local militia—and Levi A. Ward, the next in line, began adult life as their father's partners in the dry goods business. William never moved very far beyond that status (and would die early, of cholera), and so Levi became his father's partner in the banking and insurance business, his successor as public benefactor, and, as the years went by, custodian of the family fortune, as well. Henry Meigs Ward, just a year younger than Levi and more interested in reading books and writing poetry than moneymaking, was left to run the Ward "farm," several hundred acres north of town that were eventually laid out in blocks and sold off, lot by lot, to the newcomers flooding into the city.*

Dr. Ward's daughters also wielded power, mostly through the men they chose to marry. His oldest daughter, Siba, wed Silas O. Smith, the town's most prominent merchant. Her younger sister Esther married one of the town's leading attorneys, Moses Chapin. Susan married another, Samuel L. Selden, who eventually became chief judge of the New York Court of Appeals. Mehitabel and Henrietta married two unrelated men with the same last name, Charles Lee Clarke and Freeman Clarke. The first did well in law; the second did far better as bank president, director of railways and telegraph companies, Whig politician, Republican congressman, and, eventually, Abraham Lincoln's controller of the currency.†

In this highly charged company, young Ferdinand was often overlooked. Fourteen years younger than the formidable Levi, he was a frail, anxious little boy, severely nearsighted, subject to crushing migraines that often confined him to a darkened room. At eleven, he nearly died of rheumatic fever. At twelve, he developed St. Vitus' dance (Sydenham's chorea), his face and limbs twitching so uncontrollably that he was sent east to live for a year with an uncle in Guilford, Con-

---

* Daniel Hand Ward, Deacon Ward's second son, remains a mystery. He was well enough as a boy to carry mail for his father, but in the voluminous *Ward Family Genealogy*, only his name and dates (1796–1848) are given. One source suggests he was severely "handicapped," another calls him "an invalid." In any case, he seems never to have married or to have taken an active part in any of the family's many enterprises.

† Elizabeth Ward alone moved away to marry; her husband, Daniel Hand, was a Connecticut-born businessman who made himself enormously wealthy as a merchant in Atlanta. After the Civil War he would leave more than a million dollars to the American Missionary Society for the education of freedmen.

necticut, away from the forest and swampland his parents believed were the source of his illnesses. He was lonely, homesick, and chronically fearful. When he returned to Rochester, pale and still "convalescent," his mother and father thought it best to have him tutored at home by the family's pastor.

That home could be a grim place. For all his formidable energies, Dr. Ward was "constitutionally subject to low spirits,"[7] his wife said, unaccustomed to opposition, often preoccupied, and always severe. Ferdinand's mother was less forbidding, but conflicted; perpetually solicitous about his fragile health, she was also given to expressing her regret that "I had so many children," a lament not calculated to cheer her youngest son.[8]

Dr. Ward championed progress and promoted charity, but he also opposed any unnecessary change in the way life was lived in Rochester. A neighbor remembered him as the last man in town to wear the queue, ruffled shirts, and buckled shoes that had been fashionable in New England before he came west. He believed, as did many of the Yankee pioneers who helped create Rochester and most of the other towns in western New York, that the New England world from which they had come should be the model followed by everyone everywhere.

That model included unquestioning observance of the Sabbath. In the Ward homes on North St. Paul Street, everything stopped between Saturday evening and Monday morning. The elder Henry James, who would one day attend college with young Ferdinand, recalled the Sabbaths in his own upstate Presbyterian household. Sunday, he wrote, was the day on which children were taught "not to play, not to dance, not to sing; not to read storybooks, not to con over our school-lessons for Monday even; not to whistle, not to ride the pony, nor to take a walk in the country, nor a swim in the river; nor, in short, to do anything which nature especially craved. Nothing is so hard . . . for a child as *not-to-do*."[9]

Dr. Ward was not content just to observe "not-to-do" in his own home; he also wanted the Sabbath honored in every household in Rochester. He was instrumental in passing a town ordinance levying a two-dollar fine on any canal boatman who dared blow his bugle on Sunday, and when his friend and fellow Presbyterian elder Josiah Bissell petitioned Congress to halt the movement of the mails on the Sabbath, Dr. Ward's signature was near the top of list of the four hundred Rochester citizens who signed the document. He also invested in Bissell's Pioneer Line, whose canal boats and stagecoaches pledged not to operate on Sunday. (His employees would "not *swear* or *drink*," Bissell promised, and at least "some of our taverns will be *without* bars. *Hot coffee shall* always be in waiting and *free* to the drivers.")[10] Both projects failed: Congress rejected the ban on Sunday mail on the grounds that it had no power to legislate with respect to religion; the Pioneer Line collapsed for want of business.

Ferdinand's father would now frequently find himself on the losing side of such disputes. The character of Rochester's population was changing fast as newcomers flooded into town, many of them Irish Catholic immigrants, drawn to the region to work on the Erie Canal, who sought new lives but saw no need to change old ways. Still, the old man and his elder sons remained important figures in Rochester, and young Ferdinand shared indirectly in their prominence. When the Marquis de Lafayette visited Rochester in the summer of 1825, Ferdinand's father was co-chairman of the reception committee, and his thirteen-year-old son was allowed to shake the Revolutionary War hero's hand. A few weeks later, when Governor DeWitt Clinton's flotilla of packet boats arrived at Rochester, en route to New York Harbor and the official opening ceremony of the Erie Canal, young Ferdinand and his father were both invited aboard. The Manhattan parade "exceeded anything I ever saw before or expect to see again," Ferdinand remembered, and Governor Clinton himself pinned a commemorative badge on the proud boy's shirt.[11]

In the autumn of 1827, Ferdinand was fifteen and ready for college. His parents puzzled over what he might do in life. He seemed too frail and highly strung for law or business. Besides, there were older brothers enough to run the family enterprises. Nor did he show any interest in medicine, the field his father had studied at Yale before coming west. But he had always sought his parents' approval by being the most clearly pious among the boys—the quietest on the Sabbath, the most regular in attendance at Sunday school and evening prayers—and there were as yet no clergymen in the family. Perhaps the pulpit would suit him.

His father sent him to Hamilton College in Clinton, New York, two days away by stagecoach. It was a small Presbyterian institution with a curriculum perfectly suited to a would-be-minister: classical, with an emphasis on public speaking. There were one hundred students at Hamilton, all boys and famously unruly. A few years earlier, several of them had hauled a swivel gun up four flights to the top of Hamilton Hall and fired it through the door of a fellow student's room, narrowly missing him as he lay sleeping. Subsequent classes celebrated the event on its anniversary each year. At least in retrospect, Ferdinand took no pleasure in that tradition. "A boy who goes to college is ushered into a circle entirely new," he would remember, "where the motto of each individual is 'Look out for No. 1' [and] where selfishness necessarily predominates. Not enjoying the advantages of social intercourse, he soon becomes as uncivilized and as brutish as those around him."[12] So far as we know, Ferdinand's own brutishness extended only to the stealing and surreptitious roasting of a farmer's chicken, and the memory of that single "hilarity," he would write at seventy, served as a lifelong reminder of "my state as a Sinner."*

He spent only one term at Hamilton—the school's president and trustees were locked in a bitter struggle that drove away most of the student body and very nearly destroyed the institution—before transferring to Union College at Schenectady. Its president, the Reverend Eliphalet Nott, was a Presbyterian clergyman liberal-minded enough to have introduced science into the curriculum. His students were well-bred young men from all over the country.

"Here," Ferdinand assured his youngest sister, Henrietta, "I shall prepare to act a part in life so as not to be unworthy of myself or a dishonor to my parents."[13] That would not always be easy. Ferdinand's class had eighty-nine members. Twenty-one would become clergymen. But most followed more worldly pursuits. Some took up smoking. Some tried alcohol despite President Nott's earnest warning that those who did so were likely spontaneously to burst into bright

---

* His roommate, the son of a pastor from New Hartford, Connecticut, was more adventurous than he, Ferdinand remembered many years later, "innately wild and a great grief to fond and too-indulgent parents." He bought up all the bed cord in town, spent most of the night methodically tying shut every room in every building on the campus, climbed the church steeple, cut the bell rope, and waited for dawn. No church bell rang. There was no chapel, no morning recitation. The culprit was found out and expelled. "Poor boy!" Ward wrote. "He ran away from home, [went west] and was, I am told, heard of no more. Killed by Indians. His face is now before me, bright, pleasant, but with a will untamed and impulses rudderless." Ferdinand De Wilton Ward, "Letter of 1882," in Melvin G. Dodge, comp., *Fifty Years Ago*, pp. 119–120.

blue flame. Ferdinand resisted these temptations, and when his class-mates attended balls he remained in his room; dancing, his parents had taught him, was frivolous and immoral. But he did join friends in calling upon some of the town's most eligible young women. "I am much pleased with the Society of Ladies I find here," he told Henri-etta.[14] The Albany *Microscope*, a scandal sheet that specialized in gossip about nearby towns, suggested that Dr. Nott needed to "Ward-off" the advances of a certain student on a young Schenectady lady. "It is the town talk," Ferdinand told his sister. "High & Low—Rich & Poor—are all asking—Is it true that Mr. Ward is to be married to Miss H?"[15] It was not, he assured Henrietta; "*She is not a Christian. I need say no more!*"[16]

When eighteen-year-old Ferdinand came home for the holidays in December 1830, the Reverend Charles Grandison Finney had been leading a revival there for nearly three months—perhaps the first city-wide revival in American history. Josiah Bissell, Ferdinand's father's old ally in the Sabbatarian struggle, had invited Finney to town. There was a "large budget of evils rolling through our land & among us," he'd told Finney, the result of rapid changes brought by the Erie Canal. "The people & the church say it cannot be helped—and why do they say this? Because . . . they know not the power of the Gospel of Jesus. 'Through Christ Jesus strengthening us we can do all things,' and if so it is time we were about it."[17]

Finney found fertile ground in Rochester. One evening, so many listeners climbed up to the gallery of the Wards' family church, the First Presbyterian, that the stone walls began to spread and plaster sifted down onto the congregation. Panicked men and women pushed through the doors and dove through the windows for fear the build-ing was about to collapse. Other Protestant churches threw open their doors to the temporarily homeless Presbyterians so that Finney could continue his great work. "All Rochester was *moved* that winter," one clergyman remembered. "The atmosphere . . . seemed to be affected. You could not go upon the streets, and hear any conversations, except on religion."[18]

On New Year's Eve, at the newly repaired First Church, Finney's coworker Theodore Weld preached against alcohol with such explo-sive ardor that eight grocers, cowering in their pews, vowed never

again to sell whiskey to anyone. The next day, surrounded by applaud-
ing townspeople, several of them ordered their stock rolled out onto
Exchange Street, smashed the barrels, and watched the contents flow
into the gutter.

To Ferdinand, the would-be clergyman, this was a miracle, vivid
proof that Christ was at work in the streets of his hometown. And
when Finney himself strode to the pulpit two days later, Ferdinand and
Henrietta were among his most avid listeners.

Henry Stanton, a law student who had watched Finney in action a
few weeks earlier, captured the evangelist's impact on even the most
normally unexcitable listener. Tall and grave, with blue eyes that
seemed almost to glow, Stanton remembered, "[Finney's] way over an
audience was wonderful." He went on,

> While depicting the glories or the terrors of the world to
> come, he trod the pulpit like a giant. . . . As he would stand
> with his face towards the side gallery, and then involuntarily
> wheel around, the audience in that part of the house towards
> which he would throw his arm would dodge as if he were hurl-
> ing something at them. In describing the sliding of a sinner to
> perdition, he would lift his long finger towards the ceiling and
> slowly bring it down till it pointed to the area in front of the
> pulpit, when half his hearers in the rear of the house would
> rise unconsciously to their feet to see him descend into the pit
> below.[*]

Ferdinand and Henrietta were among those who rose unconsciously to
their feet that evening and then pledged themselves to Christ, just two
of the more than one hundred men and women who officially joined
the church that month alone. If Ferdinand had ever doubted that he

---

[*] Some of Finney's listeners were less admiring. Henry Stanton's future wife, Elizabeth
Cady, was taken to hear him as a young girl in the nearby village of York, and remembered him as a "terrifier of human souls."

> I was wrought up to such a pitch that I actually jumped and gazed in the direc-
> tion to which he pointed, while the picture glowed before my eyes and remained
> with me for months afterwards. . . . Fear of the Judgment seized my soul. Visions
> of the lost haunted my dreams. Mental anguish prostrated my health.

Henry B. Stanton, *Random Recollections*, pp. 42–43; Elizabeth Cady Stanton, *Eighty
Years and More*, p. 72.

should devote himself to the ministry, those doubts now vanished. Henceforth, he wrote his sister after he had returned to college, all his thoughts would be "of one class . . . Religion . . . a subject upon which we should dwell every moment."[19] He issued admonition after admonition over the next few months, excoriating Rochester's backsliders and exhorting his sister to pray, morning, noon, and night.

In July 1831, two weeks before his graduation from Union, he and his roommate walked seven miles into the countryside so that eighteen-year-old Ferdinand could preach his first sermon, to a schoolhouse filled with farmers and their wives. The text he chose could have been his life's motto: "He that is not for me is against me."[20]

Ferdinand planned to spend a year at home before entering Princeton Theological Seminary. The pulpit was now no longer enough for him. He had what he believed to be a higher calling in mind: he was privately determined to become a missionary to the heathen overseas.

The missionary ranks he sought to join had begun forming in 1810, when New England Congregationalists established the American Board of Commissioners for Foreign Missions (ABCFM). Presbyterian and Reformed churches lent their united support two years later.* Historians differ as to precisely what accounted for the extraordinary enthusiasm for foreign missions that gripped New England and upstate New York in the early nineteenth century, but it is clear that the Puritan denominations, whose old-time supremacy had been undermined at home by new and less austere faiths, found a timely new cause in mission work among Native Americans at home and unbelievers abroad. Meanwhile, the widespread belief that the End was fast approaching—Theodore Weld said it was sure to come before 1850—suggested there was no time to waste in turning the nations of the world to Christ.

To achieve this goal in Europe and Asia, Secretary Rufus Anderson of the American Board foresaw "a chain of [mission] posts, extending from Ceylon through the Tamil nation of southern India, the

---

* Under the 1801 Plan of Union, New England Congregationalists and the general assembly of the Presbyterian Church had agreed to work together, rather than compete, as the frontier moved west. The Wards had been Congregationalists back in Connecticut but had had no difficulty helping to found and enthusiastically support Presbyterian churches once they reached western New York.

Mahrattas,* the Rajpoots, and Afghanistan, Persia, Armenia, and Asia Minor to Constantinople and into European Turkey."†

The cause of Christ consumed pious young people of Ferdinand's generation. Two members of his own family would go abroad as missionaries: his distant cousin Alonzo Chapin, who sailed for the Sandwich Islands in November 1831, and his niece Maria Ward Chapin Smith, who would accompany her husband, Rev. Eli Smith, to Syria sometime later. Ferdinand was eager to join them. "No one was dependent upon me for a livelihood," he recalled. "I had a good constitution. I had a full if not an exceptional aptitude to acquire a foreign language." Above all, he wrote, he was "called *loudly* to go abroad."[21]

But when he told his parents what he had in mind they were horrified. His mother could not bear to have her youngest boy vanish overseas. His father was adamant against his going: Ferdinand's constitution was far too fragile for the foreign field. He was extremely nearsighted, anxious, still subject to migraines, and too easily agitated when things did not go his way. His father told him he could do just as

---

* The Marathi-speaking people of western India had been the earliest overseas targets of the American Board. The first five missionaries to India, three with their wives, had sailed for Bombay in 1812. Almost everything had gone wrong. While they were still at sea, one missionary couple and one of the two bachelors declared themselves Baptists and withdrew from the care of the American Board. Before their ship arrived in India, Britain and the United States went to war, so instead of welcoming them British authorities threatened deportation. One couple sailed immediately for Mauritius, where the wife died after giving birth to a dead child and her husband suffered an emotional collapse. Three members of the original party fled to Bombay, where they were placed under house arrest. The married couple, Rev. Samuel Nott and his wife, soon began complaining of economic hardship, ran up heavy debts, demanded the right to make money on the side, and, in 1815, booked passage for home. The American Board privately denounced Nott as a "spoilt child" but covered up his activities for fear of driving away funders. The lone survivor, Rev. Gordon Hall, soldiered on in Bombay until his death. Paul William Harris, *Nothing but Christ*, pp. 27–29.
† In the end, the Board did manage to establish missions in the Middle East—and in the Sandwich Islands, China, and Africa, as well. But no serious effort was ever made to link the northern and southern ends of Anderson's chain, and the rest of the field would eventually be left to other denominations: Baptists, Lutherans, Methodists—even Unitarians and Friends—all eventually staked claims to different parts of the Indian subcontinent, the minute doctrinal differences between them providing an endless source of puzzlement to those they hoped to convert. Geoffrey C. Ward, "Two Missionaries' Ordeal by Faith in a Distant Clime," *Smithsonian* (August 1990).

much good close to home as he could abroad, and that he was far too young to make so momentous a decision.

And so, Ferdinand went off to Princeton in June 1832, knowing that his father and mother were displeased with his plans. "It required a struggle of no ordinary intensity" to leave home this time, he told his sister, and "an agony of struggle at the throne of Grace to make my will bow to the decision of my conscience, a joy mingled with tears."[22]

At nineteen, he was the youngest member of his seminary class of ninety-four, severely homesick and initially disheartened by the seminary's Spartan ways: "Breakfast & Supper same, i.e. bread, molasses, cup of water—no pie!"[23] But he was also gratified that "the subject of missions is on every side and in every forum,"[24] and especially pleased when one of his teachers told the class, "We should not object to your *all* going [abroad]. Let the home churches look after themselves. It will do them good."*

A cloud of fear hung over the entire eastern United States that spring, the likelihood that the cholera pandemic ravaging the Old World was about to descend upon the New. It had begun in Bengal in 1817, reached China by 1820, Moscow in 1830, western Europe the following year. It killed at an appalling rate: fifty-five thousand died in Great Britain, more than twice that number in France. Patients who seemed fine at breakfast were often dead by dinner. Sudden, agonizing cramps led to simultaneous violent diarrhea and vomiting that so dehydrated victims they literally shrank, turned blue, and often became unrecognizable even to family members sitting helpless at their bedsides. No one understood what caused it. Common treatments like camphor, laudanum, charcoal, bleeding, and a mercury compound called calomel either had no effect or made things worse.

Americans prayed that the Atlantic might prove a barrier against it, but the first cases of cholera appeared in New York in early June 1832. Soon, a hundred people were dying in Manhattan every day and the disease was racing inland along the canals and aboard the steamboats of which Americans were so proud.

---

* In the end, seven members of his class would enter the mission field. Ferdinand De Wilton Ward, typed manuscript of *Auto-Biography No.2*, p. 3, Brinton Collection; Kenneth Woodrow Henke, letter to the author, December 16, 2008.

It reached Rochester on July 12. The first victim lived on South St. Paul Street, only a few blocks from the Wards. A second man fell ill two days later. Soon, there were dozens of fresh cases every day, so many that straw pallets had to be laid out for them beneath a crude open-air shelter on the western bank of the Erie Canal. Ferdinand's father was asked to chair a public meeting at the courthouse to see what else might be done. He was a physician as well as a leading citizen, but all he could do was call upon the family pastor to offer up a prayer. Everywhere, including Rochester, clergymen declared the outbreak divine punishment, called down upon God's chosen country for its ingratitude. "Obscene impurities, drunkenness, profanities and infidelity, prevail among us to a fearful extent," said a pamphlet rushed into print by the American Tract Society. "Iniquity runs down our streets like a river."[25] Four hundred people would fall ill in Rochester before the pandemic burned itself out. One hundred and sixteen died. More than a thousand residents fled into the countryside and found temporary homes in taverns and farmhouses as far as thirty miles away.

All of this Ferdinand was forced to learn from the newspapers. For three weeks, no one in his preoccupied family found the time to write to him. And as their silence continued, Ferdinand grew more and more fearful, convinced that the worst had happened. At the best of times, his health was "merely tolerable," he told Henrietta in a frenzied six-page letter begging for news. But now, haunted by dark thoughts of what might be occurring at home, he could not sleep, waking again and again, "sometimes screaming, sometimes weeping." He suffered "turns of fainting," too, which lasted as long as three minutes, "so that I often dread to rise from my seat lest I should fall." Even when he tried to pray, "excited feelings" deprived him of "the use of reason."[26]

In the end, cholera spared the Ward household, but Ferdinand's parents had to dispatch Henrietta to Princeton to nurse their distraught son back to health. Ferdinand's extreme anxiety and the alarming symptoms it engendered in him further persuaded his father that he could not possibly endure the rigors of mission life. Ferdinand's psychological state worried his professors, too, but they were themselves so caught up in the enthusiasm for missions that they continued to offer him only encouragement. Two of them wrote a joint letter assuring the ABCFM that in the end Ferdinand's "singular prudence and propriety" and his "deep and ardent piety" would more than make up for his delicate health.[27]

·   ·   ·

Ferdinand agreed. He was now in a hurry. The full Princeton curriculum required three years to master. As soon as the Presbytery of
Rochester licensed him to preach, in the autumn of 1833, he left the
seminary rather than wait to graduate. He then had three choices, he
recalled: undertaking an overseas mission; joining a mission among
emigrants and Indians in the American West; or taking up a tranquil
pastorate among "the cultured and reformed." His family and friends
all favored the latter, and were already selecting " '*just the place*' " for
him.[28] His brother-in-law Freeman Clarke helped arrange for him to
occupy a pulpit in Albion, New York, during the summer of 1834 to see
how he liked preaching in a small town. He didn't. The following winter, his father saw to it that he stayed with his sister and brother-in-law
in Augusta, Georgia, so that he could venture out to mission stations among the Choctaw and Chickasaw in the hopes that a season
of preaching to them might prove satisfyingly exotic. It did not. Nor
did he enjoy several weeks standing in for the pastor of Rochester's
Second Presbyterian Church or a summerlong stand at Philadelphia's
fashionable Tenth Street Church—though the latter did allow him to
study rudimentary medicine at the Jefferson Medical School, which he
hoped would help him to better withstand missionary life.

Ferdinand refused to alter his plans. "My eye is fixed upon a *distant*
point," he told his sister.[29] His mother finally, reluctantly, agreed to
let him go. But his father continued to withhold his blessing. "The
thought of taking a step which shall contradict his feelings is, to me,
most painful," Ferdinand told Secretary Anderson of the ABCFM.
"No son was ever possessed of a kinder parent. . . . I am the youngest
son—and the only one that has taken upon himself any *public duties*. . . .
My life is fast passing (22 years have already gone) [and] I must soon
be in the field."[30]

In June 1836, Ferdinand's application was formally approved, with
one proviso: before he embarked for South India that November he
must find himself a wife and marry her at least two months before
they set sail. It was unwise, the American Board believed, to dispatch
even the most god-fearing young men to exotic lands unaccompanied;
the temptations of the flesh were too strong for safety. Marriage was
"the natural state of man," in any case, Secretary Anderson had written.[31] A missionary needed a wife as much as a minister did, as "friend,
counselor, companion, the repository of her husband's thoughts and

feelings, the partaker of his joys, the sharer of his cares and sorrows, and one who is to lighten his toils, and become his nurse in sickness."[32]

"The Board say I must marry," Ferdinand complained to a classmate, "and give to that object my entire time. I do not like it. I want time. . . . You will hear if anything is effected."*

Something was effected, and with remarkable speed. In April of the previous year, while preaching in Philadelphia, he had met a young woman named Jane Shaw at the home of a mutual friend. He had liked her "better than any other young lady I had ever seen," he remembered, but he hadn't managed to see her again.[33]

Now, with the Board insisting he marry, "Something (I do not remember what) led me to imagine that Miss [Shaw] might view with favor an invitation to be my home-companion to India. I went to the city and called upon her." He was evidently slow to come to the point: "[We] had many pleasant conversations upon many general subjects and, of course, on Missions. At one time she expressed the opinion that Missionaries ought to go out *single*. That was enough for me. As I did not desire to receive a negative, I said no more upon the subject but returned home [to Philadelphia]."[34]

Then he got a note from a friend in New York: he had given up too quickly, it said; he should go back and try again. He boarded a steamboat for the city, and, as it stopped at Matawan Landing, near Fishkill, Jane Shaw herself happened to come aboard. He nervously asked if he could call. She said he could; since her father's death she had been living at the downtown New York home of her sister and brother-in-law, Mr. and Mrs. Christopher Robert. She would be glad to receive him there.†

Before he made his call, he lunched at a Manhattan restaurant with a friend of hers, Rev. Charles Hall, assistant secretary of the Home Missionary Society. They took a corner table, Ferdinand recalled, and

---

* Three years earlier, he had written his sister Henrietta to keep an eye out for a future wife for him. "She must be a Christian, intelligent & not homely." Ferdinand De Wilton Ward to Henrietta Ward Clarke, July 2, 1833, Freeman Clarke Family Papers, Department of Rare Books, Special Collections and Preservation, University of Rochester Library.

† Christopher Robert, married to Jane's youngest sister, Anna Maria Shaw, was a successful importer of sugar, cotton, and tea and would become president of the Delaware, Lackawanna and Western Railroad after the Civil War. He shared fully in his sister-in-law's Presbyterian zeal and would eventually use his wealth to fund a number of religious institutions at home and to provide the initial funds with which Robert College was established just outside Constantinople.

he nervously asked Hall whether he thought Miss Shaw might make a suitable wife for a foreign missionary. "Excellent," Hall answered. But, he continued, "*she is an heiress* and may want to go alone—independent of man or Board . . . You can try and she can but say, 'No.' "[35]

Ferdinand screwed up his courage, called upon Miss Shaw at her brother-in-law's home, and, although he had spoken with her just three times, proposed marriage—and "'ere long received a *Yes*, much to my joy."[36]

Jane Shaw was twenty-four years old that June, small, wiry, and deaf in one ear. She would always consider herself unattractive. She was slight and stooped even as a child, with a prominent nose and hands and feet larger than she liked. "Altogether I am so ugly," she would write to her daughter toward the end of her long life. "How often I wonder why I have to be subject to so *much* mortification as regards my hands and feet. When I am dead please don't let my hands be laid across my breast but close to my sides."[37]

Her girlhood in downtown Manhattan had been comfortable but emotionally parched. Her father, William Shaw, was a successful but preoccupied Irish-born shipping merchant whose fleet sailed between Belfast and New York. Her mother, Elizabeth Johnson, was a frail New Yorker with an inheritance of her own. Jane, the third of six children, lost herself in books, loved studies, developed a reputation for Christian ardor that was at least a match for that of her new fiancé, and dreamed of somehow becoming a missionary. Asked one Sunday morning while still a little girl to contribute something valuable to her church, she had placed in the collection plate a slip of paper on which she had written "Myself."

Then, when she was fifteen, her mother suddenly died. Jane was taken out of school to serve as her father's housekeeper and hostess and to act as surrogate mother to her younger sister and two younger brothers. She was too young for the task and very nearly overwhelmed. The church became still more important to her, a refuge as well as a house of worship.

When Rev. Hall was asked to assess her potential as a missionary's wife, he responded with enthusiasm; her interest in religious work was "not a spasm of romantic feeling but such as may be calculated to inspire her as long as she lives. The temptations of refined & worldly society have not hindered her from being a devoted missionary among the poor, the ignorant and repulsive population on the outskirts of our city."[38] Her own pastor, Rev. Asa D. Smith of the 14th Street Presbyterian Church, was equally positive. Miss Shaw was "uniformly good . . . uncommonly so," he wrote, and filled with "an unusually large measure of the Missionary Spirit. God . . . has been anointing her for the work to which she is now looking."[39]

Ferdinand was formally to be ordained as a missionary on August 31. He appointed the 29th as a day of fasting and renewal for himself and his bride-to-be. That evening, she wrote him a letter setting forth her reasons for agreeing to marry him on such short acquaintance. It had little to do with him and everything to do with what she believed to be the cause of Christ. Marriage to Ferdinand would make it possible for her to answer the Call they both had heard.

It was not until the spring of the previous year that she had first felt "a personal duty in relation to the heathen," she explained. Appeals for help from men and women already in the field—including John Jay Lawrence, an old friend who had sailed for South India in May—had moved her to explore the possibility of going abroad on her own. She had "comparatively few ties that bound me to my native land," she wrote, and was blessed with a small inheritance to cover her expenses, and so, "after praying with great earnestness to be led to do . . . what would best glorify God, [I] decided that *I would* go . . . if God should see . . . fit to send me."

He had not seen fit to send her, at least not at first. She made arrangements to accompany a British Baptist couple to a mission in Orissa, on India's eastern coast, only to have them rescind the invitation when they were assigned elsewhere. She consulted Rev. Miron Winslow, who was home on a brief visit after spending more than a quarter of a century in the American Board's first mission to the Tamils at Jaffna, Ceylon, to see whether she might be welcome there. She was not. He told her firmly that there was no room for single women in the mission field. Another missionary couple asked her to accompany them to Java, but "the . . . arguments of judicious friends against my going out single, led me to hold back and . . . decide on remaining at home." She had been bitterly disappointed at her own timidity, she wrote, "and my weak, sinful heart began to grow cold and selfish."*

---

* Her friends were Rev. and Mrs. Elbert Nevius. Because Mrs. Nevius was in frail health, her husband wanted another woman along to help care for her and to teach school in her spare time. When Jane Shaw backed off, his wife's sister, Miss Azubah C. Condit, agreed to go as an "assistant missionary," and became perhaps the first

Then, she told Ferdinand, he had entered her life. She saw it as a sign from God.

> My heavenly Father at length opened a way for me to the very field on which my heart was first fixed and the call seemed so decidedly one of his own making, and His providence in it so marked and peculiar that I was led to consider and pray over it until my feelings were so enlisted and my views of duty so clear, that the present determination to go in company with one of his dear servants was made, and with humble gratitude I now hold myself in readiness to do, to be, and to suffer whatever He may will concerning me. . . .
>
> Do you think that the above narration contains anything that should cause you to believe I have been called to go with you? If so, *I am yours,* for now you know all and I feel happy to think that my heart has really unburdened itself to you. I prayed that God would direct me what to say and I know and feel that He has. This has been in many respects a pleasant day to me, and I have been enabled to pray with much earnestness for my beloved Ferdinand. My heart feels lighter under the firm conviction that if it should after all be best for me not to go, God will prevent me. Oh, it is pleasant to feel that we are *His* and he will use us for Himself.
>
> Still continue to pray for me my dear friend. The time draws near when we are to take solemn vows upon us and I will need much, very much grace to qualify me for a situation so responsible, conspicuous and solemn. May God prepare you to bear the responsibilities and trials which a union with me may impose upon you. Sometimes I fear that you will not be happy with me, my disposition is yet unknown to you. The weaknesses of my character have not yet been developed, and you know but little of her whom you so tenderly love. Oh, that you may not be forced to discover any thing that will forfeit that affection. . . .

---

single American woman ever to engage in mission work. Mrs. Nevius's health did not improve and eventually forced her and her husband to abandon the mission field and return home in 1843. His sister-in-law remained overseas, however, became the third wife of Rev. David O. Allen of the Bombay mission, and died just six months later.

Farewell my much loved friend, may your heart and your trust be in Heaven.

> With fond affection I am
> *Yours,*
> Jane[40]

Two days after she finished her letter to Ferdinand, on August 31, 1836, he and another newly minted minister, Rev. Henry Cherry, were ordained as missionaries to South India in the First Presbyterian church at Rochester. The enterprise upon which they were about to embark, said the presiding pastor, promised "the *certainty of success.* The Spirit of God is with His servants, light is dawning in every quarter of the world."[41] As the two young missionaries left the church surrounded by tearful well-wishers, a hymn especially composed and performed for the occasion echoed in their ears.

> Trusting in Christ, go, heralds, rear
> The Gospel standard, void of fear;
> Go, seek with joy your destined home,
> And preach a Saviour there unknown
>
> Yes, Christian heroes, go—proclaim
> Salvation in Immanuel's name
> To distant climes the tidings bear,
> And plant the Rose of Sharon there.[42]

The congregation's tears were understandable. It was presumed that missionaries would live out their lives abroad. Withdrawal from the field, one early missionary wrote, was an admission of failure, "a lasting stigma."[43] India was at least four months away, unimaginably strange, haunted by mysterious fevers; of the ninety-one missionaries, assistant missionaries, and their wives whom the American Board had sent to Ceylon and India since 1815, twenty-one had already died, as had many of their children. Both Ferdinand and Jane arranged to sit for portraits so that if they did not return their friends and families might remember what they had looked like.

.   .   .

They were married on September 16 in New York City. Jane's brother-in-law, Christopher Robert, appeared as a witness for the couple and loaned them $300 with which to start their lives together.* But no member of the Ward family attended, and no part of the Ward fortune was given to them as a wedding gift. Ferdinand's father was still unable to bear the thought of his youngest son defying him and disappearing overseas. In a letter to Rochester written two days after the wedding, Ferdinand hoped his father would one day learn to love "My dear Jane (now my *wife*)" and be "willing to address her as Daughter."[44]

The American Board booked passage to India aboard the merchant ship *Saracen* for the Wards and six other couples, all of whom had also recently married in order to qualify for the mission field. Like Ferdinand, William Tracy had attended Princeton Seminary. Clarendon Muzzy had graduated from Andover. Henry Cherry, Edward Cope, and Nathaniel Crane had all attended Auburn, where their fellow passenger Dr. John Steele, who was to act as their physician, had studied medicine. All of them and their wives came from New England or from New England families who had settled in New York and Pennsylvania, all were imbued with the Puritan faith of their forebears, and all expected to reinforce the same new mission among the Tamils at the ancient temple town of Madura,† some 275 miles southeast of Madras.

The evening before they were to board their ship at Boston, a mass farewell meeting was held at the Bowdoin Street Church. Ferdinand, Jane, and the rest of their missionary band were ushered to the front pew. The Gothic interior was kept dim until everyone was seated. Then, a missionary newspaper reported, "precisely at the hour, an additional quantity of gas was suddenly let into the lamps which instantaneously filled the house with a glare of light. At the same moment the organ burst forth into peals which shook the whole edifice, as though the whole congregation were putting forth their acclamation of joy."[45] Several clergymen addressed those about to embark, holding them up as exemplars for all Christians everywhere. "The Lord Jesus has sent you," Rev. Hubbard Winslow told the missionary band. "He is the head and the apostles are your predecessors." Like the apostles, these new missionaries might not be "absolutely *perfect*," he continued, but they were "eminently *holy*."[46]

---

* Just under $7,000 in purchasing power today.
† Modern Madurai.

Ferdinand had written to his parents that evening, begging them to write to him often in India: "I love you notwithstanding the apparent contradiction of my conduct. Will you pray for me? I have taken a serious step. I need grace, constant grace. We may not meet again on earth. God grant we may above."[47] The next day, November 23, 1836, just moments before the *Saracen* slipped out of Boston Harbor into the open sea, he scribbled another note:

> Dear Father,
>   Pilot soon leaves. I only say, I am leaving *Native-Land, Home—Friends* to do good. My motive is, as far as I think, pure. God bless you all. Love to Mother—dear Mother . . .
> Your son,
Ferdinand[48]

His mother would write to him from time to time in India over the next few years. His unforgiving father never did.

Ferdinand remembered the four-month voyage to India as "a test of my Christian character." Each couple aboard the *Saracen* was assigned one of seven cabins in the first hold. Ferdinand bravely pronounced them "commodious";[49] in fact, each was only six feet wide, with room for no furnishings other than a chair, a table, and two berths, the lowest hung high enough so that trunks and boxes could be slid beneath it. The weather turned bad within a day or two of setting sail, and the Wards and all their fellow missionaries became violently seasick. Loose luggage slammed against the cabin walls. Portholes had to be shut and secured against the waves, cutting off the air. Vomit and seawater sloshed from one side of the heaving cabin floor to the other. The stench was almost unbearable. It took several days before most of the husbands could bring themselves to leave their cabins, and several days more before the wives felt well enough to venture out on deck. One man did not regain his feet for nearly eight weeks, and, according to Ferdinand, none of the women felt fully restored until the voyage ended.

On the whole, the owners of merchant vessels welcomed missionaries: they could be counted on to book passage in groups, for one thing, and they helped fill empty cargo space on outward-bound voyages to distant destinations that did not interest other travelers. Captains forced to spend months with them at sea were generally less enthusiastic: the Massachusetts mariner Nathaniel Ames, for one, thought missionaries "obnoxious cargo" and saw no need ever to choose sides in the ongoing "battle between Calvin and Vishnoo."[50]

Captain Joseph P. Thomson, commander of the *Saracen*, quickly came to share that view. Before the missionaries set sail, Ferdinand recalled, Thomson assured them that during the four-month voyage, "we should have as much *preaching & praying* as we chose."[51] That turned out to be a great deal. There was a full-scale church service each Sunday morning at which Ferdinand and the other missionaries took turns delivering sermons from the fo'c'sle. But every other morning of the week, the Wards and the other missionaries also held prayer services before breakfast and studied scripture afterward; there was a daily eleven o'clock prayer meeting on deck, then Bible classes after lunch, a lady's prayer meeting at teatime, and a second on-deck prayer meeting after dinner. Hymns were sung with voices raised in order to be heard over the constant barnyard clamor that emanated from the chickens, ducks, and geese kept in crates on deck, a clamor that rose to a terrified crescendo at the slightest sign of rain.

At first, Captain Thomson found his passengers at least tolerable; he and his wife even attended the Sabbath services on deck for a week or two. But as time went by, he began to find the missionaries' unremitting piety grating. They insisted on calling one another "Brother" and "Sister," and seemed always to be trying to impress everyone, including themselves, with the gravity of their endeavor. ("Sprightliness" in private might be justified in some circumstances, Ferdinand told his parents in a letter written aboard the *Saracen*, but "*levity* is *never* admissible in an *intelligent—immortal—accountable* being.")[52] And the missionaries soon made it clear to Thomson that they saw it as their duty, not only to pray among themselves but also to bring to Christ the *Saracen*'s entire crew, thirteen hard-drinking, hard-living, tough-talking seamen. To that end, they began to interrupt the sailors' work at all hours of the day, handing them tracts, offering counsel, and exhorting them to repent. As Ferdinand reported to the Board back in Boston, Thomson finally could stand it no longer.

> As we advanced about our course [of converting the crew] his
> manners changed [and] the strong enmity of [his] natural heart

began to manifest itself. He used profane language in our presence & as it was continued we unitedly remonstrated through a committee. But to that remonstrance he gave no heed, continuing a practice which by his own acknowledgment was useless & to us painful on the plea that when he was excited he did not know what he was doing. He kept an uncalled-for watch over us while conversing with the Seamen—often calling them to engage in some employment which was unnecessary & on one occasion, for a cause quite insufficient, prohibited *all* conversation with the men at *any time.*[53]

The missionaries declared a day of fasting and prayer to persuade the captain to change his mind. He did, eventually, but life aboard the ship had been tense from then on, especially during two weeks when the *Saracen* was becalmed off Ceylon, the sun merciless, the cabins airless and hot, the sea like a polished silver plate stretching away in all directions. When the ship finally dropped anchor off Madras, passengers and captain were equally glad that the voyage had come to an end.

TWO

Labouring in Hope

The Wards spent their first night in Madras in a spacious white-washed bungalow on the seashore at Royapuram, just north of Fort St. George. It was the new home and headquarters of the Reverend Miron Winslow, the veteran missionary from Jaffna who had earlier told Jane she would not be welcome if she came to Ceylon alone. He had so recently arrived at Madras to set up this new station—intended primarily to provide printed materials in Tamil—that no one aboard the *Saracen* had known it existed before coming ashore.

Now, Rev. Winslow had another surprise for the *Saracen* passengers, all of whom had assumed they were to proceed immediately to Madura. Most of the *Saracen* company would leave by oxcart in mid-April as planned, he said, but the Board had authorized him to retain two of the newcomers to strengthen the new mission run by him and another Jaffna veteran, Dr. John Scudder. He asked the brethren of the *Saracen* company themselves to decide who among them was to stay behind. At an evening meeting held at the home of Dr. Scudder, they chose Ferdinand and Jane and William Tracy and his wife, Emily.

There is no way of knowing now why the rest of the *Saracen* company voted as they did. It may have been as simple as the fact that Ferdinand and Tracy were both Princeton men, while Cherry, Cope, Crane, and Steele had all attended Auburn together and had not wished to be separated. But Ferdinand was not pleased; he felt rejected, set apart, discriminated against. According to his skeletal journal, it took him three days to conclude that "it is my duty to remain at Madras," and he finally gave in only because it had been "the unanimous opinion of the Brethren" that he do so.[1] He would never again so easily defer to his colleagues.

The Wards struggled to adjust to India. "Went among the natives with Mr. Winslow," Ferdinand noted early on. "Oh, the wretchedness & moral death!"[2] April, May, and early June marked the height of summer, with temperatures hovering around 100 degrees. Tempers frayed. "Helped wife move boxes and unpack bedding," Ferdinand noted after they moved into a rented bungalow of their own at Royapuram. "Got some cross words and quick words. Felt bad all the evening."[3]

The sights and sounds of the city streets defeated Ferdinand's powers of description; they made him feel, he wrote, just as he had after his first visit to New York City, when he "looked with wonder . . . upon the strange things of Broadway."[4] Some 400,000 people lived in and around Madras, twice the population of New York. Ferdinand commissioned an artist to paint a series of street scenes to be sent home to Rochester: the seaside bungalow in which he and Jane were living; a street barber at work in the open air; a goldsmith tapping at his miniature forge; an entertainer leading a costumed monkey on a string; a Shaivite mendicant, smeared with ash and strung with prayer beads; and another Hindu devotee in the throes of religious fervor, slashing at his own thigh as a symbol of his zeal—a sight, Ferdinand lamented, "seen frequently in the streets."[5]

He grew frustrated by the unexpected difficulty of learning Tamil. ("It is a fearfully ugly language," wrote one English newcomer, "clattering, twittering, chirping, sputtering—like a whole poultry-yard let loose upon one, and not a single singing-bird, not a melodious sound among them.")[6] And he found the languid pace of life insufferable. Patience, he wrote, "requires an amount of Christian feeling which I cannot command to keep peace with the *slow* method of doing things in this land. That the natives should [demonstrate] this spirit is not strange, but it pervades the whole country. They talk of a *week* as we do of a day."[7]

It all became too much for him. Day after day—and sometimes for
as long as two weeks without a break—he recorded his suffering from
"sick headache," "excitement," "exhaustion & fatigue," and repeated
attacks of dysentery, which he decorously called "an ailment common in this climate" and for which fifteen leeches were once applied
by a British physician, to little effect except to further weaken the
already-depleted patient.[8] Jane was often ill as well.

The Wards' frequent illness did not prevent them from taking tea
with British clergymen or keep Ferdinand from preaching several
times to the British congregation of the Davidson's Street Church in
Blacktown. And when the news reached Madras in August that William IV of England had died two months earlier, Ferdinand was able
to drag himself from his sickbed long enough to accompany Jane to
the fort to "witness the troops arrayed and hear the proclamation *that
Princess Victoria is Queen!*"[9]

Then, after five months in Madras, the Reverends Ward and Tracy
and their wives were suddenly told they were to proceed to Madura,
after all; there was no longer enough money in the treasury of the
Madras mission to pay them.

On September 19, they set out for Madura, the Hindu bastion that
was now to be their home. The journey took twenty days. Ferdinand
rode in an oxcart, careful to hew to the economic strictures insisted
upon by the American Board. But he saw to it that Jane was carried in
a palanquin borne on the shoulders of teams of six men. They chanted
in Tamil as they hurried on:

> She's not heavy, *Putterum, Putterum*
> Carry her softly, *Putterum, Putterum*
> Nice little lady, *Putterum, Putterum* . . .
> Carry her gently.[10]

A cook and a bearer named Gabriel came along too, with two coolies
to carry utensils.

Nights were spent in government rest houses, spaced a day's travel
apart and each cared for by a watchman who could be relied upon
to strangle a chicken for the evening meal. The countryside through

which they passed was lush and green after the monsoon: thick forests interspersed with rice fields and groves of coconut palms; distant blue hills reminiscent, Ferdinand told the American Board, of upstate New York, "our Fatherland."[11] They crossed the rivers that twisted across their path in circular buffalo-skin boats, thirty feet across. There were troops of monkeys, too, and a huge banyan tree alive with fruit bats. At night the weird far-off wailing of jackals reminded Ferdinand of the sound of the wolves that had haunted his boyhood sleep.

It all might have seemed like a rare adventure if the Wards' religious convictions had permitted them to enjoy any of it wholeheartedly. But signs of the faith they had sworn to eradicate were everywhere: "If we are delighted with the appearance of a fresh and shady grove," Ferdinand wrote, "our spirits sink at the sight of the images its branches hide."[12] Even the friendly villagers who came out to watch them pass— "the poor, degraded, yet immortal beings around me," Ferdinand called them[13]—inspired in him only a sense of helplessness: he was still too inarticulate in Tamil to keep them from the fiery doom from which he was sure his Gospel message would otherwise have saved them.

On October 9, 1837, the Wards and the Tracys at last came within sight of the two giant *gopurams* of the Sri Minakshi Temple at Madura. Some forty thousand people lived in the temple's shadow, most of them devotees of Shiva and his local consort, Minakshi. As the little party moved toward the city walls they fell in with a stream of pilgrims, whose joyful shouting of the names of their deities struck Ferdinand and Jane as "demonic."[14]

The Reverend William Todd greeted them within the dusty mission compound. He was just thirty-six, but seemed far older. Todd had established the American outpost three years earlier with the help of just two other missionaries from Jaffna and three Tamil-speaking Ceylonese. It had not been easy. Madura was "inexpressibly filthy,"[15] Todd had reported to the American Board not long after he got there: a tangle of narrow, squalid streets filled with refuse, permeated by the stench of sewage and stagnant water, ravaged annually by cholera. The city had once been the capital of the Pandyan kings, in whose tumbled-down former palace a mob had once threatened to kill Todd if he did not stop maligning their gods. But it was now almost exclusively a place of Hindu pilgrimage, "a stronghold of religious debauchery," Todd told the Board. "Tumultuous processions, wild and fantastic as the dreams of a maniac . . . pervade the city night and day, making the idolaters drunk with the excess of glare, noise and folly . . . all in barbarous taste."[16]

Todd's first wife had died within weeks of her arrival; he had then married a widow (who had herself already buried two missionary husbands), only to watch her die, too. His Ceylonese helpers languished from homesickness. His own physical and psychological health had dangerously deteriorated.[*]

Still, despite everything, without ever mastering Tamil and with only sporadic reinforcements from Jaffna and the United States, Todd had organized a small congregation, started thirty-five free primary schools for boys and one for girls, established a secondary school in which students were taught in English, and dispatched missionaries to establish a second mission thirty-eight miles to the northwest in Dindigul. Todd had asked Boston for twenty-seven additional missionaries to carry on and expand his work. He got just seven.

The most recent newcomers would not prove as helpful as Todd had hoped. Shortly after the Wards moved into a single room on the roof of the bungalow newly assigned to Rev. and Mrs. Crane, Ferdinand met with Todd and the rest of the missionary brethren and was told he and Jane would immediately have to shift again, to the new outpost at Dindigul.

Ferdinand was again displeased at being told what to do and where to go. This time, after at least one visit to the British assistant surgeon responsible for seeing to the health of Europeans in the district and several days of prayer and "agitating the question," he announced that he and Jane would not move. Perhaps it was fears about his health that made him do it. Dr. Steele, the mission physician, who had been sta-

---

[*] Todd's depression would steadily deepen. He eventually asked to be allowed to resign his post but then to stay on at Madura and try to find some other work. His fellow missionaries insisted he go home. They argued to the American Board that having one of their number jobless and single, no longer preaching God's word, and evidencing what they called a "diseased mind," would constitute a "blot" on the mission. Boston eventually agreed. Todd sailed home. He was bitter for a time—he refused the allowance for himself and the children of his second wife to which he was entitled—but his devotion to the mission cause never waivered. In 1858, he went west to Clay County, Kansas, where he preached until his death in 1874 in a one-room schoolhouse he named the Madura Congregational Church.

tioned at Dindigul, was about to leave for Jaffna for his own health; he was suffering from a lung ailment that would eventually be diagnosed as tuberculosis. Without him, Dindigul would be a far more dangerous place. Perhaps Jane already suspected she was pregnant—she would give birth to her first child nine months later—and he did not wish for her to be a two-day ride from the best available care. Whatever the reason, his refusal to follow orders was not popular with his colleagues, the first recorded instance of the "lawlessness" that would alienate his brethren over the years. He evidently understood their annoyance, for thereafter, when meetings of the mission were scheduled, sudden headaches often made it impossible for him to attend.

A few weeks later, the mission organized three new outstations. Rev. and Mrs. Crane were assigned to one of them. The Wards moved downstairs to take over the bungalow and assume responsibility for mission activities in and around Madura. In his journal, Ferdinand set out the "Ordinary Duties" of his day. He rose at four each morning and spent two and a half hours in his study, writing and praying. At six thirty, he visited the English school. Breakfast with Jane at eight was followed by prayer with the servants on the veranda. He studied Tamil with a local teacher for two hours, lunched with Jane, then returned to his study for two more. The Wards rode out together in what passed for the cool of the evening, had dinner, and—provided he had no services to lead—were in bed by nine. Ferdinand also preached regularly to Madura's small Anglo-Indian community, and often rode out into the countryside in a bullock-drawn bandy, practicing his still-unsteady Tamil on curious crowds and handing out tracts and pamphlets to anyone who would take them.

Hard work and hardship could be endured provided hope for the ultimate success of the mission remained high. But events back home had begun to undermine that hope even before the Wards landed at Madras. In March 1837, the United States had begun to feel the effects of the first great financial panic in its history. "No man living has seen such a prostration of business, of enterprise, of hope," Secretary Anderson warned the missions that summer. "There is yet no symptom of relief, and probably the worst is yet to come. Many of our most munificent friends are among the bankrupts. There is no alternative for us but to lay to for a time as in a storm."[17]

That storm would never fully lift. Fund-raising collapsed. To meet the immediate crisis, the Prudential Committee of the American Board passed a series of stringent cost-cutting resolutions. Recruitment and reinforcements were frozen; no more missionaries would be coming to India, at least not for a time. Each outpost was required drastically to reduce its budget and then stick faithfully to it. All twenty-five schools in Madura would have had to close had it not been for contributions from sympathetic Britons in Madras. To all of this, the missionaries at Madura reluctantly acquiesced.

But the final emergency resolution passed by the committee struck the missionaries as a personal betrayal. The Wards and all their colleagues had left home expecting to remain permanently at their posts, but with the understanding that if the state of their health demanded it, the brethren with whom they served could authorize their return to the United States at the Board's expense. Now, Boston decreed it would no longer be "proper for any missionary to visit the United States except by invitation or permission. . . . It is better that our missionaries should die on the field of battle, than to return to camp in a wounded or disabled state. . . . As the missionary does more good by living among the heathen, so he does more good by dying among them."[18]

Ferdinand and two other members of the mission sent off a strongly worded protest on behalf of their Madura brethren. A missionary's colleagues knew far more about his health than anyone in Boston could possibly know, they wrote; it took eight to twelve months for messages to move back and forth between continents, far too long to save lives; and while it might be true that dying abroad would inspire more financial support from American churches, it was also undeniable that "Whatever of evil occurs to Missionaries is joy to the Heathens." The Brahmins of Madura already liked to say that the goddess Minakshi would not tolerate missionaries: Why else would both of Rev. Todd's wives have died?

"With sincere respect and Christian affection," they called upon the committee to rescind its order.*

It would not. There was to be no easy retreat.

---

* The Sandwich Island mission was far more vehement in its response. Several missionaries resigned, charging Boston with being "monopolistic," "despotic," "anti-republican," even "anti-scriptural." Ferdinand De Wilton Ward, Edward Cope, and Nathaniel M. Crane to the Secretaries of the ABCFM, November 8, 1838, American Board of Commissioners for Foreign Missions Archive, Houghton Library, Harvard University.

Meanwhile, as Jane's pregnancy progressed, nature harassed the mission. There were monsoon rains and months of relentless heat, Ferdinand told his sister, Henrietta.

> As we have no window glass here, where light came wind & sand came, too, & it was trying indeed. There was no escape. I dislike wind & hot wind bearing on its bosom a load of fine sand which it deposits on the table—books—paper—hand—face—in food & etc. This is most disagreeable. These winds bring with them fever—headache—low spirits &c. . . . It is now evening, but the wind is whistling out of doors. Not the healthful whistle of a Genesee North Easter which, though it reddens the cheek, causes the blood to flow with a quick step & the body to assume a strong, plastic form. No, no, but hot, hot, hot.[19]

Bookshelves stood away from walls to discourage the omnivorous white ants; the legs of all the chairs and tables, bureaus and beds rested in brass cups filled with water to bar the armies of ants that filed across the bamboo matting from climbing upward. Ferdinand killed a great spider that had made its home overnight in his shoe; its body "was nearly the size of the palm of my hand, . . ." he wrote, "olive brown, and covered with a soft down." [20]

The mosquitoes began to swarm at dusk. Bats fed on them, squealing in and out of the windows and sometimes entangling themselves in the netting that shrouded Jane and Ferdinand's bed. Clouds of moths and winged ants whirled around the hissing lamps. And even after the lamps were extinguished, fat pale-green geckos clung to the ceiling, waiting for insect prey: sometimes they missed their kill and fell, hitting the floor with a smack loud enough to wake a fitful sleeper.

Jane suffered most and often found herself alone. While Ferdinand went about beneath his umbrella, she huddled inside the mission bungalow, its doors and windows darkened by thick mats of woven grass, her only companions the servants who wet down the mats with bucketfuls of water and the boy who dozed outside with the rope that pulled the creaking punkah back and forth, tied to his big toe.

Her pregnancy proved difficult. Ferdinand's journals are studded with notes that she was having "a bad day." The British doctor visited frequently.

Ferdinand recorded the final hours of his wife's pregnancy:

> July 16 Jane's "confinement" commenced at 10 yesterday morning & continued with great severity until today at 10 AM she became the loving mother of a living infant—a Daughter. Praised be the name of the Lord!

> July 18 Jane quite comfortable. The Lord is good to her in her distress. We praise Him. Wrote to *Mother.*[21]

The infant was named Sarah, after one of Jane's sisters.

A little over a month later, Ferdinand rode off on still another itinerating tour. "Oh, my beloved Husband," Jane wrote.

> How chequered with joy and *sorrow* is this life of ours! Another & another & another is hurried to eternity. . . . Brother and Sister Tracy called to [Ceylon] to bury their beloved infant—by the side of all who have died from our company since we left America. . . . [Mrs. Cherry had died by then; so had the Muzzys' first child.]
>
> Oh what feelings of horror & trembling come over my whole frame. *You* cannot know a *Mother's* feelings. Oh, if God should see fit to call our little Sarah, I think my heart would break. . . . I feel your absence very much. May the Lord help you my dear Husband & give you back to us in His own good time.[22]

Despite the toll taken by climate and worry and frequent loneliness, Jane Ward remained determined to do at least some of the Lord's work that had driven her into marriage in the first place. Ferdinand sympathized, but the American Board did not encourage it. "The first duty of a missionary's wife is to have a *smiling face,*" a veteran member of the Jaffna mission once explained. "A female belongs to her compound. That is her peculiar sphere."[23] The Board's corresponding secretary, Samuel Worcester, spelled out the important but distinctly limited role missionary wives were expected to play: it was by "example," not by active preaching, that they were to contribute to the cause. "Woman was designed," he said, "to be an help meet for man"; her proper role was "to help the Brethren" and to present always to the unconverted "an example of the purity and dignity and kindliness—the salutary and vivifying influence, the attractive and celestial excellence—which Christianity can impart to the female character."[24]

If she could not go out on her own in search of souls to save as her husband could, she would have them come to her. In this, at least, she had the backing of the Board; the one role outside the household thought fit for mission wives was what Dr. Anderson called "the whole business of female education."[25] Jane was allowed to organize a school for girls, who met on the veranda of her home each morning to learn arithmetic and needlework, reading and writing in English and Tamil, Christian scripture, and "the natural history of birds."

It was something, but it was not enough for her, not what she had bargained for when she agreed to marry a man she barely knew. "I expected to go among the people and talk Truth with them—Argue— exhort, entreat and postulate," Ferdinand quoted her as having com- plained. "But how *disappointed* [I am]. I can't speak. The language is against me. I can't get out. The *heat* and [infant] *forbid*. I have lost my strength and my nerves are unstrung, my constitution shattered. I am worthless."[26] That same sense of personal worthlessness and perpetual disappointment would recur throughout her long life, darkening the atmosphere around her, eventually affecting each of her children.

"Madura is ready to receive the Truth," Ferdinand had written not long after he arrived, "and so is *India*."[27] But, for the most part, he found that those whom he and Jane had come so far to save were impervious to his message of salvation. Members of the small Muslim minority in Madura, he wrote, were "*in manner* cold and repulsive" and "in reli- gion most bigotedly attached to [their] own modes of faith and wor- ship . . . unique, grotesque, ludicrous, senseless and pitiable."[28] The Hindu majority struck him as still more debased. "View the gods of India," he urged mission supporters back home, "false to their word, thievish, licentious, ambitious, murderous, all indeed that is repellent, malignant and vile . . . is it surprising that there is perjury, and injus- tice, and wickedness the land over?"[29]

Few of those who attended the mission schools or listened to mis- sionary sermons did so out of religious conviction: lower-caste parents sent their children to study because no other schools would take them; higher-caste boys were willing to attend the secondary school because the English they mastered there would help ensure a good job with the British. The handful who claimed genuine conversion were for the most part untouchables; already excluded from Hindu worship, they saw little to lose and at least the possibility of something to be gained in adopting the faith professed by their rulers.

Meanwhile, the caste Hindus who filled the streets of Minakshi's city saw no reason to abandon their religion, though their priests did enjoy debating doctrine with the black-clad foreign holy men, whom they called "Swami" out of courtesy. Even Ferdinand confessed that he did not always come off best in these encounters. "Many a person who can fill a pulpit in America or England with respectability and credit," he admitted, "would undoubtedly break down if called to make an attempt among the Hindoos; and this not for want of mental strength or furniture, but from the peculiar manner in which objections are presented, and the confidence with which they are uttered."

"What do you think is the reason we leave our native country, come to your villages, and expend so much in the education of your children?" he remembered asking a group of priests.

"You expect by this good deed more certainly to reach Heaven," said one.

"Oh, it is your nature," another answered, "just as it is the nature of the jackal to prowl abroad at night."[30]

By the spring of 1840, Ferdinand and Rev. Daniel Poor had dedicated a mud-walled, thatch-roofed preaching bungalow, the first in Madura,* and for the first time the girls' day school Jane supervised began taking boarding students. But traces of disillusionment had begun to appear in Ferdinand's letters home. Actual conversions to Christianity remained maddeningly elusive: William Todd, the mission's founder, had made precisely one convert in five years: a Hindu servant in his own household who converted back again soon after his worn-out master sailed for home. Ferdinand considered the stubbornness with which his students adhered to the faith of their fathers in the face of his repeated assaults a personal affront. In April, he and Jane

---

* It would soon be supplanted by the Eastgate Church, in whose belfry was hung a bell shipped all the way from Boston in the hope that it would deny "the natives [who] have no timepieces" any excuse to miss services.

rode out to watch the annual Chithirai Festival, in which thousands of devotees haul Minakshi and her consort through the streets on huge carved carts in the light of the full moon:

> I went out between daylight and sunrise to see if, among the crowd passing like a flood from the North Gate to the river, I could discern the faces of any of the members of the English School—or others in our service—I met but one lad. I asked him where he was going. "To worship my god," was his reply. I detained him long enough to tell him what I thought of his god & what the true God thought of his conduct. Again he was in the mighty current borne on to evil & death. I will not say that others of my pupils were not there—I suppose they were—for I had learned that some of them had made vows to dance before [their deity]—but their painted faces & eccentric dress forbade my recognizing them. It was painful—a heartrending spectacle. . . . It was like a mighty river filling the whole of a wide street, & continuing for many hours. "How long, Oh Lord, how long?" was the exclamation of my heart and I turned away to return home.[31]

Jane, Ferdinand reported, was also "deeply pained" at witnessing the same procession, and "had her feelings greatly wounded."[32]

She soon found herself pregnant again. Remembering the difficulties she'd had before Sarah's birth, Ferdinand insisted in September that he and his little family proceed to Bangalore, with its moderate climate and better medical facilities, to await the new baby. They would stay there four months, boarding with a British clergyman and soaking up the distinctly British atmosphere of this garrison town. "The early mornings [in Bangalore] are as pleasant as anything I can imagine," a British visitor and friend of the Wards reported. "They have all the sweetness and freshness of an English summer. The air smells of hay and flowers, instead of ditches, dust, fried oil, curry and onions. . . . There are superb dahlias growing in the gardens, and today I saw a real full-blown hollyhock which was like meeting an old friend."[33]

Jane gave birth to a son on her own twenty-ninth birthday, December 26, 1840. He was named Levi, after Ferdinand's unyielding father.

"Little Sarah, being a *native*, enjoys fine health," Ferdinand reported to his sister from Madura a few weeks later. "So plump & healthy. Levi will, we trust, be the same but not so with their parents." In a postscript, Jane begged for a "few toys & books for my little ones. . . . My cares increase & I am less & less able to put forth much active effort. . . . [The] little ones take much of my strength & care."[34]

Her strength did not improve. Her cares multiplied. In July 1841, she and Ferdinand fell ill again. They left Madura, for Trichinopoly this time, 255 miles to the north, where there was a British garrison hospital. Ferdinand's head pounded inside the swaying palanquin in which he rode, making it impossible to sleep. Little Sarah was still well, he wrote, but infant Levi was now suffering badly from "irruptions," and Jane's health was only "mediocre. . . . I often fear what the end will be. . . . The climate makes sad drafts on her constitution & especially her nervous system & *head*."[35]

Jane recovered, and they returned to Madura. But Levi died there in November 1841, at the age of eleven months, and was buried in the walled churchyard.

Ferdinand now dreamed more and more of home. News from Rochester was infrequent: "I have been blessed with a girl and afflicted in the loss of a son since hearing from Rochester," he complained in one letter, "from which you will see that *I do not hear very often*. My last information from my beloved parents is more than a year old."[36] And again: "[How] I long at times for a little quiet and a breath of fresh air," he wrote, "a Sabbath of rest, a week of social intercourse—a sight of civilized dwellings—But No! . . . Mud houses—people with *children* quite naked—shameless habits—heat dust—noise—idols— desecrated Sabbaths—fawning for favors—deceit—all, all are constantly in view. . . . To live among [Hindus] is a *trial*, a *task*."[37]

To live among his fellow missionaries turned out to be a greater trial, a harder task; it was finally they who would drive the Wards from Madura and then bar them from India itself. It is impossible now to reconstruct precisely what went so badly wrong. Much of the evidence was deliberately destroyed long ago, and only a few surviving clues can be teased from faded letters scattered through several archives.

Perhaps it was inevitable that the Madura missionaries should fall out among themselves. The *Saracen* company had all nodded in agreement when the Boston clergyman who saw them off to India declared them imperfect, but they had all also privately concurred when he called them "eminently holy." When men and women persuaded of their holiness clashed in the South Indian heat, confusion and rancor were the likely result.

They were hopelessly outnumbered, haunted by illness, underpaid, and frequently out of touch with their superiors in Boston. And because of the financial difficulties brought on by the lingering economic troubles at home, they found themselves in a sometimes bitter battle with the Madras and Jaffna missions over the few resources that remained. Jaffna thought Madras redundant, since both missions operated Tamil printing presses. Madras saw itself as a poor relation of both its sister missions. Madura, far inland, felt isolated and sometimes abandoned. There were genuine differences over policy within the missions, too; some believed the promotion of schools undercut the importance of preaching the Gospel; some wanted to attack the caste system straight on; others thought it best to work within it.

Still, they were a personally quarrelsome lot. Pronouncing judgment upon one another seemed to provide them with a kind of grim entertainment, and the Wards came in for more than their share of criticism. Although the Board officially sanctioned it, some missionary wives had found unseemly Jane's determination to make a mark in the world outside her compound by overseeing a girls' school. The brethren resented the eagerness with which Ferdinand volunteered for prolonged inspection tours that left to his colleagues the daily monotony of seeing to the schools, and they were further irritated by the too-obvious pleasure he took in writing accounts of his own itinerating for the *Missionary Herald* back home. The Wards' relative prosperity was also a source of irritation. It had taken not one, but two oxcarts to haul their household goods from Madras to Madura, and not long after their arrival they purchased a cart and four bullocks for their personal use, an extravagance still remembered in the Madura mission seventy years later. Relatives and friends in Rochester and New York sent them clothing, books, and toys for their children often enough to further anger their less-fortunate fellow missionaries. Some of the brethren evidently made their envy plain to their families back home; within a few months of the Wards' arrival, Dr. Anderson informed Madura that he was aware of rumors that "the younger missionaries" stationed there showed an alarming tendency toward "extravagance in house, furniture, style, dress, etc."[38] The Wards were the youngest missionaries at Madura by several years.

But most of all, the Wards' colleagues came to disapprove of the couple's closeness to Jane's old friend John Lawrence, whose religious ardor and unwillingness to follow orders exceeded even theirs: while out walking one morning in January 1837, while the Wards were still at sea, Lawrence had shouldered his way between two women making offerings at an outdoor shrine, called them fools for worshipping idols, and then smashed their deity with his cane. An angry crowd gathered. Pupils deserted the mission schools. Rev. Todd thought it best to send Lawrence out of town, to join Rev. Robert Dwight at Dindigul. There, Lawrence continued to do things his own way, despite growing disapproval from his brethren. Ordered to build a modest preaching bungalow, he constructed a full-scale chapel instead, using funds solicited from devout Britons living in the area. When the quarterly meeting of the mission met at Dindigul in August 1841, most of the brethren declared themselves "aghast" at what he had done, and censured him for disobedience and vainglory. Lawrence stalked from the meeting.

Only Ferdinand and one other missionary stood by him. Ferdinand's colleagues seem never to have forgiven him for that—or for the icy hauteur with which he and Jane subsequently refused, for weeks at a time, even to speak to those who dared to differ with them.

At midnight on September 25, 1842, Ferdinand sat writing to his sister Henrietta by lamplight. "I am in the sickroom of our physician Dr. Steele," Ferdinand wrote. "Consumption is hastening him to the grave. A few weeks, perhaps a few days, will close his earthly existence." He apologized for not having written lately. His head ached continuously now, he said. Jane was pregnant for a third time and still weak from intermittent fevers that had not left her since the death of her infant son eleven months before. A box sent from Rochester a year earlier had never arrived. Another, filled with mail from home, had leaked, making most of the letters illegible.

"The *sixth* year of my absence from America is hastening to its close," he continued. "How many the changes that have occurred during that period." His grandfather, Deacon Levi Ward, had died since he'd left home. So had his older brother, William. And he had only recently learned that less than a year after marrying Rev. Eli Smith, his niece Maria Chapin Smith had died in childbirth at the American Board's Beirut mission. "How close upon each other tread the footsteps of joy & sorrow," he wrote, "of the marriage greeting & the funereal sob . . . , Mary's wedding & Mary's funeral!" He had still not heard a word from his disapproving father. "How few of my anticipations of usefulness have been realized. How *little* have I done in comparison with what I expected to accomplish. The nature of mission life—its . . . magnitude of duties—its severity of trials—can be known only by *experience.*"[39]

Dr. Steele would die nine days later, leaving the Madura mission without a physician and Jane without anyone to treat her fevers or oversee her pregnancy. Over the protests of his fellow missionaries, Ferdinand insisted that they flee yet again, this time one hundred miles to the southwest, to Courtallam (modern Kuttalam] in the Western Ghats, where, Ferdinand later remembered, "during the . . . western monsoon, the clouds are so driven as to cause almost hourly showers, giving to the air a delightful and invigorating coolness."[40] While they were there, Ferdinand and Jane resolved not to return permanently to Madura. Its climate was unhealthy, there was now no doctor nearby, and, perhaps most importantly, the brethren and their wives were openly hostile.

Moving from one sparsely manned mission to another without the assent of one's colleagues was unheard of, an act of open rebellion. Rather than face his colleagues in person, Ferdinand wrote privately to Rev. Winslow, asking for permission to rejoin the Madras mission, where he and his wife could be close to medical care. He said nothing whatsoever about his difficulties with his fellow missionaries at Madura—with some of whom he was still not speaking. Always shorthanded, Rev. Winslow wrote right back, eager to strengthen his chronically overworked outpost. With Winslow's written permission in hand, Ferdinand then wrote a letter to be read aloud at the annual meeting of the Madura mission on February 2.

After "most deliberate and prayerful thought," it said, he had resolved to *"change the field of missionary labours."*

> I deem it unnecessary to go into a *detail* of reasons. These are obvious, I apprehend, to you all. It is enough to say that *health & usefulness* of myself & family & the best interests of the mis-

sion make [a move] such as this not only desirable but *absolutely necessary*. . . .

I trust there will be no opposition to the request. A longer continuance where I now am, while it may add somewhat to the numerical force of the Mission & the amount of effort put forth in the instruction of the people, will be the continuance of great unhappiness to myself & family (if not more serious consequences pertaining to health & life) & an injury to the best of causes & most important of interests.

Trusting that the request will be at once complied with,

I remain yours most truly,

F. DW. Ward[41]

The brethren were stunned at what amounted to a haughty *fait accompli*, but even though it would mean more work for everyone—the newly widowed Mrs. Steele, for example, would find herself in charge of the girls' boarding school Jane had been running—not a single member of the mission objected to the Wards' departure. "When they left Madura (without a dissenting voice)," Henry Cherry remembered later, "Brother [Levi] Spaulding [at Jaffna] wrote to Brother Dwight [at Madura]—'I consider your Mission stronger now than it was before they left.' "*

At Madras, the Wards took up residence at Royapuram—where they had spent their first night in India—and hurled themselves into mission work, as if driven to prove their dedication to Christ all over again. Their third child, William Shaw Ward (named for Jane's father), was born there on May 26, 1843. He survived. But a fourth child, a girl named Maria (named for Ferdinand's late missionary niece, Maria Chapin Smith), would die within a few days of her birth in May of the following year. Somehow, between pregnancies and periods of grieving, Jane found time to run another girls' boarding school. Meanwhile, Ferdinand preached wherever he could, supervised six day schools in

---

* Quoted in a confidential letter from Rev. Henry Cherry to the American Board, September 20, 1846. Once Ferdinand had settled in at Madras, he would write to Secretary Anderson in Boston, claiming he had been *invited* to come to Madras and had only reluctantly accepted. Both letters are in the American Board of Commissioners for Foreign Missions Archive, Houghton Library, Harvard University.

the city, regularly visited schools in surrounding villages, and preached at five services a week—four in Tamil and one in English. He also wrote—pamphlets, children's books, editorials for a Tamil temperance weekly called *Aurora*—and learned to work a printing press so that he could help the mission printer, Phineas R. Hunt, turn out millions of pages of tracts for distribution along the roadsides.

Missionaries were rarely in much danger from Hindus or Muslims.* But in Madras, at least, Roman Catholics, whom Ferdinand and his colleagues believed at best deluded, were another matter. "Protestants are the only *true* Christians," Ferdinand wrote in *The Elements of Geography for Little Children*, a little book he wrote for use in mission schools. Catholics returned his scorn: Royapuram was largely a Catholic neighborhood and sometimes when he held services in a preaching bungalow located there, angry crowds tore up his tracts, gathered outside to jeer and throw stones, and lit noxious compounds of "sulphur, pepper and deleterious drugs" outside the windows to smoke out his listeners. Once, when none of that seemed to work, they set the structure itself ablaze. Ferdinand had it rebuilt and resumed preaching.[42]

But here, too, some of the Wards' worst problems were self-inflicted. In January 1844, roughly a year after they left Madura, cholera swept through that city. At one point, more than fifty people were dying every day. Henry Cherry's second wife, Jane, was among them. So were Minerva North, the wife of Alfred North, newly arrived, and Rev. Robert Dwight.

Dwight's widow, Mary Billings Wright, moved with her children to Madras, where, after several months, Rev. Winslow, himself now a widower for the third time, proposed that they be married. The Wards were appalled; such a marriage, less than a year after Dwight's death and to a much older man who had already buried three wives, struck them as unseemly, even un-Christian. They made their feelings known.

---

* Among the roughly 1,800 American and English Protestant missionaries who preached in India between 1800 and 1876, only twenty were actually killed by the people they struggled to convert, and eighteen of those died in the Indian Mutiny of 1857, butchered more because of their white faces than their faith. Of the remaining two, one was clubbed to death by a Sikh zealot at a Punjab village fair in 1864, and the other died in Peshawar the same year at the hands of his own night watchman who, dimly seeing his master padding through the garden in his nightshirt, shot him for a prowler.

"[Mrs. Dwight's] situation in Madras is not very comfortable under present circumstances," wrote Rev. Crane that December.

> She would be comfortable at Brother Hunt's but the Wards do not approve of her remaining at all in Madras, I mean for the future. They will not easily *forgive*, either her or Brother Winslow for entering into matrimonial engagements. Perhaps I use too strong a word, but I mean to say that they are highly displeased with the arrangement that is to unite them in marriage. I regret that they should feel so, for it will only tend to make both parties uncomfortable when they might all be made most happy by the arrangement.[43]

When Mrs. Dwight refused to retreat to the mission at Jaffna, the Wards' response was simply to stop speaking to their old friend's widow. Rev. Winslow, who had cordially welcomed the Wards to India in 1837 and had subsequently arranged for Ferdinand to rejoin his mission, was understandably indignant. Ferdinand stopped talking to him, too, and did not attend his wedding in March 1845.

By then, Ferdinand just wanted to go home. "The world is a different place to me *now* than it was ten years ago," he told his sister. "So dear Papa told me it would be & so it is."[44]

He wrote to Dr. Anderson. "When I came to India it was with a wish & expectation to die here," he said. "Nothing but a strong sense of *duty* could alter my resolution in this respect." But "long & prayerful consideration" now led him to believe he could serve God, "my family & my own *soul*" best by returning to America, "at least for some time."[45] He was not yet asking for formal permission to leave, he said, and did not plan to do so until he was sure a replacement could be found, but he also wanted his superiors to start looking for one right away.

His and Jane's health deteriorated further, and their sense of futility deepened. Ferdinand wrote a long, urgent appeal for more funds on behalf of the mission, only to have it ignored. Madura received $24,000 in 1845. Jaffna received only a thousand less. But Madras got just $4,000. "It makes us *sad*," Ferdinand told Boston. "We will not condemn. . . . But we feel grieved. We urge the point, though you give us not the men, give us the *money*."[46] Boston chose to give them neither. "*What good* has resulted from all this?" Ferdinand wrote and then sadly provided his own answer: "But little that is as yet apparent. . . . Much apparent good *I do not see*. . . . It is labouring *in hope*."*

The Wards left Madras to see if several more weeks in Bangalore would again improve their spirits and restore their health. When they returned, Ferdinand was startled to find that Dr. Anderson had responded to his letter expressing his wish to be allowed to come home by writing to Rev. Winslow rather than to him. It was clear from his letter that, while Ferdinand had claimed to have told Winslow of his plans, he had not actually done so. Worse, Anderson had asked for a fuller account of his motives for shifting from Madura to Madras, and Winslow had been unable or unwilling to provide it. Further, the

---

* It is hard now not to be scornful of the Wards for ever believing that simply by preaching the Gospel outside the gates of Hindu temples they could somehow bring down the faith that built them, a faith far older than their own. Thousands of pilgrims still stream through the Minakshi temple at Madurai each day; the dark pillared halls lined with deities that horrified the Americans are now lit by electric bulbs, but the eyes of the worshippers making offerings at its busy altars are still filled with the reverence the first missionaries failed to expunge.

The first missionaries' successors would do better by expecting less, by trying to bring understanding as well as ardor to India, by blending the blessings of literacy and modern medicine and technical skill with the Gospel.

But for all their pretensions, for all the futility of the task the Wards and their colleagues took on with such high hopes and despite the passage of more than a century and a half and the stubborn immutability of India, traces of them remain even in Madurai.

Goats pick their way through the old missionary cemetery; there are several small stones among the larger ones, each identified only by a number, and, although the book that once provided the key to who was buried where seems to have been lost, little Levi Ward presumably lies beneath one of them.

The ecumenical movement has eased the old tensions between Catholic and Protestant converts, and the sectarian bitterness that divided the Protestants of Ferdinand and Jane Ward's time from one another is largely muffled, too: the Church of South India, established with India's independence in 1947, brought the major Protestant churches into a single fold, two million strong. When the author visited the old mission compound some twenty years ago, bright-eyed children still studied on the shady verandas where Jane Ward once oversaw their lessons, and the Eastgate church, just across the road, had just celebrated its 150th anniversary. "We are still reaping the harvest sewn by those first Americans," its then pastor told me, while we strolled together around the cool interior of the New England–style meetinghouse. As he spoke, the old bell began to ring, calling the congregation Ferdinand and Jane Ward helped establish to worship once again.

secretary had expressed fear that Ferdinand might simply come home without permission.

Ferdinand had again been caught flouting the rules and misrepresenting the facts and again responded with self-righteous indignation. He had thought his letter was "private," he told Anderson. He refused to be more specific about the incessant quarreling that had caused him to leave Madura: "Mrs. Ward's health was not *the* cause. . . . I left for reasons that constrained the three Brothers [at Madura] to be unanimous in their approval. Here is where the subject rested & it is enough." He was not "lawless," he added, and if he ever did ask formal permission to return to America he would do so on the same ground that had led him to India in the first place—"Duty to God and the Church."

> Surely the Committee does not wish to use their *Authority* to keep me in India when I think that this *is not the place for me*. . . . If I return to America I go not at the urging of *friends*, not for *pleasure*, but *duty*. . . . As for the charge laid against me that I am not frank, ingenuous, straightforward, &c. I regard them as all *apocryphal*. They are too freely made and I decidedly plead "not guilty." As far as necessary I am *frank*, ingenuous, *straightforward* & all else that can denote *fairness*.[47]

A few weeks later, he again shifted his ground, and formally applied for permission to come home. He was now too ill to remain in India any longer, he said. To persuade Boston—and his fellow missionaries—that he was not malingering, he sent to the American Board on May 31, 1845, a daunting catalog of ailments attested to by the garrison surgeon at Bangalore: malarial fever; "hepatic derangement and other visceral disease"; "Bowel complaint which has greatly reduced . . . physical strength" already seriously undercut by "great mental exertions in his missionary calling and deep study"; and an "overtaxed" nervous system "inducing Dyspepsia and a tendency to *Erysipelas* [and] Inflammation of the Lower Extremities."[48]

Another hot season in India, the surgeon concluded, would surely kill him. It didn't. He would spend another eleven unhappy months in Madras before the Prudential Committee in Boston finally granted permission for him and Jane to come home. In April 1846, a little over nine years after they first landed in Madras, the Wards, with their surviving children—Sarah, seven, and William, two—finally set sail for home aboard an American vessel, the *Worcester*.

Even the sea voyage proved to be filled with tension. The despised fourth Mrs. Winslow happened also to be aboard—she, too, was ill—and by pure happenstance found herself and her child occupying a cabin more spacious and airy than the one the Wards had booked. They immediately suspected Rev. Winslow of favoritism, and refused to exchange a word with his wife during the six-week voyage.*

---

* When her husband learned of the Wards' baseless charge and self-righteous silence, he felt it necessary to write a lengthy letter to Boston detailing the entirely accidental way in which his wife had found herself more comfortable than her traveling companions in case "any misapprehensions" about it should "reach the ears of its members."

The fourth Mrs. Winslow died in 1852. "Thus he is left alone," Ferdinand wrote to his brother, "one would think, for life." Wrong again. In 1858, Rev. Winslow took a fifth wife. This one managed to outlive him. Miron Winslow to Rufus Anderson, April 12, 1848, Madras Mission's Annual Report to the ABCFM, January 1, 1845, American Board of Commissioners for Foreign Missions Archive, Houghton Library, Harvard University; Ferdinand De Wilton Ward to Levi A. Ward, June 28, 1852, Ward Family Papers, Department of Rare Books, Special Collections and Preservation, University of Rochester Library.

THREE

Chastened and Sanctified

The Rochester to which the Wards returned in the summer of 1846 had been transformed. The village Ferdinand had known as a boy had become a city, home to more than thirty thousand people, only a small minority of whom now traced their families back to New England. The Ward clan's world had altered, too. They had sold their homes on North St. Paul Street and now lived clustered together in four big handsome Federal houses on a five-acre plot on the town's eastern edge they called "Grove Place." Thirteen different varieties of trees shaded the grounds. Ferdinand's venerable parents lived there, as did his older brother, Levi, and his family, and his sisters Siba Smith, Susan Selden, and Henrietta Clarke, their husbands, and their children. Cousins played and went to school together and fought to keep the children of Irish immigrants—the "Scio Street urchins," one family member called them—from jumping the back fence to steal the family's peaches and pears and chestnuts.[1]

Ferdinand made his peace with his father. It cannot have been easy. He had disobeyed Dr. Ward by going to India as a missionary, and then, by failing and being forced to come home, he had further let him down. Ferdinand moved his wife and children into the home of his sister, Henrietta Clarke, and left them there while he entered Auburn

Seminary in Auburn, New York, where he hoped to complete the course of study his eagerness to go abroad had interrupted. Jane and the children soon joined him, taking two rooms in a boardinghouse. She told her husband that she'd felt shabby and threadbare among all the well-to-do in-laws who had failed to attend her wedding, and she had worried that Sarah and William were too "jungly" for Rochester.

Ferdinand undertook a series of speaking tours by train, preaching on behalf of Indian missions, and began to look around for a pastorate. But he took time out to bring his family back to the Grove again for Thanksgiving, eager for them to experience the family rituals he remembered from his boyhood. Candles appeared in every window of his parents' home. Before the family sat down to eat, the coachman was dispatched with a carriage full of turkeys and ducks and roasts of beef for the Orphan Asylum and the Home for the Friendless. And after the last pie plate had been carried back to the kitchen, Ferdinand's father and mother were helped into twin chairs on a raised platform so that their children and their spouses, their grandchildren and great-grandchildren—more than sixty in all—could pass below and receive their blessings.

Grove Place helped safeguard the Wards against the changes occurring all around it, but it could not shield Ferdinand and Jane from the still-smoldering anger of their former colleagues overseas. Their absence from Madura may have temporarily lowered the level of acrimony among the brethren, but it had not eliminated it. Henry Cherry, the clergyman who had been ordained as a missionary alongside Ferdinand before leaving for India and then had become one of his most bitter enemies, married for a third time. His bride was the daughter of a British magistrate whose family had been in India so long that the gossipy wife of one of the Jaffna missionaries told a friend that his new bride might secretly be an Anglo-Indian and therefore likely to "steal."[2] Cherry got wind of the insult, insisted his bride was "as purely European [white] as any of our ladies,"[3] and demanded a written apology. He was so outraged when he didn't get one that he wrote to Boston demanding that his colleague and his wife both be formally reprimanded, setting off an exchange of vitriolic letters that continued for nearly three years.

Meanwhile, the Wards' rebellious friend John Lawrence and his wife had invited Alfred North, newly widowed and lonely, to live with them at Dindigul. There, depending on whom one believed, he either

made improper advances to his hostess or she acted in a wanton and
disgraceful way toward him. In any case, Lawrence threw North out
of his house. Each then complained about the other to Boston. Always
impulsive, Lawrence compounded his problems. Twice, he was authorized to oversee the construction of cottages meant to provide desperate mission families with sanctuary from the annual ravages of cholera
and malaria, first in the Sirumalai Hills and then at Kodaikanal, in the
Palnis. He paid little attention to the agreed-upon budgets and secretly
bought himself land and planted coffee trees on it in violation of a rule
that barred missionaries from engaging in private business. Then, he
put up a separate house for his wife and children with funds that may or
may not have belonged to the mission. When he was called to account
by his fellow missionaries, he refused even to attend the meeting.

Word of continuing dissension in the Madura mission reached Boston. Questions were asked. Henry Cherry, responding on behalf of
his brethren, denied they had ever been "disorderly"; all would have
been peaceful at Madura, he said, had the Lawrences and Wards never
been assigned there.* The quarrel between John Lawrence and Alfred
North continued for months. Charges and countercharges made their
slow way back and forth between South India and Boston with no sign
of compromise on either side. Finally, Dr. Anderson ordered both men
home to appear before him.

Ferdinand knew little of all this until a few days after Thanksgiving,
when he received a letter from Boston. Rev. Anderson had heard a
rumor that Ferdinand had helped provide private unauthorized funds
for his friend Lawrence and asked for an explanation. Stung once again
at the suggestion that he could have done anything wrong or acted
out of anything but the loftiest motives, Ferdinand composed a hasty
answer. Not long after he had arrived in Boston from India, he'd been
introduced to a Mr. Wordsworth, a Revolutionary War pensioner who
had asked him how he might safely send $200 in two installments to
his friend Mrs. Lawrence, who was said to be in "very embarrassed
circumstances" at Dindigul. Ferdinand had suggested a way to send
the first $100 (some $1,800 in today's dollars), using a courier whom

---

* Much of the evidence relating to the Madura mission's internal quarrels was deliberately destroyed. This summary is based on an examination of letters separately filed
under the names of the individual missionaries involved, in the American Board of
Commissioners for Foreign Missions Archive, Houghton Library, Harvard University,
including Cherry's confidential report to the American Board, September 20, 1846.

he knew to be reliable. "This is all I have to do with the case," he told Anderson. "I was not asked as to the *necessity* of the case or the *expediency* of sending the sum. I said that it would be most welcome" but had "remained ignorant as to Mrs. Lawrence's 'pecuniary state.' "

Then, unable to control his temper at having his actions questioned, and still resentful of the economies the Prudential Committee had insisted upon, Ferdinand went on to lash its members with gratuitous sarcasm.

> When I left India at least 2/3 of the members of the Madura Mission were in debt. Whether this rose from *extravagance* or the *small salaries* is not for me to say but I state the *fact*. This feature is not *peculiar* to Madura. Others of our Missions are in the same state. . . .
>
> As to Mr. Lawrence, you are informed of my opinion of him as a devoted Christian and a laborious and successful missionary. He has . . . my most sincere affection and respect. As is not unusual, he is better versed in *theology* than in *banking* and is more successful in *debate* than in *bargaining*.[4]

Ferdinand evidently felt himself in a strong position. He was convinced he'd done nothing wrong and equally sure that his old friend John Lawrence would soon be on hand to make everything clear.

He was mistaken. The Lawrences had set out for home from Dindigul a few days after Ferdinand's letter was mailed, but months of fever and severe dysentery had fatally weakened his old friend. Lawrence made it only as far as the coastal city of Tranquebar, where he died on the day after Christmas. Mrs. Lawrence, left with three children and a dead husband, saw to it that he was buried, then hurled all of his correspondence into the sea. Ferdinand was now without any prospect of having access to the papers or eliciting the testimony with which he had hoped to defend himself.

"My health is much improved," Ferdinand had assured Dr. Anderson and the Board not long after coming home. "Mrs. W. is also much better. I love India and yet anticipate a return to that land. When, I cannot say."[5]

If his former colleagues at Madura had their say, the answer would be never. Henry Cherry had already made that clear in his letter to Boston: the Wards had been troublemakers from the moment they arrived in India, he charged; they had failed to accede to the wishes of the majority, adopted a policy of "non-intercourse"[6]—that is, silence—toward those of whom they disapproved, refused to respond to the mission's calls for greater economies, openly defied regulations meant to apply to all.

Then, in the autumn of 1847, Alfred North arrived home, carrying with him a lengthy official defense of the mission's actions regarding Lawrence and his allies. "The abominable conduct of the Wards" could never be forgiven, North said; if Ferdinand were to try to return to India and reestablish friendly relations with his former colleagues, "I can assure him that the remembrance of the numerous annoyances he has inflicted upon them for these ten years is too vivid and their personal knowledge of him too intimate, to allow them to listen."[7]

Dr. Anderson sent Ferdinand a summary of the charges. He was stunned.

"I need not tell you, Dear Sir," Ferdinand wrote back, "of the bitterness of soul this document has caused me."[8] He boarded a train for Boston, stormed into Anderson's offices, and demanded the opportunity to defend himself. North refused to be in the same room with him but Anderson handed Ferdinand the document North had brought with him from India. When he saw the charges fully spelled out—"62 pages against me [that] strike directly at my ministerial and Christian character"[9]—he realized his chances of returning to India had vanished. Without the corroborative testimony of John Lawrence and other unnamed witnesses now "in their graves," Ferdinand could not see how he could mount an effective defense.[10]

Neither could Dr. Anderson, who was weary of a dispute that had now dragged on for more than three years. Carefully refraining from taking sides, he asked instead that North and Ward both sever their connection with his organization. To save face, each would be allowed to offer an official, if inaccurate, reason for his resignation: Ferdinand claimed his still-precarious health now precluded a return to the field; North developed a sudden urge to study theology at Auburn. With both resignations in hand, Anderson destroyed North's list of charges and most of the remaining correspondence so that no one would ever know precisely what had happened.*

---

* Alfred North would move on to occupy pulpits in western New York, Kansas, Missouri, and Wisconsin before his death in 1869.

.   .   .

Late in the evening of Saturday, November 5, 1848, at the end of a jarring ten-hour stagecoach ride from Rochester, Ferdinand stepped down on South Street in the little town of Geneseo, New York. The pastor of the Second Presbyterian Church, known locally as the "White Church," had recently resigned. The session—the body of ruling elders of the congregation—was looking for a replacement, and Ferdinand had been asked to occupy the pulpit on Sunday morning and speak again at the chapel service in the evening. (His late friend John Lawrence's parents belonged to the White Church and may have had something to do with the invitation.) "My own thought was a single Sabbath service, and then to return home," Ferdinand remembered. "I so expressed myself in sincere and emphatic words to gentlemen who called upon me the next morning. Having just returned from a long residency as a Missionary in Southern India, I was ill-fitted for a pastorate in a community like this. But my wishes were overruled. . . . 'It is not in man that walketh to direct his steps.' "[11]

The session asked him to spend a few days in town, nonetheless, getting to know the place. It didn't take him long. Geneseo then had fewer than one thousand citizens and just four streets—South, North, Main, and Center. Ferdinand walked them all. There were no sidewalks, he later remembered; here and there raw planks spanned patches of otherwise impassable mud. Trees were scarce, and, for the most part, houses were "few and very plain."[12]

The village was older than Bergen or Rochester, established in 1789 by James and William Wadsworth, land-owning brothers from Connecticut whose holdings stretched for thirty miles along the Genesee Valley and whose big homes would eventually anchor the opposite

---

In 1850, Henry Cherry would also be quietly forced to sever his ties with the American Board. He remained a turbulent figure. He was tried for "Oberlinism" by the synod of Geneva. In 1859, he was dismissed by the presbytery of Florida for "dishonesty, duplicity & defamation of the community" involving "serious criminality." (He claimed he'd been let go purely because he had advocated the cause of "freedom, not slavery.") During the Civil War he served in Tennessee as chaplain of the 10th Michigan Cavalry. In 1865, a church in Kalamazoo, Michigan, removed him for what it called "gross immorality." He died in Pompey, New York, in 1891.

Mary Lawrence, the widow of the Wards' impetuous ally, taught school in Ballston, New York, until shortly before her death at the age of seventy-two.

ends of Main Street. They recruited many of Geneseo's merchants and tradesmen, donated land for churches for worshippers belonging to several denominations, saw to it that their town was made the county seat, and built a high school for Livingston County children on a wooded prominence called Temple Hill. Both brothers had died by the time of Ferdinand's initial visit, but members of the Wadsworth family remained Geneseo's most eminent citizens and principal benefactors; most townspeople farmed their lands or served them in some other capacity.

A few weeks later, Ferdinand brought Jane to Geneseo to meet the congregation, see the town, and look over the clapboard house that was to be refurbished for the new minister and his family. It stood at the corner of Second Street and a muddy lane grandly called North Center Street that would one day be renamed Ward Place. To Ferdinand's relief, "Jane liked what she saw," he reported to his brother Levi, and he agreed to serve as pastor.[13] His beginning yearly salary would be just $700. Ferdinand asked his brother to invest Jane's $7,500 inheritance from her father (nearly $200,000 today), so that they could supplement his income with the interest it earned, and to keep the arrangement a secret; if the session ever learned that he and Jane had "property," he told Levi, it would never vote to give him a raise. "That the people [here] will long continue to like me as they seem to now I cannot hope," Ferdinand wrote, but he still resolved to stay.[14] Geneseo would be home to the Wards for the rest of their lives.

That summer, Ferdinand found himself involved in another controversy, this one not of his own making. In a clan so determinedly worthy and relentlessly successful as the Wards of Rochester, it was probably inevitable that at least one member would defy its conventions. Ferdinand's brother Henry Meigs Ward had always been more or less a misfit. Fond of books, uninterested in business, and relegated to running the family farm, he had married the younger sister of his brother-in-law, Moses Chapin. Her name was Eliza, and her unrelenting religiosity was thought excessive even among the Wards. Sometime while Ferdinand was in India, Henry had begun a secret affair with an Irish serving girl. When he was found out in 1846, he packed a valise, walked out the door, and vanished into the West, leaving behind his wife and three children. Weeks later, Levi received a letter from him. He was in Chicago, living alone in a boardinghouse and happily surveying town lots for a living. He missed his hometown and his children. He did not miss his wife.

Nothing remotely like this had ever happened in the Ward family before. Rochester continued to gossip about it. In the summer of 1849, Levi asked Ferdinand to go to Chicago and see if he could talk some sense into Henry. Surely three years of self-imposed exile were enough. Ferdinand found his brother shabbily dressed and unshaven but still more or less content. He still had no wish to come home, he said, but he did want access to money his father had put aside in trust for him. Ferdinand told him that "we had rather give him $50.00 at Rochester having him near us than send him $5.00 where he is. I said to him verbatim that we *could do nothing that would tend to encourage him in his present mode of life.* This I repeated again and again." Then, when Henry started complaining about how his father and the family were treating him, Ferdinand cut him off: "I cannot think it well for members of a family to be *talking* against a Parent whatever of exceptional conduct may be, in their estimation, apparent."[15] Ferdinand's other siblings all agreed. In the face of scandal, Ward solidarity was what mattered most—then, and in all the years to come.

On November 5, 1849, a year after accepting the pastorate of the White Church in Geneseo, Ferdinand wrote two letters to Dr. Anderson. In the first, intended for the files, he formally asked for "a dissolution of my connection with the Board." It was, he said, the "will of Him of whose goodness I have had too ample experience."[16]

In the second letter, he was more frank. Since he had Anderson's assurance that all the old correspondence had been destroyed "& that nothing stands upon your records to indicate what has transpired," he wanted to confide in the Board's secretary privately, as a friend, not an official, to let him "look into the secret chambers of my spirit." Although he remained stunned that his former colleagues had turned against him, he "most truly forgave them," called upon God to "attend their labours," and looked forward to the day he would be reunited with them all at the seat of Judgment.

He was still motivated by "love to the heathen," he continued, and still wished he could somehow go back to live and preach among them, but he was now resigned to seeking other ways to do the Lord's work.

Meanwhile, "I would receive this painful event as from the hand of Him who sees that I need chastisements and whose blows are fewer than my deserts. . . . My missionary life has not been *faultless*. In a company of 14, I was . . . the youngest. My temperament is ardent and I said and did much that I cannot recall with satisfaction. I merit all that I have been called to bear and the one prayer of my heart is that this trial may have the chastening and sanctifying effect which will convert it into a blessing."[17]

The Wards would always cling to the official fiction that their delicate health alone had kept them from returning to India. Many years later, looking back over his long life, Ferdinand told his son Will that "one thought is pleasant. *I never resigned a position but by protest of those whom I was serving. I was never driven out.*"[18] But both he and his wife knew they had, in fact, been driven out, by those alongside whom they had worked and lived.

They would never lose their interest in the subcontinent. Ferdinand continued to speak on behalf of the missions, persuaded British friends in Madras to send him spices so that Jane could make him the Indian dishes he had learned to love, and had already completed a book about India that would be published by Scribner's later that year. *India and the Hindoos: Being a Popular View of the Geography, History, Government, Manners, Customs, Literature and Religion of That Ancient People; with an Account of Christian Missions Among Them* is an odd volume, compulsively encyclopedic both in the number of topics it takes up—everything from fauna to funeral practices—and in the overconfident ignorance it displays about a great many of them. ("The giraffe," the author assures his readers, "can be met with occasionally in the northwest provinces";[19] while the horn of the Indian rhinoceros "projects, not infrequently, thirty inches upward. So long as the animal is quiet, this appendage lies loose between the nostrils; but when excited, the muscular tension is so great that it becomes immovably fixed, and can be darted into a tree to the depth of several inches.")[20] Still, *India and the Hindoos* is also filled with its author's fascination with the subcontinent and its people, whom, he wrote, "I love" and now would never see again. "Though there be night the 'morning cometh,' " he wrote on its final page. "This must be our motto, to warm our zeal and nerve our arm, to cheer our despondency and strengthen our faith— 'FAINT YET PURSUING.' "

.   .   .

If Ferdinand felt divinely chastened by the way he was forced from his chosen field, as he claimed he did in his last letter to Secretary Anderson, he would not show much evidence of it in his new one. The same strange combination of unchecked ardor, self-righteousness, and deviousness that had alienated those with whom he differed in India would eventually be brought to bear on the people of his Geneseo congregation and their neighbors.

Some of the problems he faced were those of the church he served. During the years he and Jane were overseas, the American Presbyterian Church had split in two. The Plan of Union, drawn up between Presbyterians and Congregationalists in 1801, had enabled them to work together to create new congregations as the frontier moved west, but it had begun to come apart even before the *Saracen* company sailed for India.

The issues between the two sides were sometimes hard to understand. "Their contentions and janglings are so ridiculous, so wicked, so outrageous," Charles Finney wrote before the final division came, "that no doubt there is a jubilee in hell every year about the time of the [annual Presbyterian] General Assembly."[21] But Calvinist orthodoxy was at the core of the debate: conservative Presbyterians began to call themselves adherents of an "Old School" and questioned the legitimacy of any congregation that dared entertain the slightest doubt about the doctrine of original sin, or permitted Congregational ways of governance to supersede Presbyterian polity, or that failed to adhere strictly to the letter of the Westminster Confession of Faith and the Larger and Shorter Catechisms. Because Old School Presbyterians deplored what they called "the widespread and ever restless spirit of radicalism,"[22] they also frowned on revivals and abhorred abolitionism.

At the 1837 general assembly, an Old School majority had finally voted to abrogate the Plan of Union and "exscind"—that is, expel—four synods, comprising 553 churches, that had been formed under its rules. This included most of the churches in western New York. The exiled New School churches then banded together to form a rival organization. For the next three decades, there would be two Presbyterian churches—Old School and New School—each insisting on its own exclusive legitimacy, each with its own pulpits and preachers, newspapers and seminaries, synods and presbyteries and general assembly.[*]

---

* Both Old and New schools followed the system of Presbytery polity developed by John Calvin in Geneva, carried by John Knox to Scotland, and brought to America by

Church historians would call it the "Presbyterian thirty-years' war," and Geneseo would become one of its battlefields. Ever since the division, two presbyteries belonging to the exscinded synod of Geneva had sought to remain above the struggle—Rochester (which had initially licensed Ferdinand to preach) and Ontario (to which his new church belonged). They saw themselves as "Presbyterian *original* [author's italics], without either of the appendages of Old or New School."[23] Although both synods were at least formally linked to the New School assembly, their ranks included a large number of conservative pastors and laymen and so neither sent commissioners to its annual meetings.

In Geneseo, the result was that each Sunday morning, the pews of Ferdinand's church were filled with adherents of both camps on the lookout for evidence that their new pastor favored one over the other. Ferdinand did favor Old School doctrine (though he would never lose his enthusiasm for the kind of revivalism that had brought him to Christ). The Wards of Rochester had always been implacably orthodox, and he had learned most of his theology at the Princeton Seminary, where the principal, Rev. Charles Hodge, liked to boast, "a new idea never originated."*

"My feelings must greatly change before I am one of that [New School] body," Ferdinand told his brother. "I say but little among the people about it, but such are my views."[24] Still, so long as the Ontario

---

Scottish immigrants. It was intended to balance authority between the denomination and the congregation.

To prevent power from ever falling into the hands of an individual patriarch, congregations elect presbyters to serve on assemblies. The assemblies, in turn, exercise authority over congregations. Regional groups of congregations form a presbytery. Groups of presbyteries are governed by a synod. Together, the synods compose the annual general assembly. Meanwhile, local congregations govern themselves through a board of elected elders called the Session. A senior minister moderates its meetings, which are headed by the clerk of session; neither official has a vote in the deliberations.

* At least in retrospect, Ferdinand was embarrassed at ever having so much as flirted with religious nonconformity. While at Princeton, he remembered, he and seven friends privately formed a club for an object he later called "quite plausible but very perilous." Four argued that Jesus was divine and therefore worthy of being "worshipped as God." The other four took the position that he was merely "a created being, great wise and good—but only to be honoured, not adored. . . . The danger was . . . that the latter four would find so much on their side that they would adopt [it as] their own." Ferdinand regretted ever taking part: "With *religious error* as with *pitch*," he wrote, "the less handled the safer." Ferdinand De Wilton Ward, typed manuscript of *Auto-Biography No. 2*, p. 1, Brinton Collection.

presbytery maintained what Ferdinand called its "masterful inactivity" and remained aloof from the New School assembly, he would do his best to keep all his parishioners content.

But just a few hundred yards south of the White Church stood a newly established outpost of Old School orthodoxy, the Temple Hill Academy. It had once been the Livingston County High School, founded by the Wadsworths in 1827, and its first teachers, recruited from Harvard, had been carefully instructed to avoid any form of religious "narrow-mindedness" that might keep a scholar from "the undisturbed observance" of his or her own faith.[25] But shortly after the Wards came to town, the Old School synod of Buffalo persuaded the board of trustees to let it take control. As Presbyterian pastor, Ferdinand was appointed to the academy board and found himself in the midst of an increasingly bitter dispute over what should and should not be taught there and what sort of relationship the academy should have with his church.

The synod intended to expand the school and transform it into a "Synodical Academy" run along strict orthodox lines, and appointed as president of its board an especially determined conservative, the Reverend A. Lloyd. Ferdinand liked him at first—he was "a superior person," he told Levi, and shared the Ward family's preference for institutions "decidedly Christian & theologically Old School Presbyterian."[26] But Ferdinand preferred that the shift toward orthodoxy be gradual—funds still had to be raised, the teachers had to be brought gradually into line—and Rev. Lloyd turned out to be rash and intractable. He sought to remove from the board anyone connected with the White Church because of its distant link to the New School synod, and even proposed that academy students be forbidden to attend services there for fear of being exposed to what he deliberately mischaracterized as Ferdinand's "odious (N. School) preaching." "The villagers [rose] up in arms against him," Ferdinand wrote, and Lloyd was eventually outvoted and forced to resign.[27] A more tactful Old School clergyman, Rev. James Nichols, was hired as principal to smooth the transition, and Ferdinand himself began teaching at Temple Hill. "I hold a catechetical class this evening & commence a course of Theological sermons next Sabbath," he reported to Levi. "1st topic: 'Nature & importance of *Truth*.' "[28]

Given the intensity of doctrinal feeling at the time, it might have been impossible for anyone to steer a successful middle course between the two factions in a town as small as Geneseo for very long. To have done so would have required extraordinary diplomatic skill and a willingness to seek creative compromise. Ferdinand had neither, but, as he told his brother, he hurled himself into his pastoral duties with all the fervor he had demonstrated in Madura and Madras.

> The last week was one of somewhat varied occupations. Sabbath morning and Saturday night I preached two written sermons, lectured twice (one written)—conducted the monthly Concert [a coming-together of the congregation]—officiated at a *wedding*, a *baptism*, & *two funerals* (addresses at each)—spent half a day in presiding over the Board of Trustees [of the academy] (as they elected me President for another year, though I said "Nay")—another half day at a [Gospel] Society meeting—wrote one full sermon & skeleton of another—made a dozen pastoral calls—rewrote & sent to press a chapter of my forthcoming book[29]—attended two Railroad meetings [to discuss plans to connect Geneseo with Avon and Rochester]—& do not neglect my own household in any apparent respects . . . my position is no sinecure. But oh, the little I do in comparison with what is needed.[30]

He was hard on himself, but, as always, harder on others. From the first, he thought his congregation ungrateful. The church elders were shirking their duty: "They are rich, can do [more] and ought to at once."[31] They didn't pay him enough and weren't sufficiently appreciative of the sacrifice he was making in agreeing to serve the spiritual needs of their little town. He threatened to leave unless his salary was raised and his church was expanded. The session eventually granted him an additional hundred dollars a month, and voted to add a brand-new steeple to the church, to enlarge it to accommodate fifty new pews, and to build a large session house on Second Street that came to be called the "Ward Annex."

He never let up on the townspeople. He deplored the stubborn persistence of "Sabbath-desecrating—drunkenness, [and] gambling" and was enraged when the Anglican Church dared welcome one of his parishioners into its fold: "I have an increasing contempt for the whole system of ecumenicism," he wrote, "and will not throw the might of influence which accompanies my personal presence in that direction."[32] He got up a petition signed by more than 450 women demanding that the Livingston County Board of Excise stop issuing licenses for the sale of alcohol; when it was voted down on the grounds that, if permits were not provided, liquor would be sold anyway, he denounced its members, some of whom had been his friends, as wicked and immoral.

At a Fourth of July celebration, he attacked the Catholic Church and the recent flood of Irish immigrants in flight from the potato famine with such vehemence that some members of his own congregation "were ready to say the parson went too far," he told Levi afterward.[33] But Judge Scott Lord, the highest elected officer in the county and a profoundly conservative church elder with whom the Wards were living until the refitting of the parsonage could be completed, disagreed. He was pleased, he said, that "the waters are mightily stirred." The address caused "quite a sensation," Ferdinand wrote. "The cry today is '*Down with Rome.*' I spoke earnestly and boldly but not hastily. May I be forgiven if I did anyone any wrong."[34]

Levi warned him to be careful: "You can lead by *kindness* better than pull by *logic*," he wrote.[35] Ferdinand laughed off his advice. It was his appearance, not his preaching, that put people off, he said. "There is . . . something about my face that leads others to think that if I am sober I am angry. My children observe it & Willie begs Father not to look so *cross* simply because I am not *laughing* or *smiling.*"[36]

Ferdinand's outbursts did not please his wife, either. She shared his loathing for "popery," but she often thought him unnecessarily harsh, too eager to preach God's wrath rather than His forgiveness, and she feared that her husband's impatience might complicate their lives, just as it had in India. Her enthusiasm for Geneseo was distinctly qualified, too. She was grateful when the family could move into the parsonage: she had had no home of her own for three years, after all, having been forced to live on the charity of her husband's relatives, with her children in boardinghouses, or with Judge Lord. But nothing else about the little town lifted her spirits. It seemed a dreary, claustrophobic place, in which she came to feel that everyone was judging her and her children. Her girlhood dreams of personally converting the heathen had died in India. She had felt keenly the disgrace of coming home under so much suspicion and lived in fear that the real story might somehow get out. She had no choice now but to live out her life as a small-town parson's wife, barred again by custom and convention from acting independently of her husband.

Ferdinand was of little help. He followed more or less the same schedule he had followed in Madura: rising before dawn and emerging from his study only to make pastoral visits, direct Sunday school, visit the Academy, and preach his sermons. There was little time for her or the children—and as her unhappiness increased, so did the amount of time he spent away from home.

In the late spring of 1850, she suffered the first of a long series of puzzling collapses. Letters list a host of complaints: fatigue, debilitated nerves, "settled neuralgia," rheumatic joints, recurring fevers, shooting pains, and more. She would undergo the same treatment for all of them: weeks—sometimes many weeks—away from Ferdinand and her family, as a patient at Dr. Henry Foster's new water-cure facility in Clifton Springs, New York. Foster was a devout Methodist whose pious regimen—formal prayers several times a day, no dancing, no card playing, no coffee or tea—appealed especially to the clergymen, former missionaries, and their wives, to whom he offered his help at a much-reduced fee.

Treatment was Spartan: a rising bell at six a.m. was followed by a bath in the spring's sulphurous waters, brisk walks, an unvarying, mostly meatless diet, and long sessions in which the patient was packed in wet sheets.

Jane did not return to Geneseo until winter, and when she found late the following spring that she was pregnant for a fifth time, she returned immediately to Clifton Springs for another lengthy stay. This new baby was almost surely a surprise and may not have been a welcome one. Jane was thirty-nine at a time when the average life expectancy for white women in the United States was only slightly over forty. Her daughter was thirteen; Will was nine. She had thought childbearing behind her, and child rearing well along. Now she would have to start all over again. Her life would still not be her own.

Nothing seemed to cheer her. In a bleak letter to her son Will, written from the Geneseo parsonage some years later, Jane Shaw Ward sought to sum up her life. "When I remember that at age 15 I was taken from school to keep house for my father and entertain company of which we had a great amount so as to seldom get an hour for reading, and that as soon as married I was taken off to live among the heathen during 10 of the best years of my life, and since my return home have been shut up in this narrow-minded village, I really wonder that there is any thing in me to interest anybody or that my children are not rather ashamed of me." Her own life, she concluded, had been "useless," and her marriage had only served to stifle her: "I do know *something* of what it is to be thrown day after day with one who differs from you so as to prevent the full and free exhibition of your own identity."[37]

It was into this home, amid these ongoing tensions, two years after his father had formally accepted a permanent pulpit and just a year after his parents finally abandoned all hope of returning to the mission field, that Ferdinand De Wilton Ward Jr. was born—on Friday, November 21, 1851.

PART TWO

ONE OF THE WORST BOYS

FOUR

A Contest for *Principle & Truth*

As an adult, the younger Ferdinand Ward—"Ferdie," then "Ferd," to his family—was rarely reluctant to talk about himself, even when the law had closed in and it would have been far better to keep his own counsel. Even so, he did not often muse aloud about his life before Wall Street. But in two letters written from his Sing Sing cell to the sister-in-law who was looking after his son, he did make suggestions about the boy's care that reflected his own memories of the way he had himself been raised.

> I have felt in my own case the evil of too strict a religious train-
> ing. Let [my boy] ever feel his Sunday School a pleasure, not a
> burden. Be temperate with him in everything. . . . My experi-
> ence in this matter teaches me that the boy, who in early years
> has religion forced on him, never grows out of the dread of
> it. I shall never get over the dread I felt in my youth of the 2
> long sermons each Sunday and the Wednesday evening prayer
> meetings. They did me no good and only added to my dread of
> such things when I got older.[1]

It was not religion itself that filled Ferdie with dread. It was the fact that the grim and often frightening exhortations to which he was subjected were delivered by his own father, and that he had to hear them in the company of his troubled, perpetually worried mother, whose conviction that the worst was yet to come rarely lifted for more than a moment. For him, as for his parents, faith seems more often to have been a source of chaos than comfort.

We know almost nothing else about his first few years. He was said to have been a blond, blue-eyed, eager little boy; his father once tried to account for what he called his youngest child's "weakness of purpose" by saying that as a baby he had been "greatly petted, for he was very handsome."[2] But he was also small for his age and frail. When Ferdie was ten months old, cholera swept through Geneseo. He caught it and nearly died. Three years later, according to his father's spare journal, he fell ill again, with "congestion of lungs" this time, and ran a fever so high he suffered convulsions; five months after that, he was again "*very* sick."[3]

Scores of letters from his parents survive; not one of them contains winsome stories about his first attempts to walk or talk or learn to get along with playmates. His older siblings' achievements or amusements are not often mentioned, either, for that matter. Their mother was rarely able to see in her children anything other than bleak evidence of her own inadequacy, while their father's life was taken up with pastoral duties and the bitter doctrinal and political quarrels that would eventually divide their tranquil town.

In April 1852, five months after Ferdie's birth, his father set out for the annual spring meeting of the Ontario presbytery. He was apprehensive. Peace among his divided parishioners continued to depend on the presbytery maintaining its neutrality by continuing to refuse to send commissioners to the New School general assembly. But neutrality was growing harder and harder to maintain. Passage of the Fugitive Slave Act in 1850 had intensified the ongoing war between the Old and New schools. In the North, both factions officially deplored slavery, but most Old Schoolers were also adamant that the church had no legitimate part to play in the struggle against it. Too close a relationship with politics of any kind, they believed, smacked of "man-worship." Clergymen who urged parishioners to hide runaway slaves from their masters in defiance of federal law were "busy-bodies,"[4] Ferdinand told his flock. He deplored what he called "Garrisonian emanations which goad the South so terribly with no good results to the cause of free-dom. . . . I do wish that church officers would keep out of violent *party politics*. . . . It is bad, bad, bad [and wounds] the cause of Christ."[5]

Now, Ferdinand had been instructed by his church's session again to do whatever he could at the meeting to keep the presbytery from aligning itself any more closely with the New School. By his own account, his was the foremost voice in opposition to change. "I spoke for half an hour," he assured Levi, "and was enabled to hold the atten-tion of all (Ladies, lots of them, & gentlemen) to the close,"[6] but in the end, he and his allies were outvoted, twenty to twelve. The *New-York Evangelist*, speaking for the New School, expressed its delight that the Ontario presbytery had at last "decided to . . . wheel into line." "The benefits and beauty of union," it promised, "far surpass, in importance and comfort, all the possible advantages of a dissociated and indepen-dent position."[7]

The benefits and beauty of union were lost on Ferdinand Ward. "The ship is high and dry on the shore of *New Schoolism*," he reported to his brother, and he now faced what he saw as a crisis of conscience. It would be impossible, he wrote, for him to pastor "for [any] length of time in a *decidedly* New School church."[8] For a year or so after the vote, he hoped his session might make things easy for him by agreeing not to "have anything more to do with the presbytery," but in the end it preferred simply to submit a "strong minute" in protest of the realign-ment and remain at least technically within the New School fold.[9]

That was not good enough for Ferdinand. The growing success of the Temple Hill Academy (which now had some three hundred stu-dents, both boys and girls) was turning the village into what he called a "center of Old School influence" and deepening the dissension within his congregation. "Church and Academy ought to be under one eccle-siastical jurisdiction,"[10] he wrote, and he began to see it as his duty to bring about that realignment—directly if he could, deviously if there were no other way. "The apple is not quite ripe though perfecting if I do not err," he told his brother. Meanwhile, he added, "it seems advis-able to be a little quiet."[11]

But Ferdinand Ward was incapable of being quiet. In early 1854, the struggle between the Old and New schools divided the faithful of the nearby Rochester presbytery, the presbytery to which Ferdi-nand had initially belonged and the last in the state to have maintained its neutrality. When its delegates, too, voted to send commissioners to the New School assembly, five of the city's best-known orthodox clergymen—all close associates of Ferdinand and Levi Ward—left to unite with the competing Old School presbytery of Rochester City.* Inspired by their example, and possibly urged on by Levi, Ferdinand startled a meeting of his own presbytery by asking for a formal letter of dismission that would allow him to join its own Old School rival.

When the church elder who had accompanied him to the meeting began to weep at the thought of the divisiveness Rev. Ward's departure was sure to cause in Geneseo, Ferdinand withdrew the request. But when he got home he repeated it, in writing this time.

A delegation of concerned elders and clergymen from the presbytery soon came to see him in his crowded, book-lined study. They stayed for two hours. Ferdinand told them that his conscience would no longer allow him to remain even distantly attached to the New School. If he truly felt that way, they said, the "honorable" course was simply to resign.[12]

He was willing to do that, he answered, provided no "outside influence" was exerted upon his church to maintain its traditional ties after he had left its pulpit. He did not say so outright, but it was clear to his inquisitors that he planned to lead his congregation into union with the Old School. The committee told him that they could not agree to such an "unpresbyterial" proposal, and would "never consent to stand still and see the church carried over to the O.S. without an effort to prevent it," one of his visitors recalled. "There was no disposition to retain him against his wish, but how could we dismiss a pastor of one of our churches to another presbytery, especially one not in correspondence with us?"[13]

Ferdinand and the committee members shook hands. Neither side had budged. They would not set him free. He did not feel he could continue for long under their jurisdiction, and he wasn't sure what to do next. The stomach trouble that had tormented him in India returned. His chronic Monday-morning migraines intensified, too, and he was forced to spend more and more time in his darkened bedroom.

A summer spent abroad, paid for by wealthy parishioners concerned

---

* Levi Ward was one of the new presbytery's prime organizers. He put up the funds with which to establish three new congregations and eventually built a fourth church of his own, St. Peter's, just across the road from the Grove.

about his health, raised his spirits,* but it would take him two years to make his next move—years during which the same division over what was finally to be done about slavery and its extension that menaced the American Union further threatened the unity of the White Church. By 1856, the anti-immigrant, anti-Catholic American, or "Know Nothing," Party, for which Ferdinand had most recently voted, was on its last legs, and the Whig Party, to which most of the Wards of Rochester had owed their first allegiance, had splintered over slavery. Like most Americans, Ferdinand's parishioners had begun to identify themselves either with the Democrats, who saw slavery's extension as a matter for the voters to decide, or with the new Republican Party, which promised no new slave states and no slavery in the territories. The New School faction within the church was overwhelmingly Republican.

Ferdinand and the Old Schoolers were Democrats, for the most part, who shared the views (if not always the vehemence) of the Ward family physician and ruling church elder, Dr. Walter Lauderdale. To him, Republicans were nothing but "political croakers . . . , lunatics who scant at the Constitution & farewell counsels of Washington & Jefferson & trample them under their feet & who wish to ride into power on the ruins of those sacred relics."[14]

Some time that autumn—and with behind-the-scenes backing from at least two prominent parishioners (most likely Dr. Lauderdale and Judge Lord)—Ferdinand quietly approached the recently established presbytery of the Genesee River, part of the Old School synod of Buffalo, with a proposal: if it was willing to add him to its roll of clergymen *without* his having been formally dismissed from the Ontario presbytery, he and his allies stood ready to bring the White Church over to the Old School. On October 15, 1856, Ferdinand was officially—and secretly—"received" into their presbytery, then sat back and waited for the right moment to persuade his congregation to join it, too.[15]

Word leaked out. The Ontario presbytery, determined not to give up its church without a fight, passed a resolution charging Ferdinand with bad faith and ordering him to surrender his pulpit. They had the

---

* In 1856, Ferdinand published a book-length account of this trip, *A Summer Vacation Abroad; or, Notes of a Visit to England, Scotland, Ireland, France, Italy, and Belgium.* It is a hodgepodge of sightseeing and Presbyterian orthodoxy: he thought Paris beautiful, for example, but sadly lacking in "a firm and enlightened Christian faith"; after a visit to St. Peter's in Rome, he boasted, "Did we kneel? Did we make a sign of the cross? *Neither!*"

synod adopt it and then sent three clergymen to the June 29, 1857, meeting of the White Church session to deliver its rebuke in person. Ferdinand sat silent as it was read out.

> *Resolved.* That Brother Ward having now left the Presbytery which installed him . . . without having asked for a dissolution of the Pastoral relation and without a letter of dismission . . . it is the judgment of this body, that though the act was disorderly, yet when he connected himself with the Genesee River Presbytery his relation as pastor [of the White Church] ceased to exist and it is only remaining for us, for purposes of order, to declare as we hereby do, the said Pastoral relation is dissolved.[16]

The session was still made up mostly of Ferdinand's allies. They passed a defiant resolution insisting that whatever happened, they wanted him to continue to occupy the moderator's chair and to remain in the pulpit as "stated supply" if he could not stay on as their permanent pastor.* Ferdinand was encouraged by their support and still persuaded that most of his congregation was with him, but he knew that to complete the desired realignment, something else would be needed. Meanwhile, the ecclesiastical standoff continued, and bitterness steadily grew between Old and New schoolers, Democrats and Republicans, those who continued to consider Ferdinand their beloved pastor and those who had begun to see him as a usurper.

During her ten years in India, Jane Shaw Ward had often suffered from the impact on others of her husband's curious combination of ardor and indirection. Now, after ten years in Geneseo, it all seemed to be happening again. When she agreed to settle there, she had counseled Ferdinand to avoid controversy and stick to preaching. Ferdinand found it impossible to heed her advice. As a result, the church to which she and Ferdinand had devoted themselves was now deeply divided. Her uneasiness over that struggle drove her to spend still more time away from home.

Depression now seemed to settle over her every autumn—grim,

---

* "Stated supply" clergymen were employed, usually at a minimal salary, to occupy a pulpit in a church that was not then formally seeking a permanent pastor.

numbing, self-hating, hopeless. "Her tendency toward *pessimism*," Ferdinand would one day lament to his daughter, "often gets the mastery & is the cause of [misery] to herself & those around her. Oh, that she was as happy in spirit as she is good in act!"[17] She had already spent at least three winter months undergoing the water cure at Clifton Springs in 1854, three more in 1855, and another five in 1856. Miss Morison, the nurse and companion most often assigned to her there, had told her again and again that with such a worthy husband and such well-behaved children, she "should be the happiest woman living," but no number of hours wrapped in wet sheets could make her believe it.[18]

In late 1857, as the rancor within the church intensified, Jane began a retreat that would stretch on for fully half a year. Her daughter, Sarah—"Sallie" to her parents—did her best to run the household in her mother's absence. She was nineteen now, attractive, soft-spoken, suitably religious, and serious beyond her years. She had spent scattered months at girls' schools in Rochester and Batavia and Elizabeth, New Jersey, attended the Temple Hill Academy, and was sometimes permitted to spend a few days away from home, visiting relatives in New York. But she was rarely allowed to enjoy herself for long. During her mother's frequent absences, she was called upon to act as hostess for her preoccupied father, take part in all the activities expected of a clergyman's daughter, oversee the Irish cook and maid, keep the house clean, make sure the washing was done, and care for her younger siblings, Will and Ferdie.

A clutch of Jane's letters from Clifton Springs survives, all written in the winter of 1857–1858 and addressed to her children. Each is filled with anxieties and admonitions and unanchored fears about the fate of her family and her own mortality. Shadowy pains kept her from sleep, she reported—in her knees, in a finger, in her left lung, her head, her back. When she did manage to nod off she was awakened by nightmares: in one, she told her daughter, a great wind blew in the parsonage door, smashing Sarah against the wall and rendering her "almost an idiot. Oh, how my heart beat with excitement & horror."[19]

Above all, she feared that rather than follow her husband into the Old School fold, his congregation might instead desert him—and force his family onto the street. Two themes run through her voluminous correspondence: the precarious state of her own soul, and bitterness about money. She always professed not to care about the latter: "The silver and gold are the Lord's," she liked to say, and "He giveth it to whom He will." But nothing angered her more than the fact that He had chosen to give it to her husband's less pious relatives in Rochester while she had mostly to make do on a parson's salary.

Ferdinand's decision to remain in Geneseo as stated supply had already meant a sharp reduction in his pay. Now, she feared that even that pittance might be snatched away. "We have had years of prosperity, perhaps now the Lord sees best to afflict us," she wrote. "Oh, may we bear it with Christian submission & cheerfulness."*

She agonized over the steady demand her weekly treatments made on the family's depleted finances, and spread guilt with every letter. Despite the cold at Clifton Springs, she had halved her bill for firewood, she assured Sarah; "you shall not be deprived of one comfort to give me two."[20] "As we are poor," she told fourteen-year-old Willie, he could expect no Christmas gifts, but he was not to mind because "whatever you do without will add so much to keeping me here. I don't like to be selfish but some of these days you shall reap the benefits of present-day denial in my stronger efforts to do you good."[21]

Her six-year-old son got a Christmas letter, too.

> Dear Little Ferdie,
>   You are a precious little darling and I love you. . . . I hope you are good and do just what is told you and do not cry at all. I will try to get well fast but you must pray for Mother every night for only God can cure me. There are some little boys here about as big as you but they are rude and wild. I love my Ferdie best. Goodbye dearest child. Don't spend your pennies for candy but give them all to Sunday School. Try to love the dear Saviour so that we may all meet in heaven.
>   Your fond & loving,
>   Mother[22]

Years of experience helped Sarah and Willie withstand their mother's morbid, often frantic fears. But it was all still new to Ferdie. He clung to his mother when she was home and was chronically frightened when she was not. His mother's melancholic holiday greeting, with

---

* The family's income had recently been further reduced as a fresh economic panic paralyzed the stock market and dried up interest payments from the investments Ferdinand had quietly persuaded Levi Ward to make on his wife's behalf. Jane Shaw Ward to Sarah Ward Brinton, March 9, 1858, Brinton Collection.

its suggestion that without his constant prayers she might not survive, so frightened him that it was thought best for Sarah to escort him to Clifton Springs by stagecoach and train so that he could undergo the water cure alongside his mother for what she called his "fearfulness."[23]

It must have been a grim business for a small boy: doused with buckets of cold water, then wrapped so tightly in wet sheets that only his head was free to move for an hour a day—"unless," his mother wrote, "he gets nervous and cannot stand it."[24]

He did get nervous, was often unable to stand it, and continued to seem terrified of almost everything. His mother blamed the Irish serving girls back home for telling him scary stories; "I have no confidence in these Catholics," she said.[25] When Ferdie was finally escorted back to Geneseo, it was with a warning from Dr. Foster that he should be kept from beginning school for a time and must not be "frightened in any way either for fun or anything else as it might affect his brain."[26]

Ferdie was often genuinely sick when small and, like his father, would remain agitated and anxious all his life. His mother's ongoing fretfulness about him was at least partly justified. But those early episodes also taught him that illness, real or feigned, would always win her anxious sympathy and help him avoid doing things he did not wish to do.

In early March, while Jane and Ferdie were still undergoing the cure at Clifton Springs, a letter arrived there from Ferdinand. He could no longer endure the situation within his church, he said, and suggested that no one, not even his wife, understood the anguish its continuing relationship with the New School caused within him.

He now thought he saw an opportunity to bring about the change he had been working toward for years and was going to risk everything and seize it. His older brother seems to have been helping behind the scenes. The Reverend James Nichols, who had helped transform the Temple Hill Academy into a citadel of orthodoxy, announced he was leaving to become principal of the Rochester Female Academy; Levi Ward was a trustee of that institution and may have helped arrange the transfer. In any case, as president of the Temple Hill board, Ferdinand was asked to find a successor. His choice was a fellow trustee and another of Levi's close allies from Rochester, Rev. Charles Ray. He was young, dynamic, and wholeheartedly orthodox—so wholeheartedly that he declared he would take the job only if the White Church agreed immediately to sever its ties to the Ontario presbytery and declare its absolute fidelity to Old School doctrine. Meanwhile, the Old School synod made it known that if Rev. Ray did not get his way it would simply close the academy. This would be a blow to ortho-dox religious education in western New York, perhaps, but a far more immediate blow to the merchants along Geneseo's Main Street, who would be denied the pocket money of between two and three hun-dred students every academic year. Pressure for change accelerated. So did what one newspaper called "anger and agitation" among Geneseo Presbyterians, some of whom had worshipped together more or less harmoniously for nearly half a century.[27]

Jane, who had consistently urged her husband to go slow, was now uncharacteristically philosophical. "I feel that Father knows what is best and we ought not to urge him any further against his conscience," she told Sarah. "He is very, very good and if he does not see it as we see it, it may be owing to our ignorance or his own weakness. Let us leave him with the Lord and try to make him happy at home for I fear some of his church members say a great deal to try him."[28] Besides, she had begun to have visions of her own, visions that seemed to confirm her husband's understanding of all that was at stake. "We must prepare ourselves for some great event," she told her daughter.

> I have felt this for 2 years past [roughly from the time Ferdi-nand secretly signed on with the Old School presbytery] and I believe it is nearer than I expected. Satan has been prepar-ing his work for some time, through Romanism, Mormonism, Spiritualism, . . . and various other erratic dogmas. Now, God is reviving *His* work, by gathering together His elect from the 4 quarters of our land & of the world. Each [side] will muster its forces ere long & there will be a grand coalescing of all the evil on one hand and all the good on the other. A contest for *principle* & *truth* will ensue and though Truth must & will prevail, the struggle will be desperate. Many who profess to be Christians will fall away while those who truly belong to Christ will either suffer death for His sake or live through all & see the dawn of the Millennium.[29]

Jane had come to share Ferdinand's belief that the worldwide contest for principle and truth was about to be fought out in the tiny village of

Geneseo. She and her husband now both saw themselves as part of the Elect, ready, if required, to be martyred in His cause.

At a meeting of the Geneseo Gospel Society a little over a month later, nineteen of Ferdinand's closest followers proposed that all male members of the congregation come together to discuss the possibility of altering the church's "ecclesiastical connections."[30] They acted, Ferdinand remembered, because they were "confident there would be little if any difference of opinion in regard to the propriety of the proposed change."[31] They were wrong. Thirteen opponents immediately countered with a "remonstrance"; there should be no such discussion, it said, since "no good reason for so important a change exists."[32]

In the end, a majority agreed that there was "piety and intelligence enough in our brotherhood to meet and discuss [even this difficult question] with candor and mutual forbearance."[33]

The meeting was held at the White Church at ten in the morning on August 25, 1858. Ferdinand's close ally, Judge Lord, proposed an informal ballot on which each member could simply note his preference between "Old School" and "New School." A prominent New Schooler responded by calling instead for "Yeas and Nays" on the proposition that "in the opinion of this church it is *inexpedient* to change its ecclesiastical relation."[34] A full day of what the recording secretary tactfully described as "free discussion" followed. Then came the vote. Ferdinand and his allies had miscalculated. They lost, thirty to twenty-six.

Outvoted and humiliated but not chastened, Ferdinand immediately offered his resignation. "It is true the field is the world," he said from the pulpit in what was meant to be a farewell sermon, "and I . . . trust I would not long be idle [but] I shall leave this beautiful valley with no ordinary sorrow." For ten years, he had baptized and married and buried members of the congregation. "Such *remembrances* crowd my memory today and stir the deepest emotions of my heart—but my brethren, my own self-respect—the dignity that belongs to my character as an ambassador of Christ—the fidelity and jealousy even with which the Christian minister should guard the honor of his *Master* which may receive a stain through him—points the way clearly and makes my path of duty plain."[35] He planned eventually to move to Rochester, he said, and officiate at St. Peter's, the Old School church his older brother had built opposite Grove Place, the Ward family compound. The *Geneseo Democrat* lamented his imminent departure: "Mr. Ward served his people as few others would," it said, but "the circumstances that induce him to leave are of a character that no other course could be pursued."[36]

But the Old School faction in his congregation wouldn't hear of his leaving. At an acrid meeting of the session three weeks later, with Ferdinand still in the chair as moderator, Judge Lord asked on behalf of "100 or more" members of the church for formal letters of dismission "for the purpose of organizing a Presbyterian church in connection with the [Old School] Presbytery of Genesee River."[37] They were unanimous in wanting Rev. Ward to be its pastor.

The session, now badly divided, adjourned without acting, still unable to agree on whether or not officially to sanction the Old Schoolers' departure. Four days later, 113 of Ferdinand's supporters, convinced that their requests for letters of dismission were being unfairly delayed, met in the Methodist chapel and voted unanimously to leave the White Church without them.

It was clear now that neither side would give ground. Geneseo's Presbyterians were irrevocably split, Dr. Lauderdale wrote, and "the materials of which the two societies [are made are] so discordant that there is no probability of a reunion, at least to all human appearance."[38] On October 25, members of the session met again—this time without Ferdinand or his three closest allies—and passed a special resolution. They deplored the Old Schoolers' action as "censurable . . . [and a] grievous [departure] from the wholesome laws and usages of Presbyterianism." But since rebels also seemed determined in their folly, the session agreed to issue the requested letters "in the spirit of brotherly kindness."[39]

By then, brotherly kindness was a rare commodity among Geneseo Presbyterians. More than half the members of Ferdinand's former congregation were appalled by what he'd done. Old friends and former parishioners crossed the street rather than speak to him or to his wife; some would continue to shun them for years. The Wards responded in kind, adopting the same self-righteous silence they had employed in India toward those who dared differ with them.

Nothing in the surviving record indicates what impact the struggle over his father's church had on Ferdie, already fearful and only seven years old. He can't have understood the doctrinal issues at stake—most of the adults involved would have been hard-pressed to explain them.

But he could not have failed to notice that old friends of his parents had become enemies overnight, that there were now neighbors with whose children he was no longer allowed to play, that his mother was even more anxious and his father more distant and preoccupied than they had been before.

Ferdinand led his reduced flock less than half a block up Main Street to the Concert Hall above the Genesee Bank at the corner of South Center (now Chestnut) Street. There, he set about creating a temporary church until a permanent edifice could be built. Before the first meeting was over, Ferdinand's followers had pledged $6,000 of the $8,000 needed to construct a new Central Presbyterian Church at the corner of Second and Center streets. Jane, now home from Clifton Springs, undertook to buy a silver communion service and began compiling books for the new Sunday school.

"We have the right material for going ahead," Dr. Lauderdale reported, "and *a more determined set of people you never saw*. Our neighbors are perfectly surprised at the result & we are somewhat so ourselves."[40]

Lauderdale's eight-year-old son, Walter Jr., described the excitement of establishing the new church in a letter to his sister.

> We had a very nice sermon today at our new church by Mr. Ward and got the Sunday School all organized and got the classes all right. . . . We took the seats today just as we could get them. . . .
>
> We kept the same singers but they are trying to get some of them out and now they are trying to get Anna Robinson out—She says that she is going to stay as long as she wants to if it plagues them. . . . We got the carpet down and cushions in and everything all nice. Mr. Ward has got a new desk and a nice cushion to lay his Bible on and has a nice marble-topped stand and a nice haircloth spring-bottomed chair to sit in. . . .
>
> Mr. Ward's sermon was about the "Pulpit." This afternoon he gave us a history of our church . . . and we liked it better than former discourses of this kind because he did not make such long obituary notices.[41]

Geneseo's ecclesiastical warfare made headlines in the religious press. Rev. Ward's action amounted to "ecclesiastical freebooting," the New

School *New-York Evangelist* declared; it was the wicked result of naked "Old School aggression" and unprincipled "lust of numbers. . . . They [the Old School] have never, by any official act, acknowledged our existence or our right to exist. . . . They receive a minister from one of our Presbyteries without any papers, as readily as they would a converted Catholic; they will constitute churches from members of our own, without letters, as readily and apparently more greedily than they would from Pagans!"[42]

A fellow clergyman published a letter denouncing Ferdinand as devious and hypocritical:

> The Rev. F. D. Ward [whom] I have always esteemed assured me, very recently, that he could not and would not preach to a *part* of [his former congregation]. He had served them when together and could not consent to be the pastor of a . . . fragment . . . ; and yet now he consents to . . . use his influence to destroy a church which he has professed to love and tried for ten years to build up, and devotes himself to exacting another church from its ruins. I fear that like Absalom, he will find that he has listened to the voice of evil counselors, and God has turned their counsel into foolishness.[43]

As always, when anyone questioned the path Ferdinand had chosen, it only confirmed his own belief that he had picked the correct one. "We [Old School Presbyterians] are right, not generally, *but also in detail*," he later wrote. "There is no other [faith] with so much to admire and so little to condemn. . . . Such purity of doctrine—such consistency of deportment—such outgoings of zeal and effort are nowhere else to be found."[44]

Outgoings of zeal and effort were the order of the day at the Academy by September 1859, when Jane Shaw Ward walked seven-year-old Ferdie up Temple Hill to enter school for the first time. Orthodoxy's grip was now complete. Each morning began with the reading of scripture and prayer; more prayers followed tea and preceded supper. Ferdinand Ward supervised Bible recitations every Saturday evening, preached to the students at his new church on Sunday morning, officiated at devotions at the school again that evening, and oversaw recitations from the Shorter Catechism each Monday morning.

Ferdie's father was ever present at Temple Hill. So was the example of Ferdie's sixteen-year-old brother, Will. He was a senior that year, and seemed to embody everything his parents might have hoped for in a son: he was an industrious student with a special interest in science and literature; a committed churchgoer about to enter the Edgehill School in Princeton, New Jersey, to begin studying for the ministry; a public speaker so gifted that even after graduation he was asked to return to the academy to give inspirational talks. (In one of them he warned his listeners against "seeking wealth and fame in this world . . . without God.")[45]

Will's "highest happiness," his mother noted proudly, "*always* derived from the Highest & Best Source."[46] She urged Ferdie to admire and emulate his older brother in all things, and insisted that Will watch constantly over his younger brother, not only to protect him from bullying by older boys but also to see to it that he behaved always as a clergyman's son was expected to behave. Over the coming years, neither the admirer nor the admired would much like the role he was expected to play.

FIVE

The Triumph of the Monster, "War"

"War! War!" Ferdinand wrote in his journal on April 13, 1861. To him, the firing on Fort Sumter was the awful but predictable outcome of antislavery meddling by the new Republican Party and its New School Presbyterian allies. He was scornful of Abraham Lincoln—whose irregular church attendance he especially deplored—and he would at least initially admire Ohio Congressman Clement Vallandigham, the Copperhead leader, whose slogan was "to maintain the Constitution as it is, and to restore the Union as it was." But, until a compromise peace could somehow be reached, he told a gathering of townspeople, political differences had to be forgotten in the interest of preserving the Union. Secession, like abolitionism, symbolized disorder and therefore had to be crushed.

That summer, the town's leading citizen, James S. Wadsworth, newly designated a brigadier general, called upon the citizens of Livingston County to form their own regiment, the 104th New York Volunteer Infantry (later called the "Wadsworth Guards").* By early

---

* General Wadsworth would be killed leading his men during the Battle of the Wilderness in 1864. While he was still breathing but unable to resist, rebel troops snipped all the buttons from his coat and stole his silver spurs, his gold watch, his field glasses, and his wallet. His corpse was eventually returned to Geneseo, where nearly every man,

autumn, some seven hundred young recruits were housed at Camp Union, a big, hastily built barracks at the east end of town.

Whenever they could, nine-year-old Ferdie and the town's other small boys walked out North Street to watch the men drill with wooden rifles and listen to the rattle and blare of the army band. Sunday mornings at his father's church were enlivened by the presence in the back pews of strangers in blue, marched to and from services by their officers. On Thanksgiving day, Ferdie helped his mother, his sister, and the serving girls deliver hot turkeys to the barracks, and on February 25, 1862, when the men of the 104th left for the war, he was among the townspeople at the depot who cheered and waved as their special train of seventeen cars pulled by a bright yellow locomotive disappeared down the tracks.

Ferdie watched his father vanish down the same tracks in July. Rev. Ward had resigned his pastorate and enrolled for three years as regimental chaplain, intending both to minister to the men and to provide readers of the *Livingston Republican* with accounts of how their sons and brothers, fathers and husbands were faring at the front. He caught up with the regiment just in time to witness its first full-scale battle, at Cedar Mountain on August 9. No one in the 104th was killed, he reported—"all escaped. *Laus Deo!*" But "I have visited the hospitals (churches that were) and Oh how sad the scene! It beggars description. Warfare like this is a tragedy. It is no gala day affair."*

Over the next few weeks, things got far grimmer. As Ferdinand reported to the newspaper, the regiment was assigned to the Union army of Virginia, under the bumbling and vainglorious general John Pope.

> You are aware that the "Army of the Virginia" under Gen. Pope, destined, as you were told, to strike a blow from which Secessionism was never to recover, marched to the Rapidan,

---

woman, and child turned out to say good-bye to the town's leading citizen. Martin L. Fausold, *James W. Wadsworth: The Gentleman from New York*, p. 9 footnote.

* The men of the 104th may have eluded death at Cedar Mountain, but it was all around them. "It was an awful sight," one private wrote home. "Some of the men was only half-buried. The stench was awful. None of the horses were buried and bushels of maggots was on them. The feet and legs of dead men was sticking out of their graves. They was not buried deep enough." Raymond G. Barber and Gary E. Swinson, eds., *The Civil War Letters of Charles Barber, Private, 104ᵗʰ New York Volunteer Infantry*, p. 81.

and then—*marched back again....* The army retraced their
steps exhausted in body and mind, and vexed almost to the
point of rage against certain military leaders.... Excessive
fatigue from long and hurried marches, scarcity of food and
that at very irregular periods, together with the deadly mis-
siles of the enemy have left our once large healthy and vigorous corps sadly diminished in number and efficiency.... In the
face of the Surgeon's declaration that it would be destruction
for soldiers to be made to march further for the present, they
are ordered further on. The 104th will not mutiny but they will
lie down and die. Such is to be the fate of many a brave man.[1]

They continued to march and to fight—at Rappahannock Station,
Thoroughfare Gap, and Second Bull Run, where a shell narrowly
missed Ferdinand while he was helping to lift a wounded soldier into
an ambulance. As the army plodded on, he found himself more and
more badly weakened by the diarrhea that had first plagued him in
India and had often recurred during times of tension since. Eventually,
the regiment's commander ordered him to go home.

Jane, Sarah, and Ferdie were all relieved that Ferdinand was out of
danger. But they were now concerned about eighteen-year-old Will.
The war was clearly not going to end quickly, and the Union needed
men. There was already talk of a draft, the first in American history.
If Congress approved it, Sarah had told her father, "there is nothing
to exclude Willie.... He is old enough.... Do you not think the
gunboat service will be altogether better for him than on the land?"[2]
Certainly his mother thought so. Jane wrote to her brother, Acting
Master Edward Shaw, who was stationed in Cincinnati, overseeing
construction of a 511-ton ironclad river gunboat, the USS *Indianola.*
Shaw pulled strings, and on October 1, 1862, his nephew came aboard
as acting master's mate.

"Do try and be faithful," his mother told her oldest boy.

> *Don't touch a drop of any kind of spirits, or be induced to smoke or*
> *play cards for a stake.* I *know* you will never be profane but smok-
> ing, drinking & card-playing are so often urged upon young
> men with such specious reasons that many are beguiled into

the first steps and then when God is offended, he sometimes leaves them. . . . There can be no ruin without the *first* step. I feel a little disappointed that you have not a room to yourself as I fear it will prevent you retiring in the day to pray alone, but I know if my brother should notice that you take a half hour of any part of the day to be alone, he will be sure not to interrupt you or to want the room at that time. 'Tis but little to give to God out of the 24. . . .

Should you go out [sail from Cincinnati] you had better take your flannel shirts and overcoat with you, for there are in every climate raw damp nights and as you have to keep watch at night sometimes you will certainly need them. Remember, you have been delicately brought up and cannot stand every thing.[3]

Will promised to be good, say his prayers—and wear his overcoat.

Meanwhile, for the first time in seventeen years, Ferdinand was without a church. An earnest young pastor named Henry Neill now occupied his former pulpit, so in November he agreed to become stated supply at Groveland, seven miles to the south. Since he planned to be away and Sarah was to spend the winter with his sister Henrietta Clarke in Rochester, Jane and Ferdie moved in with neighbors for the winter. Ferdinand wanted Jane to have a complete rest while she was there and worried that her sleep would be disturbed by Ferdie, who still climbed into his mother's bed whenever his fears overcame him. He was eleven years old.

Groveland did not suit Ferdinand. The English couple with whom he boarded was genteel enough, and "the people appear grateful that I have come among them,"[4] he told Sarah, but the village was stultifying, the congregation of farmers attentive but uninteresting. Within weeks he resolved to rejoin his regiment. The *Livingston Republican* applauded his decision. "We are glad for the sake of the brave boys who are now lying sick and wounded. We shall miss you, Dr. Ward, but go where duty calls you—go with our wishes and our prayers."[5]

The 104th was now part of the vast tent city that stretched for miles along the bank of the Potomac at Belle Plain, Virginia. Ferdinand got there just in time to describe to Will the fiasco that came to be called the "mud march."

We moved the whole Army of the Potomac under a flaming address from Gen. [Ambrose] Burnside that *"we were to meet the enemy, &c!"* At night-fall we had marched 6 miles—and at next evening *3* miles farther—& then no more! *Stuck in the Mud! . . .* Next morning we beat a retreat to our old quarters which we reached in *48* hours. Result: about four days—traveled 12 miles, saw no foe but mud—met with a defeat—cost to gov't *$1,000,000* & gained nothing but disgrace & discouragement. What *now?* Burnside is superseded by [General Joseph] Hooker. . . . The army thrown into panic. . . .

How rejoiced I am that you are not in the *infantry* ranks. . . . *Hold on.* . . . *That* is not your "Calling." Aim higher. Serve your country well *now*, but *look beyond*. I want to see you get in *public life* [as a minister]. This I cannot be denied. God bless you my dear boy with a loving heart & obedient life toward the dear Savior![6]

Ferdinand had just taken part in one of the Union's most ignominious debacles. Will was about to find himself at the center of another. When the USS *Indianola* joined Admiral David D. Porter's Mississippi Squadron at Cairo, Illinois, in early 1863, the Mississippi southward from Vicksburg to Port Hudson remained in rebel hands. Repeated attempts by Union vessels to blast their way past the Vicksburg batteries failed until February 2, when a federal ram, *Queen of the West*, managed to make it through and then began a twelve-day sortie, burning rebel stores and capturing rebel vessels up and down the river. On the night of February 13, the *Indianola* was ordered to run the Confederate gauntlet and join the campaign of destruction. Will Ward stood watch in the forward gun turret as the ironclad slid as silently as she could toward the fortified town, which overlooked a great bend in the river. A rebel picket opened fire. "As this signal passed along the shore," Will recalled, "[our] progress was marked by volleys of small arms and signal rockets. . . . Then came the blinding flash and deafening boom of the great guns." Eighteen shells were fired at the Union gunboat; all eighteen splashed harmlessly into the river. "Thus," Will continued, "the moments passed until the last of the batteries was left in the rear, and then the *Indianola*, having by a defiant whistle proclaimed its victory to friends and foes alike, passed beyond the wall of fire."[7]

The victory lasted just eleven days. The Confederates had already seized and refitted the *Queen of the West*, and they used her to help batter the *Indianola* into submission. One man was killed, and everyone else aboard was captured. Will was sent to the notorious Libby Prison in Richmond.

Meanwhile, elsewhere in Virginia, the Union army undertook a new campaign. The 104th New York fought again at Fitzhugh's Crossing and then was held in reserve at Chancellorsville. On the fourth day of that battle, Ferdinand reported to the *Livingston Republican*, he helped officiate at what was meant to be a solemn ceremony.

> At three in the afternoon the chaplains passed across the valley to hold services appropriate to the day. . . . The Brigade was drawn up on three sides of a hollow square, in columns, by division, closed in mass. On the fourth side stood the officiating clergymen, Campbell of the 107th [New York], Cook of the 94th [New York], Mr. Bullions of the 16th Maine, and Ward of the 104th N.Y. In the rear lay another Brigade, thus swelling the audience to about three thousand persons. The exercises consisted of reading the scriptures, singing, addresses which were listened to with most reverential attention and even witnessed by many across the stream, and perhaps by some among the hills who were very soon to send among us the instruments of destruction. The words of benediction had hardly passed your correspondent's lips when there came toward us the hissing shell, and then another and another—passing just above our Regiment, but doing fatal work among those in the rear. What a change! A moment since songs to the Prince of Peace, now the triumph of the Monster, "War;" now salvation to the soul and anon death to the body. There were those who heard of Jesus on that occasion for the last time.[8]

One of the thousands of Union men lined up to listen that afternoon, Major Abner Small of the 16th Maine, remembered hearing something else: "The chaplains had urged the men 'to shrink not from the terrible ordeal through which we were called to pass, brave and heroic, and God being our shield we would have nothing to fear' when came a slight puff of smoke, followed by another, and yet another, and yet another . . . just across the river, and then a rushing sound like trains of cars and terrific explosions all around us." Even these terrifying sounds, Small recalled, were "almost drowned out by the shouts and laughter of the men as the brave chaplains, hatless and bookless, with coat-tails streaming in the wind, went madly to the rear over stone walls, through hedges and ditches, followed by shouts of 'Stand firm! Be brave and heroic and put your trust in the Lord.' "[9]

Twenty days later, the crew of the *Indianola* was exchanged at Fortress Monroe, and Will started for home on leave. "How nice it is to feel that he is at last out of the hands of rebels," Sarah wrote to her father. "I doubt whether he will be contented to remain here [in Geneseo] long. The village is so quiet. . . . There are no boys of his age in it at present." A friend had told her, she continued, that a returning soldier had said "that he loved only two men in the world. One was [General George] McClellan & the other was Mr. Ward. I am not surprised to know the men are all so fond of you, Father."[10]

The men *were* fond of him and he did his best on their behalf. "Often and often when on some hot and dusty march has he dismounted from his wee little [horse] 'Charger,' " one veteran remembered, "and put up in his place some limping, tired, poor sickening boy, when the good old Dominie would trudge along with the rest and indeed it always took the stoutest to tire him out."[11] But in June, his chronic ailment returned, and as the regiment moved across Pennsylvania to help blunt Robert E. Lee's thrust toward Philadelphia, he was often forced to ride in a litter, dehydrated and unable to sleep.

On July 1, 1863, the Wadsworth Guards were camped a few miles southwest of Gettysburg. When the fighting around Seminary Ridge began that morning, 333 men of the 104th were alive and well; when it ended, 194 of them were dead, wounded, or missing. Ferdinand spent a week with burial parties, praying over the bloated, fly-blown dead. "I committed twenty-four to their hastily dug graves (twelve Union and twelve Confederates)," he wrote. "No word more perfectly describes the scene and results than *Satanic*. . . . And the lonely graves—fields covered with them. . . . Sad scenes!"[12]

When he wrote to Sarah a week or so later, those scenes were not what seemed to bother him most.

Dearly beloved Daughter, . . .

My thoughts are very much upon going home but I must be patient. I long for *liberty & quiet*:—neither is to be found in the army. . . . The great sins of our army (Generals and all) are *intemperance, profanity* (*blasphemy*, rather). . . . Last week was one of great mental suffering (in part bodily, from the great heat) arising from

1. nearness of quarters to the tents of several of the most blasphemous, immoral persons I ever heard. How could you endure being where at each moment you are compelled to hear the name of God & Christ & hell in the most irreverent, loathsome connections. Oh, may you be spared the *necessity*!

2. The fear of being sent *South*. I am as far downward as I want to go. If commanded, I of course, must go. But I pray not;

3. & greatly—our reduced numbers. Some 60 to 70 on parade rather than 600 & more. It depresses greatly. The officers almost all gone. It is sad, sad—So small a *parish*—So little to do. All these things create an almost intolerable sadness—shall I say, homesickness. Perhaps I ought not to name [these feelings]. They are *unsoldierly, childish*. I hope that I am not wholly useless—but I long to be at home.[13]

In the end, the 104th did march further south, into northern Virginia, in vain pursuit of Lee's retreating columns.

On September 15, as Ferdinand struggled to keep up with his regiment, his eldest son undertook what was meant to be a gallant errand some one thousand miles to the southeast. He was now stationed aboard the USS *Choctaw*, a 280-foot side-wheel steamer that had recently been refitted as an ironclad. After Vicksburg finally surrendered to U.S. Grant on July 4, the *Choctaw* was assigned to guard the mouth of the Red River. It was warm, sleepy duty interrupted only occasionally by guerillas sniping from the forested shore. The day before, a man in a rowboat under a white flag had brought a scrawled note for the *Choctaw*'s commander, Lt. Com. Frank M. Ramsay: a young woman was requesting permission to visit a dying relative upriver. Ramsay ordered Will Ward to take several men ashore and deliver her pass in person.

"When we reached the shore," a sailor named Daniel F. Kemp

recalled, "one man and myself were left in charge of the boat with orders not to leave but to keep a good lookout and be ready to shove off." Will ordered Landsman Andrew Ryan to keep watch from a ridge, then disappeared from view with Seaman William Gill, headed for the woman's house—and walked into a trap. Scores of rebel guerillas were hiding in the woods. "We saw Ryan . . . motioning and calling to Mr. Ward," Kemp remembered, "and heard loud voices behind the ridge and saw Ryan throw down his musket and run down . . . towards the house. This was the last we saw of them." Out of sight, Will and his companions were captured and led away at gunpoint.[*]

Jane got the news in a letter from the *Choctaw*'s commander on October 6. She wrote to Will at once, though she had no idea where his captors had taken him: "You may well suppose that my heart *ached* over such intelligence. . . . I have always said I had rather have you shot than fall into the hands of a lawless band of men who show no mercy. For an hour or more my heart bled for you and it seemed as if my brain would go wild."[14] Then, the postman brought her a second envelope from the *Choctaw*. Will was no longer being held by the guerillas; they had turned him over to Confederate General Thomas Green, who, in turn, sent Will and his companions on to a prison camp near Alexandria, Louisiana.

His mother did her best to hide her concern. Outwardly, she remained the selfless, tireless Christian worker she always tried to be, overseeing a women's book circle, collecting supplies for missions overseas, winding bandages for the wounded. When diphtheria tore through the village, she stoically tended to the sick and dying, too. "One of your little pets has fallen a victim," she wrote to Will.

> Dear little Harry Lord was taken ill on Monday and died the following Sunday night. I was with him a good deal. One of his recollections of you was . . . a funny face you had taught him. He made up the face and said, "Willie Ward showed me." Poor little fellow, he suffered terribly at [the] last. I dressed his

---

[*] In the aftermath of this incident, Lt. Com. Ramsay was formally reprimanded by Secretary of the Navy Gideon Welles for having "endangered the lives of his officers and men unnecessarily or without an object connected with the public interest or welfare which would justify it." Despite this official scolding, he ended his naval career as a rear admiral. Daniel F. Kemp, Civil War Letters, A64–97, Buffalo and Erie County Historical Society Archives.

corpse and decorated it with flowers which he carried down with him [into] the cold and cheerless earth. Mrs. Lord bears it like a Christian. Freddie Pearson is also dead by the same disease. Little Emma Dean, too, was taken in less than a week. I hope it may not enter our house.[15]

Sarah, off visiting relatives, shared that hope. It had been irresponsible for Harry Lord's mother to ask her mother for help, she wrote. Jane professed to be unafraid.

> Your long & excited letter reached me last evening & what shall I say? God sometimes calls us to make personal sacrifices for our friends & His children, and why should we shrink? Has He not set a time for us to die and will He call us away before that time because the force of circumstances and the demands of friendship lead us into danger? Does He not prove to *us* especially, every day, that no situation of exposure is beyond His control? Has he not kept dear Father & Willie . . . from perils by land & by water, by gunshots or sickness? *I* have no fears of Diphtheria or any other malignant disease so long as I can ease the mind of anxious friends or relieve the agony of a sufferer. In my attendance upon dear little Harry Lord I was very careful to wash & change my clothes before coming into Ferdie's presence and now that the little fellow is dead & buried 4 days, I am as well as ever & Ferdie, too.[16]

Ferdie may physically have been well as ever, but the absence of his father and brother at the front and the sudden, capricious deaths of boys and girls he had known and played with all his life can only have added to his terrors. So did the morbid, crippling self-doubt his mother carefully hid from outsiders but could not keep from pouring out onto her children.

When Sarah innocently confessed that worry over diphtheria back home had upset her stomach, her mother immediately blamed herself; the cause of her daughter's indigestion was over-spiced food she had unwisely served when Sarah was a little girl in India, she was sure of it. Everything she did as a mother turned out wrong, she said. "In view of the mistakes I have made in bringing up my children . . . life does not contain much for me. I often & often wish I had been blotted from it as soon as born and not been made the mother of suffering children. My heart goes up, too, in Thanksgiving that God took two of my children in their infancy & thus spared me & them from the results of living."[17]

With the rest of the family away, Ferdie was unable to escape hearing variations on that theme over and over again. He was now his mother's sole companion in the dark parsonage. It was fragrant with spices imported in wooden boxes from India, but the carpets and curtains and furnishings were drab and worn, shabby testimony to the truth of his mother's teaching: no one should expect virtue, no matter how conspicuous, ever to be rewarded in this world.

Will and the two sailors captured with him were imprisoned for six weeks before they were exchanged, long enough for him to develop intermittent fevers and persistent diarrhea. When they got back to the *Choctaw*, Daniel Kemp remembered, "the two boys seemed as happy and healthy as if they had been on a picnic and . . . seemed to enjoy the notoriety it gave them, but Mr. Ward, poor man, was simply a living skeleton. . . . I never saw a live man more emaciated. Whether he ever recovered from the experience I am unable to tell."[18] When Will failed to get better within a couple of weeks, the vessel's surgeon recommended he be sent home.

The same week that Will staggered back aboard the *Choctaw*, his father found an army surgeon in Washington willing formally to certify his own "ongoing trouble" as incurable, and to recommend that he, too, be allowed to go home, just as, twenty years earlier, Ferdinand had found a physician willing to testify to his inability to remain in Madras. The ailment that was responsible for this forced retreat, he assured the readers of his newspaper dispatches, was "not dangerous, though exceedingly irritating and troublesome, rendering life anything but a blessing. Having endured it for *five* months, I could bear it no longer."[19] He was discharged for disability on Christmas Eve, 1863.

Three weeks later, Will was formally discharged from the navy on the same grounds. The war continued, but neither father nor son would see any more of it.

A little over a year earlier, Freeman Clarke, the husband of Ferdinand's youngest sister, Henrietta, had been elected to Congress as a Republican. Jane—who shared her husband's loathing for that party and whose jealousy of the Rochester clan had so intensified over the years that she found it hard to visit there, even for the holidays—sent Henrietta her carefully qualified best wishes.

> My dear sister:
>
> As I am not going to Thanksgiving this year & shall not be able to present my congratulations, in person, for your good husband's triumphant election, please therefore accept them in writing. I shall be sorry to miss you from the Rochester circle, though I seldom see you when I visit there now.
>
> I want you to come and make me a visit this winter all by yourself, for though I have no girl, I make out to get enough for ourselves to eat and whatever friends may come in. Besides, I do not care much what I give those who, like you, get every luxury at home and so can well afford to live on gravy for a few days. Now *do* come and let us have a nice quiet cozy visit together which we may both remember with pleasure when you will be mingling with the gay and brilliant diplomats of the great Republic, and I shall be plodding on in my country kitchen among the pots & kettles.
>
> With ever so much love . . .
> Your sister[20]

Perhaps understandably, Henrietta Clarke chose not to come to Geneseo for that cozy visit. But a year later, she invited twenty-four-year-old Sarah Ward to stay the winter with her family in Washington. Ferdinand had been delighted. "*Enjoy yourself* just *as much as possible*," he told her, "consistent with your duty as a Christian."[21] Her mother professed to be pleased, too; a prolonged visit to Washington would provide Sarah with "an opportunity to see the world"—an opportunity, she never tired of telling her daughter, that her own life as a clergyman's wife had denied her.

Sarah would remain part of the Clarke household for the better part of three years. She loved being there. It was a lively, bustling place; there were seven offspring in the house, ranging in age from seven to twenty-nine. The Clarkes were sufficiently religious to reassure Sarah's parents but open-minded enough to welcome people of all kinds into their parlor. Sarah made her debut at the home of Postmaster General

Montgomery Blair, attended a levee at the executive mansion, shook hands with the Lincolns and with General Grant, and, after checking with her mother to make sure that occasional theater- or opera-going would not make her an "inconsistent Christian," was escorted to see Edwin Booth play *Hamlet* and to hear Gounod's *Faust.*[22] She attended balls, too, but, like her father before her, always resisted the temptation to dance. "While I have never seen the time when I would yield the point still I have felt it," she confessed to her mother. "But 'tis the only thing I have denied myself which has cost real effort. And I am pleased I have done it for perhaps it has been the 'mark' which has told me to be a Christian."[23] "Washington is no place to be good in," she added. "The tide in the other direction is too strong."[24]

Above all, she followed the fighting, poring over battle maps in the newspapers, talking with the young officers who came to call, joining a party of some fifty women who toured the Bull Run battlefield in carriages. Eventually, she came to share her uncle's Republican attitude toward the struggle: "I know Father will think me pretty violent," she confided to her mother. "I hate secessionists as much as radicalism."[25]

"There is nothing thought of [here] but the war," she wrote home during the summer of 1864, just after Washington's defenders had beaten off an attack by Jubal Early's Confederates.

> You at the North do not realize it as we do here. . . . Here all are more less affected. . . . Trains of wounded in ambulances are passing through the city in regiments and brigades. . . . The city is filled with soldiers and the sights one sees in passing the hospitals are sad enough. I can't express how glad I am to have been in Washington at this eventful period. . . . I know of no place I would have preferred to be in Europe or America.[26]

The war and the wider world to which her aunt and uncle had introduced her made her want to remain in the capital as long as she could. Besides, there was something else at work, as well.

Sarah had a serious suitor. Brigadier Surgeon John Hill Brinton was six years older than she and descended from a Quaker family that settled in Pennsylvania in the late seventeenth century, only a few years after the first Wards reached New England. Gen. George Brinton McClellan was his first cousin, and John had initially hoped to join his staff. But he had been sent west early in the war, instead, to serve first under Gen. John Charles Frémont (whom he thought "un-American" because of his fondness for gold braid and brass bands), and then as medical director of the Cairo district under Grant, whom he admired from the moment they met for being "plain, straightforward, peremptory and prompt."[27] He faced enemy fire at his commander's side at Belmont and during the Siege of Fort Donelson and the Battle of Shiloh and defended him against the charge of alcoholism, cementing a friendship that would last well beyond the war. Then, he had been assigned to Washington to begin a multivolume *Medical and Surgical History of the War of the Rebellion* and to help establish the Army Medical Museum, for which he supervised the collection of thousands of examples of "morbid anatomy" from the battlefields—shattered skulls and severed arms and legs.*

Despite his strong prejudices—he disliked Jews, dismissed black troops as slow-witted, and thought most women who volunteered to nurse the wounded worse than useless—he was much admired in Washington: he helped found the exclusive Metropolitan Club, was welcome at the executive mansion, and counted Lincoln's secretaries John Nicolay and John Hay and the widow of Stephen A. Douglas among his closest friends.†

When he began to call on Sarah Ward in 1864, some in her circle were wary of this older bachelor with such strong opinions. One of them sought out Grant himself to ask about the doctor's character and

---

* Brinton became an expert on gunshot wounds and the world's leading authority on the eerie phenomenon he called "frozen death"—the strange spectacle of soldiers who had been shot through the brain but whose bodies remained on horseback or in kneeling positions, sometimes clutching their pipes between their teeth, as if still living. "These attitudes were not those of the relaxations of death," he concluded. "But were rather of a seemingly active character, dependent apparently upon a final muscular action at the last moment of life, in the spasm of which the muscles set and remained rigid and inflexible."

His museum became a Washington tourist attraction. Amputee veterans sometimes dropped by with their families to see their missing limbs, preserved in jars. For forty-one years, Gen. Daniel Sickles, who had lost his leg on the second day at Gettysburg, made a point of visiting what was left of it on the battle's anniversary.

† Brinton was a formal, unsmiling man, but he did have a sense of humor about himself. One of his favorite stories had him removing a wounded man's arm at a Washington hospital with such swift skill that a junior surgeon complimented him. Then, Brinton wrote, "I remember well being startled by the voice of [President Lincoln] behind my back, making the solemn inquiry, 'But how about the soldier?' " John H. Brinton, *Personal Memoirs of John H. Brinton*, p. 265.

received what the general later remembered as his "favorable endorse-ment."[28]

Sarah was intrigued by Brinton. But there was a problem: although his ancestors had been Quakers, he was an Episcopalian. He and his widowed mother and three sisters only sometimes attended Sunday-morning services at the Holy Trinity Church near their Phila-delphia home and did not otherwise keep the Sabbath. Worse, wine was drunk at meals, and brandy and cigars were sometimes served afterward.

Over and over again, Sarah begged her mother for guidance.

> Mother, you know me almost as well as you know yourself. . . .
> Do you think my piety is of such [a] deep sort that it can grow
> and thrive if transplanted from my present home where reli-
> gion is the [central] element to a home where I will not be
> sheltered from this world's attractions! Do you think God has
> allowed my education to be what it has been so that I might be
> able to have the test that life would put me to! Do you think
> my sphere of life would be wider? The world does not possess
> the charms it used [to] for me. I think in my very heart I can
> say that I have never wished to change my life for that of those
> brought up in wealth and temptation. My sincere wish is to
> do God's will. I know, Mother, you will say, "God will guide
> you right." But do you think these doubts I have come from
> Him? . . . It is almost cruel but I feel that I must look to you for
> advice for there is no one else.[29]

Jane, who had met Dr. Brinton at least once and found him danger-ously "worldly," urged her daughter not to marry him simply because of his devotion to her. "We make a great mistake when we immolate self on the altar of a desire for the happiness of another," she wrote. "God never made it necessary that charity to one should involve cru-elty to another of his creatures, even if that creature be oneself. It is false or morbid heroism that prompts to this. . . . But above all dear Sarah, be true to God. If the interests of your soul are endangered by [this] union . . . , beware how you run into a snare. This is to me the grand point at issue and *for this I have prayed more than any other*."[30]

Jane was especially upset when Brinton—who had watched scores of men die during the war—told Sarah that in his experience professed Christians were no more serene in the face of death than those who had never been converted. "We *must not* listen to worldly arguments against Christianity," she wrote. "We know the word of God is true and that His promises are yea & anon in *Christ Jesus alone*."[31] The two women exchanged anguished letters about Dr. Brinton's lack of religious zeal for nearly two years, Jane insisting again and again that Sarah not allow her feelings for him to overwhelm her love of Christ.

When Congressman Clarke's term ended, Lincoln appointed him his comptroller of the currency, so Sarah was still living in Washington in January 1866 when Dr. Brinton insisted she make up her mind about marrying him, one way or the other. "I cannot blame him for wanting my decision as soon as possible," Sarah told her mother. "He has been waiting two years for it and feeling that it is time I knew my own heart and so it is—but I [fear] I shall never know it."[32]

Ferdinand, who had hoped his daughter would marry a Presbyterian clergyman, traveled to Philadelphia to look into Dr. Brinton's reputation. He may privately have been disappointed to find the prospects of his daughter's suitor bright and his character unassailable, but he finally advised her that marrying him was the right thing to do. Dr. Brinton obviously loved her and was undeniably a "gentleman"; marriage was a "heavenly appointment"; she should not keep him waiting further; "it is not right. His manliness is compromised."[33]

Her mother took longer to grant her blessing and would never give up the hope that her daughter's example might one day bring Dr. Brinton into the Presbyterian fold. In January 1866, Sarah finally said yes. "It is indeed a relief to feel that the question of almost two years is decided at last," she told her mother, "and, though I know it involves much unrest, still I have been more at peace than for months past." She continued,

> I have a proof of Dr. B's love I could not otherwise have had and he knows that he is marrying one who loves her religion better than him. I know he values me more now than if I had been easily won. The idea of marrying him is no longer repulsive and tho' I do not love him with the ardor of a young girl [she was now twenty-seven] I know that I do care for him more than for others, and it is only when the thought of leaving you comes that my heart sinks. How can I do that?[34]

.   .   .

She did finally do it. Sarah and John Brinton were married at the Grove in Rochester on September 23, 1866. They honeymooned at Niagara Falls, then moved into his mother's Philadelphia house. The groom's mother assured Sarah that no one in her home would ever intervene in her *"form* of worship. Christ has but one church on earth and all who love him . . . are his disciples and the mere form by which we approach Him is of very minor importance—you will not in the least be interfered with."[35] The newlyweds would do their best to work out a compromise: they agreed to attend different churches on Sunday, but if visitors turned up later in the day, Sarah retreated upstairs so that her Sabbath, at least, would remain inviolate. When wine was poured for dinner guests, she quietly turned her glass upside-down. But Dr. Brinton never forgave his in-laws for the delay they had helped cause in his courtship and actively grew to dislike his mother-in-law, whom he considered small-minded and intrusive.

The senior Wards never really warmed to their daughter's in-laws, either. When Sarah became pregnant with her first child, George, Jane asked to be allowed to come to Philadelphia to help with the delivery. Sarah turned her away as gently as she could; her mother-in-law, she said, simply had no extra room. Ferdinand was furious. "That [Mother] has not been there or *any of us* since your marriage awakens surprise & would *especially* if it were much longer delayed. She must go & see you. The question is as to *the place of her residence while there. Mrs B., you say, has no room. If she were a Minister's wife she would have to find room*—a nook, a closet, somewhere. . . . There are times when a daughter should have *her own mother.*"[36]

By then, nothing seemed to be going well for the senior Wards. Ferdinand had returned from the war without a job. On weekends he served as stated supply in the tiny town of Phelps, preaching to a congregation his daughter described as "oh so contracted and bigoted."[37] He earned so little, Jane wrote, they were forced to live on the fees he earned at weddings and funerals and had to pay Will's tuition out of the dwindling principal of her inheritance. Ferdinand made things still more difficult by plunging himself into another long acrimonious battle in Geneseo, opposing the establishment of a free state normal school that seemed sure to make his beloved academy redundant: "When will the New School folks stop this trying to crush the Academy?" he asked Sarah. "They can't do it. It is folly & wickedness."* He lobbied Freeman Clarke hard to help him land a new job as secretary of the Philadelphia Board of Education and paled visibly when it went to someone else.

Then, when Dr. Neill, his successor at the Central Church, decided to move on, some parishioners urged Ferdinand to return to the pulpit he had left five years earlier.

Jane was adamantly opposed; she could not bear the thought of stirring up the old resentments his restoration was sure to inspire.

He overruled her: "I am again pastor here," he wrote Sarah in December 1866, "much apparently to the joy of the people but not those nearer home. For the *latter* I am sorry. But what could I do? . . . I do wish that Mother were happier. She does not *mourn* but it is *submission* rather than cordial approval. . . . Mother is too *intellectual* to be attendant on my preaching, I do not satisfy her, I wish it were otherwise but I do my best and can do no more."[38]

By then, Presbyterians across the country were working toward reunion between the Old and New school assemblies. The once-divisive Plan of Union with the Congregationalists had long since been abrogated. The question of slavery had been settled on the battlefield, and hundreds of thousands of freedmen comprised a promising new mission field. The only issues remaining struck most laymen as abstruse and unimportant: who should interview prospective clergymen, for example, or how much leeway those clergymen could have in elucidating the Westminster Confession. In the summer of 1869, all 257 American presbyteries, both Old and New school, would be polled as to whether they wished to reunite; all but three voted to do so. The Presbyterian thirty-years' war was coming to an end.

But not in Geneseo. "As to the *Union* between the OS and N Schools," Ferdinand told his daughter, "I have no doubt that this will eventually be accomplished."[39] But he saw no need for haste. Doctrinal minutiae still mattered to him. He wrote a defiant twenty-page tract, "Why I am an Old School Presbyterian." demanding that the

---

* They did do it, and the normal school eventually put the Temple Hill academy out of business, just as he had feared it would. Ferdinand De Wilton Ward to Sarah Ward, November 20, 1862, Brinton Collection.

Old School hold out until the New School surrendered on each and every point, and then he made sure every member of both churches in town received a copy. When the Reverend Isaac Sprague of the rival White Church tried to organize union services, Ferdinand did as little as he could to comply without seeming obdurate. Privately, he and Jane thought Sprague "dictatorial" when he began to call his church "reunited."[40] It would take the Geneseo churches another eleven years to come back together formally.

The Wards' fondest hopes for their children rested on Will, whom Jane called her "Darling Child" and whom both she and her husband believed destined to follow him into the pulpit. Not long after returning from the front, Will entered the Williston Seminary, in Easthampton, Massachusetts, as a junior in the classics department, then moved on to Princeton, just as his father had. His parents were delighted when he said he shunned the company of "tipplers." But he had learned to smoke in the navy, and both his father and his mother exhorted him to stop: a smoking clergyman would never do.

Will's real interest was not religion, but science, and, he confided to his mother, he had more and more trouble reconciling the Bible with the new discoveries in geology, archaeology, and church history that seemed to turn up in every morning's paper. Jane was alarmed at first. "I do not want you to tempt God by the faintest semblance of a doubt,"[41] she wrote. But she also tried to be reassuring. While the Bible was "somewhat mystically written,"[42] she wrote, its essential moral truth was unassailable. She hadn't realized that there were different translations of God's word, but she wasn't troubled.

> Why not take that one which favors the facts of science most, so long as its other statements do not conflict with the grand & essential truths of the one *we* adopt? A mere mistake in chronology or in man's understanding of the length of periods could make no difference in reality, nor nullify the testimony of all the rest. As to the pre-adamite men I cannot see the discrepancy of their existence more than that of pre-adamite animals. Indeed, the wonderful exhuming of cities with people in them of which we have never heard in history, is rather evidence of a pre-Genesis earth altogether, which might have existed for

ages and been destroyed or thrown into the chaotic mess that is described . . . as "without form & void."[43]

When Will eventually transferred from Princeton to the newly estab-lished Columbia College of Mines his parents were not unduly alarmed. Their hope was that he would emerge from his studies as something altogether new: a man of God whose faith was only deepened by sci-ence; a scientist who never lost sight of the Creator.[*]

---

* For all his orthodoxy, Ferdinand had never seen any serious conflict between science and theology, if properly understood. In 1853, when Henry Augustus Ward, the teen-age son of his ne'er-do-well brother Henry, alarmed some of the more orthodox mem-bers of his family by declaring his interest in becoming a geologist, Ferdinand saw to it that he studied science at the Temple Hill Academy, paying the tuition from his own minister's salary. Henry Ward went on to become an explorer, museum builder, pio-neer taxidermist, and proprietor of Ward's Natural Science Establishment, supplying colleges and universities with geological cabinets and biological specimens from all over the world. Roswell Ward, *Henry A. Ward: Museum Builder to America*, pp. 38–39.

SIX

Suspected of Evil

Ferdie had turned fifteen on November 21, 1866, less than a month after Sarah married John Brinton and moved to Philadelphia and Will entered the Columbia School of Mines in New York, and just a few days before his father formally resumed the pastorate of the Central Church. The boy was already a cause for concern. Older parishioners saw only Ferdie's quiet good manners. "*Everybody* who speaks of him (outsiders) give him the best character in this respect," his mother told Will. "He never bullies little boys or does any such cowardly things."[1]

Boys his own age were less generous. He "never applied himself to study," a Temple Hill schoolmate remembered many years later. "He simply fooled away his time. About the only thing he did well was to write the other boys' names in books in a Spencerian hand, an accomplishment of which he was very vain."[2]

He blamed nearsightedness for his poor grades. His parents eventually withdrew him from school for fear he would damage his eyes. Private tutoring and "oral learning" did not seem to help. But somehow—despite his supposedly weak vision and inspired perhaps by stories of his father's work with the mission press at Madras—he took up printing and launched a four-page monthly of his own, the *Valley Gem*.

"Ferdie Ward, Editor and Proprietor" addressed his readers directly:

"If the 'Gem' has not met the expectations of its many readers the cause may be traced to the lack of ability, not of desire and effort on the part of its youthful Editor."* The *Gem* cost forty cents a year, "payable quarterly in advance," and was assembled rather than written. Just one copy—dated October 1866—is known to survive. It includes verse by Thackeray, riddles ("Why is a writer of fiction a queer animal? Ans. Because his tale comes out of his head"), and tall stories ("There is a town in Maine where the climate is so good the cemetery committee were obliged to shoot a man to start a graveyard. . . . A man in Illinois was so absent-minded that on retiring, he put his boots to bed and set himself outside the door").

"Ferdie busy at the press though unable to [see well enough to] read," his puzzled father noted. "I don't know what we shall do with him." Neither of his parents could disguise their disappointment that he showed none of the "peculiar interest in religion" they expected from all their children. When his mother insisted he go to Rochester to hear the "Sweet Singer of Methodism," Ira D. Sankey, preach on judgment, she reported that he returned to Geneseo more "rebellious and stubborn" than he had been before boarding the train. She was further distressed when he refused formally to join his father's church on the grounds that the congregation was filled with hypocrites.

But it was more than that. It was increasingly clear within the family that something more than weak eyes or the "nervousness" and tendency to fall ill he had displayed since infancy was wrong with Ferdie. His parents had always known he had a "timid spirit," Jane wrote, but now there was evidence of a "weak conscience" as well.[3] He had begun to spend money that was not his. "Ferdie very wrongly hired a cutter two or three times without our knowledge," Jane wrote Will the following spring, "amounting to five dollars! [More than $90 today.] He has promised to pay it from his press & I shall keep him to it."[4]

---

* A Rochester editor, mindful perhaps of the power the Wards still wielded in his city, welcomed the *Gem* to the region's "newspaper circle" with the hope that its "youthful conductor" would be successful, saying his "little paper is filled with good original and well-selected matter, and would be a credit to an older head and hand."

No one knows how long Ferdie printed the *Gem* or how many subscribers it had, but the monthly was successful enough that he was invited to write and print a book of his own the following year, its subject and title now lost. "It is nothing but a sensation tale all of his own concoction and worth nothing except as it gives him something to do," his mother told Will.

But she did not keep him to it. Nor did he pay it back. Instead, he ran up more bills and left them for her to find out about and be forced to pay. She would always indulge him, partly perhaps as a form of unacknowledged penance for what she believed to have been her own failure as a mother, and partly because it seems to have suited her to keep him dependent on her. And he, in turn, never seems to have evinced the slightest genuine remorse for anything he did. The cumulative trauma of his childhood—his father's remoteness, his mother's depression, the tension between his parents and between them and many of their neighbors, the constant dread of death and damnation that hung over the dark parsonage—evidently helped convince him early on that no matter what happened he was always a victim, perpetually blameless. He was "weak," he would sometimes admit, but he was never wicked.

It was impossible for Jane Shaw Ward ever fully to understand her son. His father saw him simply as "an enigma."[5] But both were right to be worried about his conscience; it would eventually become clear that he had none.

At the Columbia School of Mines, Will was struggling with his own conscience. His faith remained strong—many years later, his younger son would remember him as "a strict Presbyterian" and "a Calvinist through and through"[6]—but he did not hear the call to preach. For months, he wrestled with the question of what to do with his life. So did his mother—weeping, praying, sometimes feeling so helpless, she told him, that she wished for death.

> Such a consciousness of wasting energies that can never be recovered, such a sense of utter nothingness, took possession of me yesterday that I cried unto God with my whole heart to be taken to Him. It never seemed to me such a *reality* that the world could not & would not miss me, and that it would be "far better to depart & be with Christ." I felt so anxious for this change that it was a real disappointment when I waked this morning to find myself still here, and I could not restrain my tears.[7]

In the end, despite his mother's morose letters, in the face of his father's repeated declaration that "there is no employment on earth which

[can] compete with that of *preaching Christ*,"[8] Will abandoned the idea of becoming a clergyman. Instead, after he graduated, he worked for an inventor who shared a patent with him for an improved bottle for nursing infants and then commandeered the profits. He left that job to become directing chemist at the Rumford Chemical Works near Providence, Rhode Island, overseeing the manufacture of a lemon-lime tonic called Horsford's Acid Phosphate, then gave that up and went to work as an assayer in the United States Assay Office on Wall Street, under the supervision of his uncle Dr. John Torrey.* He would remain at that post for ten years. His father eventually got over his disappointment at his son's failure to follow in his footsteps: "I now only hope that you may do good through your scientific attainments. . . . Aim at the highest attainment in goodness and intellect. You have rare qualities. Use them with industry. God will bless you."[9]

Neither of the older Ward children had fulfilled their parents' dreams—Sarah had married outside her church, Will had given up the clergy. Only Ferdie was left. He was sent off to Edgehill at sixteen, just as his older brother had been, and with the same aim in mind: to prepare him for the pulpit.

His first letter known to have survived was written to Will at the start of his second term there on September 7, 1868. In it, the pattern he would follow all his life was already established. He was determined always to be seen as the Good Boy everyone insisted he must be. In order to maintain that fiction, he would always be willing to misrepresent the facts.

> I am all right and not at all homesick but would nevertheless like to be at home. . . . I have endeavored to make friends with all the boys and think I have, at least they often come to me for advice which I think shows that they look to me a little. The only thing that I object to here is the way the boys keep the Sabbath. They play a good deal which I do not like. I shut

---

* Dr. Torrey was married to Jane Shaw Ward's elder sister, Eliza. He was an explorer, teacher, and America's leading botanist as well as chief assayer. Despite his kindness to young Will, relations between him and his wife and Will's parents were sometimes strained, since the Torreys were enthusiastic members of a New School congregation in lower Manhattan.

myself in my room as much as I can but my chum [roommate] brings boys in and they get to fooling which I do not like for you know I have always been brought up at home to reverence the Sabbath. . . .

I remain your loving brother,
Ferd[10]

In fact, Ferd had made few friends at Edgehill, and most of his class-mates had learned to distrust him. He was "one of those fellows whom you can never tell whether they are telling the truth or not," one remembered years later, after his crimes had been uncovered.[11] It was he, not his chum, who got to fooling, profaned the Sabbath, and got into trouble for it. He was miserable at school, hostile to the whole idea of becoming a clergyman, and happy to exploit his mother's chronic worry in order to get back home. He told her his eyes were now so weak he couldn't see well enough to study after sundown.

His mother insisted he go to Philadelphia and have them examined. Somehow, he managed to convince an ophthalmologist there that he was not only nearsighted but might, in fact, be going blind. The school sent him home. "It is a *very great* disappointment to me," his mother wrote to Sarah, "and will be, I fear, to Ferdie, that he cannot ever look forward to an education. . . . I had fixed my hopes on Ferd for a min-ister and now must give that up."[12] Still worse, she wrote, the towns-people who were always watching her and her children for any sign of weakness were now sure to accuse the Wards of pampering their younger son, of "vacillating" and "irresolution."[13] To silence them, she prevailed upon John Brinton to write her a letter attesting to the boy's poor vision so that she could show it to any Genesean who dared express doubt openly.

There was little for a seventeen-year-old to do in or near Geneseo. Farmers had few odd jobs in winter. Shopkeepers rarely needed clerks. Ferdinand could not even become an errand boy in Freeman Clarke's or Levi Ward's banks, his mother complained, because Rochester members of the Ward clan always got their pick of those positions. Above all, she believed, it was important that her son find something to do in the open air, away from what she called "street influence."[14]

Finally, a post was found for him as apprentice to a local carpen-ter named William McBride, "a nice, respectable man, a good deal above the common run," his mother assured her daughter.[15] She comforted herself with the thought that carpentry was not necessarily an end in itself: "It *may* be the stepping-stone to [becoming] an architect which . . . is a good and respectable business."[16]

And so there he was in the winter of 1869, back home, bundling up and setting off through the snow each morning with a box of tools bought on credit, helping to rehang doors, replace broken panes, repair chairs and tables. At the end of his first two weeks he brought home his pay—one dollar and fifty cents. Jane allowed him to keep fifty cents for "pin money"; the rest she laid by for the future. "I am determined to keep him at it," she wrote, "for I do not like a vacillating character, and this is in all respects the best thing for him now." But she remained acutely solicitous of his health, and he made the most of her exaggerated concern. When he said he was overtired, she let him lie late in bed, and once even permitted him to skip the Wednesday-evening church service—something, she vowed, "he will not need to do when he gets more used to work."

In the lamplit evenings, while his father bent to his writings in his upstairs study, Ferd worked away at a carpenter's bench set up off the living room. As he worked, sanding a chair leg or fashioning a trinket box for a neighbor, his mother sat in a nearby rocker reading improving literature aloud to him. "It is very pleasant to have him so near me," she told Sarah, "and under such good influences while at work."

The good influences did not take. Life in the Ward parsonage had taught Ferd that virtue was rarely rewarded, at least not in this world. Vice offered livelier possibilities. Ferd found ways to slip out of the house and elude his mother's fearful gaze. "When he ceased going to school," a Temple Hill classmate remembered, "he spent all his time with the [young] ladies. . . . If the word had been coined . . . he would have been known as a dude. He was simply an exquisite with nothing to be exquisite on. . . . His accomplishment was polished manners. He was . . . very extravagant and always running up bills for his parents to pay."[17] And when he could no longer get credit from one merchant or another for his extravagances—monogrammed handkerchiefs, trinkets for local girls, unauthorized buggy rides—he began to borrow money around town, using sums cadged from one person to pay off another, embarrassing his parents, causing more talk among his father's parishioners.

In January 1870, in hopes of relieving Jane's anxiety and straighten-
ing out his eighteen-year-old son, Ferdinand escorted him to another
boarding school, the Bellefonte Academy in Bellefonte, Pennsylvania,
in the heart of the Appalachians. "Distance [from Geneseo] short (225
miles)," his father reported to Sarah, "but requiring *six* [railroads] to
reach, & 19½ hours time."[18] The school was housed in a handsome
pillared hilltop building and run by an old friend, Rev. James Potter
Hughes, who had been Will's headmaster at Edgehill. It promised to
provide the atmosphere of a Christian home. "F. ought to be contented
& improve," his father told Sarah.

> I was pleased by it all, better pleased I fear than F. will be, espe-
> cially until initiated. No letter from him yet, but rather doleful,
> I apprehend, when it comes. I am not unwilling to have him
> feel keenly his absence. His going was of his own seeking. He
> could have stayed at home and learned just as much *had he so
> willed.* . . . It pains me much to have him away, though a relief, I
> think, to Mother. When here he has to be watched hourly, day
> & night. He little knows what cause of anxiety he was to his
> Mother, to say nothing of self.
>   Though a father has less demonstration, he feels equally
> with a Mother. . . . I left you at Elizabeth, W'm at Edgehill &
> F. at Bellefonte & wept to do so. We Fathers *do* feel, though
> accused of . . . lack of heart.[19]

Jane Ward had steeled herself as well. "I feel a very great relief . . . in
having Ferdie at school," she told Sarah. "He would have been ruined
here for I was not strict enough with him and now I feel as if God
would take him up. He writes me that there is a good deal of religious
interest in the village and some of the boys are giving their hearts to
Christ and I hope he, too, may become a Christian."[20]
    To Will, she was more frank.

> I hope you will write to Ferdie & encourage him to stay [at
> school], for I feel a great weight lifted from my heart in hav-
> ing yielded him to the care of others under God. . . . On no
> account send him any money for some time to come, and then
> only a very little. He *must* be taught the value of money, and
> nothing will teach it so effectively as the want of it. I wish

Mr. Hughes might be advised to see that Ferd does not spend money without his knowing just where it goes, and also that he will not allow Ferdie to write home to anyone but Father & me without letting us know it. All this, too, without Mr. [Hughes] knowing (if possible) that we suspect Ferdie of *evil*.[21]

As his father had predicted, Ferd's letters from school were a torrent of complaints, mostly centered around the "pork & codfish diet," which he claimed was making him ill.[22] He wanted to come home. At first, his mother ignored his pleas. "It will do him no harm to be disciplined on this line," she told Sarah.

He has been humored far too much and his character is consequently not a strong one. This reminds me of your remark about "wondering why God had not given your Father & me more of this life's comforts when we have always served Him." It is just as necessary for God's children to be disciplined by privation and want as for ours, in order to [build] their strong characters. Too much indulgence would make us selfish, inconsiderate and weak, just as it has in Ferdie's case and in all indulged children, so that it is one of the strongest proofs of His love that he does not give us all we want or seem to *need*. I have been led to feel this in seeing how wrongly I have favored Ferdie and I am content with God's dealings toward me.[23]

Her contentment did not last; neither did her resolution. When another self-pitying letter from Ferdie arrived three days later, she sent it to Will right away.

It shows, dear Willie, a terrible nervous state . . . arising I suppose from home-sickness which he has not yet been able to shake off. I begin to feel that by persisting in his staying there perhaps we may be acting wrong and the consequences may be bad. . . . Ferdie is of such a nervous temperament and has been so long now under a state of excitement about his ill conduct and worry about the food there that perhaps we ought to regard the matter in a different light. . . . It may seem changeable in me, Willie, but . . . prolonged homesickness, without anything else will often produce death, and in such a nervous system as

Ferdie's it might be fatal. If he were a good Christian like you I would not feel half the anxiety for him that I now do.[24]

Neither Will nor Sarah believed Ferdie was in mortal danger. Both warned that his troubles at school were not just dietary, that he could well be, in Sarah's carefully chosen words, "using arguments that are not true" in order to persuade his parents to bring him home again.[25] "I cannot bear to think," his mother answered, "that in the midst of his seeming repentance for the past he is still going on in lying and deceit. It seems at times as if I would be crushed by the hopeless prospect there is before me in regard to him."[26]

Sarah and Will were right. In early March, Rev. Hughes personally escorted Ferdinand to the depot and put him on the train for home. We don't know what he had been caught doing, but the infraction was so grave in the headmaster's eyes that there was no question of Ferd's ever returning to the school; he was formally expelled, not merely suspended. "He himself says he transgressed on purpose," his mother explained to Sarah, "because he could not stand the food and was sick all the time. . . . It seems as if he were one of the worst boys and in the most hopeless condition. . . . What shall we, what *can* we do with him?"[27]

Will wrote that it was his mother's infinite solicitude for Ferd's weaknesses that had brought about this latest humiliation. Sarah urged her mother to show her displeasure by silent disapproval at the very least. She couldn't do it. "I cannot be angry all the time, for my own sake & others even if Ferdie would mind it," she wrote. "I used to pursue such a course sometimes when you or Willie vexed me, but it did not make you feel as badly as I felt myself." Besides, she was now convinced her boy was really ill. "The Dr. says he 'has all the symptoms of Dyspepsia and it must be cured at once,' " she reported. "He looks pale and his lips whiten & redden alternately. . . . He declares that he came home only because of this distress which made him cross and low spirited all the time, indeed completely wretched. But I will say no more now. Only *pray.*"[28]

By January 1871, Ferdinand was well enough to be sent back to boarding school—to Edgehill again, which had moved in 1869 from Princeton to Merchantville, New Jersey, just outside Camden. He lasted just two months this time, before being sent home for reasons that had something to do with an unauthorized visit to a young lady in Philadelphia.

He had now been sent away three times and three times been sent home again. This time, there were at least superficial signs of repentance. His father noted in the spring of 1871 that the "special blessing of God in revival" was at work within his church. Fifty-one persons entered its congregation on confession of faith. Nineteen-year-old Ferdinand was one of them, at last.

And in the fall, another of his father's hopes for him seemed about to be realized—a real job. One of his former teachers at Edgehill got him work as a clerk at the Meridian National Bank in Indianapolis, Indiana. "When you write to him beg him to be *accurate* in his accounts," his father urged his daughter, "not attempting to do things *fast* & not have money lost by carelessness or burglary when in his care."[29]

Ferdinand was home again within two weeks, personally dismissed by the bank's president. Thirteen years later, the banker would explain that he'd fired Ferdie simply because he smoked and whistled on the job; young men with such weaknesses could not be trusted around money. But it's hard to believe that proximity to cash hadn't proved too tempting for Ferdie to resist. In talking to the press when his former clerk had become a notorious swindler, the bank president might simply have been reluctant to admit that his depositors' funds had ever been at risk while in his care.[30]

Hoping, again, to keep Ferdie away from bad companions and teach him the virtues of hard work, his father prevailed upon his old commander, Colonel John R. Strang, to try him out as a clerk in the upstairs office at 51 Main Street he shared with another attorney, James B. Adams. "Ferdie is doing well at the Law Office," his mother reported to Sarah a few weeks later, "but [doesn't] quite like the business."[31]

He turned twenty-one on November 21, 1872. Jane was away, visiting Will in New York. Ferdie evidently had several friends in to celebrate. When his mother returned she found him at home, dutifully boiling water for her tea. She was, as always, happy to see him. But that evening, she noticed something amiss in her storeroom. The previous summer, she had placed on a high shelf six full bottles of sweet wine sent to her husband by his brother Levi, exclusively for use at communion. One was now missing, she told Sarah, and the rest had been partly emptied and then clumsily recorked. "I said to Father, 'So you have been using up my wine since I was gone.' He looked quite surprised and when I told him the facts he said he had not touched a drop of it. I said, 'I wonder who could have taken it then.' "[32]

"My heart felt quite worried," she told Sarah, "and I feared that perhaps F. might have been helping his friends out of it. . . . I told him I missed my wine and . . . wondered if [one of his friends named] John Conway could have used it. . . . He said there was no wine used . . . and that he did not believe John would take anything. As to himself, he said he did not know there was any wine in the house. I knew this last was true when I left at any rate, and as the wine was on a high shelf, way back, I did not believe he could have found it or thought of looking for it."[33] The culprit, she finally decided, had been Katy, her daughter's Irish nurse, who had stayed in the house when Sarah and her two children had visited the previous summer. "From the way the [remaining] bottles were used, each one a half or 2/3 gone and not any one quite empty," she explained, "I suspect . . . also that she must have done it as no thief outside would have done exactly that way but rather have taken bottles and all. I therefore feel sure she is not strictly honest but as wine like that would not make her drunk I cannot of course affirm that she took it."[34] In a subsequent letter, Jane would beg her daughter not to mention the pilferage to Katy—who remained a valued part of the Brinton household for years. Once again, she had been unable to blame her errant son for anything.

A few weeks later, smallpox broke out in Geneseo. Schools closed. Churches stood empty Sunday morning. The stores on Main Street did little Christmas business. On December 17, at the height of the epidemic, Ferd suddenly announced to his parents that he was going to flee the village and spend Christmas with an old Temple Hill friend who now lived in Jersey City.

Jane struggled to explain his unexpected departure to Sarah.

> He had been working in the Office very hard of late, day & night, so, since the smallpox had appeared in the village and business of all kinds became terribly dull, Mr. Strang told Ferd he might be excused till after the holidays. He had been made terribly nervous and fearful by hearing men talk about the smallpox until he got into such a state—intensified by hard work and confinement—that he would seem all in a terror when he came home. I tried reasoning and persuasion in vain, for I did not think he ought to spend his money so long as he

owes it to others. . . . [But] as soon as Ferdie *determined* to go I did what I could do to cheer him off and today I received a letter from him which was written in good spirits. I feel now that I may throw off some of the responsibility—and anxiety—that I have borne for Ferdie for so many years. For he is of age and must judge for himself. I believe he wants to do right. But he is of a terribly nervous and timid constitution and some allowance must be made.[35]

His mother would always find a way to make allowance for Ferdie, no matter what he was accused of doing.

Then, on Christmas Eve, while staying with his friend in Jersey City, Ferd received a terse note from Colonel Strang: his services were no longer needed. The day after Christmas, Jane Ward swept up Main Street to confront her son's employer in his office. How could he have treated her boy so badly? Colonel Strang was tactful but unyielding. He liked Ferd very much, he assured her; her son had done everything asked of him "and done it quickly and well." The problem was simply "pecuniary." A young law student named Hopkins had asked to be allowed to work for Strang & Adams "without any pay in order to learn the profession." He had been there some weeks before Ferd went to New York, and after he had left "Mr. A & S talked the matter of their business over and concluded that they could not afford to keep a [paid] clerk when they could get one without pay. [Strang] never asked Ferdie or Father whether Ferd would work for nothing but gave the preference to Hopkins. . . . Mr. Hopkins goes to that [New School] church which I think is the real reason. God will judge them for such injustice."[36]

No new jobs opened up. His father's friend and Old School ally Judge Scott Lord gave him occasional documents to copy. A plan to go to work for a judge in nearby Dansville failed to materialize. Will suggested Ferd study law on his own. He dutifully borrowed a copy of Chancellor James Kent's *Commentaries on American Law* and began leafing through it in his room in the evenings. He seemed "in earnest," his mother wrote, and, though it meant "our house will have to go without carpets, my windows without curtains, my furniture without repairs and both Father's and my wardrobes without replenishing," his parents were willing to support him for another two years, if at the end of it her boy would have a profession—"a real life work."[37]

Meanwhile, his parents insisted he run for the post of clerk to the church board of trustees. Those plans, too, went awry. "You 'feel anxious about Ferd,' " Jane wrote Sarah in late January. "So do I. He lost the election to the clerkship. . . . The New School folks [some of whom evidently now found it more convenient to attend the Central Church] overcame him. . . . He is weary of idleness. Father gives him copying to do . . . but he feels worried not to have some *regular* work.[38]

Ferd was now a grown man continuing to lead the life he had led from early boyhood: he was without work, expected to help his parents entertain visiting clergymen, to sing in his father's choir and accompany his mother to church and prayer services several times a week. "Ferdie is wholly dependent on us now," his mother told Sarah with what seems to have been a blend of concern and satisfaction. "He has not even 25 cts a week for pocket money unless we give it to him."[39]

Her husband shared all of her concern and none of her satisfaction. Neither he nor Jane was well. His old stomach complaint continued to nag at him. Jane experienced "a nervous tremor over my system," she told Sarah, occasional chills and "a good deal of head-ache," and therefore was too ill to travel to Philadelphia, where Sarah was about to give birth again—to twin boys, it turned out. "I am growing old fast," she wrote, "and am more & more to shrink into myself and withdraw from those whose society I most enjoy."* And rumors reached the Wards that their youngest child was secretly running with Geneseo's equivalent of a fast crowd. He was seen spending time with his boyhood friend Herbert Wadsworth, the eccentric and hard-drinking son of the late General Wadsworth.† He hunted birds with some of the town's wealthiest and most worldly gentlemen, including Judge Alfred Conkling, the father of New York's Republican senator Roscoe Conkling. And he had even been spotted stepping into the tavern of the American Hotel for a quick beer with his friends. All of it alarmed his parents.

Ferdinand wanted work for his boy, serious work, away from home

---

* This was at least in part face-saving on Jane's part; according to one of his descendants, Dr. Brinton wanted to see as little as possible of his mother-in-law. Jane Shaw Ward to Sarah Ward Brinton, April 18, 1873, Brinton Collection..

† Herbert Wadsworth grew into a would-be inventor and dilettante poet who boasted that he had "written more, in bulk, than Tennyson," but rarely published any of his output. Alden Hatch, *The Wadsworths of the Genesee*, p. 119.

and right away. He prevailed upon Will to see if he couldn't try harder to find something for him in New York.

Nothing materialized. Then, on March 10, 1873, Professor John Torrey—Jane's brother-in-law and William's employer at the Assay Office—died at seventy-five in New York City. Will represented the family at the funeral, and afterward encountered S. Hastings Grant—called Seth—an orphaned missionary's son whom Torrey and his late wife had helped to educate. Grant had just been appointed superintendent of the newly reorganized Produce Exchange on Whitehall Street in lower Manhattan. Will saw his chance. Ferd was bright and eager, he assured Grant; he had fine penmanship and considerable experience in accounts and office work; only his bad eyesight had kept him from college, perhaps even the ministry. Grant said he needed a secretary. If the young man would come to New York right away, he would try him out—and pay him $100 a month. After all, he was almost a member of the family.

Ferdinand could not have been more pleased. Seth Grant was just the sort of employer he had hoped to find for his unsteady son. He was a deacon of the Old School Madison Square Presbyterian Church, a life member of the American Bible Society, and for seventeen years had been librarian at the Mercantile Library Association, established to provide young clerks like Ferd, newly arrived from the countryside, with improving literature to keep them from succumbing to city temptations.

On June 20, 1873, Ferdinand noted in his journal, *"Ferd left for New York!"* "The sky is clear," he told his son. "To become a felt & admitted *necessity* is a prime attainment. That you may become more & more so. *N.B.* Punctuality—*care in penmanship & figures—courtesy to all & unimpeachable integrity.* I know you will keep these in view. Look upward for all needed moral qualifications."[40]

PART THREE

THE YOUNG NAPOLEON OF FINANCE

SEVEN

The Avaricious Spirit

The Produce Exchange, at Whitehall and Pearl streets in lower Manhattan, where Ferd now went to work, was everything Geneseo was not: clamorous, frantic, fast moving. Its heart was the vast high-ceilinged "call room" in which hundreds of brokers and shipping agents in top hats crowded around long tables examining samples of grain, then raced one another to one of three telegraph offices in the building to wire bids to other brokers and shipping agents in Omaha and Chicago and Kansas City, Liverpool and London. It was a minute-by-minute business, prices rising and falling as brokers tried to outguess one another as to what the future, final price of a commodity might be. Critics charged that its hectic pace, made possible by the telegraph and the postwar explosion of railroad building, encouraged reckless gambling. The president of the Exchange, Franklin Edson, was unmoved: "Most people in this country have a desire to become rich quickly," he said. "We are born speculators, as likely to gamble on grain as to speculate in stocks."[1]

At his stand-up desk adjacent to the superintendent's office, Ferd struggled to keep track of it all, recording in enormous ledgers the big profits being made buying and selling carloads of flour and corn and wheat, bacon and butter and cheese, that brokers never even saw.

He did well enough to make himself a "felt & admitted necessity" to his exacting employer, just as his father had hoped he would, and was soon promoted to confidential clerk, privy to every transaction. But the work was arduous—Mr. Grant prided himself on the fact that no mathematical errors were *ever* committed in his office—and the hours were long. Ferd left the Fourth Avenue rooms he shared with Will early enough every morning to reach work two hours before the opening bell, and he kept at it long after the building emptied.

The pace was unlike anything he had ever known. And he resented the close watch his mother insisted his brother keep over him. Will, she reported happily to Sarah, "sees just how [Ferd's] money goes, how much he sends home to pay debts and what he denies himself to do it. I know that this lesson will be good for him."[2]

From the first, he seems to have been conflicted: excited to be at last away from home and out from under his mother's prying eye but frightened of failure; weary of being treated like a child and at the same time unable to imagine being treated any other way. He sent home a stream of querulous letters suggesting it was all too much: his weak eyes were getting worse; a doctor had told him that a painful boil on his neck had been caused by "city air" and could not be cured so long as he stayed in New York.

His father, who had finally left his church after a combined total of twenty years and taken up new duties as district secretary of the American Bible Society, insisted that Ferd stay where he was.* "The clouds have been dense," he told Sarah, "but a little light dawns. He was in Geneseo quite long enough."

His mother was less sure. "He told me something of his weakness and poor health but the half was not told," Jane told her daughter after Ferd made a brief visit to Geneseo during the summer of 1874. "He is

---

* "*I* think the [congregation is] getting tired of him," his wife had confided to her daughter shortly before Ferdinand resigned. "Many never *relish* him." The departure was not an entirely happy one, at least from Jane Shaw Ward's point of view. The session provided a parting gift of just $100, a sum she thought ludicrously grudging. And, she told Sarah, although several parishioners had given farewell dinner parties in their honor, "I have not heard one person say 'We are sorry *you* are going to leave us, Mrs. Ward' but always, 'We are so sorry Dr. Ward is going to leave us.' I do not feel badly over this—God knows. . . . '*My* record is on high.' That was David's comfort & shall be mine." Jane Shaw Ward to Sarah Brinton Ward, n.d. 1873, Brinton Family Papers, the Historical Society of Pennsylvania, November 2, 1873.

really miserably thin, pale and dejected, cannot eat, does not care to go out and seems terribly depressed."[3] Even a visit to a cousin's cottage on nearby Hemlock Lake failed to revive his spirits, she told Will:

> He came back entirely exhausted so that when I went to call him at 8 o'clock this morning he still felt all worried and complained of pain in his back. . . . It is the result of a whole year's standing on his feet and leaning over a desk. Why is it that these grasping money-makers are so hard-hearted? Why cannot they feel enough for a weak clerk, to say nothing of a strong one, to let him *sit* at his desk? How can they see the young withering down under their exertions and undermining their competition for life just to please a whim? I think you ought to speak to Mr. Grant and tell him that Ferdie is not able to bear it.[4]

Neither of Ferd's siblings took his lamentations seriously. Both believed he was up to his old tricks, malingering to avoid work, elicit sympathy—and winkle funds—from their mother, whose indulgence of his excesses still seemed boundless. Neither his alleged ill health, his aching back, nor his old debts kept him from running up more bills while he was at home—at the tailor's, the boot maker's, the livery stable. "I do not believe ten thousand a year would suffice him," his mother admitted to Will. "May God correct his avaricious spirit, and never let him feel as many have done as [if] we are off on a picnic."[5]

"All of his years have been lived in our flush times," a Wall Street veteran would write ten years later, trying to explain Ferd's actions amid the wreckage of Grant & Ward.

> He came with the impulses of youth into the very center of business, starting at the Produce Exchange . . . where men were "on the jump" during business hours and there is not time to stop and read character, but each man takes every other man to be perfectly solvent because he is there in the building, doing business. In this life of action without much forethought, young Ward instantly matured, like a beefsteak broiled on the fire which comes to us both rare and done. All he wanted was

capital to carry out the ideas he saw as clear before him as his nose in the glass.[6]

Ferd would never stop complaining that he was being worked too hard, but his proximity to the big money being made all around him only intensified the avaricious spirit about which his mother worried. He had also begun to see opportunities afforded to him by his position at the Produce Exchange. As confidential clerk to the superintendent, he was empowered to buy the membership certificates of retiring members for $240 to $250 apiece, then sell them to new would-be traders eager to try to make their own fortunes at a profit of anywhere from $10 to $50. And he was convinced early on that these memberships would appreciate steadily in value. (Business at the Exchange was steadily expanding; plans were already being drawn up for a vast new headquarters to be built opposite Bowling Green to accommodate it all.)

All he needed was cash to get started. The quickest way to gain access to it was to find himself a wealthy wife. He went about his search with a kind of steady, calculating resolve he'd never shown before. To seem more prosperous and more promising than he really was, he wrote home for money with which to buy a suitably elegant new overcoat and trousers. When his mother gently suggested he wait until at least some of his hometown debts were paid before incurring new ones, he responded with icy defiance.

> Dear Mother
>   Your last is at hand. I will have to act as necessity requires, but will not buy the clothes until absolutely necessary. I shall have hardly enough left this month to last me a week, so if I am entirely out, I *must* borrow. I will say no more to Mother on the matter. . . .
>
>   In haste.
>   Goodbye
>   Your loving son
>   Ferdie[7]

To forestall further borrowing, his mother ordered George Goode, Geneseo's best tailor, to make up the clothes he had asked for in secret; they would be a "surprise gift," she told his exasperated older brother.[8]

Ferd wrote home again. He was now unable to pay any part of his share of the rent, he said. Will, forced to come up with the money out of a salary that had recently been cut, was furious, and saw to it that his brother moved to cheaper lodgings at 72 Clinton Street, across the East River in Brooklyn Heights.

Will may have meant the move as punishment: he would wash his hands of his brother's affairs many times over the coming months, only to find himself drawn back into them again, unable to resist his mother's pleas to help nudge Ferd back toward the straight and narrow. But his younger brother could not have been more pleased with his banishment to Brooklyn. He liked its shady streets lined with handsome brownstones and he liked still more the glimpses he got of the splendid lives being led behind their doors. An elderly resident remembered Brooklyn Heights as it was when Ferd first moved there.

> Sumptuous drawing rooms with . . . beautiful mirrors, crystal chandeliers, heavy furniture, Moquette and Aubusson carpets in patterns woven for the room, costly ceilings decorated by Italian artists; . . . grand receptions, the house filled with flowers, soft music, with gracious women . . . to help receive, and the dining room tables gleaming with cut glass and silver, with tempting edibles in as fascinating array as a French chef could devise. Terrapin was then in vogue, with champagne freely flowing. No matron of those days would think of introducing her daughter to Society, other than from her own home. The invitations . . . were delivered from house to house by the hostess in her carriage, coachman and footman wearing white gloves, the latter running up and down the front steps delivering the invitations with great ceremony. . . .
>
> Those were the days of beautiful horses and fine harness with mountings of silver and brass. How many buckles would the gentleman have on his new harness? Would he have single letters or monograms? . . . Very fast horses were the fashion, *pater familias* having a pair of horses for the family use, with two or three fast horses for himself.[9]

Ferd was determined to be a part of all of it. He cultivated a moustache to make himself seem more mature, accelerated his purchase of stylish clothes on borrowed funds, and joined one of the most fashionable churches in the neighborhood, the Church of the Pilgrims, at the corner of Henry and Remsen streets. It was Congregational rather than Presbyterian, but Ferd's father admired the preaching of its celebrated pastor, Rev. Richard Storrs, nonetheless. "There are no jokes nor stories to provoke laughter, no sudden outbursts nor apropos allusions to excite applause," a contemporary wrote; Storrs was "a Puritan preacher [who] dispenses the Word of God soberly and piously to the sons and daughters of the Puritans."[10] And Ferdinand especially liked the fact that the church's New England origins had been so important to its congregation that the architect had included a fragment of the actual Plymouth Rock in its lobby wall.

This was the kind of world Ferd knew well. He was expert at mingling with parishioners; he had been doing it all his life. He was amiable, soft-spoken, well mannered, and eager to fit in. "I have made many kind friends [within the congregation]," he assured Sarah, "and they all seem to take an interest in me." When he volunteered to help with the Sunday school as a "means of doing good," the superintendent was so impressed by his rare combination of apparent piety and accounting skill that he made him its treasurer.[11]

Each weekday morning, Ferd made his way down to the Montague Street Ferry slip with the other junior clerks and office boys to catch the first boat to Wall Street at seven. The fare was a penny. It doubled after nine, when the older, more successful, passengers came aboard—bankers, brokers, chief executives, the privileged owners of the homes and stables Ferd envied, who smoked their cigars and read their newspapers and had their boots blacked as they steamed toward Manhattan. A young man knew he had advanced in business when he joined the rank of the two-cent-fare payers. Ferd Ward saw no reason to wait.

On the evening of March 18, 1875, he sat up late in his Brooklyn boardinghouse writing a long, agitated letter to Will across the river. His search for a well-to-do wife was gathering steam. He'd already clumsily tried to ingratiate himself with a wealthy young woman named Webb, cadged a ring from his sister to present to her, and then somehow done something that so alarmed her parents that his mother felt compelled to write them a letter to "exonerate" him.[12]

Now, he had zeroed in on another young woman from Brooklyn Heights. Her first name is lost but her last name was Robinson. The frenzied late-night letter inspired by his infatuation with her—and with the world of luxury and comfort an alliance with her would open up to him—revealed more about his turbulent inner life than anything else he ever wrote. He is, by turns, obsequious and aggrieved, a perpetual victim whose status somehow makes him immune from ever doing wrong, rendered giddy by thoughts of money and the guilty pleasure he gets from spending it—especially when it does not really belong to him.

Dear Will,

It is 11 o'clock and I have just returned from a lovely, and need I say, most pleasantly spent evening with Miss Robinson. I received a note from her day before yesterday asking my company this evening, and I have been [to see her] and now here I am in my room, too excited to sleep, for I feel that I have made myself agreeable to her. . . .

You may wonder that I write to you, yet I must, for although encouraged by her, I feel that I am not encouraged by you, and I deserve to be left to my own ways, yet do be lenient with me Will, for I cannot bear to feel that *your* love and interest grow less. I used to see so much of you and now I see so little. Why is it? I know my tendency to extravagance displeases you yet I ask that you will not give me up. If I were to lose your love, I would care but little for this life. I *do try* hard to do right, yet I seem to fail, but I *am* doing better than before and with your help I can some day come out all right.

You do not know, Will, how I try, and you can never know, for you are so different than I am. You know my life at home has been one of indulgence;—I have had everything that home could afford, and my misfortune has always been that of self-indulgence. It seems second-nature to me and it is not easy to break myself of this habit of extravagance. I feel it deeper than you can ever know, and it is only by slow perseverance that I can ever hope to come out a better man. I love money not so much for the pleasure it gives me but for the pleasure it gives others. I spend money for other's pleasure as well as my own and it is hard for me to reason before acting. I get a thing & give it away and not till after it is gotten do I feel the remorse of having done wrong, but I suffer afterwards.

You probably think me foolish in not having the will to think before acting; this I acknowledge, it seems at times almost like a disease of which I can only be slowly cured. One cannot break himself of a habit without a long and earnest effort; so with me. I say to myself that I will resist certain things & the next minute I will be doing those very things. I have no power to resist and I feel that this can only be cured by slow and hard self-will.

Now Will, I *cannot believe* that I am losing your love, yet I feel that I deserve to, for I do so many things you disapprove of. Remember that I am weak in many points and if possible bear with me for I know that some day I will come out all right.

I love to dress well, and especially when I go among people like the Robinsons. I do not like to look shoddy but I like to be neat in my dress. In order to be [I] have to spend money and so find it goes faster than I suspected it would.

I will show you, Will, how in the last month I have spent my money so that you may see where it goes.

You know that my new coat which I got from home was too short in the sleeves, so I took it to Evans the tailor (the place where you told me to go). He let the cuffs down a little and charged me $2. Now, I little thought he would charge me so much or I would not have gone to him.

I also found that I must have some new stockings and cuffs, so I got them and they cost me $2.50.

I have been suffering very much of late with a decayed tooth which has pained me so that I have been kept awake at nights with it. I . . . made up my mind that I must have it out, so I did & it cost me $2.

I also felt that I must take some exercise as my strength was growing very weak. I have therefore bought some dumb-bells which cost me $1.50.

The other night Mr. Atwater [his Brooklyn landlord] asked me if I would go with his wife to see the "Big Bonanza" at the Academy. He had a meeting at hand and could not come in till late. I went, supposing he would pay my way, but he took the $1 I offered.

Yesterday two more copies of the Shakespeare came in and I paid $1 for them.

I was invited, as I said, to the Robinsons & know I must have light gloves so I had to pay $1.75 for them.

Thus you see, Will, I have spent $11.75 for these things. [A total of $244 in today's terms.] They may seem useless to you yet I did really need most of them & so my money goes.

What can I do? I want to do right but it seems my fate to do wrong.

Oh bear with me, Will, a little longer & I will try harder to do better.

If you could have been where I have been tonight and have received the encouragement I have received from Miss R. you would be more lenient, I know.

She has asked me to make myself at home at their house. She has asked me to get music and come and she would play while I sang. She has begged me to try & visit Sister [Sarah] at Narragansett [where the Brintons spent their summers] next summer so that we might see each other there. She has consented to go to the watercolor exhibition with me. Her father & Mother have asked me to call whenever and as often as I want to, and when at their house I am happy. Can you blame me then if I feel a desire to look well when with them? I love to go there for they are all so kind and Miss R. and I seem to have so much to say to each other that the evenings with her are to me so pleasant, and if I felt you loved me as ever I would be so happy. Oh Will, I feel all I say & know you will deal justly with me and I will try to do the best I can.

Forgive my many faults & believe that with God's help I will come out all right.

You are the only one I have here to go to, so bear with me, for without you I would be all adrift.

I love you Will & cannot bear to think that we are drawing away from each other. It spoils all my happiness & I care but little for what comes to cheer me if you draw away from me.

Forgive me if I have spoken too plainly and believe that I

feel what I say deeply. I know my faults are many, but not so many that they cannot be lessened by your help.

Goodnight my own dear Brother. May God lead you to be lenient with your

> Truly grateful & loving
> brother
> Ferd[13]

Within weeks of his writing to Will, the Robinsons withdrew their hospitality, just as the Webbs had. Precisely what Ferd did to shake their confidence is unknown, but it was made clear that he was no longer welcome in their parlor.

He wrote more dolorous letters home. His mother feared for his sanity. Then he seemed to brighten again. When Sarah, now the mother of three children, including three-year-old twins Ward and Jasper Brinton, asked him in July what sort of young women he was meeting in Brooklyn, he eagerly responded.

> I appreciate, dear sister, the interest you take in the young lady acquaintances I make and I shall profit by experience and try to select one suited to all when the time comes. I have become acquainted with a Miss Green, who is a charming young lady, of good family and a Christian girl. We have seen a good deal of each other and I found great pleasure in being in her society. She has gone to East Haddam for the summer and they have kindly invited me to visit them which I shall do. . . .
>
> She is rich in her own name and on this account I have to be a little guarded for we are being gossiped about already.[14]

Ella Champion Green was quiet, attractive, dark-eyed, empathetic, a teacher in the same Sunday school Ferdinand served as treasurer. Like the Wards, the Greens took extravagant pride in their ancestry; not only had at least one collateral member of the clan arrived in America aboard the *Mayflower*, but, an enthusiastic family historian claimed, three direct forebears had signed the Magna Carta. Ella's branch of the family was founded by Captain James Green, a merchant and shipbuilder whose substantial wood-and-stone house, high above the Connecticut River, dominated the village of East Haddam. Its lower floor housed the town's first bank. The captain had eleven children, six of whom were also prolific, so that by the 1830s Greens and their relatives by marriage filled so many local offices that one by one, all six of his grandsons had to sail downriver to seek their fortunes.[*]

Ella's father, Sidney Green, started out as a cotton broker before the Civil War. By 1875, he was a director of the Union and Marine National Banks, a trustee of the Church of the Pilgrims, and a pillar of Brooklyn Heights society. Ella and her three siblings lived with their parents in an elegant three-story brownstone at 37 Monroe Place; its dark rooms were crowded with expensive furniture, its plaster ceilings handpainted with floral garlands, its tables and mantelpieces thickly forested with statuary.[†]

It was everything for which Ferdinand yearned. Yet for all its elegance, the Green home was not a happy place. There was something introverted, pinched, isolated about the family. Sidney Green was sixty-four and failing by the time Ferdinand first met him. His wife, Mary Gleason Green, was four years younger than he but already showing signs of dementia. All but the youngest of their children were in their twenties; none was married or engaged. Mary, the oldest, was moon-faced, snappish, and reclusive; she would never wed, and until her death at the dawn of the flapper era, insisted on wearing the elaborate hairdos, rigid stays, and rustling floor-length skirts of her girlhood. Fred was nervous, slender, and serious minded, a junior clerk in a Wall Street firm with little aptitude or enthusiasm for business; his proudest boast in later years was that as a schoolboy he and his younger brother, Sidney, had once crossed the East River on the swaying catwalk of the unfinished Brooklyn Bridge. Sidney was the youngest, the pampered child of his parents' middle age; like Mary, he would remain single, a fat, largely luckless investor, fond of bird shooting (if it didn't require too-strenuous exertion) and of food—which he insisted on having served to him piping hot, his plate brought gingerly to the table on a heated stove lid by a servant wearing special gloves.

---

[*] One of them—William Webb Green—did so well that he retired to a splendid home at 235 Central Park West at the age of forty-nine, a millionaire many times over.

[†] Nettie Lauderdale, daughter of the Wards' Geneseo physician and Old School ally Dr. Walter Lauderdale, dropped by the Greens' during a brief visit to Brooklyn. "We called on Miss Green, Ferd Ward's intended," she told her brother. "She has a beautiful home. The parlors are grand. What she can see in that man is too much for me." Nettie Lauderdale to John Vance Lauderdale, John Vance Lauderdale Papers, Western Americana Division, Beinecke Rare Book and Manuscript Library, Yale University.

In such a household, Ferd seemed a fresh breeze. He had a gentle, confiding air, told amusing but decorous stories, dressed in modest good taste, and, with Ella seated at the piano, sang the right sort of parlor love songs in a pleasing tenor. He also began quietly to talk business with her father. He explained the easy profits he could make buying up membership certificates on the Produce Exchange and then lending them to men who wanted to do business there temporarily. All he needed was a little capital. Mr. Green agreed to provide some and was initially delighted with his half of the profits—$2,500 ($50,000 in today's dollars) in the first year alone.[15]

Sidney Green was a director of one of the city's largest financial institutions, the Marine National Bank at 78–80 Wall Street. In the late spring of 1875 he agreed to serve for a time as its chief cashier. Ferd began to stop by to see him there at lunchtime, and his frequent visits and intense whispered conversations eventually drew the curiosity of the bank's president, James D. Fish.

"Green, who is that young man?" he asked after one of the younger man's visits.

"That is Ferdinand Ward," Green answered. "I regard him as a very bright young fellow. In fact, I expect that if everything turns out well, . . . [he] will marry one of my daughters."[16]

On August 14, 1875, Jane Ward got a frantic letter from Ferd. Two weeks spent standing in for his vacationing employer had been more than he could bear, he wrote; he'd been to the doctor, and had been advised to flee the city for a week of "quiet time all alone."[17] He thought he would spend it in East Haddam. Ella Green was there— though he did not tell his mother so—spending the season with her family at a summer hotel overlooking the Connecticut River, named the Champion House after one of her maternal ancestors; he'd already been there to see her once that summer. His mother sent Ferd's letter to Will, with instructions to consult the doctor to see if her youngest son was telling the truth about his condition and, if so, to advance him the money for his passage upriver if he really needed it.

Ferd went to East Haddam and, ten days later, wrote a formal letter to his parents announcing his engagement. They were delighted—and relieved. His mother was happily seated at her writing table, halfway through a letter welcoming Miss Green to the family, when a telegram arrived from Ferd: "Do not act till you hear further from me."[18]

"Is the poor boy to be disappointed again?" she asked Will. "Has he any secret enemy who dogs his movements and creates barriers to his happiness?"[19] He was his own worst enemy, of course, and evidently had been seen to be moving too quickly. It took several days before he and Ella could persuade her startled parents that they were serious, and his prospective father-in-law insisted that Ferd pay off all his outstanding debts before the wedding could take place. Ferd assured him he had nothing to worry about.

His father wrote a letter to Sidney Green immediately afterward, meant to reassure him about his son and the family from which he came.

> Fathers are less demonstrative than Mothers but your daughter may be assured that what is lacking in this direction will be fully made up by Mrs. Ward, my dear Mrs. Dr. Brinton of Phila., and others in my large household. I have but one daughter and she is very dear to me—as I doubt not this second will soon become. I am quite ready to pledge to you and Mrs. Green all I can do to make your dear child happy. She will, as F has, I presume, told you, be introduced to a large circle. . . .
>
> We are a united household—not an element in the least divisive—and are *all* [church] communicants—principally Presbyterian. If my son ever goes astray—if he ever brings sorrow to your daughter or yourselves (which I do not predict)—it will be under protest of his entire family for three generations.
>
> If apology is needful for introducing these facts—as to F's family, it is that you may know to whom your daughter is to be related, We are a plain—New England (on my side)—household.
>
> As to my son, he has been taught that *integrity—industry—courtesy—*and *economy* are essential—to success and happiness. So long as his Mother lives he will have a rare counselor. I cannot but think that your daughter is safe (under God) in committing herself to him and I know that she will be to him a great blessing. We long to greet [her]—as we promise her a large place in our heart and a cordial welcome to our home. And the same to her Parents.

That our son has satisfied his employers at the "Exchange" appears in a unanimous vote to raise his salary. If not too prosaic in such a letter allow me to suggest through you to your daughter that he be not ever with her *too late* in the evening. He is not strong and needs all his strength that sleep brings to his daily duties. He ought to be (I tell him) in his own room at 10 o'clock. You and I have been as he is and know the difficulty of parting with one we dearly and early love. Pardon this very practical suggestion.

A long letter this and far from sentimental. I write as I would speak. Pray make my true esteem acceptable to your *wife—daughter—household.*

Hoping in our time to meet you all and that there may be before our children a long—happy life.

Affectionately yours,
F De W Ward[20]

Will was by no means sure Ella Green would be safe under Ferd's care; nor was he convinced integrity and industry were essential to his brother's nature. Neither was Sarah. She wrote an anguished letter to her parents: she felt uncomfortable with what was happening; Ella was evidently a lovely girl; the Greens were innocent people; shouldn't they at least gently be alerted to Ferdinand's weaknesses?

Her father replied to Sarah right away. The family was to say nothing. "Ferdinand *is* an enigma," he admitted, writing in his big, overwrought hand. "I cannot understand him," but "I want to *emphasize* just one point."

It is about F & saying this I will [say] no more. We *all* know F. well—too well for him to deceive us & sufficiently to enlist all our patience. F. is greatly lacking in frankness & true nobility. It is hard to trust his word or confide in him as to anything. This we know too well. There is no use in *denying* it & it cannot but affect us. (I mean—Mother—W'm—you—and me.) *But* what shall we do? Cast him off? This we cannot do. He is a member of the family. "If one suffer so do all."

My idea is 1) pray for him—daily—fervently. This is fundamental.

2) *Write to him*. Frankly—cheerfully—encompassingly. Don't tell him his faults—but have them in mind when writing. Urge him to be noble, open-hearted, thankful for what he has.

3) Above all things there must be family *oneness*. That is our family trait. "*Ward clannishness*" is our title & one in which we glory. We don't agree on politics—business—&c &c, but as a family we are & must be *one*. It is not so in all households but must be so in *ours*. Don't turn a cold face to F.

4) Write to *Ella G*. If near . . . go at once to see her

The future of F. we cannot surmise. But we must *do our best* to keep him right. Don't let him have to say that *any one of us cast him off*. We may keep to ourselves what we think but act toward him frankly. F. loves Wm greatly & I am not at all surprised. But enough on a painful subject. There are but three of you. *Oh, be a unit in affection!*[21]

There would be no warning for the Greens. Ferd's true nature, like Ferdinand's own disgrace in India, would be kept a closely guarded family secret. Instead, Ferdinand traveled to Brooklyn to meet his son's prospective bride. "I was *very much* pleased with Ella," he wrote to Will afterward. "If she *is* as she appears F. is to be congratulated & may he be worthy of her. This should be our prayer. I had to tell Mother (she asked) if there was wine. I *did not* see F. drink. Perhaps he did, but not to my knowledge."[22]

Despite Ferdinand's diplomacy, his son's courtship did not go smoothly. The wedding date was put off from the spring of 1876 to that winter, then again to the spring of 1877, entirely because of what his father called Ferd's "queerness and wrongness."[23] Ferd exaggerated to Ella the amount of money he was making and was found out. His debts rose rather than fell. He now claimed one eye had been blinded by overwork, that he was rapidly losing sight in the other, and that he would have to seek some other kind of employment unless further financial help was forthcoming. When his mother, who believed marriage "might be the making of him," came up with the money for an engagement ring, his father approved: "I want him *settled in a home*," he wrote.[24] Again and again, Ferd claimed he was about to pay his debts, failed to do so, was found out, asked to be forgiven, then ran up more bills. At one point, he let slip to Will his intense interest in gaining access to the Green family fortune—in just one year his prospective father-in-law had earned the modern equivalent of almost a million and a half dollars[25]—and got a sermon from his father: "I warned him against any intimation or hint that he ever *thought* of Ella's money," the old man told Will.

> It would disgust her & her friends. *Also*, he must not be allowed to *incur a dollar's debt* to be liquidated by what he may get through her. *He* needs earnest warning in that direction. . . .
>
> As to F., we must take him as he is. He has peculiarities of disposition & manner that we would wish were different. With these we must strive to be patient. I think that Mother has made up her mind not to notice his dolorous letters. He is not strong & comes home *tired* of course (8 AM to 6 PM) & then sits down & pens what he regrets after.
>
> I had a letter from Mr. Grant which was *complimentary* of F. in this, that there are things he *alone* can do & therefore he can't part with him *more* than four days. As kind a letter as a *businessman* can be expected to write. I agree with *you* in this—if F wants to *retain his position* he must *stay right by*. Let a waiting man (& they are "legion") take his place for a week & F is "nowhere" afterwards. If F. gets married to Miss G he may be rather more independent—*not now*. You have been a good . . . and generous brother to F. & he feels it but is at times too high-strung to say so. Now, keep on good terms. Do not let a wall rise between you. See the Greens often. God bless you, dear boy.[26]

Jane continued to send checks to cover Ferd's bills, and provided new "loans" whenever he asked for them. After all, she told Will, "he is still the baby, you know."[27]

Then, in March 1877, with the wedding day just weeks away, there was more trouble. Investments Ferd had made for himself and his prospective father-in-law evidently went sour. Ella's father complained about Ferd's unsteady nature and bad advice, and said he was tempted to call off the marriage. "I have no doubt that Mr. G. has lost considerable money of late," Jane told Will, "which may make him suspicious and perhaps crusty and fearful of everybody." She continued,

It will be best, I think, to let everything shape itself and not attempt any arrangement for [Ferd and Ella]. If they are to be married it will be all brought about by a [Power] wiser than we and if not, we must fear lest . . . we be found "fighting against God." . . .

I look for a little explanation of the sentence in your last "How much this failure of F's may have to do with Mr. G's *change of [heart]*" &c &c. I tremble lest the family admit any ground of suspicion against him. I think he really means and hopes to succeed when he starts. But risks are so precarious nowadays that no one is safe. . . . When F does come to you to talk over matters try to sympathize tenderly with his present position. It is really very trying and if he [has] brought it upon himself it is all the more depressing and hard to bear. We all need sympathy in our failures as well as in our successes.[28]

In the end, the engagement was not ended—but the wedding was postponed again, this time to the fall. Then, a couple of months before the ceremony was scheduled to take place, Ferd suddenly had money with which to cover all his bills back home, begin paying $30 a month for a handsome gold watch and chain for himself, and buy his bride glittering wedding gifts, including a pearl necklace and a diamond cross that cost $350—$7,400 in today's terms.[29] When his mother asked how he had managed it all, Ferd said some of his investments had unexpectedly paid off. Jane was delighted but wary. "If he told you what he told me *and you believe him*," she wrote to Will, "it will relieve your mind as to the honesty of his gains."[30]

Will's mind was not relieved, and a week before the wedding he somehow learned that at least some of Ferdinand's sudden solvency was due to his having siphoned funds from the Sunday school of the Church of the Pilgrims. He spoke to Ferd about it. Ferd angrily denied he'd done anything wrong. Will told his father, nonetheless. The old man tried to reason with his younger son, then reported back to Will.

I have had a talk with F. quite as satisfactory as I could expect. I think that he will resign the treasurership. He said that he offered to do so last Sabbath week but Mr. [Charles E.] Hull [the church's overall treasurer] said no. . . . I shall do my best

but it is a delicate & hard case, as F. is of age & in a new relationship. . . . We must hope—pray & wait. Oh, that all may be
right!*

Jane tried to reason with Ferd too, and urged him once again to confide fully in his older brother. Of course he wanted to be independent,
she said, but he should follow his father's example; Ferdinand Ward
was always his own man, but since returning to America he had never
made an important decision without consulting his own older brother,
Levi. This time, Ferd responded with something like hauteur. He did
plan to resign as Sunday school treasurer, he wrote, but "as to going to
Will with my business affairs *this cannot & will not be done. I am sorry,
Mother dear, to refuse anything you ask, but I am *determined* on this
point. If Will is ever troubled about any of my bills let him come to
me & I will explain to him. Ella & I will always be glad to see him at
our home."[31]

Ferd and Ella Green were finally married at the Church of the Pilgrims on October 20, 1877. For the elder Wards it was not an entirely
happy occasion. No member of the Rochester clan bothered to attend:
"It is *too* bad that none of the family feel interested enough to spend a
little time and money for this occasion," Jane wrote Will, "but so it is
and we must bear the mortification."[32] The ceremony itself went well
enough: Ferd's father shared the officiating with Dr. Storrs. President

---

* All was not right, and some years later Mr. Hull—who was a vice president of
the Howard Insurance Company as well as the treasurer for the Church of the
Pilgrims—told a newspaperman what had happened. Several times Ferd presented
bills for the same Sunday school books and supplies and then professed astonishment
at the "mixup" when caught. He also persuaded the church to provide him with funds
for having scriptural verses written out by a calligrapher, elaborately matted, and
framed and hung on the walls of the Sunday-school room. When the bill came back
unpaid he muttered that "there's been some mistake" and begged for forgiveness. "We
did not like his way of doing things," Hull said. "He lied. He evaded matters. We took
him to task and he resented it and he finally resigned." Eventually, Hull wrote him a
letter urging him to "effect a radical change in his methods of doing business."

  Afterward, when Ferd seemed more prosperous and overdue bills continued to
turn up at the church, he was allowed quietly to pay them. The Church of the Pilgrims
remained scandal-free. Ferdinand De Wilton Ward to William Shaw Ward, October 17, 1877, Brinton Collection; *New York Tribune*, October 9 and 19, 1885.

Fish of the Marine Bank was among the guests. But at the reception afterward, as Jane had feared, Sidney Green could not be dissuaded from serving champagne to his guests: "I hate the thought of going to see it drunk," she had written before leaving for New York.[33]

A few days after the wedding, the elder Greens invited Will to dine with them and the newlyweds, hoping bygones could become bygones. Will was too "wounded" by his brother's actions to attend, he said.[34] It would be months before the brothers reconciled. When it did finally happen, their mother wept with gratitude. So long as Will continued to look over his younger brother's shoulder, she wrote, she felt certain Ferdie would not be "tempted to do wrong."[35]

EIGHT

The Bonanza Man

If Ferd Ward married Ella Green in large part because he hoped one day to get his hands on her family fortune, he didn't have long to wait. On January 20, 1878, just three months after the wedding, his father-in-law, Sidney Green, died of peritonitis, at the age of sixty-seven. Ferd and his brother-in-law, Fred Green, were the executors of his sizable estate—thousands of dollars in cash and stock and tens of thousands more in real estate in Brooklyn, Manhattan, and Chicago. Fred Green was two years older than Ferd but only a minor clerk in a small-time investment firm and deferred to him when it came to decisions about the family's finances.

That suited Ferd perfectly. His first move, made just a day or two after his father-in-law was buried in Green-Wood Cemetery, was to persuade his grieving mother-in-law that she should allow him to use family funds to purchase on her behalf thirty Produce Exchange certificates at $300 each. The Exchange was on the rise, he assured her; over time, the certificates were sure to make her an independently wealthy woman. Five years later, talking to a reporter at the height of his celebrity as a successful stockbroker, he would point to this purchase as proof of his early shrewdness: the certificates were already worth nearly $4,700 apiece, he said then, and were still steadily appreciating; he saw no reason they shouldn't be worth $10,000 each before too long.

In fact, he had not bought a single certificate. Instead, he had deposited his widowed mother-in-law's money into his own personal account. Later, he would do the same thing with most of the rest of her inheritance, falsely claiming to have invested it in stocks and Chicago real estate. She was just the first of hundreds of victims to be ruined by his false promises.

A few days after pocketing his mother-in-law's money, Ferd wrote an apparently anguished letter to the president of the Marine Bank, James D. Fish. He felt lost, abandoned without his late father-in-law's guidance, he said; he was only twenty-six, still too young to succeed in business on his own or to shoulder the burden of his wife's family. Mr. Fish was fifty-eight, almost twice his age, and had been Mr. Green's closest friend. If he could consult the older man from time to time to help keep him from making the kind of mistakes into which his inexperience might otherwise lead him he would be forever grateful. Years later, Fish would dismiss this letter as "pathetic," but at the time he was flattered—and intrigued by the idea of working still more closely with a newcomer whose "enterprise and push," he said, reminded him of how he himself had been when young. He agreed to do all he could to help. "From that time on I provided Ward with all the money he needed to carry on his dealings in Produce Exchange certificates," Fish remembered. "Sometimes he would buy two in a day. He always turned over my half of the profits promptly."[1] Ferd soon proposed a fresh notion—buying up odd lots of flour from big-time dealers eager to get rid of them at fifty cents a barrel less than market value, then reselling them at a profit. Fish again loaned him the cash. "It was a very sound-looking scheme . . . and we made a nice little thing of it."[2]

Like Ferd, Fish had once been a small-town boy struggling to make good in the big city. He, too, came from an old Connecticut family; Fishes had populated his hometown of Mystic since 1674. He was the eldest of nine children of Squire Asa Fish—schoolteacher, state legislator, probate judge, and ship's chandler, supplier of everything from soap to sailcloth to the fleet of fishing smacks that filled the mouth of the Mystic River each morning and evening. James had come to Manhattan at the age of twenty-two in 1843 to help run a chandlery across from the Fulton Fish Market on South Street. Captains and crews from Mystic and neighboring towns were his first customers, and they often left cash in his vault between voyages because there was then no bank at home.

At first, he had felt homesick and intimidated by Manhattan. "Sunday nights were the hardest times," Fish remembered. "Here I was, a young man in a large city, with nowhere to go. I had been to preaching so much in my boyhood that it gave no pleasure to me to hear a heavy discourse at the end of the day."[3] That was like Ferd, too. Instead of going to church, he went to the theater, most often to Mitchell's Olympic on Broadway between Broad Street and Grand, just off the Bowery. It was a small house, half the price and half the size of its rivals, "a tiny show-box for vaudeville and burlesques,"[4] Charles Dickens wrote. It was a favorite both with the swells who sat upstairs and the poor streetwise "b'hoys" who crowded into the pit to see shows known for what one critic called "coarseness and obscenity."[5]

"I paid one shilling," Fish recalled, "and took my seat in the pit, and I saw around me men who have since been worth millions."[6] His favorite performer was a winsome soprano named Mary Taylor—"our Mary" to smitten and impatient admirers like Fish, who sometimes drowned out the other performers by chanting her name to bring her onstage before her scripted entrance. She was a capable singer but best known for her "tender side-long looks" and for her splendid legs, whose outlines could be seen when she played "breeches roles"—daring men's parts that required her to appear in tight trousers. "When that woman married," Fish recalled, "I somehow felt that it was a personal blow at me."[7] Even as an old man, he kept an ambrotype of her hanging in his office, and he would be drawn to opening nights—and young actresses—all his life.

In 1843, Fish married Mary Esther Blodgett, a hometown girl, and moved to a house on Henry Street in Brooklyn. She bore him seven children before she died at forty-six. By the time he met Ferd he had married again, to Isabelle Rogers from Illinois, who had given him still another son.

Meanwhile, his progress in business had been slow but steady. He expanded his chandlery to outfit ships from everywhere and made more money by selling cargo salvaged from wrecked vessels. He chartered freight and passenger ships of his own, too, and then, in 1853, helped establish the Marine Bank. Many of its first depositors were his friends and neighbors from Mystic. In 1861, the directors elected him its president; five years later, under his leadership, it became part of the new national bank system, created to provide a reliable means for marketing the federal bonds that helped fund the Civil War. (Ferd's uncle Freeman Clarke supervised it for a time as U.S. comptroller of the currency.) National banks were meant to be more reliable and conservative than their competitors and therefore had to submit to quarterly inspection by a federally appointed national bank examiner; they were also discouraged from lending against real estate collateral and required to hold roughly one-quarter of their deposits in reserve against emergency.

By the time Fish befriended Ferd, the banker was "one of the best known figures about Wall Street," a friend recalled, "a stout, short, pleasant-faced man," bald, with a white fringe of Quaker-style beard. Competitors muttered that his bank was a sort of Fish "family asylum"[8] because he named his brother, Benjamin, chief cashier, and created posts for two of his sons, as well as his brother-in-law, daughter, and nephew. But most agreed that when it came to overseeing everyday business, Fish remained "a perfect autocrat, . . . able, shrewd and honorable."[9] When he took over the bank it had less than $500,000 in deposits; by 1880, it had nearly $5 million ($108 million in today's terms). Because the Marine Bank still took days to conduct its meticulous quarterly audit while more up-to-date banks completed theirs within hours, some on Wall Street considered it "somewhat old fogeyish."[10]

Fish was especially proud of his reputation for rectitude. Over some forty years in business, he once said, "I never failed to pay 100 cents on the dollar whenever any obligation became due . . . and I often paid when I could have wriggled out of it. . . . I have had the settlement of many trusts as executor, administrator, receiver, and trustee. No claim was ever made of unfaithfulness that I can remember."*

---

* Fish's memory was selective. After the president of the failed Brooklyn Trust Company killed himself in 1873 rather than face embezzlement charges, Fish and two other members of the board of directors were accused of having personally contracted to finance completion of the New Haven, Middletown and Willimantic Railroad, using funds improperly loaned by the bank.

Again, in the spring of 1875, a committee appointed by the bondholders of the bankrupt Chicago, Danville and Vincennes Railroad charged Fish and his fellow directors with failing to lay the length of track for which they'd contracted, pocketing

For all his hard work, "Mr. Fish had never made great money," a friend recalled. "He believed in waiting and letting things develop."[11] When Fish began working with Ferd the U.S. economy was still gripped by a severe depression that had begun within a few weeks of the younger man's arrival in New York in 1873. More than three million men remained jobless. Wages for those still working had fallen. Banks and brokerages and insurance houses had gone out of business. Half the railroads in the country were in receivership. Part of Fish's initial willingness to ally himself with Ferd seems to have been that even in the worst of economic times the younger man seemed so certain big money could still be made. "If at any time you feel that you must call in these loans on certificates, I will raise the money," Ferd assured Fish during one of their earliest dealings, "but I feel the larger the venture in our hands, the better it will be for us, for I watch them carefully and as things look now there is every chance of their going up. . . . They are a splendid thing when watched."[12] Fish agreed. Happy with the tidy profits Ward paid to him each month, he did not call in his loans.

Fish would follow that pattern for the next six years, believing himself Ferd's enabler and sometime co-conspirator—but ultimately becoming just another of his dupes.

For a twenty-eight-year-old from a small upstate town, Ferd was doing remarkably well in Manhattan. Thanks to his late father-in-law, he now had access to money with which to work, and he had the financial backing and the kind of cover only a seasoned, apparently conservative Wall Street veteran like James Fish could provide. Fellow plungers on the Produce Exchange began calling him "Futures Ferdinand"[13] for

---

company funds, and issuing fictitious reports to cover up their malfeasance. The bondholders sued to recover the money. Fish and James W. Elwell, vice president of the Marine Bank and a fellow director of the bankrupt railroad, countersued for moneys they claimed were owed them by the bondholders. Illinois banks and other railroad companies got involved. The case would drag on for fifteen years, finally reaching the U.S. Supreme Court in 1890. It upheld a lower-court decision that had called a halt to the litigation and forced Elwell to abandon his fight for the funds.

In neither case was the question of Fish's guilt or innocence resolved in court. *Middletown* (CT) *Daily Constitution*, September 19, 1873; *Financier*, April 17, 1875; *Elwell v. Fosdick*. No. 216, Supreme Court of the United States, 134 U.S. 500; 10 S. Ct. 598; 33 L. Ed. 98; 1890 U.S. LEXIS 1989; argued March 19, 20, 1890/decided, March 31, 1890.

his apparently uncanny skill at seeing which way commodity prices were going to go. Without quite saying so, he gave the impression to them and to Fish that he was being guided by inside information gleaned from his close working relationship with influential men like his immediate boss, S. Hastings Grant, and the president of the Produce Exchange, Franklin Edson.

Still, he was not satisfied. More success required more connections. It fell to Will Ward to provide them. He had landed Ferd his first job in New York and then made him stick to it, had tried his best to keep him away from temptations and out of trouble in the big city, just as their mother had hoped he would. Now, he would unwittingly make it possible for his kid brother to give in to temptation and get himself into trouble on a scale even Jane Shaw Ward could not have imagined.

By the late 1870s, Will had grown restless. Every morning for nearly a decade he had gone to work at the U.S. Assay Office at 30 Wall Street, where he helped ensure the purity of the gold and silver bullion used to make coins at the Philadelphia mint. It was exacting, tedious work, and before long, he had begun looking for ways to rekindle his imagination and supplement his income. He served as part-time science editor for *Appleton's Journal* for a time, and wrote on scientific topics for that magazine, *Scribner's Monthly*, and the *American Encyclopedia*. He helped organize a laboratory at the short-lived New York Aquarium at Thirty-fifth Street and Broadway, too, and began investing in small blocks of mining stocks that performed well and whetted his appetite for more.

In April 1878, three months after Sidney Green's death and while Ferd and Fish continued to speculate in Produce Exchange certificates and odd lots of flour, Will moved into new quarters, an elegant flat in the brand-new Bella apartment building at the southwest corner of Twenty-sixth Street and Fourth Avenue.* Thanks to dividends from his mining investments, he was able to afford $300 rent in advance, a fact that brought out all his mother's buried envy.

> Why Willie, dear, you do not know how big such a sum seems
> to me, nor what it would do for us here in the country. Shall

---

* The five-story building, built in two sections with two large apartments on each floor, promised its tenants a "revolution in living." Louis Comfort Tiffany took the top floor of one section and turned it into a Moorish-style palace, its walls painted Indian red, its foyer lit by stained-glass windows. Robert A. M. Stern, Thomas Mellins, and David Fishman, *New York 1880*, p. 542.

I tell you? Well, it would put two coats over all the outside of the house. It would also paint the 15 sets of window blinds, newly roof with shingles the house, kitchen and wood-house, would get a new carpet for my parlor and lower hall which they greatly need, and leave me $50 to spend on outside 'fixing,' etc.! And yet this all seems a small sum to you. Well Dear, I am glad you have it, much more glad than if I had it myself, and you have earned it by hard labor which gratifies me much more than if some good fortune or windfall had given it to you without effort. Since you have no home of your own [because he was still unmarried] surely your bachelorship entitles you to comfortable, respectable and even luxurious quarters, if necessary. I know you thank God for all you have and as He gives it to you He wants it to be used for your happiness, as well as that of others.[14]

Will had a new roommate as well as new digs: twenty-five-year-old Ulysses S. Grant Jr., the second of three sons of the ex-president of the United States. Nicknamed "Buck" by his father because he'd been born in Ohio, the "Buckeye State," he was nine years younger than Will Ward. As early as the winter of 1877 they had planned together to produce a history of the Civil War, and General Grant—who liked Will as soon as his son introduced him—had promised to provide them with fresh anecdotes to set it apart from its competitors. Will's father was sure the result would be "a most *interesting* & *popular* & *saleable* volume. . . . The promise of General and Ex. Pres. Grant to *aid you* is an omen of success."[15] In the end, the plan had come to nothing—upon leaving the White House in March, the ex-president and his wife had begun an overseas journey that would stretch on for nearly three years—but the two young men remained close.

Buck Grant was round-faced, soft-spoken, and genial—"without enemies," a Chicago newspaper said, "amiable and stalwart."[16] But he was also always unsure whether people were responding warmly to him or to his illustrious name. His elder brother, Colonel Fred Grant, had been closer to his father; he had accompanied the general during the Fort Gibson and Vicksburg campaigns, attended West Point, and risen to the rank of lieutenant colonel before marrying a beautiful Illinois heiress, Ida Marie Honoré. Meanwhile, Buck had been largely under the care of his mother, Julia Dent Grant. A reporter who covered the White House during the Grant presidency remembered him as "a modest, retiring lad, as sensitive and kindly as a girl, . . . so sensitive that a cross word was more of a punishment to him than a severe chastisement would be to most boys."[17] He attended Phillips Exeter, Harvard, and the Columbia Law School and acted briefly as his father's private secretary, but it was a word from his mother to the wife of one of the senior partners that had won him his first job, as a clerk in the Manhattan law firm of Davies, Work, McNamee & Hilton, specialists in real estate and tax law. (He and Will first met at a dinner held at the home of the firm's senior member, Julian T. Davies.)

Neither Buck nor his employers believed quarrels over the titles to brownstones or suits for damage done to local businesses by the clamorous new elevated railroads would hold him long. Buck had begun to court Fannie Chaffee, the daughter of Colorado's Republican senator, Jerome B. Chaffee, who had made millions in mining stocks over the years and saw no reason why he—and his prospective son-in-law—shouldn't make millions more. Buck agreed, and with advice from Chaffee and the ex-president's other friends in the mining business, and with written instructions from the general himself, traveling in Europe, earned enough money investing in the Nevada Comstock Lode to send his parents $600,000 with which to extend their tour all the way around the world. When the Comstock mines began to peter out in 1879, Buck joined a syndicate of other ambitious young men on the lookout for fresh opportunities at the site of a potential new bonanza: Leadville, Colorado, a played-out gold camp eighty miles southwest of Denver that now turned out to be rich in silver mixed with lead.

"Mining securities are not the thing for widows and orphans or country clergymen, or unworldly people of any kind," wrote Charles H. Dow, the savvy newspaperman who would one day help develop the Dow Jones Industrial Average. "But for a business man, who must take risks in order to make money; who will buy nothing without careful, thorough investigation; and who will not risk more than he is able to lose, there is no other investment in the market today as tempting as mining stock. And among mines there are none the value of which can be more fully foreshown than those in Leadville, Colorado."[18]

A Leadville mine called the "Evening Star" was up for sale at what seemed a very low price. Buck's syndicate was eager but wary. Mining was always a gamble: General Grant himself warned that it was "beyond humankind to judge with accuracy as to what lays hidden in the bowels of the earth."[19] And Leadville, like every other mining camp, was alive with thieves and confidence men; ever since the California gold rush of 1849, eastern investors had joked that the definition of a mine was "a hole in the ground with a liar on top."

Before he or any of his friends wrote a check, young Grant said, they should have the mine thoroughly examined by a seasoned assayer whose integrity could not be questioned. His friend Will Ward was just the man. Watson B. Dickerman, a successful broker who happened to have been Will's classmate at Williston Seminary, seconded the motion. Bored by the Assay Office, eager to apply his skills in the field and to make some real money on his own, Will agreed to take a month's leave, head west, and have a look at the Evening Star. He returned with good news: the mine seemed very promising. The syndicate bought it and asked Will to become its manager.

On January 1, 1879, he resigned from the Assay Office and signed a five-year contract to run the Evening Star. Only afterward did he tell his parents. His father was displeased at first; the depression was only just coming to an end, and he was concerned that his son was giving up a "permanency" at the Assay Office. His mother was more supportive—"you may become a *millionaire!*" she told him—but she also begged him to take a temperance pledge before leaving home, worried he was about to enter a world of "temptations, . . . rough society [and] the want of moral restraints."[20]

That world was very real. When Will got to Leadville in February 1879, claim jumping was common. So were street holdups, pickpockets, confidence men, and Saturday-night brawls. Everybody wore a gun. Saloons and gambling houses never closed their doors. Whorehouses advertised openly: the women at the Red Light Hall were billed as "rounder, rosier and more beautiful than elsewhere. . . . You don't care a cent whether school keeps or not just so the girls are there."[21]

Will seems to have stayed away from all of it. He proceeded with greater care than most of his rivals, ensuring that every foot of the five mine shafts he ordered sunk was securely timbered and every vein of ore his miners exposed was meticulously assayed before declaring the first monthly dividend of $25,000—more than half a million dollars today.

Will also made it possible for his younger brother to buy a large block of shares at the bottom price, just $2 a share; within a few months, they would be worth $50 apiece. Monthly dividends rose steadily, too. Thanks to Will, Ferd now had an income of his own to add to the funds he was quietly taking from his wife's family's estate.

The Evening Star's grateful owners were soon asking Will to scout out new properties (in which both he and Ferd also invested), and he had become one of the camp's leading citizens. He built himself a gabled double-storied house on Capitol Hill, overlooking Leadville at 220 West Eighth Street. He first thought to call it "Indianola," after the ironclad aboard which he'd served during the Civil War, but settled for "Cloud-rift Cottage" because of its sweeping mountain views. One frequent visitor to Will's porch never forgot the "great silencing sunsets" that could be seen from there each evening.[22] The couple living in the log cabin next door provided Will with congenial and cultured company. Arthur D. Foote was a fellow mining engineer, trained at Yale. His wife, Mary Hallock Foote, was an illustrator and writer whose work, like Will's, had appeared in *Scribner's Monthly*.* She found her neighbor "cheerful, refined, clean-souled," she told a friend, "and he *wears* wonderfully well."[23] When he asked if he could build a covered walkway from the Footes' cabin to his house and invited the couple to board with him, taking advantage of the cook the Dickermans had sent west to serve him, Mary happily agreed. In turn, she helped him buy carpets and curtains for his new home—his "*trousseau*,"[24] she called it—and acted as his hostess and chaperone, permitting him to invite the right sort of young women to dine. "He entertains a great deal," she wrote to a friend, "and we see an amusing procession of New York bondholders and capitalists, tourists, newspapermen, mining men, and men of all descriptions."[25] J. Watson Dickerman and his beautiful wife, Martha, came west to see how their mine was doing—and seemed delighted with everything. Buck Grant visited, too, and Mary Foote found him "extremely modest and very sensible."[26]

Among those who also dined at Will's table that summer were the two daughters of Judge Jasper Delos Ward, a former Republican congressman from Illinois, who owned another mine on Carbonate Hill, the Little Giant, and presided over the brand-new Leadville courthouse as district judge. The judge's elder daughter, Emma Jane Ward, called

* Mary Hallock Foote was the model for the heroine of Wallace Stegner's Pulitzer Prize–winning novel, *Angle of Repose*, in which both Will and Ferdinand Ward make brief appearances under their own names.

"Kitty" and "Kate" by her family, caught Will's eye. She was "a handsome girl of the (I sh'd fancy) English country house style," Mary Hallock Foote told a friend. "Admirable on horseback—beautiful hands and feet and head—thorough-bred looking—descendant of General Artemas [Ward] who came near being the father of his country."*

Will courted Kate on horseback, galloping with her back and forth across Tennessee Park, a mile-long meadow blanketed with wildflowers that stretched along the Lake Fork of the Arkansas River. By December 1879, Mary Foote noted, "they had become engaged. . . . They are as foolish as usual and as happy as it is rather unusual to be." Will's father was happy as well. Everything he and Jane had heard about his son's fiancée and her family was reassuring. "Rather singular that her name should be Jane Ward," he told Sarah. "He always said that Jane Ward [his mother] was as good a wife as he wanted & he has found her."†

William and Kate Ward were eventually married in her father's Chicago home at 285 S. Ashland Avenue. Three hundred guests attended and afterward danced to the music of Hand's society orchestra. Will's father officiated. His mother did not attend, perhaps because of the great distance involved, more likely because champagne was served

---

* General Artemas Ward was a worthy but ponderous patriot from Shrewsbury, Massachusetts—he had considerable difficulty getting on and off his horse—who directed the defenses of Boston until George Washington arrived there in July 1775. Ward was not pleased when the Virginian assumed command, regarding it, according to Washington's biographer James Thomas Flexner, as "an insult not only to himself personally but to that only admirable and virtuous section of the universe, New England." Although he would later become a Federalist and a member of the House of Representatives, he never got over his personal resentment at being supplanted by Washington. During his last days he suffered greatly from gout. "This day," he wrote from Philadelphia on February 22, 1792, "is the President's birthday & there is a mighty fuss in this City on that account. Being unwell I am excused from taking any part therein, & that gives me no pain, but rather pleasure." Rodman W. Paul, ed. *A Victorian Gentlewoman in the Far West: Reminiscences of Mary Hallock Foote*, p. 197; James Thomas Flexner, *George Washington in the American Revolution, 1775–1783*, p. 29; Charles Martyn, *The Life of Artemas Ward*, p. 305.

† Jane's enthusiasm was more qualified than her husband's: she was relieved to know that his future daughter-in-law's family was "*thoroughly respectable*," but she remained troubled that Kate "lacks in the one thing needful"—she was a Congregationalist, not a Presbyterian. Jane Shaw Ward to Sarah Ward Brinton, December 27, 1879; Ferdinand De Wilton Ward to Sarah Ward Brinton, December 31, 1879, Brinton Collection.

at the reception. "The presents were unusually numerous and fine,"
reported one Chicago paper, "among the number being . . . two bronze
vases and a solid silver and gold-lined ice-cream set from Ulysses Grant
and a magnificent set of solitaire diamond earrings, brooch, and ring
from the groom."[27]

Will's full-time mining career in the West meant that he was now only
nominally involved in his younger brother's affairs, and could no longer exert the kind of caution he had once insisted upon. Ferd was free
to act as his instincts and his conscience—or lack of it—dictated.

Sometime late in 1879 he told S. Hasting Grant, his employer at the
Produce Exchange, that he was leaving his post after six years in order
to go into the brokerage business on his own. (Even as he left, he was
careful to maintain his ties with Grant, lending him several thousand
dollars with which to import Jersey cattle; he always tried never to
alienate anyone who might prove useful to him in the future.)

As a favor to his friend and classmate Will Ward, J. Watson Dickerman allowed Ferd to set up his own desk behind a heavy curtain in the
corner of the office he shared with his partner, Benjamin Dominick, at
74 Broadway.

At first, James Fish doubted Ferd would do well on Wall Street,
where, as he said, "very few men succeed and thousands fail."[28] The
young man's boldness and inexperience were likely to do him in. But
Ferd was reassuring, Fish recalled: "He said that he would do nothing
that was risky and that he had some very good backers who . . . gave
him pointers and were willing to let him into good things."[29] David
Dows was just one of them, Ward said. The retired patriarch of the
New York grain trade, Dows had made himself two great fortunes,
first in commodities and then in railroads. Now, according to Ferd,
he enjoyed offering the young man his investment advice just for the
fun of seeing his predictions come true. "Ward declared that Dows
had . . . advised him to buy Rock Island stock," Fish recalled. "It
turned out that Rock Island was a splendid thing and this [impressed
me]." Fish lent Ferd more money with which to speculate: "He was
remarkably successful and for a long time he made me about $200 a
day [$4,300 in today's dollars]."[30]

Rock Island stock did do well, but there is no evidence that Ferd
had ever so much as shaken hands with David Dows, who had become

famously reclusive and had come to see the stock market as inherently unsafe in any case. But Fish evidently believed his young associate's story and marveled both at the way he seemed able to befriend so many powerful older men and at the energy with which he bought and sold stocks, apparently at their direction. "He would sit by [his own stock ticker] daily from ten o'clock till three," a visitor to the Dominick & Dickerman offices remembered. "Even while talking to a visitor he would slip the tape through his fingers and write orders. . . . It was generally thought in the office that when a fellow went behind that little curtain with Ward that Ward was in no danger. The friends of the other fellow . . . often got uneasy."[31]

Among those who frequently joined Ferd behind his curtain was Buck Grant. Will had introduced Buck to his younger brother before he left for Colorado, and they had since become better acquainted as fellow investors in the Evening Star and other Leadville mines. "Buck didn't know anything about stocks and he asked me to advise him on a good many things and make his investments for him,"[32] Ferd remembered. He eagerly complied. Flour, railroads, mining stocks—Ferd seemed able to record big profits on them all. Buck was amazed: "Why is it that you always come out ahead?" he asked Ferd one day.[33] Ferd just smiled. Buck asked that nearly every dollar he made be reinvested, and promised to come up with still more money for Ferd to work with.

Will Ward regarded Buck Grant as a friend. Ferd saw him, as he saw everyone around him, as someone to be exploited, a means to achieving his own ends: if properly managed, this naïve, overeager young investor with the famous name and close links to his father's influential friends could help attract almost unlimited capital. And if Ferd could persuade both the son of the ex-president of the United States *and* the president of the Marine Bank officially to go into business with him, he was sure millions could be attracted to the firm. "You know the old saying is true that the more one has the more one wants," he told Fish, "and this is so with me."[34]

He first needed to bring Buck and the banker together. Will Ward innocently made that possible, too. In December 1879, the Evening Star syndicate summoned Will back to New York to make a presentation about the mine's future to potential investors at the Union League Club. Ferd and Ella were glad to see him: Will spent Christmas with them in Brooklyn, and the brothers sent a barrelful of brightly wrapped gifts to their parents in Geneseo with cards signed by both of them.

But before the Evening Star dinner began, Ferd made sure that the seats were arranged so that Fish and Buck sat next to each other.

Fish got up from the table that evening convinced both that he should invest heavily in Will Ward's mine and that a partnership that included Buck Grant would be a good idea: it was clear that the general's son could bring in big money and equally clear that he wouldn't interfere with business. "Things seemed to look very bright indeed," Fish remembered.[*]

But when Ferd made a formal offer of partnership, Buck surprised both him and Fish by turning them down. He believed Ferd was already "a very rich man,"[35] Buck later explained, far too rich to "attach himself to a slow-coach like me."[36] Attaching themselves to that kind of "slow-coach" was precisely what Ferd and Fish wanted to do, of course, and Ferd promised Fish he would keep trying to change young Grant's mind.

Buck Grant's belief that he wasn't in Ward's financial league was understandable. In the spring and summer of 1880, Ferd was *acting* like a very rich man. He returned to Geneseo, checkbook in hand, apparently seeking at one stroke to erase the stain of martyred poverty that had clung to his parents throughout his boyhood and to impress the townspeople who had once gossiped about the feckless preacher's son who would never amount to anything. His stunned father reported to Sarah just some of what he did for them during his brief, showy stay.

> F in his characteristic kindness put enough to my account in the bank (same to Mother's) that we are relieved of all anxiety at least for a year. . . . F is the wonder and the theme of Geneseo for what he did . . . & still proposes to do. It seems a myth, his financial success. His *income* for four months is equal to *my father's whole estate*. It is amazing and the end is not yet. And his generous heart! It does not seem to me possible. His late visit (including gifts . . . House-repairing &c) will help *scores*

---

[*] Fish's decision to invest in the Evening Star, at least, turned out to be a good one: on investments of $500, profits of $14,000 were realized in "a very short period time." Charles B. Alexander, "Argument on Defendant's Motion for Judgment," in *George C. Holt, as Assignee, &C., against William S. Warner, and Others*, Supreme Court, City and County of New York, p. 52; *New York World*, July 2, 1886.

to live with more comfort. William would do the same if he had it. . . . How opportune to *us all* are the [Evening Star] and other mines! Our *house & surroundings* when completed as F has directed & arranged will (I think) be equal to any in the village with the possible exception of Mrs. Ayrault. . . ."*

I have seen so many financial reverses that it [is] with "fear & trembling" I view F & W's success. All that we can do under Providence is to 1.) urge their putting *now* in a place *beyond peril* a sum sufficient for their comfortable support if the worst comes. $50,000 is less than a quarter's income to F & yet $50,000—at 6 per cent—[would be] enough to support F & E comfortably in a village like Geneseo [and] 2.) use what they give us in a way that shall be permanently beneficial. . . . But enough upon all this. Let us be grateful—joyous & hopeful.[37]

Ferd professed to admire his father, but he rarely paid attention to anything he said. He never even considered putting away money in order to live comfortably in a village like Geneseo. He and Ella had been renting a four-story brown-stuccoed house at 81 Pierrepont Street, just two blocks west of the Green home on Monroe Place in Brooklyn Heights. Now, he bought it, for $40,000 ($866,000 today), and then feverishly began filling it with the sort of art and oriental carpets and ornate furnishings with which he'd dreamed of surrounding himself since his boardinghouse days.

He started a collection of rare books: original elephant folios of Audubon's *Birds of America* and *Animals of America*; multiple leather-bound sets of Dickens and Shakespeare; Bibles in Arabic, Persian, Urdu; four sets of *The Arabian Nights*, one with six hundred tipped-in engravings. A book dealer marveled later at how "impulsive and decisive" Ferd was; it had taken him just three minutes to decide to buy a volume that cost $1,600.[38]

He haunted Goupil's art gallery on Broadway, bringing home etchings, bronzes, and canvases by fashionable European artists.

---

* Mrs. Ayrault was the wealthy widow of the town banker, Allen Ayrault, whose large, handsome house on Main Street would later become the Big Tree Inn.

Ferdinand did not list all of Ferd's gifts; he also bought the disused old Session House for his father and had it lined with shelves to house his father's library, and he purchased a horse and carriage and hired a coachman so that his parents no longer had to make their way along the village's muddy streets on foot.

Twenty-seven paintings hung in the parlor alone. Most were conventional views of fashionable young women, fox hunts, still-lifes, and landscapes. But Ferd's prize canvas was *Christ Raising Jairus's Daughter*, by Gabriel Max, bought for him by an agent in Paris for $4,500 (almost $97,000 in modern terms). Four feet high and nearly six feet wide, it depicts Christ at the bedside of a teenage girl whom he is about to wake from the dead; a meticulously rendered fly on her arm is meant to make the viewer understand that she is lifeless, not merely a pretty girl asleep.* It was a theme perfectly suited to remind guests (and potential investors) that, for all his apparent wealth, Ferd remained a clergyman's pious son who could be trusted to do the right thing, that their money would be safe in his hands.

A visitor remembered the Ward house as "one of the richest and most complete in its interior appointments that I have ever seen."[39] Four Irish maids kept the oriental carpets clean and dusted the books and artworks. A French chef and his wife ran the kitchen. An Irish butler announced callers, saw that the wine cellar was fully stocked, and ensured that the staff maintained the lofty standards of service expected by residents of Brooklyn Heights. And in the Ward stable on Love Lane, just behind the house, where Ferd kept four horses, an Irish coachman made certain that the silver mountings on the harness were kept gleaming for the carriage rides Ferd and Ella took through Prospect Park and Green-Wood Cemetery every weekend.

Ferd was asked to join the Brooklyn and Kingston country clubs. "He was not what would be called . . . a society man," a fellow member of the Brooklyn Club remembered, "though with his family, he moved in refined circles. He was a generous friend of all charitable movements, contributed liberally, and Mrs. Ward participated in many fairs held to give aid to charitable institutions."[40] The Wards gave generously to the Church of the Pilgrims, the Mercantile Library, the Eye

---

* Vincent van Gogh, who saw a photograph of this painting in 1877, told his brother it was "particularly fine." A New York critic who looked over Ferd's collection when it was auctioned off after the crash took a very different view: "Mr. Ward's pictures," he wrote, "were largely rubbish, the sort that a rich man without much taste would be likely to buy. . . . Gabriel Max's 'Raising of Jairus's Daughter'—including the carefully painted fly on the young woman's arm—was sold to a gentleman who, not inappropriately, presented it to the Presbyterian Hospital, although he would have done better still had he sent it to the Morgue." The painting is now at the Montreal Museum of Fine Arts. *The Art Amateur: A Monthly Devoted to Art in the Household* (February 1885).

and Ear and Homeopathic hospitals, and the Brooklyn Association for Improving the Condition of the Poor. Ferd especially pleased his father by helping to pay for revival services held at the Brooklyn Academy of Music that were aimed at bringing the young, still-impressionable clerks of Wall Street to Christ. Ferd himself did not bother to attend.

Brooklyn neighbors took to calling him the "bonanza man."

The same year that he renovated his parents' parsonage and bought and began furnishing his own home, the Wards also purchased, in Ella's name, the Champion House in East Haddam, the country inn where Ferd had proposed marriage five years earlier. The quiet old Connecticut River town was the ancestral home of the Green and Champion families; since childhood, Ella and her family had spent summers there to be near relatives and friends. When she learned that the inn was scheduled for demolition, she set out to save—and transform—it. She turned the battered old hotel into what its brochure would describe as a haven of "comfort combined with quietude": thirty double rooms, all gas lit "at a cost of nearly two thousand dollars"; a formal dining room with dumbwaiters to carry food up from the kitchen and "eliminate all odors of cooking"; a private wharf at which steamboats from New York and Hartford stopped twice a day; a specially built fifty-foot steam launch named the *Ella C* in her honor that carried guests wherever they wanted to go; and on the terraced lawn the words "Champion House" spelled out in clipped greenery, in living letters large enough to be read from Goodspeeds Landing, half a mile upriver.

The newly renovated Champion House was advertised as a "select and refined retreat" for well-to-do New Yorkers—the kind of New Yorkers Ferd needed to finance his schemes and among whom he had always craved to be counted. It served another purpose for Ferd as well. He persuaded Ella's brother, Fred, to take it over as manager, keeping him busy outside the city and away from the family finances, which he was at least officially supposed to help oversee.

On July 1, 1880, as work got under way on the Champion House, the brokerage firm of Grant & Ward was formally established for "the purchase and sale of stocks and bonds and in any legitimate mode of making money."[41] The new firm's profits were supposed to be divided equally each month, but Ferd was to be the managing partner. He, and he alone, was to sign the checks, keep the books, and conduct the day-to-day business.

It had taken months to persuade Buck Grant to sign on—months during which Ferd had privately grown more and more anxious. Rev. Ward's "fear and trembling" about his son's ability to hold on to his fortune had been fully justified. Ferd's personal account at the Marine Bank now held less than $2,000. The money he had spent on homes and furnishings and gifts for his parents had almost all come from the funds Fish and Buck and a handful of others had invested with him. The profits he claimed to be holding for them—more than $50,000 owed to Fish, nearly $100,000 to Grant (over $1 million and $2 million, respectively, in modern terms)—were only partly real. If either man had demanded full payment, Ferd's Wall Street career would have ended early, in disgrace. Only by persuading them that far bigger revenues would result from this new partnership was he able keep the facts from coming out.

Grant & Ward was fraudulent from the start. Ferd, Buck, and Fish were each supposed to contribute $100,000 as capitalization. Young Grant dutifully turned over his full share, including $30,000 in cash and more than $60,000 in valuable Evening Star stock. Fish—who had been encouraged by Ferd to believe that he was shrewdly taking advantage of young Grant's naïveté—did not contribute a penny in cash; more than half of his "contribution" consisted of IOUs from Ferd, whose share was also almost entirely paper, much of it worthless.

Fish and Ferd had grown closer. The banker's second wife had died in December 1879, and soon afterward he had moved from the house he had shared with her in Brooklyn into a small flat above his Wall Street bank. Ferd assured him he should consider himself part of the Ward family, and the lonely old man began crossing the East River back to Brooklyn by ferry each morning to have breakfast with the Wards. A portrait of a bull's head hung over the sideboard, a fierce-eyed symbol of the Wall Street optimism upon which Grant & Ward would rely. Ferd was unfailingly solicitous. "If the [morning] was very slippery in winter," Fish remembered, "he would assist me [back] down the hill to the ferry. 'I've got to be very careful of you Mr. Fish,' he would say, 'for you are my benefactor. I can't afford to lose the best friend I have in the world, the man to whom I owe all I have.' "

A special telephone line was installed between Fish's office at the bank and Ferd's desk at Grant & Ward so that the two men could talk business several times a day. The firm did well at first, investing in the stocks of two railroads, the St. Louis and San Francisco (of which Fish was president) and the Third Avenue Elevated (of which he was a director). Both exceeded expectations. Ferd claimed to be reaping other big profits, too, in mining stocks and flour contracts—all of them the result of fevered buying and selling, the details of which he kept even from his breakfast guest.

When Buck Grant tried to play a more active role in the firm's business, Ferd pulled him up sharply. "I supposed at first I was going to find opportunities to make money," Buck remembered.[42] One day he stepped behind Ferd's curtain to tell him that on behalf of the firm he had bought shares in the Manhattan Railway Company. Ferd told him he'd done wrong. The stock was a poor risk, and in any case only Ferd himself was authorized to act for Grant & Ward. Buck ruefully reassigned the transaction to his personal account—and promptly lost $6,000. "The result made me think Ward smarter than ever," he recalled; after that, "I was reduced to doing nothing. I was sort of a customer of the firm."[43]

He was a happy customer, though—so happy that after less than three months he wanted his father to share in his good fortune and join Grant & Ward. The senior Grants were coming to Manhattan in late October, when Buck was to marry Fannie Chaffee. The groom-to-be wanted the general to meet Ferd and Fish while he was in town. Nothing could have pleased them more.

NINE

The Imaginary Business

In 1880, Ulysses S. Grant was still the best-known American on earth. He and Julia had been back in the United States for more than a year at that point, after a triumphal tour of the world that had seen big crowds turn out to cheer them from London and Paris to Benares and Tokyo. Life in the modest home the people of Galena, Illinois, had built for them now seemed hopelessly humdrum. Thanks mostly to poor timing and inept political advice, the ex-president had been denied his party's nomination for what would have been a third term in the White House in 1880. He had loyally campaigned for his party's nominee, Ohio Congressman James A. Garfield—although he privately believed Garfield hadn't "the backbone of an angleworm"[1]— then checked into the Fifth Avenue Hotel, still harboring hopes of somehow winning back the White House in 1884.

Meanwhile, at fifty-eight, he needed to make some money—in those years, ex-presidents had no retirement funds to fall back on.* He had been forced to give up his military pension when he became a civilian to enter politics, and Democrats had blocked repeated efforts

---

* They would receive no pensions until Harry Truman left office in 1953 and the Democrats in command of both houses of Congress voted to grant one to him—and to all his successors.

by Republican congressmen to restore him to the army roster after he left the White House.

Twenty Wall Street admirers raised a $250,000 trust fund for him in gratitude for his service to the Union; its income was meant to make it possible for the Grants to live comfortably in Manhattan. Meanwhile, a second group of wealthy men, including the Philadelphia publisher George W. Childs and the New York bankers Anthony Drexel and J. Pierpont Morgan, put up another $100,000 to help the Grants buy a brownstone at 3 East Sixty-sixth Street, just off Central Park. "It was much larger and more expensive than we had intended," Julia would admit, "but it was so new and sweet and large that this quite outweighed our more prudential scruples."[2] The Grants filled it with symbols of the general's victories in battle and the gifts he had received during their long sojourn abroad: medals and decorations and a miniature gold version of the table on which Robert E. Lee had signed the articles of capitulation to end the Civil War; gold-headed canes and presentation swords in scabbards studded with diamonds; framed documents granting him the freedom of most of the major cities in the British Isles; a gold-enameled cigar box from the king of Siam; a pair of immense elephant tusks presented by an Indian maharaja; and a library of some five thousand leather-bound volumes given to the general by the people of Boston.

But it was not enough. Many of the men who now sought Grant's company were rich beyond the imagining of an Ohio tanner's son—and seemed to be growing richer by the minute. Neither the general nor his wife would be satisfied until he could take his place among them.

Buck Grant was certain that cutting his father into Grant & Ward's profits was the quickest way to make that happen. On October 20, he escorted his father downtown to James D. Fish's rooms above the Marine Bank for a private luncheon with his partners. For all his fame, U. S. Grant was an unprepossessing figure—short, rumpled, reticent, and unimaginative. (Venice would be a lovely place, he'd once said, if only someone would drain its canals.) But he had been a superb military commander, an implacable realist about combat and its costs who had earned his nickname, "Savior of the Union," at Fort Donelson, Shiloh, and Vicksburg; the Wilderness, Spotsylvania, and Cold Harbor; Petersburg and Appomattox. "The art of war is simple enough," he once told John Brinton. "Find out where your enemy is. Get at him as soon as you can. Strike him as hard and as often as you can and keep moving on."[3] Nor had he ever lost sight of what was at stake beyond the battlefield. When, during Grant's visit to Germany, Chancellor Otto von Bismarck suggested to him that the Civil War had been fought merely to preserve the Union, the general politely corrected him: "In the beginning, yes. But as soon as slavery fired upon the flag it was felt, we all felt, even those who did not object to slaves, that slavery must be destroyed. We felt that it was a stain on the Union that men should be bought and sold like cattle."[4]

He was the only president since Andrew Jackson to have completed two terms, and when he left office in 1877—feeling like a boy let out of school, he told a friend—he could point to some solid achievements. He had held steady during the Panic of 1873, restored relations with Great Britain that had been badly strained during the Civil War, tried to bring peace to the western plains, sent soldiers south to protect the rights of at least some freedmen and remained concerned about their plight after most members of his own party had lost interest in them. "To Grant more than any other man," wrote Frederick Douglass, "the Negro owes his enfranchisement and the Indian a humane policy."[5]

But from his early days in the army—when a fast-talking fellow soldier did him and three friends out of their savings—he had shown a fatal inability to recognize dishonesty among those who purported to be his friends. Shortly before the Civil War he'd been gulled again, swapping a sixty-acre Missouri farm for a house in St. Louis that was not actually owned by the man who made the deal. " 'No,' to him was the most difficult word in the English language," an old admirer remembered;[6] capable of sending thousands to their deaths without blinking, he seems to have been made deeply uneasy by one-to-one confrontation. His personal honesty was never questioned, but his presidency nonetheless witnessed so many scandals involving his appointees that editorial writers coined a new word for political corruption: "Grantism." More puzzling than the amount of highly placed malfeasance that surrounded him was Grant's reaction to it: he remained stubbornly loyal to many of those forced to resign in disgrace, and seems to have seen them all as comrades-in-arms upon whom it would have been wrong to turn his back while they were under fire.

Now, when his son's partners promised him big money for very little work, he believed them. "The great captain of the Union's salvation," wrote the financier Henry Clews, "was as helpless as a babe when Ferdinand Ward and James D. Fish moved upon his works."[7]

The firm was recapitalized. Once again, Ferd and Fish contributed mostly valueless paper, Ward explaining that all his ready money was tied up because he was actively interested in so many businesses. Buck paid in another $100,000. The general deposited $50,000, and when Grant's youngest son, Jesse—just twenty-one but already speculating in mining stocks and on the Produce Exchange—asked to join, he put in another $50,000.

Each of the Grants was guaranteed $2,000 for living expenses ($43,000 today) every single month, no matter how the firm was faring; in 1884 that sum would grow to $3,000. The rest of their profits were to be left with the firm as working capital.

Fish, however, now insisted on being treated differently. He wanted every penny of his share turned over to him every month. "That did not strike me as a good arrangement and I told him so," Ferd would say much later. "But Fish stuck to that point and I finally yielded."[8] He would later claim that his objection had been based on sound business practice; Fish's insistence on having cash in hand every month meant that a quarter of the firm's profits was unavailable for reinvestment. In fact, he was against it because it meant that at least one partner had to be regularly paid off in cash, not promises. Fish used most of the money to buy up buildings and building lots all over the growing city.

Shortly after signing on with Grant & Ward, General Grant accepted the presidency of the Mexican Southern Railroad, meant to link Mexico City with Guatemala, the Pacific, and the Gulf of Mexico. As soon as he opened a railroad office on the second floor of the United Bank Building at the corner of Wall Street and Broadway, Grant & Ward moved into a suite of its own downstairs.

Neither Fish nor the general nor either of his sons was to be found there very often. But Ferd was almost always on the premises, polite, energetic, and eager to add new investors to the firm's books. The depression had ended. Wall Street was optimistic, expansive, volatile. Ferd had an outsize pair of horns from a Texas longhorn bull hung in the outer office as a symbol of the surging market he hoped to ride to riches. Business mushroomed, attracted by Grant's name and Ward's energy. John M. Bradstreet listed Grant & Ward as "gilt-edged." Its credit was unquestioned. Ferd invested in railroads and silver mines, coal and commodities. "It is my plan to build up a great firm that shall live long after . . . its founders have passed away," he assured Buck.[9]

"To all of us," a Wall Street veteran remembered, "[Ward] seemed a lusty, good-natured boy, an amiable visionary who had landed in an accidental prominence as General Grant's partner. That he was evil-dispositioned not one of us ever conceived . . . not till jury evidence heaped higher than the Catskills."[10]

Ferd continued to lavish gifts on friends and family: $100 to help rebuild his cousin Rev. George K. Ward's church in Danville, New York, following a fire; $200 to buy brass instruments for the East Haddam concert band; a big oriental carpet for the parlor of the Brinton home in Philadelphia. "What an elegant present Ferd gave you," his mother wrote to Sarah. "It does me twice the good that it would had he given it to me. He is indeed a noble-souled boy to give among his relatives when it is needed and when it will not be noised abroad in the world. . . . I feel the comfort of his generous kindness in the dividends that come from time to time."[11]

The summer after the general joined the firm, Ferd bought and furnished still another home, a twenty-five-acre country estate called "Rosemount" on elm-shaded Strawberry Avenue, the most fashionable street in Stamford, Connecticut.* A gatekeeper kept out unwanted visitors. His small house, with its tall, narrow windows and mansard roof in the Second Empire style, mirrored in miniature the big, three-story, twenty-two-room main house that stood several hundred feet back from the road. There were shade trees and formal terraced gardens, too, a fountain, and a windmill. An Irish couple, Mr. and Mrs. Joseph Dyer, moved down from Geneseo to occupy the house year-round: Mr. Dyer was the coachman; his wife did the cooking. Another Irish couple, named Shepherd, oversaw a greenhouse meant to keep both Rosemount and the Wards' Brooklyn house filled with fresh roses all year 'round. Ferd's stables and barns housed some two dozen horses, including a $10,000 pair of fast mares belonging to General Grant. There were also donkeys and donkey carts, carriages of nearly every kind and size, a herd of Jersey cattle, and fifteen Irish setters that set up a fearful barking whenever a stranger turned up at the gate.

Jane Shaw Ward found it all too much. "Ferd has had another

---

* Ferd bought the house for $49,220 from James D. Fish's younger brother, John D. Fish, cashier of the Marine Bank, who was also serving as executor of the previous owner's estate. Only its gatehouse survives. *New York Herald*, November 28, 1885.

horse taken to Stamford," she reported to Sarah, "and has sent for still *another*! The young man who took down the last one [from a horse breeder in Livingston County] says, 'Mr. Ward was dressed in *short* pants (to the knees) and long stockings with low shoes!' I am sorry he will enter into every new fashion so readily. It must make a fool of him."[12]

But most of Ferd's neighbors, summer commuters like himself, seemed to enjoy his company and could not have failed to be impressed when General Grant himself paid visits to play poker and drive the fast team he kept in the Wards' stables. The Reverend Richard P. H. Vail of the Presbyterian Church and his wife became among the Wards' closest friends. Ferd and Ella joined other young couples sailing off Shippan Point, bought shares in the stock company formed to build a new club for what the *New York Times* called the "wealthy citizens of this town,"[13] and liked Stamford so much they bought a second, far smaller, house on South Street in Ella's name as an investment.

Many years later, a fellow commuter remembered riding the train back and forth from Stamford with Ferd.

> He liked to talk of the stock market. Was in no way a know-it-all, but he had his theories that he reveled in expatiating on. He was the first Wall Streeter I ever knew to go in for charts. He was just as glib about "cycles" as are the patterers today. One morning I said to him: "Do you really think you can bob a lot of lines up and down a foolscap sheet, illustrating what you call past performance, and from those ink tangles tell what's on the way for tomorrow?"
>
> And he answered:
>
> "Sure markets! Markets are just repeating echoes."
>
> I pursued: "Have you ever tried your notions out—put your funniness into action, with real dollars up?"
>
> He came back: "Yes sir, I have done that"—and what an ingratiating smile he flourished!—"I am going to keep at it right along till, being plenty patient, I prove I'm right."[14]

In the summer of 1881, Rev. Ward traveled west again to visit Will and Kate. (Ferd had paid for his train tickets and also arranged for a subsequent voyage to England.) Leadville was still a wide-open boomtown.

Ferdinand can't have been pleased with the downtown casino which featured a stained-glass window and called itself "the Little Church on the Corner." He must have deplored the big, jostling crowds of miners who still elbowed their way in and out of the saloons and gambling rooms on the Sabbath. And he couldn't help being concerned that whenever his son went out after dark, he still carried a pistol in his pocket. But the mountains were beautiful, the weather "perfect," and there was a handsome redbrick Presbyterian church just down the street. (Will had helped fund it and attended services there every Sunday.) The old man was astonished by the progress that had been made in less than three years: the population had grown from fewer than fifteen hundred to almost sixteen thousand. There were now twenty-eight miles of streets; some thirty mines and fourteen smelters working day and night; thirteen schools, six churches, and three hospitals; gaslights and water pipes and telephones; and a post office with fourteen full-time clerks, which, Ferdinand was told, "did a larger business than any other between St. Louis and San Francisco."[15]

In a letter to his daughter he could not contain his pride in the part his elder son was playing in it all.

> W & [Kate] . . . & their friends most agreeable @ W's delightful home on Capitol Hill, the pleasantest location "by all odds" in this "camp." . . . As to *William* I w'd say this that if ever a family had cause to be *proud* of a Son & Brother we have of William. Take him "all in all" I never knew his superior. He unites in a rare degree of intelligence, courtesy, simplicity, enterprise & *immovable principle.* Meet him in the street, on horse or afoot & you w'd judge from his dress that he was a day laborer and yet for authority in mines &c he is at the *head.* A common looking man said to me yesterday "all of *W.S.'s* (as all style W) family may be well proud of him," adding this: "His two excellences are (1) He is *the same to all*—high & low & (2) he can [not] be bought. . . ." In a long conversation with *Gov Tabor** he told me that [the Evening Star] was the best managed

---

* Horace Austin Warner Tabor, known as the "father of Leadville," was a Vermont-born veteran of the western gold and silver camps who had become a multimillionaire as owner of three of Leadville's richest mines—the Little Pittsburgh, Chrysolite, and Matchless. He had been elected lieutenant governor of Colorado in 1878. Had Rev. Ward met him two years later, he might have laid less stress on Tabor's judgment of his

mine in camp & Wm the *first* man for character & influence in Leadville."[16]

Eventually, William would manage or share ownership of other mines: in Leadville, the Morning Star and the Kennebec and his father-in-law's Little Giant; in Adelaide City, the Terrible Mining Company; in Independence, the Farwell Consolidated Mining Company; and, in Gunnison, the Ward Consolidated Company, the Adams Prospecting Company, and the Sterling Mining Company.

Sooner or later, Mary Hallock Foote wrote, "persons who got rich in Leadville moved to Denver." The William Wards did so, too, in December 1881. William built himself a big, handsome house at 1280 Grant Street, just two blocks from the state capitol, in the heart of the city's most fashionable neighborhood. He also bought a 2,500-acre ranch not far from town and called it "Alfalfa-Fields," and he established the William S. Ward Fellowship in Economic Geology at Princeton in order to encourage young alumni to seek the kind of success that study and hard work had won for him in the mining field.

"How prosperous W & F are in business & how generous!" their father told Sarah. "Strange to see two country boys hand in glove with Pres. Grant—[William H.] Vanderbilt—&c &c. while Jay Gould pronounces F as one of the *rising* men of NY.[*] W & F are in business conservative & cautious—honest & shrewd. If it be the will of God may their prosperity continue & above all may not wealth imperil their spiritual interests! For this, let us ever pray."[17]

Will Ward was everything his father said he was. Ferd was not.

In mid-December 1881, Jane Shaw Ward received a letter from Brooklyn. Ella was about to give birth. There had evidently been an earlier miscarriage, and for this delivery Ferd seems to have wanted his mother nearby. For some reason, perhaps because she did not feel Ella really wanted her, she did not go. "I think that Mother makes a *mis-*

---

son's character; in 1883, Tabor divorced his first wife in order to marry his mistress, a divorcée named Elizabeth Doe—"Baby Doe"—who would one day become the model for the opera *The Ballad of Baby Doe.*

[*] Jay Gould may well have said this—certainly Ferd was thought to be doing astonishingly well—but an extensive search has failed to find any record of it in the newspapers of the time. Ferd may simply have invented it to impress his father.

take in not accepting Ferd's *beseeching* invitation," his father told Sarah. "But she must do as she thinks best."[18]

The baby was born dead on December 19 and buried the next day in the Green family plot at Green-Wood. None of Ella's letters from the years before the crash survive. Nor do anyone else's that might have cast light on how she or her husband felt about their loss. But the next evening, Ferd evidently felt well enough to stroll over to the flag-filled banquet hall of the Brooklyn Academy of Music on Montague Street and take his place at table G at the big New England Society dinner held to celebrate the 261st anniversary of the landing of the pilgrims. General Grant was the guest of honor but left most of the speaking to what he called the "unadulterated Pilgrims"[19] who surrounded him. The speeches and toasts, brandy and cigars went on well past midnight.

Some six weeks after the baby's burial, Ferd's mother left home for a rare visit to her children in Philadelphia and Brooklyn. Jane disliked travel, always thought herself too drab for the big city, and was never able to keep to herself her disapproval of even the slightest departure from her sense of piety and decorum. Her husband could not accompany her—he was now serving as stated supply in the tiny village of Rushford—so Maggie, the senior Wards' Irish housekeeper, served as her escort.

Their first stop was the Brinton home at 1423 Spruce Street in the Society Hill district of Philadelphia. The narrow three-story brick house was alive with grandchildren: George, already nearly six feet tall at thirteen; John, eleven; Ward, nine; Jasper, three; and Sarah, not quite two. There were three servants, too, as well as Sarah, the doctor, and his unmarried sister, Mary. Somehow, room was found for both visitors.

Several years earlier, Dr. Brinton had commissioned his friend Thomas Eakins to paint portraits of himself and his wife. Each captured something of the sitter's essence. The bearded doctor's full-length portrait dominated the dark office in which it had been painted. He was a formidable man: a highly respected surgeon at the Jefferson Hospital, he had already helped establish the Philadelphia Academy of Surgery and the American Surgical Association, and he would soon succeed the celebrated Dr. Samuel D. Gross as chief of practical surgery at Jefferson Medical College. He was "devoted to the patriarchal," one of his boys remembered, a member of Philadelphia's oldest clubs who saw himself as the "faithful guardian of the House of Brinton." Ancestral portraits lined his walls. Specially built cabinets held ledger books and parchment deeds dating back to the 1680s. The children were forbidden to climb onto two chairs in the front hall because George Washington and Lafayette had sat on them. Brinton was also interested in the history he himself had witnessed, and especially revered his old commander, General Grant, whom he considered "one of our nation's greatest men."*

Sarah's somber, pensive Eakins portrait hung in the parlor. "She was slight in figure," her son Jasper recalled, "but her frail body sheltered an indomitable spirit. She was never ill, that is to say, she never admitted it; nor did any sorrow—and she had heavy ones—permit her to add to others' grief by a surrender to her own."[20] Her son did not exaggerate the number or weight of the tragedies she would endure. When she posed for Eakins in 1878, she had already survived her first sorrow: two years earlier, Ward Brinton's twin brother, the first Jasper Brinton, had fallen from the third-floor nursery window and died.

She seems to have grown into the kind of woman Jane Shaw Ward had often wished she herself had been: calm, reassuring, fond of reading her children to sleep in a low, beautifully modulated voice they never forgot. She saw to it that they and all the servants gathered together before breakfast to say their prayers and taught them their ABCs before sending them off to one or the other of Philadelphia's most exclusive schools. On the Sabbath, she made sure every child who was old enough memorized five new Bible verses, then led the whole family to the Tenth Street Presbyterian Church at Twelfth and Walnut streets—the whole family, that is except for her husband.

"My father, as his father had been before him . . . was an Episcopalian," Brinton Jasper explained many years later, "and we had a pew in the gallery at Holy Trinity Church. This was occupied by all of us on the rare occasions when my father's professional duties led him to announce his intention of going to church. Then we would accompany

---

* In 1891, Brinton would write a vivid, anecdotal account of his service in the Civil War, intended for his children and grandchildren alone to read. He wanted them to understand, he wrote, that "*then*, the War, to all of us, was *everything*, it was all in all. The past was forgotten; the future we scarcely dared to think of; it was all then the grim present, in which everyone tried to do his best and in which almost every gentleman felt it his duty to take his share." The book was not published until 1914, seven years after Dr. Brinton's death. John H. Brinton, *Personal Memoirs of John H. Brinton*, p. 11.

him in family procession—up Spruce Street and across [Rittenhouse Square]—a very important occasion."[21]

Such occasions were very important in part because they were so infrequent. Dr. Brinton was neither a Presbyterian nor a weekly church-goer, and he refused to pretend otherwise when his mother-in-law came to town. Evidently, she complained during her visit. He responded with some heat. Sarah was caught in the middle. "It is just as you say about worldly men," Jane told her daughter after she had left, "and I don't think arguing does the least bit of good. Let us both go to God with an earnest desire for Dr. B's conversion."[22] Perhaps not surprisingly, Dr. B. did not welcome her back to Spruce Street.

Jane and Maggie moved on to Brooklyn, where Ferd did everything he could to impress his mother with how well he was doing. He arranged things so that when she stepped off the ferry, Watson B. Dickerman's top-hatted coachman and gleaming coupe were waiting to whisk her and her companion up the cobblestoned hill to 81 Pierrepont Street. There, even though it was midwinter, her son and daughter-in-law were waiting in the doorway with bouquets of roses fresh from their Stamford greenhouse.

"Ferd and Ella received me with open arms and seemingly *warm* hearts," Jane reported. The butler served her an elegant lunch and afterward Ferd proudly led his mother from room to room so that she could see "all the improvements." The Ward home was even more opulently furnished now. General Grant had presented his young partner with some of the surplus gifts he had gathered during his world tour: tiger and leopard skins and a velvet-seated piano stool from India with gilt legs in the shape of long-trunked elephants; a Japanese ceremonial sword and a bamboo fire screen hand-painted with a map of the world.

"[Ferd] certainly *seems* to take great pleasure at my being here," Jane wrote on stationery embossed with her son's address.[23] It can't have been easy for him to give that impression. With his mother present no cigars could be smoked, no wine could be served. Ella—still weak after the loss of her baby—had to listen without complaint to her mother-in-law's exhortations to pray more often and more earnestly for Ferd's conversion. She spent as much time as she dared out of the house, taking the air—under doctor's orders, she said.

Harriet Clarke, Ferdinand's youngest sister, came to Brooklyn for a few days. Sarah, who had lived with her beloved "Auntie Harriet" in Washington during the Civil War, came north to see her. The unabashed enthusiasm with which Mrs. Clarke was greeted evidently did not sit well with Jane. "I only wish *I* was more agreeable to outsiders," she told her daughter afterward. "All here extol Auntie as such a lovely & agreeable lady. I am glad *always* to hear others praised but I would like to be worthy of a *little* myself."[24] It must have been with some relief that Ferd and Ella saw her and Maggie to the train that took them back to Geneseo.

Ferd went back to work. He was slender and intensely blond with deep-set blue eyes and a pale, drooping moustache. He dressed well, spoke softly but moved fast, and enjoyed the same fine Havana cigars Fish had shipped to General Grant by the barrel. But he also sometimes showed signs of the high-stakes tension under which he constantly lived: he tapped his teeth absently with the earpiece of the spectacles he wore to correct his old nearsightedness and sometimes compulsively opened and closed a gold-handled pocketknife marked "U.S. Grant," a gift from the ex-president, who had watched it being made for him in Sheffield, England.

"Young Ward has a rather old face," wrote a Wall Street veteran who knew him well, "like that of a man who sacrificed youth for business ambition and had not been much in the company of 'the boys.' "

> Of a serious nature, laboriously in earnest, with his eyes set upon a fortune, he is typical of hundreds of young men who come to New York and put no measure to their hopes of fortune and power. Discovering how easy it is to do things they had esteemed difficult, they have never known the distress nor the training of one who has lost money after slowly acquiring it. Made buoyant by juvenile success, with young brains full of blood which can race they often fall over a precipice because they had not tripped up at some friendly snag or hole earlier in the start.[25]

That precipice seemed very close in early 1882. For all the enthusiasm with which he had displayed his treasures to his mother, Ferd and his business were in terrible trouble. Some of it was the fault of the Grant family. The general's fondness for old friends had led him to reward some with unwise speculations: at his insistence, for example, the firm had bought the Southern Coal Company with mines in West Virginia from his old Confederate adversary, General John Bell Gordon. The firm would lose $150,000 (in modern terms more than $30 million) before it could extricate itself. And there were other unfortunate investments in mines that failed, railroads that never got built.

Ferd would one day blame Fish and the Grants for most of the firm's losses. Despite their "recklessness," he claimed, the firm's standing remained "unimpaired and its business good because the general run of business in my hands turned in a most gratifying profit for the benefit of the entire firm."[26]

In fact, there had been no genuine profits since 1880. In order to make it seem otherwise, at least in the firm's ledgers he showed to his partners, he had begun rehypothecating the firm's securities, pledging the same paper over and over again to borrow money, paying the interest on one loan out of the principal for the next, hoping that things would somehow balance out one day. So long as everyone got paid it was not illegal, but it was considered a dangerously risky practice, unworthy of a prominent brokerage firm. Ferd was careful not to let his customers know that he was doing it.

Fish, however, did know. He had already begun authorizing bank loans to Ferd and the firm, then permitting his young partner to take back to the Grant & Ward office the securities that were supposed to remain in the Marine Bank vault as collateral so that he could pledge them for a second or third time. As early as September 1880, just two months after Grant & Ward was established, he had to remind Ferd to return a bundle of bonds temporarily so that the national bank examiner would be satisfied that its loans were all properly secured. "We are not so rich as we ought to be at the bank," he told Ferd, "and I do not want to put too much for appearance's sake in bonds and securities that are not available. . . . We expect the Bank Examiner daily. He is very arbitrary [and] likes to show his power."[27] Ferd did as he was told—he slipped the bonds back into their loan envelopes at the bank and left them there until the examiner had finished his work, then carried them back to the office to use to raise more money. "Mr. Ward rehypothecated everything, the moment he could get his hands on it," George W. Spencer, the firm's clerk, recalled.[28] Grant & Ward had struggled along in this way for a little over a year.

But now, the bull market had ended. Wall Street was again sliding steadily downward. Investors were no longer inclined to take the kind of flyers Ferd had routinely taken. Some called in their loans. Creditors clamored to be paid. "I was in a corner," Ferd would recall. "These people held our paper. They expected their tremendous profits and I was anxious to retain the reputation I had gained." That, he said, was the moment when he began what he called "the imaginary business."[29]

No one was more concerned about the firm's prospects than James Fish, and when he turned up for breakfast in Brooklyn on Wednesday, February 1, 1882, he was relieved to learn that his resourceful young partner seemed to have come up with a brand-new money-spinning plan. Given the disturbing trends on Wall Street, Ferd said, he thought it best that the firm shift its focus from stocks and bonds to government contracts. Whatever happened elsewhere, the federal government still had to buy vast quantities of wheat and oats, hay and pork, and other supplies to feed and outfit soldiers and sailors and reservation Indians. Cities and towns signed contracts, too, continuing to undertake costly civic improvements—roads and bridges, waterworks and gas lighting.

It was ordinarily a risky, fiercely competitive business. Suppliers had to fight one another for contracts. But the potential profits were so great, Ferd explained, that contractors were willing to offer sizable shares of them to anyone who would advance them the money they needed to get started.

Grant & Ward was in a unique position to do just that, he assured Fish. Thanks to the behind-the-scenes influence of General Grant and his powerful friends, including Buck's father-in-law Senator Chaffee and New Mexico Territory's former congressional delegate Stephen B. Elkins (in whose New York law office Buck was now a junior partner), the firm could get far more than its share of government business.

Not even Ferd—who always wanted the world to believe the worst of everyone he wronged—dared hint that the general was aware that his young partner planned to exploit his name in this way. In fact, Grant would later testify that he had expressly forbidden Ferd ever to seek government contracts for the firm; while there was nothing inherently wrong about dealing in them, he said, he had told Ferd, "I had been President of the United States and I did not think it was suitable for me to have my name connected with government contracts."[30]

But the picture of potential profits Ferd painted for Fish proved so irresistible that he evidently didn't ask whether Grant was actually willing to cooperate. Massive infusions of new money would be needed, of course. That was where Fish came in. Ferd proposed that the firm issue notes, which Fish, as president of the Marine Bank, would immediately endorse and get discounted. For fear of alerting rivals, Ferd continued, he thought it best never actually to sign contracts in the firm's name; rather, he would take them on assignment from third parties and Fish was to keep a separate "special" set of ledgers at the bank so that the contract business would not get mixed up with whatever else the firm was doing.

Fish was intrigued. Before the week was out, Ferd reported that he already had an order from the U.S. government for 2,500 barrels of flour. It would require a considerable investment, but he thought the firm could clear $5 a barrel, for a total of $12,500 (more than $271,000 in today's terms). "Shall we take it?" he asked. "There won't be many more of these orders given until spring, so we had better take what we can get."[31]

Fish said take it by all means, saw that his bank loaned Ferd all the money he needed, and set sail for Cuba for two months in the sun. He was delighted that his young partner had once again figured out a novel way to make big money in hard times.

He had not. There were no government contracts—none. He never intended that there should be. He planned simply to keep the firm afloat and himself out of jail by pyramiding its funds; past investors were to be paid their supposed profits out of money freshly deposited by gullible new ones. "In reality," one reporter remembered, "Ward was borrowing from the next victim to pay off the victim of several months back who was hotly pressing for his money."[32] His only hope, Ferd later admitted, was that "I might, through a more active stock market in the future get even again."[33]

Until this moment, James Fish had understood—and actively encouraged—a good deal of Ferd's trickery. He'd overlooked the coming and going of securities from the vaults of his own bank, for example, and had authorized the loan to the firm of so much of his depositors' funds that it sometimes cut into the bank's reserves deeply enough to imperil its status as part of the national banking system. He had also allowed Buck Grant to believe that he and Ferd had each contributed $100,000 to capitalize the firm when they had not. But from now on, Ferd would have to make sure Fish remained as deeply in the dark about the true nature of the business he was doing—or pretending to be doing—as were his intended victims. Since the contracts didn't exist, he needed to come up with a plausible reason why his partner must keep secret every detail of the firm's supposed dealings with the government. "Now, as to grain orders," he wrote Fish on February 26, "I note your advice to take all the government contracts I can get, and I have done so since you went away."

> I fully agree with you that we must make hay while the sun shines, as we may not be in favor long [because the Democrats might win the presidency in 1884 and Grant's name would no longer carry the same weight in Washington], so I shall take these orders when I can get them. . . .
>
> Now, a word about the General. You know the Senate has passed the bill to retire him on [the] pay of [a] general, and it is now going to the House. If some of those fellows down there who oppose this bill should get wind of our having these contracts they will use it as a tool to defeat the bill, so I am very careful and have cautioned [James R.] Smith [the member of the stock exchange Grant & Ward used formally to buy and sell stock] against saying anything. As long as we keep quiet and do this business in outside names and in a quiet way, the General will stick by us.
>
> We have a bright prospect ahead if we are careful. We [presumably he and Buck] fully appreciate your kindness in aiding us in getting the money. I shall always look out for your interest in these matters, and if I get going too fast at any time or seem too anxious to make money you must check me, for although I am very cautious, still I know that discretion is the better part of valor. We are fast gaining a foothold in Washington and if some day we can get some of those Indian contracts I will be happy, for the profits on one of them is enough to set us up.[34]

Three days later, he wrote Fish again to drive home the need for silence: "The Government contract business is progressing well but we need to 'keep it mum' for if we don't the papers will give us fits. Some of our friends . . . have their suspicions that we are getting something rich . . . but I keep it quiet."[35]

Fish, too, kept it quiet, at least at first. (Later, he would occasionally confide in potential investors he knew well, thinking he was doing both them and himself a favor by letting them in on such a good thing.) And

Ferdinand De Wilton Ward, newly ordained as a
Presbyterian minister and about to sail for India as a
missionary, sat for this portrait by an unknown painter
in 1836 so that his family would remember what he
looked like if he were to die overseas.

Portrait of Jane Shaw *(above)*, painted just before her marriage to Ferdinand Ward, and *(opposite page)* paintings of three Indian street scenes—an entertainer, a Hindu mendicant, and an ox-drawn cart—commissioned by her husband for his parents back home in Rochester, New York. The scrawled captions are in his own overconfident hand.

American Mission Premises at Mdura East Home

The Wards would return from India in disgrace in 1847, but these reminders of the lives they had led there hung in the parlor of their Geneseo, New York, parsonage to the end of their days: the one at the left depicts an overnight encampment on their journey from Madras to Madurai; the other, painted by Ferdinand himself, depicts the Madurai mission where the Wards occupied East House, the structure at the left.

On his way to Europe for a
vacation in the spring of 1855,
Ferdinand *(left)* stopped at
a New York studio to have
his likeness captured by the
brand-new ambrotype process.
The elegant gloves, German
binoculars, and ivory-handled
umbrella were gifts from
wealthy parishioners. Three
years later, he would shock
his benefactors by splitting
their church *(right)* and
seizing control of Temple Hill
Academy *(below)* in the interest
of Old School Presbyterian
orthodoxy.

Plank Road.

Temple Hill Academy
in the fifties.   Geneseo N. Y.

This engraving *(above)* from the early 1880s, made from a photograph long since lost, is the earliest known image of Ferd Ward. His marriage to Ella Green *(at right, photographed by Napoleon Sarony)* gave him entrée to the rarified world of Brooklyn Heights; her family home, 37 Monroe Place, is the house with the brick façade at the right of the photograph below.

The elaborately furnished dining room and formal
parlor of the Green residence, where Ferd wooed and
won his wife—and then talked his widowed mother-in-
law into letting him manage the family fortune

Ferd's elder brother, William Shaw Ward, and his fiancée, Emma Jane Ward, in Leadville, Colorado, 1879. Will Ward's success in the silver-mining business—and the wealthy friends it won him—would help make Ferd's swindles possible.

Souvenirs of Ferd's brief heyday: *(above)* a stereo view of a weekend visit to an investor's country home (the Wards are the couple at the right); the art-filled Ward parlor at 81 Pierrepont Street in Brooklyn Heights *(opposite page, bottom)* (the samurai sword and elaborate fire screen were gifts from Ulysses S. Grant); and an elaborate hand-painted menu for a dinner at which Ferd was seated among some of the richest and most powerful men in America. It occupied pride of place on the wall of his Sing Sing cell.

DINNER

TO

Gen'l PORFIRIO DIAZ

BY

Gen'l U. S. GRANT.

UNION LEAGUE CLUB, April 4, 1883.

+GUESTS.+

Sr. Romero Rubio,
Dr. Eduardo Liceaga,
Sr. José M. Rascon,
Gen. J. B. Frisbie,
Gen. Cañedo,
Hon. J. W. Foster,
Col. F. D. Grant,
Mr. U. S. Grant, Jr.,
Mr. Jay Gould,
Hon. Roscoe Conkling,
Hon. Wm. M. Evarts,
Mr. C. P. Huntington,
Gen. G. M. Dodge,
Mr. H. M. Alexander,
Mr. F. Ward,
Hon. Franklin Edson,
Mr. T. Masac,

Sr. Salvador Malo,
Mr. J. H. Work,
Mr. Russell Sage,
Gen. E. F. Beale,
Mr. Henry B. Hyde,
Mr. Julien T. Davies,
Mr. Clarence A. Seward,
Mr. Victor Newcombe,
Mr. James D. Fish,
Gen. Horace Porter,
Gen. Lloyd Aspinwall,
Sr. Matias Romero,
Mr. W. H. Hurlburt,
Hon. J. A. J. Creswell,
Mr. Isaac H. Bailey,
Mr. Hugh Hastings,
Mr. Algernon S. Sullivan.

James Dean Fish, Ferd's mentor, partner, and enabler: a seasoned banker with a reputation for cautious conservatism, he conducted a secret liaison with Sallie Reber *(opposite page)*, a Gilbert and Sullivan star who bore him a daughter, Alice Reber Fish *(below)* and then died, just as his trial got under way in Federal Court.

In 1878, Dr. John H. Brinton commissioned his friend Thomas Eakins to paint portraits of himself *(left)* and his wife, Ferd's older sister, Sarah Ward Brinton *(right)*. Six years later, in the spring of 1884, Ferd's sister-in-law, Emma Jane Ward, began sitting for Eakins, too. Then, Grant & Ward collapsed, her brother-in-law was arrested, and she was never able to return to the artist's studio. The painting remains unfinished.

Angry depositors and anxious onlookers crowd Wall
Street as rumors spread that the Marine National Bank
and the firm of Grant & Ward have simultaneously
crashed, May 6, 1884.

The collapse of his firm ruined Ulysses S. Grant; throat cancer would kill him. Every detail of his illness, including visits by his doctors *(right)*, was reported in the press. Just weeks before the general died on July 23, 1885, he and his family appeared on the porch of their borrowed cottage at Mount McGregor, New York *(below)*. Ferd's gullible partner, Ulysses Grant, Jr.—known as "Buck"—sits at the left, just below his mother, Julia Dent Grant. His sister, Nellie Grant-Sartoris, wears the light dress; his brothers Fred and Jesse are to the general's right.

The New York crowds that lined Broadway to watch Grant's funeral on August 8, 1885 *(opposite page)* dwarfed those that grieved for Abraham Lincoln twenty years earlier. Ferd was somewhere in the throng, having bribed his guards at the Ludlow Street Jail so that he could watch his partner's coffin pass by. His trial for grand larceny began some six weeks later. In this courtroom scene from *Frank Leslie's Illustrated Newspaper (above)*, Ferd's flamboyant attorney, W. Bourke Cockran, questions a prospective juror while Will Ward whispers into his brother's ear.

THE "LITTLE NAPOLEON OF WALL STREET" IN EXILE.

The Friends of His "Flush" Days Don't Care to Know Him Now.

The public clamored to see Ferd punished: the comic artist Frederick Opper published the cartoon *(opposite)* while Ward was still on trial. After his conviction, *Leslie's* staff artists followed him to Sing Sing, where one picked him out of a line of convicts depositing their spoons after dinner *(above)*, and another caught him trying to cross the prison courtyard without being recognized *(below)*.

FERDINAND WARD
MESSENGER

Ferd's crimes and imprisonment bewildered his parents, shown here in their later years. Rev. Ward wears his Civil War chaplain's uniform on the day he was called upon to preside over a memorial service for U. S. Grant, the commander his son had ruined. The horse and carriage *(below)* was a gift from Ferd that his creditors allowed them to keep; Will, home on a brief visit, holds the reins.

Ella Ward, shamed by her husband's crimes and
harassed by his relentless demands for money, aged
rapidly while he was in prison. When this photograph
(opposite page) was made shortly before her death in 1890,
she was not yet thirty-eight. Her son, Clarence *(above)*,
was just five then, and had no memory of his father.

Clarence Ward at eleven *(opposite page)* and the handsome
Federal-style home in Thompson, Connecticut, where
he lived with his uncle and aunt, Fred and Nellie
Green. After his father tried to kidnap him, he had
orders to run to the barn at the left and hide whenever a
strange carriage came up the street.

Despite Ferd's crimes, the townspeople of Geneseo
continued to treat him as one of their own. In 1895, he
took part in a minstrel show meant to raise funds for the
Livingston County Historical Society—he's the small man
with the large adam's-apple seated third from the right in
the second row. A decade later, he would be forced to flee
his hometown after he was caught stealing money from
seventeen citizens, including several of his fellow minstrels.

Ferd Ward in 1911 *(left)*, about
the time he finally ran out of
schemes for seizing his son's
assets, and his son, Clarence
(below), reveling in his own
children, Frederick Champion
Ward and Helen Ward, on
the lawn of their home in
New Brunswick, New Jersey,
that same year.

Ferd seemed to be doing spectacularly well, reporting the purchase of more and more contracts that promised ever-larger revenues—so many lucrative contracts, he told Fish, he thought it best to refer to them only by number to ensure total secrecy. In April, for example, he wrote to remind his partner that a "ten thousand dollar note is due today on Contract No. 16, and we will carry it over to Contract no. 5."[36] Fish never fully understood what such notes meant—neither "Contract No. 16" nor "Contract No. 5" existed, after all—but he also never failed to try to find the money Ferd asked for, making loans from his own bank and approaching friends in the banking business, as well.

Sometimes the strain showed. In May, Fish evidently caught Ferd selling off some shares of his stock without informing him. Ferd was abject, at least on paper, his tone exactly the same as it had been when he was a boy and his mother or his brother had caught him in a lie.

> Now Mr. Fish, you know that I appreciate too deeply the kindness you have shown me since Mr. Green's death to ever be guilty of trying to take advantage of you. I have always looked upon you as a second father to me, and I fully appreciate your kindness. You have been the sole means of placing me where I am, and I can't stand it to feel that you think I would take advantage of you if I could.[37]

A week or so later, Fish wrote Ferd another stern note. The bank directors, he said, had begun asking awkward questions: "For instance, [the loan] to Sidney Green [of] $86,137.50. . . . There are things in that loan that I know nothing about. . . . And then the check of yours in cash since May 6. These things are not what they should be."[38] Ferd apologized again.

Others also began to worry about the pace Grant & Ward seemed to be setting. On July 5, Fish got a letter from Thomas L. James, the president of the Lincoln Bank, from which Grant & Ward had borrowed large sums on Fish's recommendation. James asked Fish to clarify his relationship with the firm: Was he a general partner and therefore responsible for all its actions and for its debts and obligations, or merely a special partner, liable only for the sum he'd invested in it? It was clear that James had grown suspicious.

Fish worried that others would become wary too, and for the first and only time in the history of Grant & Ward, he wrote to the general, asking if they might get together and talk over what their young partners were up to. He evidently wanted to be sure Grant was fully committed to the contract business he thought Ferd was conducting behind the scenes.

[PRIVATE]

My dear General:

You and I don't often meet to talk over business matters, or for any other purpose, but I trust that you are well aware that the failure to do so is not for any want of respect, esteem or friendship on my part. We are both pretty well occupied generally, which explains it. I think, however, it would not be amiss for you and me to counsel a little occasionally in regard to the business of Grant & Ward, as our conservative influence, if not beneficial, would do them no harm as they [Buck and Ferd] are so much younger than ourselves.

I have often been asked by friends and business men whether you and I were general or special partners. We were for a time advertised as special, but I think we are virtually and actually general partners, and I think legally we would find that to be our status. The enclosed letter to me from President James of the Lincoln Bank . . . was received by me and I send you a copy of my reply. . . .

You may be aware that I am on the notes of G & W as indorser, which I have discounted myself and have had to get negotiated to the extent of $200,000 in aggregate at the same time and at once, which is not a trifling amount for me. It is necessary that the credit of G & W should deservedly stand very high. These notes, as I understand it, are given for no other purpose than to raise money for the payment of grain, etc., purchased to fill the Governmental contracts. Under the circumstances, my dear General, you will see that it is of the most vital importance to me particularly that the credit of the firm shall always be untarnished and unimpaired. I will be happy to meet you at almost any time you may name to talk these matters over. . . .

> With respect and esteem, I am,
> sincerely yours
> James D. Fish[39]

The following day, an answer arrived in the general's own handwriting.

> My dear Mr. Fish:
> On my arrival in the city this a.m., I find your letter of yester-
> day with a letter from Thomas L. James, Pres. of Lincoln N.
> Bank, and copy of your reply to the latter. Your understanding
> in regard to our liabilities in the firm of Grant & Ward is the
> same as mine. If you desire it, I am entirely willing that the
> advertisement of the firm shall be changed so as to express this.
> Not having been in the city for more than a week I have a large
> accumulated mail to look over and some business appoint-
> ments to meet, so that I may not be able to get down to see you
> today. But if I can, I will before 3 o'clock.
>   Very truly yours,
>   U. S. Grant[40]

Grant never did turn up that afternoon, and his letter made no reference, one way or the other, to the government contracts Fish had asked
about. He would later testify he had no memory of ever even reading
Fish's letter—that most likely Ferd had "summarized it" for him, leaving out any mention of the contracts, before he wrote out his response.

It had been a close call for Ferd, but he also saw in it a way to turn
things to his advantage. That same day, he handed the hastily scrawled
draft of a second letter to the clerk George Spencer and asked him to
copy it out right away in his own hand. It was also ostensibly from the
general to Fish. Spencer did as he was told, although he later testified
that it had been the only time in the history of the firm he'd been asked
to do such a thing. Ferd placed the letter on the general's desk with
several others awaiting his signature. A few minutes later, Grant stuck
his head in the door and asked if there was anything that needed doing
before he left for a few days at his summer home at Long Branch, New
Jersey. Ward told him he had several routine letters he'd like to have
signed; nothing urgent, but it would be good to get them into the mail.
The general did not bother to read any of them; he signed them so fast,
according to Spencer, that he barely even sat down. The all-important
letter read as follows:

> My dear Mr. Fish:
> In relation to the matter of discounts kindly made by you for
> [the] account of Grant & Ward, I would say that I think the

investments are safe, and I am willing that Mr. Ward should derive what profit he can for the firm that the use of my name and influence may bring.

Yours very truly,
U. S. Grant[41]

After the crash, Fish and Ward would clash angrily over the authorship of this letter. Fish claimed he'd known nothing about it; it had been Ferd's idea and Ferd's alone. But Ward said they'd cooked it up together. Fish had dictated the original draft, in fact, and then gone over it carefully, suggesting changes they'd both agreed to make. When the general signed it, he would claim, both he and Fish had been delighted.

No one will ever know for certain who was telling the truth. In any case, Ferd now had a letter signed by the general himself perfectly calibrated to reassure wavering investors. Grant seemed to be in on everything; all the firm's investments were "safe," it said—presumably including the government contracts—and he appeared to have authorized Ferd to use his name and influence to land still more.

Ward's pace quickened. "If I get that government contract it will be for 150,000 bushels No. 2 oats," he told Fish in early August, "and they will cost about sixty-eight cents, profits about $102,000. . . . If you think best I will try this, if not I will let it go."[42] Fish continued to think it best.

Once, when Fish expressed momentary qualms, Ferd threatened to liquidate the firm: "In this case, of course, I would find a man who would take up all our government notes ($170,000) for which we would give him the profits. I could close the whole thing up in ten days . . . and then your mind would be relieved."[43] Fish immediately backed down; he could not bear the idea of passing on such profits to anyone else. The younger man might be impetuous, but the results he seemed to be producing remained dazzling—Fish had taken home $100,000 in 1882, and would end up with three times that amount the following year ($2,160,000 and $6,490,000, respectively, in modern terms).

Colonel Fred Grant had now come aboard, as well, not as a partner but as an eager investor. Increasingly envious of the astonishing returns his father and younger brothers seemed to be making, he hoped to get in on the action himself, he told Ferd, but he first wanted to be sure the firm was as solvent as everyone said it was. Ferd just smiled and led him into the safe. He opened a canvas satchel and showed him its contents: a jumble of beautifully engraved bonds and stock certificates. How much was all that worth? Grant asked. Oh, about a million and a half, Ward answered; he'd never had the time to total it all up. The colonel wrote him a check for $10,000 on the spot. Before it was all over, he would advance to Ferd and the firm almost a million and a half dollars of his own.

The Ward money machine still had constantly to be fueled by fresh cash from new investors, the richer the better. When Ferd learned that General Grant was having a dinner for a few business acquaintances, including Cyrus W. Field and William H. Vanderbilt, and that he was not invited, he determined to meet them anyway. Late that evening, just as the Grants and their guests were getting up from the table, the doorbell rang. It was Ferd in formal dress. Might he see the general, just for a moment? Grant appeared in the foyer. Ferd apologized for interrupting. He had stayed in the city to attend the opera, he said, and just wanted to step in to tell the general that he'd "managed to make a little turn today—nothing to do with the firm—but just a little outside speculation and I put you in." The stock he had shrewdly picked had tripled in value by the close of business. Grant's share of the profits was $3,000 (nearly $70,000 today), and Ferd thought, since he was in the neighborhood, he might as well just drop off the check. Grant was understandably delighted and insisted that his young partner join his guests in the parlor. There had been no actual investment, of course. The evening cost Ferd $3,000—but, he later said, he considered it "cheap at the price."[44]

At least twice a week thereafter, Ferd traveled uptown to join the general's nearly nightly poker game. Other regulars included old army friends and a handful of just the sort of "men of prominence and influence" whose company Ferd always sought: City Chamberlain J. Nelson Tappan; former New York senator Roscoe Conkling; Stephen Elkins; Bird W. Spencer, the treasurer of the Erie Railroad; and Commodore Cornelius K. Garrison, a onetime riverboat captain who'd made millions in shipping and railroads and gas lighting. All of them would eventually invest heavily in Grant & Ward.

"I think [poker] appealed to [Grant] because he had to bring to it some of the same qualities which caused him to . . . 'fight it out along this line if it takes all summer,' " Ferd recalled.

> Five of us were playing . . . [including Grant's old comrade Phil Sheridan]. After the cards were dealt we all came in with the regular ante and we all stood for the raise. When cards were drawn General Grant took three and General Sheridan stood pat. He bet the limit. We all dropped out with the exception of General Grant. With his usual black stub of a cigar in his mouth he . . . quietly looked Sheridan over, saw his bet and raised the limit. Sheridan promptly came back with another boost. . . . General Grant saw that and raised again. Then General Sheridan with his pat hand called. General Grant showed a pair of nines and won the pot. . . . [He] laughed and said, "I knew you were bluffing, Phil, and I would have kept it up until I had staked my pile."[45]

Privately, Ferd claimed to find such evenings wearying. "General Grant liked to have me up to the house and I was anxious to please him," he remembered. "But there was not much fun in going clear over from Brooklyn and getting home from sixty-sixth street at one or two o'clock in the morning."[46] Still, it wasn't all wasted time. Between hands one evening, Ferd spied a vase on the mantelpiece filled with $800 in $20 gold pieces given to the general for attending directors' meetings and then turned over to his wife to help with household expenses. Ferd took Mrs. Grant aside. That money shouldn't be allowed to just sit there earning nothing, he said; it should be invested on her behalf. Besides, leaving cash out in the open was a terrible temptation for the servants; you couldn't be too careful these days. After midnight, when he boarded the early-morning ferry for home, his pockets were weighted down with gold.

CHAPTER TEN

Tears of Grateful Joy

Ferd's partner, James Fish, liked to tell people, "I sleep over the bank."[1] It implied an unusual degree of devotion to his business, presumably comforting to depositors. When he left his old home in Brooklyn, with all its memories of life with two wives and eight children, and moved in above his office, his business associates had thought they understood. His two rooms were elegantly fitted out. An Irish housekeeper saw to his daily needs. The Wall Street ferry was close by, and most mornings he rode it back to Brooklyn to breakfast with the Wards. But the financial district fell silent after the close of business, and some in Fish's circle worried that he must be lonely.

He was not. He had had another reason for moving to Manhattan: it brought him closer to the night world of the theater that had drawn him since the early 1840s. He told one interviewer that his interest in the performing arts was largely philanthropic: "In the course of time I have often assisted some of those actors who were improvident and [had] exhausted their strength and reached old age poor and unhealthy," he said.[2] But it was actually young actresses, not old actors, that interested him most. He had "the reputation about town of being 'one of the boys,'"[3] one newspaperman reported; another described him as "one of the most conspicuous young-old gallants whose recreation is found on the front rows or boxes of theatres and among actresses behind the scenes and elsewhere."[4]

His favorite place was the Casino at Broadway and Thirty-ninth Street. A Moorish fantasy featuring a vast horseshoe-shaped theater and New York's first roof garden, it was the brainchild of the producer and composer Rudolph Aaronson, but it had been built with funds Fish and Ferd had helped collect from some of New York's biggest investors: Morgan, Vanderbilt, Field, Pierre Lorillard, the tobacco king. Both the Marine Bank and Grant & Ward had invested in the place as well. Ferd, Fish, and Ed Doty, Ferd's boyhood friend and sometime clerk brought down from Geneseo, served on its board of directors. William McBride, the onetime Geneseo carpenter whose apprentice Ferd had been when he was a schoolboy, was appointed treasurer and delivered the box office receipts to his former student every morning at eleven. Ferd and Fish had a special box at the Casino all their own. Fish occupied it nearly every night.

Aronson hoped the Casino would become the nation's leading showplace for light and comic opera, but it was the chorus—statuesque, boisterous, lightly clad—that the mostly masculine audience turned out to see. The mother of Lillian Russell, who would one day become the Casino's greatest star, offered a cold-eyed assessment of the managers for whom her daughter worked. They hired people only "to make money out of them," she said. "Most of the young men [they] call 'dudes' who frequent the Casino are stockholders . . . in a small way, having paid in a few hundred dollars—the dividend returned being an introduction to the women on the stage, and a promise to make them solid with the same."[5]

Fish acted at the Casino more or less as the other dudes did. After the show was over, he was said sometimes to walk one or another of the chorus girls across Thirty-ninth Street to a hideaway in the Mystic Flats, an apartment building he was constructing and had named in honor of his hometown.

Clearly, he did not always sleep over the bank. He did not confine himself to the Casino, either. On November 25, 1882, he attended the New York premiere of Gilbert and Sullivan's *Iolanthe* at the Standard Theatre. The critics didn't like it. They thought the show—a lampoon of the House of Lords disguised as a fairy tale—too British for an American audience. The company was mediocre. Miss Sallie Reber, who played the female lead, was picked out for special criticism:

one critic called her "wooden," another said she "acted and sang very badly."[6]

James Fish thought she was wonderful, and the air of personal tragedy that surrounded her only added to her appeal. She had been singing in public since her debut at fifteen in her hometown of Sandusky, Ohio. In her mid-twenties she was a featured performer with Patrick Gilmore's Famous Band at Gilmore's Garden on Madison Square in Manhattan: "She is pretty," one critic wrote after seeing her there, "has a good voice and was rightfully encored whenever she appeared."[7] She had gone on to become a star with Ruben's Grand English Opera Company and the D'Oyly Carte organization. Then, at thirty-one, she had abandoned her career to marry Franklin F. R. Laing, a wealthy suitor from Brooklyn. It was a terrible mistake. His parents cut off his allowance rather than accept an actress into the family, and he turned out to be an alcoholic, often abusive, unable or unwilling to earn a living. The couple took a room in a boardinghouse on West Thirty-fourth Street. She went back to work to pay the rent. Laing's brutality sometimes drove her out into the street at night. He made a nuisance of himself at the theaters where she played, spent three months in a home for inebriates, and emerged from the experience drinking still more heavily. Sallie had the sympathy of the whole theater world; earlier that year, friends had organized a "Grand Complimentary Concert to Miss Sallie Reber" at Steinway Hall to raise funds on her behalf.

At sixty-three, Fish was one year short of twice Sallie's age, but he was smitten, nonetheless: she was an actress, beautiful, delicate, and in need of help. He came back to see her several times, sitting in the front row and sending armloads of flowers backstage. When she was replaced in *Iolanthe* by a younger actress in January 1883, he provided sympathy, as well. And after Sallie's husband died of drink that autumn, he attended the funeral, where, he later said, "I saw some members of her family and confirmed the impression I already had, that she was a well-bred girl, that I need not be ashamed of her company."[8] He started to call regularly at the boardinghouse where she and her younger sister, Alice, were living. "As a friend of Miss Reber, I naturally felt interested in all her troubles," he remembered. "I occasionally took her out to dine and had reason to think that my association with her was agreeable. The more I saw of her the more I appreciated her good qualities and the more my regard for her increased. I may say that the feeling was reciprocated." Soon, he seemed to be accompanying her everywhere.

Fish genuinely loved the theater but never permitted his love for it to outweigh his concern for revenues. Early in 1883, he and Ferd bought the Booth Theatre at Twenty-third and Sixth for more than half a million dollars. The creation of the great tragedian Edwin Booth, it had once been the most elegant showplace in America, with a lobby and grand staircase carved from Carrara marble, frescoes and busts of great actors and favorite characters from Shakespeare, seats for 1,750 spectators, and a stage on which shoals of supernumeraries had room to move without bumping into one another. At the theater's opening in 1869, the *New York World* had declared that "no such temple consecrated to the drama has ever been reared before."[9] Booth went bankrupt in 1874; the theater hung on for nine more years under a series of unsuccessful managers before finally having to close its doors. Fish and Ferd attended the final performance, an actor's benefit of *Romeo and Juliet* starring Maurice Barrymore and the Polish-born star Madame Modjeska. "We sat in a box together," Ferd remembered, and after the final curtain an actor stepped forward and "denounced Mr. Fish and myself as men of deep avarice. . . . We were more amused than disturbed."[10] They ordered the theater razed and installed on the wall of the business block with which they replaced it a brass plaque that read "This Building was Erected by James D. Fish and Ferdinand Ward."

That pairing pleased Ferd's parents. Their younger son's success continued to delight them, though each worried that with Will living so far away, Ferd might still be tempted to stray from the right path or fritter away the fortune he was making: "William McBride [the Casino treasurer] is here," Ferdinand once nervously reported to his daughter. "He *thinks* that F's doing well in business. He *thinks* that he does not use up his income. I hope he does *not*—for reverses may come."[11] Once, during a visit to Manhattan, Rev. Ward stopped by the Marine Bank to introduce himself to Fish. He praised the banker as his son's "guardian and benefactor," and said he was grateful to God that Ferd was under the daily influence of a man whose caution and experience and integrity would keep him from reckless speculation. "Mr. Fish," he told him, "we pray for you and yours always."[12]

Ferd's mother shared in those prayers, but she remained frightened by her boy's continuing refusal to adhere to God's laws. When Sarah and her sons visited Ferd and Ella in Stamford, and Sarah gently refused to go out driving with them on Sunday, Jane was delighted.

I knew you would try to keep the Sabbath and have the children do so as far as possible so that Ferd might see you regard the day with some degree of reverence. He has himself so little conscience about it that I tremble for him, as I *know* God will not honor him if he does not honor God and his laws. . . . Oh, how I long to see him converted.[13]

Looking back, writers would suggest that Ferdinand Ward had a "hypnotic presence," an "uncanny power" over even the most seasoned veterans of Wall Street. He was unquestionably good at reading people. He knew whom to flatter and how to coax, and seemed to understand by instinct just how far he could go with each prospective victim. He knew the power of the subtle suggestion and secretive wink that opened purses and emptied pockets, and was masterful at spinning out the kind of particulars that made his supposed contracts seem plausible. James Fish remembered how

> Ward used to tell me rainbow-colored stories of the prospects which seemed to be opening up. He declared that through Mayor [Franklin] Edson [who had been superintendent of the Produce Exchange when Ferd worked there] he was going to get a contract to supply the Department of Charities and Correction with flour. He submitted an estimate of what the flour would cost, what it would be sold for and what the profits would be. He calculated cartage and all the other details. It was one of the great points in his method that he always was prepared to give you facts and figures in the most extreme detail, and they always seemed reasonable and based upon good business principle.[14]

But in the end it was neither Ferd's personality nor his skills as a fabulist that did the trick; it was the astonishing yields he promised—and seemed able to deliver.

"It is marvelous," wrote Wall Street veteran Henry Clews, "how the idea of large profits when presented to the mind in a plausible light, has the effect of stifling suspicion."[15] Clews set down the experience of one old friend. The man was a friend of General Grant's, too, and on the eve of a family trip to Europe in the spring of 1883, he stopped by the firm's offices and deposited $50,000 with Ferd to invest as he saw fit. Back in New York after six months, and having heard nothing about how his investment was doing, he came into the office and asked to see Mr. Ward.

Ferd greeted him warmly enough, but said he could not recall offhand what had happened to his money. The press of business made it impossible for him to remember every little transaction that came along. He was sure his visitor would understand. A little annoyed—$50,000 did not seem like a small transaction to him—the man agreed to wait while Ferdinand retreated to an interior office to check the books.

Moments later, Ferd returned with a broad smile and a check for $250,000. The man insisted there must be some mistake: he had invested just $50,000. No, Ferd assured him, the sum was correct. Sizable returns like that were more or less standard for the customers of his firm.

The investor pocketed the check and emerged onto Wall Street in a pleasant daze. His money had grown five times in six months. If he'd left it with the firm and things continued at that rate, he would be a millionaire by the end of the year. He was too keyed up to sleep that night, and when Grant & Ward opened for business the next day he was waiting outside the door. Ferd smiled as he let him in, took back the check, and made a note of the reinvestment in his books. The investor apologized for giving him so much extra work to do. Think nothing of it, Ferd said. No trouble at all.*

---

* Ferd's technique was not foolproof. "I'm a smarter man than Ferdinand Ward," one young investor told a reporter after the crash.

"My wife who has got more sense than a dozen men, heard about the big profits that Grant & Ward paid their customers and kept at me until I put $500 into their government contracts. Pretty soon I drew out $1,000. Then I put it back and there came out $1,500. Back that went and out came $2,000. This seemed like picking blackberries. Back it went and out it came again, just as natural. . . . It beat any game I ever saw, and I have tried them all. . . . I put it all in again and the bigger it got the more it seemed to grow. . . . At last my $500 had grown to $10,500. Then my wife said, 'Take out that $10,000. It's my speculation and I claim that money. We will have a brown-stone before next Saturday.'

"I told her she was crazy, and I was never so mad at her in my life. She insisted that we should take our profits and leave in the original capital. . . . I felt very sheepish when I called on Grant & Ward for my $10,000. I told Ward his business beat anything that human brain ever conceived, and that I was sorry that I had to take the money; that I thought my wife was about the biggest goose that ever lived; that she didn't know the alphabet of speculation, but that it couldn't be helped. I expressed my determination to leave in the original capital, and promised him that I would never draw it out until he said so."

.   .   .

By the spring of 1883, all of Grant & Ward's alleged profits were said to be coming from government contracts. At least one big contract, he whispered, had been secured personally by President Chester A. Arthur (who had succeeded Garfield after his assassination). General Grant may not have known about the supposed contracts, but it is clear that his sons did and were delighted at what they thought they were earning.* On May 17, 1883, Buck reminded Ferd that "I have some *contract* money coming in today and want to re-invest it. . . . Be a good boy and make some money today, as Mr. Fish says."[16]

Three days later, Fred Grant wrote Ferd, "I will take $50,000 to $55,000 in the new contracts, just as you wish. . . . With love for you and my regards to Mrs. Ward, your friend."[17]

In July, Buck asked Ferdinand to invest in them for him again: "Will send you $3000 more . . . and give me as large an interest on a $35,000 good contract as my finances will cover."†

The Grant sons were clearly discussing the supposed contracts among themselves, they were frequent visitors at their father's home, and, as Fish himself once said, "it does seem strange that the General never heard about them."[18] But Grant seems only to have been dazzled by Ward's ability to make money for his family. Fish remembered making one of his rare visits to the Grant & Ward offices and finding Fred

---

"Has he ever said so?"

"Not yet. He still has got the original capital, but I have been smart enough to beat his game out of $9,500."

"And your wife?"

"Well, she has got the brown-stone."

Boston Daily Globe, June 9, 1884.

* Much later, Buck would claim that in early May 1883, he told Ferd expressly that the firm should have nothing to do with the contract business for fear his father's name might be dragged into it. "Mr. Ward almost shed tears when he thought I would believe he would do anything to the injury of my father," Buck testified. "He said my father's honor was as dear to him as it was to me, and he intended to make the firm . . . a great success and never have any scandal attached to it in anyway." Ferd sounds very like himself in this recollection. But the letters from Buck and his brothers show that they, at least, were knowing and enthusiastic investors in contracts of all kinds. *Chicago Daily Tribune*, November 11, 1887.

† At least one big investor, Captain Elihu Spicer Jr., testified that both Buck Grant and Ferd had personally promised that he would profit handsomely from government contracts. Spicer would lose a quarter of a million dollars when the firm collapsed. *New York Herald*, October 8, 1885.

Grant sitting in the waiting room. He asked the colonel how he was. "I feel grouty," he said. He jerked his thumb at the general, at work behind his desk: "I don't like the way he speaks about Ferd Ward. Last night we were all together—father, mother, Buck and Jesse [and our wives]. Someone said something about Ward, and father said, 'Mother, I'd give anything in this world if our boys were as smart as that young Ward.' Mother said: 'How can you say such things?' "*

James Fish was dazzled, too, so pleased by his earnings that in June 1883, he wrote a note to Ella, on notepaper embossed with a golden bird feathering its own nest.

> Dear Mrs. Ward,
>   I have for a long time been thinking of some present that I could make you—something that you don't already possess.
>   I thought a piano might be acceptable and have directed that one be sent to you at your Stamford home. I hope it will please you. It is only a small return for the many acts of kindness received from you and your husband.
>   Sincerely,
>   your friend
>   James D. Fish[19]

That summer, Ferd and Fish got more good news. If they played their cards right, they could win potentially unprecedented access to a fresh source of big money, the treasury of New York City itself. Millions in municipal funds were on deposit in financial institutions all over town. James Fish had always hoped that his bank's share of them might be enlarged, but before any additional deposits could be made the signatures of two officials were required: the city chamberlain and the comptroller.

J. Nelson Tappan, the longtime chamberlain, was already an ally. The fifty-six-year-old broker had been Fish's friend and business

---

* Others told similar stories about Grant's faith in Ferd. General Horace Porter, an old friend of the general's who now headed the Pullman Company, dropped by his home one afternoon, intending to warn Grant that the revenues from his investments simply seemed too good to be true. But just then Ferd wandered in to report that profits were continuing to rise. The general beamed with pleasure at his prospects. Porter retreated without saying anything. *New York World*, July 2, 1886; Jean Edward Smith, *Grant*, pp. 619–20.

associate for thirty years; he remained a director of his bank, and had begun investing heavily in Grant & Ward's supposed contracts. Tappan understood that the more municipal money the Marine Bank held, the better he himself was likely to do: the value of his stock in the bank would rise and, by deepening the pool of available cash, he would make more money available for loans to Grant & Ward that would help boost its profits as well. But thirty-two New York banks were officially designated depositories, many of them larger than the Marine Bank, whose capital—assets minus liabilities—was less than $400,000. Nevertheless, by the summer of 1883, Tappan had already seen to it that the Marine Bank held $241,000. He dared not try to deposit any more without the active cooperation of the comptroller.

Then, Mayor Franklin Edson named a new man to that office. Edson was himself well disposed toward Ferd and Fish: in addition to running the Produce Exchange when Ward went to work there, he had also served as a director of Fish's bank until he was elected and cut all his ties to private business for the sake of appearances. Whether or not the mayor was deliberately showing favoritism to old friends by his choice for controller, Ferd and Fish couldn't have been more pleased. S. Hastings Grant had been Ferd's immediate boss at the Produce Exchange for six years; he owed his former employee several thousand dollars, and he, too, was already investing in Grant & Ward's contract business. The partners were so eager to have him in office that they put up half the $200,000 bond required so that he could accept the post. "*This,*" Ferd told Fish, "is the biggest thing for us."[20]

It was. Over the next ten months, Tappan and Grant would increase city deposits at the Marine Bank six times, and Fish would permit Ferd to draw upon them again and again to fuel his frantic dealings.

Rumors now spread through the financial world that Ferd was paying profits of 10, sometimes 20 percent a month. No one quite understood it, but virtually everyone wanted to get in on it. The great cartoonist Thomas Nast invested his life's savings in the firm at least nominally headed by the ex-president he had once championed with his pen. So did scores of Union veterans and their widows. William R. Grace, the shipping magnate and former New York mayor, was pleased enough with the profits he made that he asked to become a partner; Ferd turned him away, probably because he wanted no one in the firm who might insist on a real accounting.* Bird W. Spencer, treasurer of the Erie Railroad, did so well investing in the firm on his own that at Ferd's urging he deposited hundreds of thousands of dollars' worth of company bonds in the Marine Bank and assigned their sale to Grant & Ward. Ferd's uncle by marriage, Freeman Clarke, the former comptroller of the currency, was sufficiently impressed by what he'd heard about the firm that he deposited $50,000 of his own money with his nephew.

And at Ferd's urging, Buck Grant talked his father-in-law, former senator Chaffee, into turning over to the firm bonds worth $500,000 on which to raise still more money. "As there were great profits in prospect it would be better to use the money of our friends than to borrow from those for whom we did not care," Buck remembered Ferd telling him; besides, Ferd was now so rich, young Grant told Chaffee, that he would safeguard him against even the possibility of loss.†

Democratic senator Allen G. Thurman of Ohio suggested that since young Ward was "the most successful financier thus far produced" in America, the next president, Democrat or Republican, "would make a stupendous blunder if he did not make Ferdinand Ward Secretary of the Treasury."‡

---

* Grace had proved himself a more demanding investor than most. Missed deadlines and bright promises of bigger profits just around the corner did not satisfy the ex-mayor. "I want to wind up that loan made [to Grant & Ward] a year ago . . . ," he told Ferd in June 1882. "'Tis six months since we were to have wound this up, and now I am *desirous of positively closing it out.*" Ferd did as he was told. Marquis James, *Merchant Adventurer,* pp. 206–07.

† Chaffee himself sometimes worried about how his son-in-law's firm could be doing so well. "I can't imagine how you can make so much and do it safely," he told him, and again, "I am afraid there must be a bad end of this cash business, because I don't see how anybody or anything can pay such interest for the use of money and end well." But the former senator did not ask for his securities back. *New York Times,* December 28, 1884, February 1, 1885.

‡ Now and again, Ferd's exaggerated sense of himself got in his way. One of his early investors, a broker named W. H. Bingham, once challenged him. "See here, Ward, what is there in these contracts?" he asked. How much money was in them? How did it all work? "The relations of General Grant and the firm to the government are of a very delicate nature," Ferd answered. "If I could tell what those relations are I could get millions where you could get [only] thousands." Bingham made no further investments in the firm. *New York Times,* August 24, 1884; *New York Tribune,* May 23, 1884.

.   .   .

Most of those who invested most heavily in Grant & Ward were veterans of Wall Street far older than he, Ferd remembered. But perhaps his most useful individual source of ready cash was a rough contemporary. William S. Warner was the fat, hulking son of a well-known Manhattan merchant. He spoke with the complacent anglophile accent of a wealthy old New York family, but he had failed at everything he'd tried since leaving school. The big dry goods merchant A. T. Stewart had let him go. His own brokerage had done so poorly that he had had to sell his seat on the stock exchange. Now, thanks to his brother-in-law, J. Henry Work, a partner in the law firm Buck Grant had joined when he first came to New York, he had a glorified clerk's post in the Mexican Southern Railroad's office on the floor above Ferd's office. But he had maintained links with the members of his father's well-to-do circle and was still eager to find some way to make money on his own.

One afternoon, Buck Grant brought him downstairs and left him with Ferd. Ward laid out for him the clandestine contract business in which he pretended to be engaged. A project that called upon a contractor to expend a total of, say, $500,000 might require an advance of $100,000 to get under way, he explained. That was where Grant & Ward came in. The big contractors with whom he did business, however, wouldn't even talk with him unless he was willing to provide the entire advance at once. Sometimes that could cause a problem. Ordinarily, the firm had plenty of cash on hand, but it was a fast-moving business, and when Grant & Ward could come up with only, say, half of a big advance on a given day, Ferd was always willing to let a few trusted and discreet investors in on the big profits grateful contractors were willing to provide.

Warner was intrigued. Ferd encouraged him to talk to his friends. He couldn't reveal any details about the numbered contracts, of course, but if they pooled their funds and allowed Warner to invest them with him on their behalf, he could promise remarkable returns. Warner began in late 1882 with an investment of $15,000. Ferd returned it with a profit of $3,750 in just thirty days. Warner came back right away with a larger sum borrowed from friends. It did just as well. Thereafter, he would return several times a month with ever-larger sums that reaped ever-larger profits. He bought himself two grand homes, one on Fifth Avenue; the other in Long Branch, New Jersey. J. Henry Work began collecting money from his friends, too. Ferd insisted on only one thing from Warner and Work: they should bring their business to the office only after hours, when the firm's clerks had gone home. No one else was to know what they were doing; no one else must understand how desperate Ferd was to keep fresh funds flowing in. He began to carry a pencil and a little notebook in which to keep track of how much money he had promised to whom to be delivered when.

At Grand Central Station on the evening of November 15, 1883, Ferd joined a group of seven prominent men aboard the *Ramapo*, the elegantly appointed private railroad car belonging to the president of the Erie Railroad. General Grant and his son Fred were aboard. So were James Fish and three of Grant & Ward's biggest investors: Mayor Edson, City Chamberlain Tappan, and the financier J. R. Smith. Greeting them at the door of the car was their host, the Erie's treasurer and another major investor in the firm, Bird W. Spencer.

He and Ferd had planned the trip. Grant & Ward had an interest in the Bradford, Eldred and Cuba Railroad, a feeder line for the Erie that had recently built the tallest, longest railroad bridge on earth, across Kinzua Creek just south of Bradford, Pennsylvania. At 301 feet high, 2,005 feet long, and built entirely of iron, the Kinzua Viaduct was billed as the "Eighth Wonder of the World" by local boosters, who ran excursion trains out to see it. Ferd and Spencer hoped a well-publicized visit from General Grant would help to increase tourist traffic and maybe promote the sale of some stock, as well.

But as the special train pulled out of the station, Ferd told his fellow passengers that the object of the trip was to provide everyone aboard with a well-deserved good time. This was to be a vacation. Porters would make sure their glasses were full, their cigars lit. Fresh packs of cards would always be available.

Above all, no one was to talk business. Ferd smiled as he said it, but he was deadly serious. Everyone aboard was involved in one way or another with Grant & Ward. Should anyone riding in that car question another about what he knew or didn't know about the shadowy contract business, everything might collapse. And so, as the train rattled along, Ferd moved tirelessly from group to group, asking General Grant to reminisce about battles he had won, encouraging Fish to tell stories about Manhattan business before the Civil War, urging the mayor to talk about the challenges of running City Hall.

Years later, in a rare moment of candor, Ferd would say that this three-day trip to upstate New York had marked the high point of his business career, because he had managed to keep any of his fellow passengers from asking about the behind-the-scenes transactions from which all believed they were benefiting. He lovingly listed the risks he had run so successfully.

> Mr. Fish had invested with Grant & Ward, ... some $2,000,000 which he supposed was in government contracts secured through General Grant, and still all through the trip he never said a word about them to [the general]. Col. F. D. Grant at that time had invested ... some $1,500,000 in city and other contracts, procured through the influence of Mayor Edson and J. N. Tappan, and still he never mentioned the fact to either gentleman throughout the trip. J. Nelson Tappan ... had invested some $300,000 in government contracts which he supposed were secured through the influence of General Grant and his sons and still he never mentioned the fact to the General or any member of his party. Mr. B. W. Spencer had some $300,000 invested in the same way, and still said nothing. ... J. R. Smith, ... too, remained silent, though he had $100,000 invested. So ... here were a party of eight gentlemen who were travelling together for some four days on the closest social terms, five of whom had invested some $4,000,000 at some 10 to 20% per month in a business which they supposed was procured and sanctioned by others of the same party, and still not a word was said by one to the other about the business.[21]

The visit to the Kinzua Viaduct proved anticlimactic. Heavy snow blanketed the landscape. The general got down from the train, bundled in a greatcoat, cigar jutting from his jaw. Gripping the handrail to keep from slipping on the snowy wooden walkway that ran alongside the tracks, he led the little party out onto the towering bridge. When he reached the middle he stopped and gazed down at the whitened valley for a time. Shivering in the cold wind, everyone waited to hear what he thought of it all. "Judas priest!" he finally said. "How high we are!" His fellow passengers quickly agreed and followed him back to the warmth of the *Ramapo*.

The special train pulled into Rochester the next afternoon. Union veterans lined the platform to cheer their old commander, just as they had at every small-town depot along the way. The passengers made their way through the crowd of well-wishers and climbed into carriages that were to take them to the Rochester Club. There, Ferd's cousin, the banker Levi F. Ward, was to host a formal luncheon. Ferd's uncle Freeman Clarke was among the waiting guests. So was Ferd's proud father, who had come to town that morning from Geneseo. The Wards of Rochester had often treated Ferd's branch of the family as poor relations, as his mother never tired of pointing out; they had not been willing to give Ferd a job in Rochester when he needed one, nor had they thought it worth their while to attend his wedding. Now they had to watch as he took his place at the head table with his business partner, the former president of the United States. His once-dismissive relatives now had to admit that he really did belong among the rich and influential men whose company he'd sought from the moment he moved to New York, that he really was what other investors were now calling him, the newest "Young Napoleon of Wall Street."*

Later that month, George Alfred Townsend, a much-admired business reporter for the *Philadelphia Inquirer*, interviewed Ferd and Fish about their apparent success. Ferd was just thirty-two years old, he wrote, but already "one of the phenomenal young men in [New York]" who has "kept the confidence of every employer and friend he began with."[22]

Ferd was eager to assure potential investors of his caution and reliability. Grant & Ward was a "quiet house," he claimed, wary of Wall Street's risks, interested in "investments rather than speculation."[23] That, he said, was why the powerful Erie Railroad permitted the firm to handle its brokerage operations and the city of New York was happy to have it take care of so much of its fiscal business. But he also wanted readers to know that he was constantly in search of what he called

---

* Bird Spencer was so grateful to Ferd for helping to organize the trip—and for the opportunities Grant & Ward had given him to make money for himself—that on Ferd's thirty-second birthday, a week after the railroad excursion ended, he had delivered to his home in Brooklyn a cane with a silver handle from Tiffany's. It was marked with the date—November 21, 1883—and featured Spencer's own initials. It was fashioned in the shape of the head of a long-beaked bird, a pun on Spencer's first name. Author's collection.

"energetic communities," which were interested in improving themselves and willing to put up the money to make it happen. To that end,
he was already working to provide gas lighting to the people of his
own hometown of Geneseo, had helped underwrite a new salt mine in
Warsaw, New York, and was president of companies that were going to
provide clean drinking water to the Kansas City suburbs of Wyandotte
and Armourdale.

Fish spoke of his partner's "sagacity," his remarkable ability to make
money for himself and for the firm: "I hardly suppose [Ward] was
worth over $1500 [when I first knew him]. Today he is worth a million
and a half [almost $33 million in modern terms]. He has a magnificent
home at Stamford, and is one of the active young fellows of our day."[24]

Ferd returned the compliment. "[Mr. Fish] has been a uniformly
kind man, his advice sound," he said. "I attribute all my success to him
alone."

What made the banker such an effective partner?

His "decision" as well as his "caution and conservatism," Ferd
answered. "I generally make propositions for business to him, and
he almost always puts himself in opposition for a little while, . . . not
merely for obstinacy but to bring out the truth."[25]

But it was revenues, not truth, that mattered most to the partners
of Grant & Ward. "I think we have made more money during the past
year than any house in Wall Street," General Grant told Fish, "perhaps
in the city."[26] Grant assured his wife in December that she no longer
needed to worry about saving money for their children. "Ward is making us all rich—them as well as ourselves," he said—so rich he thought
it might be a nice gesture to buy "comfortable little homes" for a few
of their old friends.[27] "The necessity of strict economy does not exist,"
he assured his daughter, Nellie, that same month, and as if to prove it,
he sent each of his four granddaughters a Christmas gift of $2,500.[28]

James Fish was generous at holiday time, too, transferring to five of
his children some $100,000 worth of Manhattan real estate.

In Brooklyn, Ferd ordered the Green family coupe heaped with so
many brightly wrapped gifts it took nearly an hour for the servants at
Monroe Place to unload them, carry them into the parlor, and arrange
them all around the tree.

Christmas of 1883 also brought a rich harvest of gifts to the Geneseo parsonage. All three children seemed to be doing well now, and
all had been generous with their parents. "Not one indifferent or val-

ueless thing," Jane noted in a letter to Sarah, "and so indicative of the most thoughtful and generous kindness. Surely there was no 'dark side' for me to look at."

But it was Ferd's "princely" generosity, Jane continued, that made the holiday so memorable: an elegant black silk dress with jet trimming, *two* pairs of gloves, she reported, *two* bottles of cologne, *two* boxes of guava jelly, *two* painted china pitchers, and "five photographs of paintings," including "one of that expensive painting [Ferd] has, 'Christ Raising Jairus' Daughter,' each 10 inches by 8 inches."

That evening, the old couple spread their gifts before the fire in the second-story study of the old Session House, which adjoined their home—itself Ferd's gift to his father—so that neighbors and former parishioners might drop by and admire them. They were there, talking quietly with friends, when the doorbell rang. It was Will Shepard, a young lawyer friend of Ferd's, home from New York. He came in, stomping snow from his boots, and climbed the stairs to the warm study. He had an envelope for each of the elder Wards, he said. He wished them a Merry Christmas and hurried on his way.

When he had gone, they tore open the envelopes. Each held a thousand-dollar check from Ferd ($22,000 today). Jane wept with happiness, she said, and "even Father shed tears of grateful joy."[29]

ELEVEN

The End Has Come

On March 11, 1884, in Brooklyn, Ella Ward gave birth to a healthy baby boy. She and Ferd named him Ferdinand Grant Ward, after his father and his grandfather and for the general and ex-president whose great name seemed to be making a reality of what Ferd's mother would call her son's "life-long disposition to be rich."[1] General Grant himself was said to be especially pleased the boy was to bear his name: Ferdinand Ward, he continued to tell anyone who asked about him, was the ablest young businessman he'd ever met.

But two days after the baby was born, Ferd quietly transferred the title to 81 Pierrepont Street to his brother-in-law Sidney Green, for a dollar. And Green, in turn, put the house in the name of his sister, still recovering from childbirth in her upstairs bedroom. Ferd already knew what was coming, even if no one else did. Grant & Ward was insolvent; it had been almost from the beginning but never on such a massive scale. Angry creditors would soon crowd in on all Ferd's assets. By transferring his home to his wife he hoped at least to be able to keep a roof over their heads.

Outwardly, he continued to live his life as though nothing had changed. He and Ella attended a performance by the Jewell Brothers, illusionists, at the Brooklyn Club; they loaned several canvases to a fund-raising exhibition for Bartholdi's Statue of Liberty; and presented a gray wolf and several other stuffed animals to the Long Island Historical Society, all purchased from his cousin Henry A. Ward's Natural Science Establishment in Rochester.

But since the first of the year, Ferd had been working at an ever-more-frenzied pace to stave off disaster. He grew still thinner, still more pale, and seemed always on the move, racing between his office, the Marine Bank, and the offices of investors and city officials all over southern Manhattan. An old friend visited James D. Fish at his bank early that year and watched Ferd dash in, rush up to the cashier's desk, sign something, and then race back out again, too distracted to speak to anyone. "I wouldn't lose my nervous temperament like that young man for all his money," the visitor said.

The banker disagreed. "Ah," he said, "that is a great man; that is a very great man."[2]

Fish still believed in his young partner's extraordinary ability as a businessman: the steady stream of revenues he had received each month since 1880—at least $585,000 in all ($13.2 million today)—was all the evidence he needed. But he remained concerned about Ferd's methods and the damage they might do to the reputation of the bank. For more than three years now, he had been playing hide-and-seek with the national bank examiner, permitting Ferd to hold on to securities so that Grant & Ward could raise more funds with them, provided he got them back into their loan envelopes at the bank in time for the quarterly inspection. It had always been his hope that the need for such loans would lessen as the contract business in which he believed Grant & Ward was specializing grew. Instead, it seemed steadily to increase. The firm's account with the bank rose and fell alarmingly: one day that winter Grant & Ward had $4,365 in the bank, the next it was overdrawn by $145,547, and the following morning it was well into positive territory again. Fish's exasperation sometimes showed. "I suppose we can stand it a day longer," he had written Ferd at one point toward the end of 1883, "but I am afraid there is trouble ahead. . . . If you know of some acceptable man who wants to be President of a small bank down the street, I can find a place for him."[3]

He hadn't meant it—the bank was his life's work—but he did fret. At any moment, one or another of the bank's directors might challenge a loan made to Grant & Ward and ruin everything. There were fifteen directors, including Fish, an amiable, easygoing group who often did business with one another outside the bank and were not prone to questioning each other's actions. Most attended the twice-weekly meetings largely because after an hour or so of formalities they were treated to a long, leisurely lunch at Delmonico's.

Still, Fish took no chances. Among the directors, he and City Chamberlain Tappan could already be counted on to give Grant & Ward the benefit of any doubt, but when the annual election of directors came up on January 11, 1884, Fish made sure that Buck Grant, Bird Spencer of the Erie Railroad, and Ferd himself were all also voted onto the board. To better the odds against raising suspicion still further, Fish also saw to it that Ferd was appointed to the committee that met every three months to ensure that loans were backed by suitable collateral, with all the securities tucked neatly into their envelopes. Ward was a "very active" member of that committee, one director recalled, much "quicker than the rest of us in handling the securities."[4]

Even that was not enough. The firm needed far more money from the bank than it could ever legitimately justify, and so, on February 15, Fish had called his loan clerk, Nathan Daboli, into his office and asked him to shut the door behind him. Ferd was already inside and did all the talking. Over the next few weeks, he said, the Marine Bank would be making a series of loans that would require what he called "special handling." The bank records were to show that Grant & Ward had deposited securities to cover each of them, but in reality the firm would continue to hold on to the paper. He explained that Grant & Ward was engaged in so many businesses simultaneously, decisions had to be made so quickly, and large sums had to be raised so fast that it was necessary to keep good securities readily to hand. Mr. Daboli was a man of the world; surely he could understand that. In any case, he needn't worry: the loans were to be paid back from the millions Grant & Ward was making by the purchase of government contracts—transactions that, of course, were never to be discussed outside the office. All he needed to do was bring them to Mr. Fish for his approval.

Daboli did as he was told. Over the next two months, Fish would grant loans from the Marine Bank totaling $375,000—$4.6 million today—to eight individuals: Buck Grant; Will Ward; Ella Ward's brother, Fred Green; the firm's clerks Walter H. Mallory and George E. Spencer; Edward E. Doty, Ferd's friend and sometime assistant from Geneseo; and Charles H. Armstrong, the former Pullman porter who called himself Ferd's "private secretary" because he was entrusted with carrying his canvas satchel filled with paper securities and sup-posed contracts back and forth between the office and the bank. None of them ever saw a penny. All the money went to Grant & Ward—and much of it went from there to Ferd's personal account.

After hours, he continued to collect large sums from William War-ner and his blind pool of rich friends, as well. He was so desperate to have their money he began allowing Warner to dictate the percentage of profit he would get when the notes came due. "When Warner once got twenty per cent a month," Ferd remembered, "he never would take less."[5] During March and April alone, Ward would write eighteen checks to his shadowy visitor, totaling $943,166, and two more, total-ing $50,000, to Warner's brother-in-law J. Henry Work. All twenty represented large advances returned along with exorbitant interest.

Ferd borrowed from major institutions as well as private individu-als—$4,650,000 from four big trust companies and the Equitable Life Assurance Society between January 28 and April 25. Each loan was for six months at a high rate of interest. At least one also involved an addi-tional off-the-record payment by Ferd to the executive who agreed to let him have the money.

He continued to dangle new contracts in front of potential inves-tors, too. He and Fish had begun negotiations to purchase a rocky island off the Maine coast, he told them; the federal government planned a sprawling Romanesque-style post office in Brooklyn; thanks to Grant & Ward's connections, the firm was guaranteed to win the multimillion-dollar contract to clothe it with granite, and the part-ners wanted to increase their profits by being able to quarry their own island. Ferd was already peddling municipal revenue bonds to pay for construction of a new aqueduct to bring additional water to the growing city from the Croton Reservoir, and he also began talking up another, far more lucrative scheme to tap the Ramapo watershed in the Catskills. Because "certain members" of the commission looking into improving the city's water supply were "associated with the firm," he said, "we [will] complete the contract . . . receive $35 million," and earn "a certain profit of 17 million."*

---

* The figures Ferd used were, as usual, wholly imaginary, but in this case real profits seem to have been at least possible. In January of 1881, six New Yorkers had burned to death in a fire that engulfed the seven-story Potter Building on Park Row. Fire-men blamed low water pressure for their inability to put out flames on the upper floors. A consortium of insurance underwriters and dry goods merchants, worried that

.   .   .

The unsecured loans made to Ferd by the Marine Bank, the sums advanced by William Warner and his voracious friends, and the moneys borrowed from financial institutions and advanced by individuals eager to get in on the contracts that Ferd described so vividly all helped Grant & Ward stay in business. But Ferd and Fish were now relying most heavily on the unique and illicit arrangement they had worked out with Comptroller Grant and Chamberlain Tappan to tap directly into municipal funds.

The mutually beneficial scheme that Ferd and Fish, Tappan and Grant worked out together in early 1884 was simple. Grant was authorized to issue 3 percent municipal revenue bonds to pay city expenses in anticipation of taxes to be collected during the current year. Ferd turned up at his office from time to time to purchase them in large numbers—$7,450,000 worth between January 1 and May 2, 90 percent of all the bonds issued by the comptroller's office during that period. The law required that he pay for them with certified checks. But Grant—who would eventually invest at least $320,000 of his own money in Grant & Ward's supposed contracts ($7,220,000 today)—made Ferd's purchases as painless as possible. He was allowed to pay each bill with several Marine Bank checks certified by Fish, some of which would then be deposited back into the Marine Bank. He did

---

Manhattan buildings were sure to go still higher, proposed to increase water pressure in the city by bringing water down from the mountains by gravity alone. Mayor Edson appointed a two-man committee to look into it. One member was Comptroller S. Hastings Grant. Both he and the mayor may initially have been inclined to favor the scheme. Ferd had worked closely with both of them; each had profited personally from that friendship. But on May 7, 1885, just as the decision was due to be made, Grant & Ward collapsed. Less than two weeks later, Comptroller Grant joined his fellow commissioner in advising against the Ramapo scheme on the grounds that it would be too costly, take too long to complete, and leave the city's water supply in the hands of private speculators. Edson quickly accepted the committee's recommendation. Whether the decision was affected by the potential embarrassment of having the press uncover Ferd's role behind the scenes if the go-ahead had been given, no one will ever know.

In 1899, a similar scheme was proposed by another private syndicate—and was rejected for the same reasons. In 1905, the state legislature finally created a public board of water supply empowered to acquire land and begin construction. Twelve years later, New Yorkers in all five boroughs were drinking and bathing in water from the Catskills. *Proceedings by New York (N.Y.) Sinking Fund Commissioners*; Ferdinand Ward, "General Grant an Easy Prey for the Wolves of Finance."

so seven times between January 1 and March 29, 1884, for a total of $954,000.

When other investors turned up at Grant's office interested in buying bonds, the comptroller's subordinates were instructed to tell them they would have to go to Grant & Ward's to make their purchases. The comptroller's deputy would one day be asked whether rival would-be purchasers had ever complained. They had, he said: "They had been customers a long time [and] thought it rather hard to turn them off and send them to brokers' offices."[6] Ferd always did his cheerful best to make potential customers welcome at 2 Wall Street.

Even with the collusion of the city's top financial officials, Ferd found it more and more difficult to satisfy creditors like William Warner who insisted he make good on his gaudy pledges, on time and in full. When Ferd and Warner began their murky after-hours transactions, Ferd had been firmly in charge and Warner simply grateful to be making such remarkable returns on funds borrowed from his friends. But as the months went by, their positions had slowly reversed. Ferd needed more and more money to stay ahead of his investors and was forced to promise more and more to get it. It now took just twenty days for a $20,000 investment to grow to $36,000; $433,000 became $519,000 in only thirty days; a month after that saw $450,000 become $540,000.

Grant & Ward's balance was so erratic that Ferd often did not have the cash on hand to make good on Warner's largest investments. Whenever that happened, he now offered a new arrangement: to keep Warner from demanding his money, he would guarantee delivery of the matured principal by a new date but would also pay Warner 20 percent per month *in addition*. On a single loan of $640,000 that would not mature until October 1884, for example, Ferd had to find $125,000 every thirty days to satisfy Warner and his friends. Warner, not Ward, was now in control of their relationship.

By the end of March, both Ferd and Fish were feeling desperate. "If this goes on this way," Fish told Ferd, "the situation will not only be serious but dangerous."[7] Four days later, he wrote to Ferd again. "Do you know that your account is overdrawn $80,000 this morning? Our affairs seem to be drifting entirely beyond my understanding or comprehension."[8]

Then, Chamberlain Tappan suffered a heart attack. His doctors urged him to sail for Bermuda to see if a month's rest there would restore his health. While he was gone, Ferd returned four times to the comptroller's office. He bought a total of $2.5 million in revenue bonds during those visits—and, with Grant's approval, the city of New York deposited a million more dollars in the Marine Bank in four installments, each deposit made on the same day the bonds changed hands.

By April 25, thanks to Comptroller Grant and with the acquiescence of the absent Tappan, Grant & Ward was able to borrow against some $6 million worth of municipal bonds and the Marine Bank was holding $1.6 million in city funds ($36,100,000 today). This was more than twice as much as any other depository in the city—so much more that Isaac S. Barrett, a veteran clerk in the comptroller's office who had several times expressed concern about the growing imbalance, finally felt compelled to intervene. "There's no use talking, Mr. Grant," he told his boss. "There is altogether too much money in that bank."[9]

Grant reluctantly agreed. People were beginning to ask why the city favored one bank and one brokerage house over all the rest, and he had no ready answer. Municipal funds—and his own reputation—were at risk. Something had to be done.

J. Nelson Tappan returned from Bermuda two days later. He was still so weak that he had to be carried off the ship. His deputy (and brokerage partner) F. W. Gilley, who met him at the dock, remembered that Tappan "expressed no surprise" at the amount of city money in the bank of which he was a director. But not long after he was put to bed at his home on Lexington Avenue, Comptroller Grant got word to him that there was serious trouble, and that the Marine Bank's holdings had to be reduced—and quickly.

On Thursday, May 1, the city withdrew $300,000.

The next day, Friday the 2nd, Fish got a second letter from the chamberlain's office, signed by Deputy Chamberlain Richard W. Montgomery on behalf of his ailing boss.

> Mr. Tappan finds it necessary . . . to draw on the Marine Bank an additional $300,000, and we have notified them of the draft for that amount on Monday [May 5], to come through the Clearing House Tuesday A.M.* We regret the necessity, and

---

* The New York Clearing House, established in 1853, centralized banking activity in the city. Checks representing tens of millions of dollars were exchanged there each morning and accounts were kept to insure the financial health of each participating institution.

if unexpected receipts should make it possible to diminish the draft will be glad to do so. As the account of receipts and payments now stands, the draft is unavoidable.[10]

Several million dollars in Grant & Ward loans were to come due on Monday. Ferd's ability to continue drawing on the Marine Bank now represented the difference between life and death for the firm, which had been overdrawn between $80,000 and $115,000 nearly every day for the previous two weeks. If further city funds were withdrawn and could not be replaced by matching sums from some other source, the bank would go under. Ferd had been scurrying after money for weeks. Now, he became frenzied.

Ferd first thought he would try Comptroller Grant one more time. He wrote two checks totaling a million dollars and took them to Fish to certify. Fish hesitated: Grant & Ward was now overdrawn by more than half a million dollars. Ferd tried to reassure him. It was only a momentary problem, he said; besides, he claimed, the firm still had a million and a half in negotiable securities as collateral. Fish said he would certify the checks—the crisis was too grave for him not to try to help—but he insisted that Ward bring all of the securities to the bank before the close of business that day.

Ward raced to City Hall, bought more bonds, and then pleaded with the controller to countermand the chamberlain's action: the Marine Bank needed more city money, not less. This time, Grant said he was powerless to help: it was all up to Mr. Tappan, and Tappan was too ill to see anyone.

Ferd returned to his office and fired off a message to Deputy Chamberlain Montgomery. "I had a talk with the Controller," he wrote, "and he said that he was perfectly agreeable to anything the Chamberlain did. . . . I want you, if possible, to put $100,000 or $200,000 in the Marine Bank today until Monday, as I have sold lots of bonds to be delivered [then]. Let me know what you can do."[11]

Montgomery refused to do anything.

Things were falling apart. Ferd hurried back to the bank, with Charles Armstrong struggling along behind, carrying the canvas satchel supposedly filled with the securities Fish had demanded to see. Ferd's nerves were beginning to fray. He stalked into his partner's office. "*There!*" he said, in what Fish remembered as "a very petulant" tone. "There are over $1,400,000 worth of securities in there, and I hope you're satisfied."[12]

Ward had Armstrong loudly drop the bag in a corner of the directors' room next door. Then he called Nathan Daboli over. "This belongs to *me*," he said, "and I'll want it when I come for it."[13] About an hour later, he and Armstrong quietly returned and took the satchel away again. No one ever bothered to look inside to see what it actually contained.

The next morning, Fish pleaded with Ferd: "Get in all [the money] you can and hope to see better days."[14] It was Saturday. Ferd wrote eleven more checks, ostensibly to his employees, but in fact so that he could pay Warner and at least some of the other investors clamoring for their money. The checks totaled $796,112. The firm was now overdrawn by $392,000. Funds were still flowing out. None were coming in.

"I have arranged with a party up-town for a loan of $200,000," Ward assured Fish that evening, "but I will not get the check till I get to his house tonight. I will however be able to deposit it by 9:00 Monday morning."[15]

Fish did not know it, but the uptown investor, like the government contracts in which he still believed, was imaginary.

On Sunday afternoon, the doorbell of the Grant townhouse on East Sixty-sixth Street rang. A maid opened the door. It was Ferdinand Ward, hat in hand. Might he speak to the general?

He was ushered into the dark, crowded parlor. Buck Grant was home too. Both he and his father were always glad to see Ferd. He rarely turned up uninvited, and when he did he usually brought good news: an unexpected dividend or a quick Wall Street turn that had benefited the firm—and fattened the Grants' finances.

Not this time. Ferd was soft-spoken and deferential, as always. But there was a problem. The Marine Bank was in trouble. The city had unexpectedly withdrawn city funds. The bank was now running on its reserves.

The general was sorry to hear it. But what business was it of his?

"We have $660,000 on deposit there," Ferd answered, "and it would embarrass us very much if the bank should close its doors."

"They're good for it, aren't they?" Buck asked.[16]

Of course they were—no worries on that score, Fred said. But it would take time before Grant & Ward had access to its money again. And that could cause problems as its loans came due.

Ferd had plenty of securities in the firm's vault, he said, and he had already raised $230,000 on his own. (In fact, he'd been turned down flat by Stephen B. Elkins and others earlier in the day.) But he hoped General Grant might be able to borrow another $150,000 right away. For appearance's sake, the check needed to be dated Saturday. It would only be needed for twenty-four hours, in any case, long enough for the bank to call in a host of outstanding loans that would return it to solvency.

That might not be easy on a Sunday afternoon, Buck said.

True enough, Ferd replied. "But I know the General can borrow it if anyone can."[17]

Getting around was not easy for General Grant these days. He had slipped on the ice in front of his house on Christmas Eve and badly reinjured his left leg, initially damaged when his horse fell on him after the Battle of Vicksburg. He was still leaning heavily on crutches, but he called for his hat and hobbled out into the street. Ferd and Buck trailed along behind and joined him in his carriage.

They clattered south along Central Park and entered Manhattan's most fashionable neighborhood, Fifth Avenue in the fifties. H. Victor Newcomb, president of the United States National Bank, lived in a handsome house at 683 Fifth Avenue at Fifty-third Street. The general considered him a friend—Grant served on his board of directors—and thought he'd try him first. While Ferd and Buck waited in the cab, the ex-president got down, made his halting way up to the door, and rang the bell. The banker wasn't home.

Grant wasn't sure to whom to go next. Ferd suggested William H. Vanderbilt. His newly built turreted palace stood just one block south, between Fifty-first and Fifty-second streets. Seven hundred men had worked on it for more than two years; 250 of them had done nothing but carve the interiors of its fifty-eight rooms. The house was so overstuffed with art that when its proud owner paid to publish a book detailing its contents, two volumes were needed just to list them all.

Grant did not know Vanderbilt well, but he was master of a railroad fortune estimated at more than $200 million ($4.5 billion today). It would do no harm to ask. While Ferd waited in the cab, a startled butler led the general and his son into the parlor, its walls and coffered sixteen-foot ceiling tricked out in gilt, crystal, and mother-of-pearl.

Grant explained why he was making this unannounced and embarrassing visit. Vanderbilt was as blunt as he was rich. He could not recall ever having made a personal loan to anyone, he said. It was not good business. "I care nothing about the Marine Bank. To tell the truth, I care very little about Grant & Ward. But to accommodate you personally I will draw my check for the amount you ask. I consider it a personal loan to you, and not to any other party."[18]

General Grant promised to have the money back to him in a day or two. He, Buck, and Ferd rode uptown together as far as Sixty-sixth Street, where the general sent for a pen and endorsed the check over to Grant & Ward.

Ferd pocketed the check and climbed back into his own coupe. Everything would be all right now, he assured the Grants. They needn't be concerned.

That evening, he wrote a note to Stephen Elkins. Thanks to his own efforts and some money Fish had allegedly raised separately, the bank would survive, he said. "I shall see," he vowed, "that that institution does not get into such a fix again. I can run my own business, but I cannot take care of other people's."[19] He was not to blame for anything that was about to happen; all the fault lay with James Fish and the Marine Bank.

The Marine Bank opened its doors as usual at ten the following morning. Ferd was first in line at the window of the teller, John H. Carr. He handed over the Vanderbilt check with a flourish. It was "gilt-edged," he said, because it bore the signature of the railroad millionaire on one side and was endorsed on the other by Ulysses S. Grant. It went into his personal account. He turned as if to leave, then came back to ask a little favor. Over the weekend, he said, he had deposited an uncertified check drawn on his account at the First National Bank for $80,000 to cover a transaction that had subsequently been canceled. He asked that it therefore not be sent to the Clearing House, where all of the city's bank transactions were settled every morning. The teller told him he was sorry, but it was too late. The bank's cashier, John Fish, had already certified a check on the Marine Bank against it. Ferd seemed "very anxious" that the certified check not be used, Carr recalled. Together, they went to see James Fish. He and Ferd conferred in low tones. "Well, John," Fish finally said, "Mr. Ward says it is all right and I suppose it is."[20] He ordered the teller to withdraw the check from the exchange. Ferd thanked him, promised he would bring in a great deal more money by the end of the day, and hurried out.

As he left, he ran into James Fish's brother and chief cashier Benjamin on the front steps. "I have just deposited old Vanderbilt's check for $150,000." Ferd said. "How's that? We're all right now."[21]

They were not all right, and Ferd knew it. The transaction that Ferd said had been canceled had actually gone forward. Within a few minutes the certified check came back, already paid and charged to the Marine Bank. Fish called Ferd on the telephone line that linked their two offices. Ferd expressed astonishment. Clearly, there had been some stupid mix-up, he said; he was very busy just then, but he would come down and sort things out as soon as he could.

After lunch, Benjamin Fish brought his brother evidence of another troubling transaction. Ferd had deposited his own uncertified check for $75,000, drawn on the First National Bank, and then, before it could clear, had written William S. Warner a check for $71,800.

Again, Fish telephoned his partner. What was going on?

"Those checks are all right," Ferd said. "The money is at the First National, and the $75,000 will be paid."[22] But the money was not at the First National; Ferd had less than $2,000 in his account there. Yet before the day was over he would write a total of $215,000 worth of checks against it.

"I have secured a loan of $250,000 from a private investor up-town and will take the securities up to him to get a check," he told Fish in a scrawled note meant to reassure him. "But I may not get to the bank until late in the afternoon."[23]

Fish waited for him until five o'clock. Ferd never turned up and when he couldn't be found at the Grant & Ward office either, Fish set off for Brooklyn in search of him. He wasn't home. Fish left a note insisting that Ferd come to his flat that evening, then returned to the city to wait.

Ferd was in Prospect Park, taking Ella for a long, quiet carriage ride. It is impossible to know how much or how little Ella knew about what her husband had been doing for the past few years. She was aware that he was often anxious, hypochondriacal, and not always truthful; she had learned all that during their courtship, with its odd stops and starts. But for all his foibles, he had managed to provide her with an extraordinary life: two opulently furnished homes and a grand summer hotel, staffs of servants, a circle of acquaintances that included not only other up-and-coming young couples in Brooklyn and Manhattan and Stamford but celebrated figures, including the ex-president of the

United States. And now they had an infant son, less than two months old. Just a week earlier, Ferd had bought for Ella several thousand dollars' worth of diamonds at Tiffany's in apparent celebration of the birth of their child, and as an early gift for her thirty-second birthday, now just three days away.

Ferd knew that most of the world he had created for her was about to vanish. How much he told her about what was about to happen or the real reasons for the coming disaster as they drove together beneath the big shade trees no one will ever know.

They got home just after dark. Ferd wrote two more letters and ordered them to be hand-delivered to Fish and Buck Grant. "I will get two hundred-and-fifty-thousand dollars checks tonight if possible," he assured his older partner, though he had no real prospects of making good on that promise. "Am doing my best to put matters through and make [the] bank easy. I am not leaving a stone unturned."[24]

With Buck he was more frank. "I am very much afraid that the end has come," he wrote, "and that unless something is done tonight everything will be over tomorrow. Now take it cool, old boy, and don't get excited, but remember that we don't want our names to go down, and we will fight before it comes." He listed securities allegedly on hand, adding up to $1,323,700, and urged Buck to return to Mr. Vanderbilt that evening and see if he could get half a million dollars more on the promise of $800,000 or $900,000 worth of them. The check was needed by morning; the securities could be delivered to Vanderbilt the next afternoon.

> I am going to start out myself and see several men and may be able to do something—so go right at it, Buck, and remember that if it is not done it will be the end of our business career. This is the last [withdrawal] Mr. Tappan will have to make, but if we don't pay this $500,000 tonight it will be our last blow. I will be down sometime during the night, for I shall go everywhere, so send me word what you succeed in doing, and if you get a check send it over by a messenger. Mr. Vanderbilt can draw on the Chemical bank if he wants to. We must have the loan for 10 days, anyway, till we can get the bank straight. I am going to several bank men myself and will be home late, so don't try and find me, but try to get all you can.
>
> This is our last hope, Buck, so do all you can.[25]

Ferd did not "go everywhere," as he had promised Buck he would; nor did he track down "several bank men." Instead of knocking on more doors, he strolled over to the Brooklyn Club, sat quietly in its reading room until it closed, then returned home and got ready for bed. The end had come as he had feared, and he was powerless to do anything about it.

Buck Grant did not return to William Vanderbilt's home in search of more money, either. But he did remember that Grant & Ward had $50,000 worth of bonds belonging to his father-in-law, Jerome Chaffee. If the firm really was in trouble, he wanted them back. With his wife and Stephen Elkins, who was acting as Chaffee's counsel, he climbed into a carriage and headed for Brooklyn. Ella greeted them. Ferd wasn't home yet, she said. She directed the servants to set out wine and slices of cake for them to enjoy while they waited. Ferd entered the room well after midnight. He was sorry, he said, he had been all over New York trying to raise more money for the Marine Bank. Sadly, he'd had no luck. All three men agreed the bank would have to take care of itself. Grant & Ward would ride things out on its own.

But, Elkins said, for the time being at least, he wished to have his client secured and therefore wanted his bonds handed back to him. Ferd said he'd be glad to turn them over, but "I don't see the need. Senator Chaffee can have his money at any time on demand."[26]

Elkins insisted. Very well, then, Ferd said, Chaffee's bonds were in a strongbox at the office. He'd meet Buck and Elkins there first thing in the morning and hand them over. They could keep them until things calmed down.

It was nearly three o'clock in the morning when the visitors climbed back into their carriage. Young Grant was relieved. But Elkins was troubled: "The whole thing is suspicious," he said. "Did you observe he had his slippers on? He was in the house all the time. And was afraid to come down and see us."[27]

Just as he had most weekday mornings since 1880, James Fish boarded the Wall Street Ferry shortly after six on Tuesday, May 6, and headed for Brooklyn. He had heard nothing from his partner since the scrawled note he'd received the previous evening, and had slept only fitfully in his room above the bank that night. Ella met him at the door. He had to see Ferd at once, he said. She said her husband had been out late and was still asleep. Fish insisted. They argued back and forth for a minute or two. Finally, he pushed past Ella and started up the staircase. By the time he reached the second floor, Ferd's bedroom was empty—he had taken advantage of the argument to race down the back stairs and out the basement door. The maid he had rushed past said he hadn't told her where he was going.

Fish put his hat on and went back to Wall Street to face the coming disaster alone.

The directors gathered at the Marine Bank at ten thirty for their regularly scheduled Tuesday meeting. Everything seemed normal, though some at the table thought it odd that neither President Fish nor young Ward was present.

Ferd wasn't at his office, either. Buck and Stephen Elkins asked George Spencer where he was. He didn't know—he had stopped by Ward's house on the way to work, he said, and found Mrs. Ward in tears. Her husband was missing. He'd left a note saying only that the Marine Bank was going to fail today and he would not be home. She feared he might kill himself.

Elkins called for the key to the strongbox. Spencer said Ferd had it. The attorney sent for a hammer and chisel and broke open the box. Most of Senator Chaffee's bonds were missing.

Meanwhile, Fish had gone to the Clearing House with a bag full of cash and a big bundle of the bank's securities, hoping somehow to borrow enough money from his fellow bankers to make up for what was now a $900,000 shortfall, due almost entirely to unsupported checks written by Ferd on behalf of Grant & Ward. Fish was "acting like a man dazed with fright," the Clearing House president remembered.[28] The sum he needed was simply too large. The Marine Bank, to which he'd given thirty-one years of his life, would have to suspend operations.

At the bank, the directors' meeting broke up at eleven o'clock. Ten minutes later, a janitor pulled down the iron shutters and locked the door. A crowd of baffled depositors began to grow outside, eventually closing off both Broadway and Wall Street. Customers banged on the door. Rumors swept the financial district. The bank was wrecked. So was Grant & Ward. "My God," one man in the stunned crowd said, "if that's true, I'm ruined."[29] The stock market plunged 3 percent overnight. Within ten days, the survival of two other New York banks would be in question, in each case because of misdeeds by their own corrupt officers.* Several major brokerage house and banks in Newark and Pittsburgh and elsewhere collapsed. A brief but unsettling panic followed, caused, said the *Commercial & Financial Chronicle*, by "a complete loss of confidence . . . in the stability and soundness of various institutions and firms."[30] No one had done more to undermine that confidence than James D. Fish and Ferdinand Ward.

At around noon on the day of the crash, General Grant turned up at 2 Wall Street. The crowd of curiosity seekers that now filled the street fell silent and parted so that he could make his way inside. Newspapermen had already stationed themselves in the hall and reception room of Grant & Ward. A young financial reporter named Alexander Noyes never forgot seeing the general arrive:

> The outer door slammed open. It admitted General Grant, followed by his Negro servant. Moving rapidly across the room on crutches . . . the general looked neither to right or left. He made for his partner's private office, unaware that [he wasn't] there. . . . As he moved across the room . . . he held tightly clutched between his lips a cigar that had gone out. Nobody followed him, or spoke to him but everyone in the cynical "hard-boiled" group took off his hat. It was not so much a tribute of respect to a former Chief Magistrate as spontaneous recognition of the immense personal tragedy which was enacting itself before our eyes.[31]

Buck was waiting for him behind Ferd's office door.
  "Well, Buck, how is it?" he asked.

---

* On May 14, a week after the collapse of Grant & Ward and the Marine Bank, there was a run on the Second National Bank of New York, when it was revealed that its young president, Amos R. Eno, had lost $3 million of his depositors' money speculating on Wall Street. The bank was saved only when Eno's father, Amos R. Eno, stepped in and personally paid back every penny. Young Eno fled to Canada. He was arrested there, but released again because the extradition treaty between the two countries then covered neither defalcation nor embezzlement. He would remain across the border for nine years, until he was sure the indictment against him would be quashed, then returned to Manhattan and inherited what was left of his father's fortune.

On May 16, the Metropolitan Bank had to close its doors; its president, George Seney, had lost most of his depositors' money dabbling in railroad stocks.

Swallowing hard, Buck answered: "Grant & Ward has failed, and Ward has fled. You'd better go home, Father."[32]

Without a word, the general turned and slowly stumped his way back out of the office, past the silent reporters, into the elevator that carried him upstairs to his office at the Mexican Southern Railroad. He stayed there, all alone, till five o'clock, when he called for George Spencer, Grant & Ward's clerk.

Spencer found him slumped behind his desk.

"Spencer," he murmured, "how is it that man has deceived us all in this way?"

The clerk had no answer.

"I have made it the rule of my life to trust a man long after other people gave him up," the general continued. "But I don't see how I can ever trust any human being again."[33]

He buried his face in his hands.

When Grant left home that morning he had believed himself a millionaire. When he got home in the evening he had $80 in his pocket. His wife had another $130. There was nothing else.[*]

Ulysses S. Grant would never come back to Wall Street.

Ferd had fled, just as Buck Grant told his father he had, but he hadn't gone far. After slipping out of his house to avoid meeting James Fish early that morning he had crossed the East River and taken the train to Stamford. He "felt there would be trouble with the Marine Bank," he remembered, "and I wanted to avoid the excitement."[34] In fact, he was paralyzed with fear. He spent most of the day holed up in his big house on Strawberry Hill Avenue. "It seemed to me that I was dreaming," he recalled later, "and sometimes, when I look back at some of the transactions, that I was out of my head."[35]

In the late afternoon, he pulled himself together and boarded a train back to the city. All around him, passengers were reading the afternoon papers. The Marine Bank's collapse and the failure of Grant & Ward dominated the front pages. Ferd feared he might somehow be recognized. As the train slowed in the Manhattan railyards, he

---

[*] The $250,00 trust fund, created earlier to provide the Grants with a comfortable life in Manhattan, had been invested in bonds of the Wabash Railroad—which was about to go into default.

jumped off, made his way across the tracks to Second Avenue, rode the elevated railroad to Twenty-third Street, ducked into a livery stable, and ordered a closed carriage to take him across the newly completed Brooklyn Bridge and home to Brooklyn.

When he saw that newspapermen and curiosity seekers filled the sidewalk in front of his house on Pierrepont Street, he asked the driver to take him around the back to Love Lane. He got into the house through the stable without anyone spotting him.

Bill Shepard, the boyhood friend who sometimes served as his attorney, was waiting for him in the parlor. He brought a message from William Warner's brother-in-law, J. Henry Work: Work wanted to see him right away. Ferd was trembling so badly that Ella administered a double dose of chloral hydrate to calm him down, but since Work was a partner in the law firm that had represented Grant & Ward, as well as an investor in the supposed contracts, Ferd agreed to see him. Work got there around nine thirty. Warner turned up a few minutes later with a stenographer.

It was not a friendly visit. Work was acting now as Warner's spokesman, not the firm's lawyer. Warner and the anonymous investors he represented had done spectacularly well in their dealings with Ferd, collecting some $1,255,000 more than they had put in (better than $28 million in modern terms). But they still had obligations totaling $578,000 with the firm, he said, and were unwilling to forgo a cent. Work warned that if Ferd did not turn over to Warner every bit of his property in exchange for those obligations, the shadowy but powerful men whose interests he represented would do everything they could to destroy him. Shaking, panicked, incoherent, Ferd signed over the deeds to his Stamford estate and everything it contained, to his half of the Booth Theatre block, and to sixteen house lots at 121st and Madison Avenue as well. He tried to argue that he had already conveyed his Brooklyn home to his wife, but Work insisted she sign a paper turning it and all its contents over to Warner, regardless.

Thursday was Ella Ward's birthday. She spent it with three friends at 81 Pierrepont Street packing up the few personal possessions she had brought to her marriage so they could be carried to her family's home at 37 Monroe Place. It began raining late that afternoon, but a crowd gathered to watch the servants struggle down the stairs with an upright piano and a bedroom set that had been part of Ella's trousseau. After dark, a closed carriage carried her and her trunks the block and a half to her mother's house to avoid her neighbors' stares.

It rained steadily all that night and into the next morning. Seven detectives, assigned by a Supreme Court justice to ensure that Ferd not escape before a warrant for his arrest could be issued, took what shelter they could in doorways and under trees in the cobbled square bounded by Monroe Place and Pierrepont, Clinton, and Clark streets.

Around eight thirty, a fast-moving cab splashed to a stop in front of the Greens' Monroe Place house. The door flew open. Ferd dashed down the steps, climbed in, and ordered the driver to hurry off again toward the ferry landing. The detectives broke into a run. One jumped onto the back of the cab. Another seized the horse's bridle. A third pulled open the door. "Mr. Ward," he said, "you must pardon me, but I'll have to put one of my men on the box."[36]

Over the next few days, as Ferd moved back and forth between his mother-in-law's home and his lawyers' offices in Manhattan, a city detective would always be at his elbow.

No documents survive that reveal how Ferd's parents took the first news of the disaster, but subsequent letters make it clear that they blamed James Fish for most of their son's troubles. Ferd was weak, not wicked, fatally susceptible to temptation. "Oh, how I tremble lest [Ferd] should have to be tried," Jane Shaw Ward would tell Sarah. "I cannot tell you my dear child how many hours of heartache I have over the thought of dear Ferdie's guilt in conniving at any of Mr. Fish's frauds."[37]

The editor of the *Livingston Republican* expressed the feelings of many of the Wards' neighbors when they heard what had happened:

> Dr. and Mrs. Ward, the father and mother of Ferdinand Ward, receive and are entitled to the heartfelt sympathy of their many friends and of the entire community in Geneseo and vicinity over the great blow which the failure of Grant & Ward has been to them. Dr. Ward has lived here thirty-six years and the greater part of that time he has ministered among the Presbyterian brethren of Geneseo. He has baptized, married and buried them and there is no occasion for rejoicing or mourning where his presence is not looked for, to laugh with those who laugh and weep with those who weep. His gray hairs are respected by rich and poor alike and he is looked on and believed to be a Christian and a gentleman.

The talk on the street generally expresses surprise that the failure had not occurred before, the success of Ward having always been looked on as phenomenal and ephemeral, but the extent of the failure seems to startle people. Ward's charities in this his home, which have been mainly distributed through his mother, command the feelings of many of the citizens. He has given money and remunerative positions to his friends, men of his own age from Geneseo, and he and his family have many friends left here.*

In Philadelphia, Dr. Brinton was devastated. General Grant, his friend and old commander, had been ruined. Worse, his own brother-in-law was responsible. He talked of resigning from his clubs, even leaving the city. The Brintons did not go out in public for weeks.

In Denver, Will Ward boarded a train for New York, forced once again to try to get his brother out of trouble. After he had done so, he told a reporter, he hoped to bring Ferd and Ella and their baby west with him to start new lives on his alfalfa ranch outside of town.

At first, newspapermen were able to find friends and acquaintances willing to speak well of Ferd: a naval officer who had known him for ten years volunteered that he was a "square, straightforward man";[38] a fellow member of the Brooklyn Club declared him modest, reliable, and "without any bad habits";[39] even Buck Grant initially believed his former partner would somehow set things right.

But on Saturday, the national bank examiner issued his preliminary report. The Marine Bank was hopelessly insolvent. Depositors were owed $5.2 million. The bank's assets—including cash on hand, properties bought for the bank by Fish, and the bank building itself—added up to just slightly more than half of that. Meanwhile, Julian T. Davies, the lawyer who had once been Buck Grant's employer and had now been appointed receiver for Grant & Ward, estimated that the firm owed at least $14.5 million to its many creditors and possessed less than $60,000 in assets. Until then, the *Brooklyn Eagle* reported, "Mr. Ward still retained a few friends on the Street, but now it would be

---

* Fish's hometown paper was equally kind to its native son. "Mystic people were sadly surprised and shocked" at the collapse of the bank in which so many townspeople had been stockholders and depositors. But it had been heartening to hear from many quarters "entire confidence expressed in the integrity of President Fish." *Livingston Republican*, May 10, 1884; *Mystic Press*, May 8, 1884.

hard to find any person willing to uphold his cause. Never before has such a downfall been witnessed in financial circles. . . . His most boon companions have deserted him."[40]

That evening, Ferd climbed the stairs above the shuttered bank to which James Fish had devoted most of his adult life and asked to see him. The housekeeper showed him to a chair. Fish entered, accompanied by two of the bank's other directors. By then, he had had to absorb still more disturbing news: the government contracts that had been at the heart of Grant & Ward's supposed success had never actually existed; virtually everything Ferdinand Ward had told him over the past four years had been a lie.

Ferd began to talk, words spilling over one another. He wanted to explain, he said, wanted to say how sorry he was. He didn't know how it had happened. Fish was his best friend, had been like a father to him. He had been unable to resist temptation, could not seem to help himself. Why hadn't someone stopped him?

Fish cut him off. Ferd had ruined him and his family, he shouted. Several of his sons had lost their savings investing in the shattered firm—and his own reputation had been destroyed forever. Ferd was an ingrate, a liar, a thief. "I said to him that I could kill him if he were not such a contemptible miserable viper," Fish remembered. "I took up [a] chair and raised it over my head as if to strike him, and he crawled and fell on the tiles of the floor and begged me not to kill him. . . . He kept on his knees and whined."[41]

What should he do? How could he make things right?

It was "one of the most exciting affairs I ever saw," one of the witnesses told a reporter. "Ward cringed and slunk like a whipped cur."[42]

The banker eventually put the chair down. "I advised him to go and commit suicide," Fish remembered. "Drown himself, hang himself."[43]

Ferd fled down the stairs and out into the empty street.

PART FOUR

THE BEST-HATED MAN IN THE UNITED STATES

TWELVE

A Magnificent and Audacious Swindle

It was now clear that serious crimes had been committed. "Every day has developed some new and startling phase of dishonesty," the editor of the *New York Times* wrote on Sunday in a call for the immediate arrest of both Ferd and Fish. "What was originally supposed to be a large bank failure, involving the downfall of an enterprising business firm conducted upon legitimate principles, now resolves itself into a magnificent and audacious swindle."[1]

It was also evident that as creditors warred over the spoils, the courts would soon be clogged by suits and countersuits. There were separate receivers for the Marine Bank and for Grant & Ward, different assignees for each of the firm's partners, a phalanx of lawyers representing the Erie Railroad, the First National Bank, former senator Chaffee, and dozens of other investors. Chamberlain Tappan hired lawyers too, determined to get back at least some of the $320,000 he'd personally invested.

Ferd himself soon added to the tangle. Will Ward had just come in from Denver. "Till he arrived, Mr. Ward had not the courage to take any decisive step," one of Ferd's attorneys said. "He had been constantly alone . . . and even now is in constant fear of violence."[2] Now, Will insisted that his agitated brother make a second, separate assignment of his property, to a Manhattan attorney, George C. Holt. Having Mr. Warner get everything was unfair to Ferd's other creditors, Will said, and the assignment to him had, in any case, been made under duress. Sidney Green agreed: on the night of the crash his brother-in-law had been "laboring under great mental excitement [as well as] misrepresentations, if not threats," he told a newspaperman. "But whether he was out of his mind or not, I am unable to say."[3]

The first suit to reach the New York Supreme Court was that of Fish's assignee, John H. Morris, against Grant & Ward. A justice appointed an eminent attorney, Hamilton Cole, as referee, empowered to take evidence and try to determine who was entitled to what.

On Wednesday morning, May 14, a week and a day after the crash, Ferd was called to testify in Cole's big fourth-floor office in the Metropolitan Bank Building at Third Avenue and Seventh Street. Framed lithographs of British barristers in wigs lined the black walnut–paneled walls. Attorneys for all the parties sat along both sides of a long wooden table heaped with ledgers and bundled checks. Behind them were rows of newspapermen and creditors, all craning their necks to see Ferd step into the room.

He seemed nervous as he took his seat at one end of the table; he swallowed hard, his prominent Adam's apple rising and falling. One reporter, who had last seen him in Stamford the previous summer when "his acquaintance [had been] courted by a great many people,"[4] thought he had aged ten years.

Ferd had reason to be fearful. The diminutive white-bearded lawyer who rose from his seat at the other end of the table to interrogate him was Francis N. Bangs, said to be the most relentless cross-examiner in the city.

Bangs went right at him. Ferd did his best to be an elusive target.

Did Ferd keep businesslike books? Yes. But the contract business did not appear in them. Those transactions were recorded on several pages of foolscap he had kept in his locked desk. He no longer knew where those pages were. He thought Work might have taken them during his late-night visit to the Wards' Brooklyn home. He didn't think the firm had owed Warner anything like the $575,000 Work and he had claimed, but without his records he couldn't say for sure.

He said he couldn't remember when he'd bought his homes or what he'd paid for them, didn't know how he'd come by his other properties, wasn't able to recall how much he'd paid for his share of the Booth Theatre.

"Can't you remember within $100,000 or $50,000 or $25,000 or $10,000?"[5]

Ferd said he could not. He sighed and shut his eyes when pretending not to remember things. He said he had also forgotten precisely how the conveyances to Warner had come about—except that when he'd agreed to Work's demands the night of the crash, he had not "been fit to talk or to be talked to."

"Tell us about the government contracts," Bangs said.

"There are no such contracts. There never were any. I never had any contract with the government, neither personally nor as a member of the firm."

"Then what was meant when the investors were given to understand that there was a contract?"

"Nothing at all."

"Did the money go into the bank with your personal deposits?"

"Most of it."

"It was not put into specific investments?"

"Oh, no."[6]

What made him pay such immense interest for money loaned to the firm?

"That's hard to tell. I had to rob Peter to pay Paul."[7]

He had been forced to borrow at exaggerated rates to pay debts already incurred. For more than two years he'd been unable to pay his bills without doing so. He'd known all along that the crash would come.

He was so depleted by the end of his first day's testimony, so pallid and shaky, that Bangs told him to go home and get a good night's rest.

He needed it. The next morning, Bangs returned to the attack, emphasizing each phrase by rapping his knuckles on one of several ledgers fanned out across the referee's table.

"So, then, the real nature of your business consisted in discounting the fanciful prospects of imaginary profits to be derived from fictitious contracts, founded on manufactured artificial contributions of altogether imaginary money. Is that so?"

The lawyers in the room laughed. Ferd laughed too, but said nothing. "Well, why don't you speak? Doesn't that adequately describe the business you were in?"

"Some—some of it was conducted on an imaginary basis, yes."

"And was not that known to anyone besides you? Do you mean to say that you hadn't any confederates?"

"I think that was the case."[8]

How did he persuade people to invest in contracts that they had never even seen?

"Take Tappan, for instance. How did you get him in?"

"I didn't get him. Mr. Fish got him. Mr. Fish was the first man associated with me in the business."

"Well, how did you get Mr. Fish?"

"I simply represented to him the business I proposed to carry on, based on government contracts, and asked him to share in the profits."[9]

Ferd couldn't recall how much Fred Grant or Tappan or anyone else had invested in the contract business. Nor had he ever bothered to explain to any of his investors the supposed details of the business he was doing.

Bangs was incredulous: no one had *ever* asked to see the contracts?

"None of them. No, sir, not even Messrs. Warner and Work."[10]

Ferd had claimed that the ledgers and heaps of checks on hand did not tell the full story, that his personal record of the contract business had somehow been lost.

But it wasn't. As Ferd's fourth day of testimony began, Judge Ashbel Green, representing Assignee Davies, presented the referee with an envelope sealed with wax. In it were four sheets of paper clipped together, on which Ferd had recorded in black ink each investment in the supposed contracts as well as the initials of the man who had made it and the date repayment was due. Supposed profits were recorded in red. The investors and the sums they had invested were genuine; the profits were fictitious.

The identities of most investors were straightforward enough— "J.D.F." was James D. Fish, for example, "W.S.W." was William S. Warner—but one set of initials drew Bang's attention.

Did "C.A.A." stand for President Chester A. Arthur?

No.

Had Ferd told Fish they did?

He couldn't remember.

The total of "Profits on Contracts" was given as $1,928,716.92. Ferd admitted he'd once shown that figure to Fish, but he didn't recall telling him how the money was obtained. Bangs turned the page. Still more profits were listed.

"Mr. Ward," Bangs asked, "was there any rule, arithmetical or geometrical, which you followed, or did you simply divide up all the money you had on hand or could raise?"

Ferd smiled. "We had no rule," he said.[11]

He was especially forgetful when it came to what he'd done over the last days before the crash. He had no memory of writing checks for a million dollars on May 2, for example, and couldn't remember telling Fish he had $1.4 million in securities on hand, or bringing the satchel supposed to contain them to the bank—or taking it away again.

"Isn't your memory remiss about matters generally which occurred about that time?"

"I can't answer that."

Bangs had no more questions.[*]

---

[*] Some months later, when a federal grand jury examined Ferd about the same matters, it got more or less the same answers. According to the foreman, the future publisher George Putnam, he showed Ferd one of his ledgers while he was on the stand. Many years later, he reconstructed the exchange that followed:

Your book of contracts opens with "No. 157." Where are the earlier 156 contracts entered?

There were no earlier ones.

Why did you use 157 instead of 1?

It looked better.

Who and what did No. 157 represent?

It didn't really represent anything.

Do you mean that nothing was bought or sold, that no service was rendered?

Nothing whatever.

How then did you obtain the $23,000 "proceeds" that were entered?

There were no proceeds.

How come these figures are called "profits."

I wrote them there so as to please our investors.

Didn't customers draw on their accounts?

They were so pleased with the show of big profits that they were only too glad to have their apparent winnings pyramided. They liked my showings very much.

Did General Grant know anything of how your business was being conducted?

He knew nothing. He took my word. He had the same information the customers had—and he had the same happiness, while it lasted.

Ward "interested and amused us all by his perfect frankness," Putnam remembered. "He evidently felt a sense of pleasure in having been able, youngster as he was, to outwit a number of shrewd, experienced business men." George Haven Putnam, *Memories of a Publisher*, pp. 315–317.

.   .   .

Any pleasure Ferd may have felt at completing his testimony before Referee Cole cannot have lasted long. Just before he entered the hearing room that morning a deputy had handed him a subpoena. He was to appear before a grand jury looking into civil charges against him the next day, Wednesday, May 21. J. Nelson Tappan, the ailing city chamberlain who had helped him and Fish loot New York City funds, had filed a complaint through his attorney, John R. Dos Passos,* demanding return of the $320,000 he had invested with Ferd in supposed government contracts.

Ferd testified for just one relentlessly forgetful hour and was arrested that same afternoon at his lawyer's Wall Street offices. When Deputy Sheriffs Brown and David McGonigal turned up with the warrant, he was "much affected, almost wild,"[12] according to an eyewitness.

"Don't take me to jail," he begged. "Can't I go to a hotel till something can be done?"[13]

He could, McGonigal murmured, but it would cost him a hundred dollars—$2,260 today. Ferd quietly agreed to pay. The three men crossed town by carriage and under assumed names checked into room 13 at the Sinclair House at Broadway and Eighth Street. They ordered up dinner and drinks from room service. When it came time to sleep, Deputy Sheriff Brown summoned his own father to keep watch all night in case the prisoner tried to escape. The room was crowded and filled with the sound of snoring. "I didn't like the arrangement all," Ferd remembered, "especially at the steep price I was paying."[14]

For the next eight years, he would be at the mercy of prison officials willing to provide him with special treatment for a price. He resented them all but never failed to come up with the money, almost all of it provided by others. The world might see him as a common criminal, but he refused to be treated like one.

He entered Ludlow Street Jail the next day. His bail had been set at $300,000. Ferd's attorneys believed he might still be capable of raising it, but they counseled him not to do it. There were likely to be so many additional warrants, each with its own demand for bail, that eventually the total would be far too great to meet. If he were going to remain locked up, Ludlow Street was the place to be. Built of red brick at the

---

* The novelist John Dos Passos was his illegitimate son.

corner of Ludlow and Broome streets, it had originally housed debtors and looked more like a library than a jail. Ordinary prisoners occupied eighty-seven ten-by-ten-foot cells upstairs, but "tip-top types"[15] like Ferd, willing to pay as much as a hundred dollars a week for their board plus more for what were called "extras" and "extraordinaries,"[16] were provided with a first-floor suite, where, as the *New York Times* said, there was "nothing suggestive of imprisonment."[17]

"There are three rooms in [Ward's] suite," a visitor noted, "all nicely furnished and very comfortable."

> His reception-room, almost as large as an ordinary parlor, has soft sofas and lounging chairs scattered about a marble-topped centre table. The hangings of the room are of a soft neutral-tinted brown, very restful to the eye, and accord well with the heavy Brussels carpet. Through the open windows a cool breeze floated in between the bars, rendering the apartment delightfully cool and stirring the pages of the magazines on the table. [The keeper] declared emphatically that the rooms were "cooler than in any hotel in the city because the walls are so thick."[18]

From the moment he arrived, carrying an alligator-skin valise filled with papers, Ferd seemed at home. He paid to have a cage of canaries and his favorite black-and-white setter brought in to keep him company, procured a piano so that he could enjoy the sing-alongs he'd always liked, imported a barrel of Havana cigars and cords of wood for his three fireplaces, and greeted a steady stream of visitors—his wife, his brother, his brother-in-law, teams of lawyers, newspapermen looking for headlines, old friends from Wall Street. He seemed happy to see them all. "He sat half-buried in the depths of a great arm-chair, with his legs on a table," one reporter noted. "He was in his shirt-sleeves, had a long cigar in his mouth at an angle of 45 degrees, and chatted away cheerfully, listening to the gossip that his friends brought from the outside world. . . . He pressed his guests to stay for dinner, promising them a meal almost equal to any Delmonico's might serve, and offering to send for any brand of wine they chose."[19]

When guests didn't come to him, he went to them. For $15 and up for an evening, Warden Phil Kiernan or Sheriff Alexander Davidson would escort him wherever he wanted to go. He attended the theater (sometimes occupying his old box at the Casino), took long carriage rides through Central Park, dined with friends uptown or at Delmonico's, and, whenever he felt like it, strolled along Grand Street to the Bowery, where he bought rounds of drinks at the bar run by his friend Patrick Frawley, the Tammany alderman who got a cut of all business done in his district, including profits made from wealthy prisoners like Ferd.

His seventeen months at Ludlow Street would cost tens of thousands of dollars. At first, the money came from his life insurance policy; he'd cashed it in right away, he later reported, because Grant & Ward's receiver, Julian Davies, was about to "pounce" and "I thought I might as well get the benefit."[20] When he ran through that money, he threw himself on the mercy of his relatives. Unless they wished to see him cruelly mistreated, he said, they would have to provide him the wherewithal. They did. Ella got several thousand dollars in cash past the guards. Will brought him money, too. Billy Jones, the Ludlow Street janitor, remembered Ferd sending him to Patrick Frawley's saloon to cash thousand-dollar bills for him and his guests. And when that money, too, began to run low, he persuaded Ella to smuggle a chamois bag filled with her jewelry in to him beneath her clothing—earrings, brooches, necklaces—which he doled out one by one to his jailers, who converted them to cash, always keeping a piece of the action for themselves. "It is the same in jail as everywhere else," Ferd recalled, "money talks and with it you can do most anything."[21]

On the afternoon of May 27, General Grant's doorbell rang. A maid opened the door and was startled to see Ferd again standing on the steps. Sheriff Davidson stood just behind him. Ferd offered his card and asked if he could speak to the general. He would only need a minute or two. The maid took the card inside and returned. The answer was no. General Grant had nothing to say to him.

No one now knows what Ferd hoped to gain from speaking with the man whose family he had ruined and whose reputation for honesty he had at least temporarily tarnished. But it was probably just as well that he wasn't ushered inside. Jerome Chaffee remembered the general's mood in the weeks following the crash: "He would suffer for hours in his large arm chair, clutching nervously with his hands at the arm-rests, driving his finger-nails into the hard wood. . . . One day he said to me, 'Chaffee, I would kill Ward, as I would a snake. I believe I should do it, too, but I do not wish to be hanged for the killing of such a wretch.' "[22]

"We are all paupers now," General Grant told another visitor not long after the crash.[23] He was not exaggerating. Buck and Fred Grant lost their homes to creditors. The general's sister lost her savings. He and Julia retained their houses on East Sixty-sixth Street and in Long Branch, New Jersey, only because William Vanderbilt—to whom they had insisted on turning over all their property as partial payment of their debt to him—urged them to stay on in them as long as they liked. Gifts from friends and strangers paid their household expenses. Grant considered them loans, and pledged to pay them back as soon as he could.

The financial blow had been bad enough. But James Fish had just done still more damage to the general's reputation. The banker had been arrested the previous evening on a federal warrant, charged with "misappropriating a large sum of money belonging to a National Bank." He had not stayed behind bars for long; three friends came up with his $30,000 bail within an hour of his arrest, and as soon as he was released he sought to lighten his own burden of guilt by implicating Grant. "I have in my possession documentary evidence sufficient to fully vindicate me in every particular," Fish told a reporter. He then had his lawyers produce the two-year-old letters, signed by Grant, that seemed to suggest that the general had been aware that Ferd and Fish were engaged in the dubious government contract business and hoped to profit from it personally.

Democratic newspapers jumped on the story. "The Grants profess to have been entirely ignorant of the tricks that Ward was playing in their names," said the *Rocky Mountain News*, "but it requires a tremendous strain on the charity of the public to believe what they say."[24] "Is Ulysses S. Grant Guilty?" asked the editor of the *New York Sun*, and then provided his own answer: James Fish was Grant's innocent victim, he wrote, "misled by the written word of a man who has twice been chosen President of the United States. . . . For the love of money the greatest military reputation of our time has been dimmed and degraded by its possessor. The people look on with shame."[25]

Privately, Grant himself was ashamed. "I could bear all the pecuniary loss if that was all," he wrote to a friend, "but that I could be so long deceived by a man who I had such opportunity to know is humiliating.

Then too to have my name and that of my family associated with what now proves to have been nothing but a fraud for at least two years back."[26]

He was forced to offer a pained public explanation of the two letters to Fish. He had no recollection of either one, he said, but he admitted that he had signed them both. "My confidence in the integrity and business qualifications of the members of the firm of Grant & Ward was such that I have not hesitated to sign my name very often to papers put before me, on a mere statement of the contents without reading them, I am very well aware this was not business-like, but it is the fact. . . . I have never directly or indirectly sustained a Government Contract taken by the firm of Grant & Ward."[27]

Grant's denial never quite caught up to the charge. Even his closest friends were embarrassed for him: "He has lost everything," William Tecumseh Sherman wrote, "and more in reputation."[28]

On June 1, three days after Ferd made his peculiar visit to East Sixty-sixth Street, the Grants closed up their house and moved to their cottage at Long Branch for the summer. The general was glad to be away from headlines and editorials but badly in need of some sort of income. Earlier, he had turned down an offer from the *Century Magazine* to write articles about the great campaigns he'd led during the Civil War; he disliked revisiting his past and hadn't really needed the money. Now, when the offer was renewed, he eagerly accepted. He agreed to write four articles for $1,000 each. He would spend the whole summer at it, Julia Grant remembered, "writing, writing, writing for bread," and even began to think there might be a book in it.

But as he wrote, something else was bothering him. The day after the Grants arrived at Long Branch, he bit into a peach and recoiled in pain so intense he thought a wasp had somehow been hidden in the fruit. The pain subsided but did not entirely disappear. Dr. Jacob M. Da Costa of Philadelphia was visiting Grant's next-door neighbor, and was asked to have a look at the general's throat. (Da Costa happened to be Dr. John Brinton's brother-in-law as well as his colleague at the Jefferson Medical College.) He was an eminent internist, but no expert on lesions, and when he noticed an unusual-looking growth on the roof of Grant's mouth he prescribed something to ease the pain but urged the general to see his own physician for a more thorough examination as soon as possible. The Grants' doctor was vacationing in Europe and not expected back till fall. Grant was busy writing. The appointment would have to wait till October, when his doctor had returned and the Grants were back home in Manhattan.

On the afternoon of July 23, Rev. Ferdinand De Wilton Ward had an unexpected visitor of his own. James D. Fish had come up from New York to Geneseo, hoping to have a talk with his errant partner's father. The maid showed the visitor into the dark parsonage parlor and asked him to wait; Rev. Ward was upstairs in his study. He came down the steps slowly, grim-faced, without extending his hand. The two men sat. Fish reminded the older man of how often Rev. Ward had expressed his gratitude for all that Fish had done for his boy, how many times the minister had said he was in his and Mrs. Ward's thankful prayers. Now, he had a favor to ask. Fish wanted him to persuade his son to "come out manfully and say that I knew nothing about the inside affairs of Grant & Ward. I have lost everything . . . but my good name. I want to keep that."

Ferdinand rose from his chair. "I can't listen to anything against my boy," Fish remembered his saying. "The law will hold you equally liable."

"Yes, equally liable in a business sense, but not in guilt."

Ferdinand repeated himself: "I won't listen to anything against my son."

"Oh, Dr. Ward," Fish recalled saying. "I have done so much for your son. All I want is that he shall do this one act of justice to me. Let him tell the truth. I am a beggar now, but I want to be a beggar with an honorable name."

Ferdinand's expression never changed. "I can't do it," he said. "My son, William, will spend his last cent to defend Ferdie, and I will stand by him. Good morning." Ferdinand stalked from the room. For him, then and always, Ward solidarity took precedence over everything else; whatever sins Ferd might have committed, his son's accusers would get no help from him.

Fish showed himself out. He stumbled up Ward Place toward Main Street, turned right, and started toward the depot to board the evening train for New York. "[Rev. Ward] left me alone," he recalled, "and without one word of kindness or of sympathy. It was one of the most cruel experiences that I have endured in all my misfortunes."*

---

* When Fish gave an account of his doomed mission to Geneseo to a reporter for the *New York World* a year or so later, Rev. Ward was indignant. To publish such a story,

Fish's misfortunes were multiplying that summer. His trial was still months away. Without Ferd's willingness to exonerate him, he saw little chance of ever clearing his name. And he was lonely: after the crash, Sallie Reber Laing, the lovely actress with whom he had kept company since her husband's death the previous autumn, had left the city and returned to her family in Sandusky, Ohio.

On August 6th, she took to the stage again for a one-night benefit performance as the lead in *Patience* to raise funds for the city's poor. "It was a matter of general remark among those who knew her," the *Cincinnati Inquirer* would later report, "that she was not the Sallie of the year before in point of healthful appearance."[29]

In fact, she was three months pregnant. Her baby was due in February.

James Fish was the father. He was in the audience that evening and may have escorted Sallie back east a day or two later: the *Hartford Courant* reported that she "sang at a number of private entertainments" in and around his hometown of Mystic later that month; presumably, he would have been with her.[30] In any case, by late September she was occupying an elegantly furnished apartment in the brand-new Albert Flats at 23 East Tenth Street, arranged and paid for by her far-older lover, who spoke to no one when he visited and came and went only after dark.

On October 22, General Grant returned home to Sixty-sixth Street from two downtown appointments. He had news for Julia, both good and bad: he had visited the *Century* offices, where he'd been offered a

---

involving as it did "aged and heart-oppressed parents," had been in "*bad taste*," he wrote in a letter to the editor. He had indeed once been grateful to Mr. Fish, he said.

> Country-born and country-bred, [my son] was ill-qualified to encounter the pecuniary perils of Wall Street. To have such a counselor seemed to F.W.'s family a fortunate circumstance. He was repeatedly asked in strong terms to have an eye to F.W. lest he make unfortunate investments and, above all, engage in dangerous speculations, and he said that he would. It is not at all impossible that I asked God's blessings upon him. I often met him at my son's table at Brooklyn, where he was an ever-welcome guest and was treated as a member of the household.

He had been forced to remind his surprise visitor "under whose roof you are," but he denied having been rude: "I was not cordial (how could I be under the circumstances lately occurring) but ungentlemanly I was not." *New York World*, July 2 and July 31, 1886.

contract for a full-fledged memoir that was sure to ease their financial situation, but he also had been told by a specialist to whom his family physician had sent him that the throat pain he'd been experiencing since June was caused by a disease that was "serious, epithelial in character," and only "sometimes capable of being cured."[31] Though his physician was careful to avoid the term, Grant was suffering from cancer of the tongue. Twice-daily treatments with muriate of cocaine could mask the pain, but nothing could be done about the cancer's steady growth. The general stopped smoking his beloved cigars and redoubled his efforts to finish his book, hunched over in a little room at the top of the stairs, writing or dictating all morning, preparing notes for the next day's writing every afternoon. When Grant's old friend Mark Twain heard that the Century Company had offered him only an author's standard royalty of 10 percent—no more, he said, than "they would have offered to any Comanche Indian whose book they had reason to believe might sell 3,000 or 4,000 copies"[32]—he resolved to better the offer and publish the book himself. He pledged 70 percent of the profits and, to demonstrate his seriousness, gave the general an advance of $10,000.

Grant stuck to his relentless writing schedule all winter, working hour upon hour without so much as a drink of water because of the agony swallowing caused. His condition steadily worsened. He lost weight, felt weak, and wore a knitted cap and a shawl across his knees to fend off the cold that gripped him now, even with all the house fires lit. Battlefield dreams and fear of choking interrupted his sleep. "My tears blind me," Julia Grant confided to a friend in January. "General Grant is very ill. I cannot write how ill."[33]

Rumors of his condition began to reach the newspapers in February. His doctors denied them at first. Mark Twain dropped by on the 21st. He was shocked by the general's appearance—emaciated, gray, shrunken—but he complimented him on the news stories suggesting he was on the upswing. "Yes," Grant smiled, "if it had only been true."[34] One of Grant's physicians, Dr. John Hancock Douglas, happened to be on hand. Twain asked him if he believed cigar smoking had caused the general's affliction. There were several causes, the doctor answered, but the most damaging had been the continuing grief caused by his financial disaster. The general took up the subject, his initial anger at Ferdinand Ward now replaced by sadness. He spoke of his former partner as if he were talking about an offending child, Twain noted, without venom or vengefulness, while Twain himself was "inwardly boiling all the time. I was scalping Ward, flaying him alive, breaking him on the wheel, pounding him to jelly, and cursing him with all the profanity known to the one language I am acquainted with, and helping it out in times of difficulty and distress with odds and ends of profanity drawn from the two other languages of which I have a limited knowledge."[35]

Three days later, on February 24, 1885, Sallie Reber gave birth to a baby girl in a rented room in an old farmhouse on the outskirts of Carlstadt, New Jersey. Everything had been arranged in secret. She had quietly left her downtown flat ten days earlier and moved across the Hudson into the home of a nurse-midwife to await her delivery. She told the nurse and attending doctor that her name was Nellie, that her husband had only recently died; Franklin Laing's name, not James Fish's, appeared on the birth certificate as the father, even though he had been dead for eighteen months.

Fish was preoccupied that month, huddling each morning with his lawyers, preparing for the trial that was about to begin in federal court: he faced twenty-five counts, all of them having to do with his willingness to approve fictitious loans without collateral in defiance of the National Banking Act. But every other day or so during Sallie's confinement he had found time to take the train out to Carlstadt, bringing fruit and flowers. After Sallie gave birth he went again and again to see his new daughter—and ninth child.

His trial was finally to start on the morning of March 11. As the banker left his apartment in the Mystic Flats to go to court, a messenger handed him a telegram. It was from Carlstadt. Sallie Reber had died the previous evening. She had fallen ill two days earlier, suffering from a sudden fever that soared so high she became delirious. Fish had been at her bedside the previous afternoon. Dr. J. W. Phelps of Rutherford Park, the attending physician, who had been reluctant to get involved at all, listed "acute gastritis" as the cause of death. It is impossible to know the truth, but it seems more likely that she suffered from puerperal (or "childbed") fever, the form of fast-acting septicemia that was the leading killer of childbearing women in the nineteenth century. There were two possible motives for the doctor to have misrepresented the facts: to spare an unmarried woman's family the knowledge that she had given birth in secret, or to cover up his own incompetence, since puerperal fever was most often the result of careless medical care.*

Fish was stunned. His trial was about to get under way. "I had little time to consider what was my duty," he remembered. In fact, he did nothing at all for twenty-four hours, then sent a wire to Sallie's brother-in-law, Frank A. Layman, telling him of her death. Layman, who was the editor of the Sandusky *Evening Journal*, wired back that he and Sallie's unmarried sister, Alice, would arrive in New York the following evening. As soon as he got there, he summoned Dr. Phelps to the Mystic Flats and asked him what had happened. (Fish left the room as soon as he arrived; Alice remained out of earshot as well.) The news that Sallie had been pregnant came as a shock; so did the fact that her baby had survived. Layman begged the doctor to say nothing about any of it; the news would only add to the grief of his aged mother-in-law and Sallie's sister: "For God's sake," he said, "don't tell Alice."[36] Phelps and Layman agreed that everything would be kept secret, but if either ever suspected the truth was going to get out he was to wire the other immediately with the message, "Breakers Ahead," so that they could get their stories straight.

Fish temporarily entrusted the infant to the brother of Fish's first wife, J. Blodgett, who was the janitor of the Mystic Flats.

Meanwhile, Sallie's corpse had been shipped to Luke Clarke's Sons, undertakers, on Twenty-third Street in Manhattan. "The body was prepared in my rooms," Clarke remembered. "Mr. Fish was present when the girl was laid in her coffin. She was kept here until the following Sunday [when Layman and Alice Reber escorted her home to Sandusky for burial], and he came to look at her every day."[37]

The United States Post Office and Courthouse at Broadway and Park Row was not the tallest building in Manhattan, but it was among the

---

* In an interview conducted after the story broke more than a month later, Dr. Phelps went out of his way to blame the victim. She had suffered from chronic stomach trouble, he said, and had been warned to be careful what she ate. "I went to see her the morning of March 9 and found her much worse. . . . She told me she had eaten a dozen oranges, some stewed clams and . . . ginger ale. I . . . told her that in her delicate condition it was enough to kill her. She was a little petulant . . . and told me she knew what her stomach could stand much better than any doctor could tell her." By the next evening she was dead. *New York Times*, May 8, 1885.

most conspicuous and certainly the most grandiose. Built to embody federal might in the aftermath of the 1863 draft riots that had threatened to destroy the city, it was a trapezoidal Second Empire architectural extravaganza, a full city block of balconies and pillars and walls ten feet thick, topped by an array of Mansard roofs and canopies, a tall lantern, and a still-taller central dome. The Astor House across the street looked as it if could be stowed away in some corner of its basement, one critic wrote, and it seemed to shrink nearby City Hall to the "size of some old-fashioned toy."[38]

A sixty-foot ceiling dwarfed the lawyers and witnesses, newspapermen and curiosity seekers who crowded each day into the second-floor courtroom in which James Fish was being tried before federal judge Charles Linnaeus Benedict, a veteran jurist appointed to his post by Abraham Lincoln.

The prosecution was led by Elihu Root, the forty-year-old U.S. attorney for the Southern District of New York, ambitious, able, and eager to win a conviction in what was sure to be a headline-grabbing courtroom drama.* "It was a great case," he recalled half a century later, great in the public interest it inspired and "great in the sense of the mass of evidence to be examined."[39] So many checks and securities and contradictory ledgers were in evidence that it had taken Root six weeks just to get them into some kind of order. An aide remembered him sifting through it all at his enormous desk, "on which he had a dozen spindles, a dozen different colored pencils and little pads. . . . From time to time he would make a little note and stick it on a red spindle, . . . he would make another note and stick it on a yellow spindle."[40]

Root and his assistants needed to convince the jury that in approving fictitious loans to Grant & Ward's employees and close associates without collateral, Fish understood that he was breaking federal law. They also wanted to at least suggest that he had known and approved of everything Ferd was doing. In its opening brief, the prosecution pledged to prove that the loans had been as "unwarranted, as clandestine, and as flagitious as though a conduit had been laid and operated from the vaults of the Marine Bank to those of Grant & Ward and was kept constantly in operation."

Fish sat silent, gazing up at the lofty ceiling, polishing his spectacles,

---

* Root was also a friend and early political ally of young Theodore Roosevelt, who would one day make him first his secretary of war and then his secretary of state.

sometimes taking notes. His attorneys, led by Stanley G. Clarke and
Edwin B. Smith, had to persuade the jurors that their client might have
been careless and certainly had made "mistakes,"[41] but had never been
deceitful or larcenous. Instead, Fish had been Ferd's luckless dupe:
"Gentlemen," Clarke told the jury, "if anybody is to be punished for
these things, let it be Mr. Ward."[42]

It took the government nearly two weeks to lay out its case. Nathan
Daboli, the Marine Bank's former assistant cashier, was the principal
witness. He told of Fish's suspicious willingness to sign off on unsecured loans to Grant & Ward employees and to let Ferd mislead
national bank examiners by returning rehypothecated securities to the
vault just before their visits. He also described the "special" Grant &
Ward account book Fish kept that showed the firm was often overdrawn by hundreds of thousands of dollars and was never shown to the
directors.

The defense countered by doggedly leading Daboli up and down
the pages of the bank's mammoth ledgers—eighty-one of them were
stacked waist deep around the witness stand—in search of earlier loans
to Grant & Ward that had been paid back with interest. By listing
successful transactions, Clarke hoped to show that Fish had not been
recklessly risking his depositors' money when he made loans to his own
firm, that Grant & Ward would have somehow paid off its outstanding loans of $1,373,000 had not unfortunate circumstances intervened.
The money flowed both ways, he claimed. Yes, U.S. Attorney Root
shot back, "but the money the firm paid into the bank was previously
drawn out of it."[43] During this phase of the trial, one juror's wife complained, the attorneys moved through the endless columns of figures
so slowly and in such detail that she couldn't sleep at night because of
her husband's constant tossing and turning and muttering about stocks
and securities.

The government called five former directors of the Marine Bank to
the stand to demonstrate how poorly run the bank had been and how
casually they had taken their responsibilities: they'd never questioned
a single loan made by the bank, had never opened a loan envelope to
see if securities were actually present, and claimed not to have known
that Fish had an interest in the firm to which millions were being lent
or to have recognized the names of the Grant & Ward employees to
whom the loans were allegedly granted, even though at least two of
them had invested in the supposed contracts and had been introduced

to everyone who worked in the firm's office. On March 24, Root rested the government's case. If he had had his way, the district attorney said, the bank's ex-directors would have been in the dock alongside its former president.

Court was adjourned the next day so that the judge and attorneys could travel uptown to take the testimony of General Grant. He had written to the U.S. attorney expressing his eagerness to speak about what Fish and Ward had done to him and his family. He greeted the lawyers in his library, huddled in front of a hickory-wood fire, wearing a skullcap, dressing gown, and slippers. Everyone agreed to waive the oath. The questioning went on for three-quarters of an hour. Grant's voice was low but steady. Once or twice he winced in pain.

He reiterated that the letters that bore his signature and that Fish had claimed would prove his innocence did nothing of the kind. He made it clear again that he had been consistently and adamantly opposed to dealing in government contracts—federal, state, or municipal. When, not long before the crash, he'd heard what he called "whispers" about what Ferd was doing, he had called him aside and been assured that "he wouldn't do anything that was going to injure me, . . . and . . . he had no contracts anywhere."[44] Had Fish ever asked him about the business? Only once, he thought, during their railroad trip together to the Kinzua Viaduct: "I made a remark . . . to the effect that Mr. Ward was a man of wonderful ability, wonderful business capacity or something like that, and Mr. Fish said he had never got anything so good in his life before."[45] Fish had never told him Grant & Ward's account in the bank was badly overdrawn, never advised him that the firm was borrowing large sums, with or without collateral. The general had had so much confidence in his partners that he had not even bothered to read the monthly reports of the profits he had believed he was making. On the morning of the crash he had "supposed that I was worth well nigh to a million dollars."[46] He and his sons had lost everything.

As his visitors rose to leave, one newspaper reported, a lawyer told Grant, "You're certainly looking remarkably well."

"I don't know about that," Grant answered. "I am conscious that I'm a very sick man."

Grant's testimony was read out to the jury the following morning. There was nothing new in it. But the effort he had made to answer every question had a profound impact inside the courtroom and beyond. When he seemed suddenly to be sinking two days later, one of his physicians publicly blamed the great effort he'd made to be responsive to his visitors for sapping his strength. Newspapermen began a death watch outside his house. Every day's developments were described and improved upon by the headline writers: "Grant Failing"; "The Old Chieftain at the Door of Eternity"; "The Hero Still Fighting His Unconquerable Foe."[47] He eventually rallied, but Ferd, reading the newspapers every morning at Ludlow Street, understood the impact reports of the general's near death were likely to have on his own chances for public forgiveness. When he heard that a lawyer representing his assignee in a suit against William Warner still hoped to examine the general, he wrote begging him to drop the idea.

> The public have already been so ungenerous as to attribute the General's sickness to his troubles with Grant & Ward and when the examination was made for Mr. Fish the other day, the papers said it did much to aggravate his troubles. This is so hard for me to bear that I can't help but ask that you will do what you can to save me from any more such insinuations.[48]

Plans for Grant's testimony were dropped, but Ferd had every reason o be concerned. "The public reads about [the general's] throat and thinks of him only as a sufferer from cancer," the *New York Times* would write a few days later. "In one sense it is true that cancer will kill him, but those who know him best know that Ferdinand Ward is morally responsible for his . . . sufferings."[49]

When Fish testified on his own behalf, he presented himself as his former partner's hapless dupe. He had joined forces with Ferd only because he had been his late father-in-law's friend. He had never much wanted to become partners with either Buck or General Grant. He had believed absolutely in the genuineness of Ward's government contracts and had played no part in drafting the fraudulent letter that seemed to authorize them, signed by the general. He also had never knowingly made any loans without collateral, and had thought those he had arranged for Grant & Ward in the names of its employees were "as safe as I ever made. I never had any suspicion of Grant & Ward's soundness and I believed all Ward's representations to be perfectly true."[50]

Then, Elihu Root began what turned out to be four days of brutal cross-examination. Fish denied everything. Profits had sometimes seemed swollen, he admitted, but he'd never questioned them. Although he and his partner had breakfast together most mornings and often dined with one another as well, he had never once asked Ferd where he was finding such vast amounts of flour and other commodities, or who was paying for them, or how they were to be stored or shipped. He had never asked to see the firm's books, either, and had always believed that the securities on any loans he approved were in the envelopes where they belonged. On those rare occasions when they were found to be missing, Fish said, he assumed they would be brought to the bank "as soon as it was practicable. Mr. Ward was always rather remiss in these matters."[51]

How had Fish's curiosity not been aroused immediately after the firm's founding when the first profits were being divided and yet Grant & Ward's account with the Marine Bank held just $280? It hadn't worried him at all, he said; he'd just assumed that the bulk of the firm's funds were in some other bank. He had always believed that Ward had outside agents handling the contract business, too, though he'd never asked about it.

Root handed him a heap of checks, all drawn by Ferd against the firm's special account, and asked if he could find a single one meant to pay for the purchase, transportation, or storage of government supplies of any kind. Fish went through them, one by one. There were none.

Root bore down.

"Did you believe these to be honest contracts?"

"For government contracts, I did."

"What do you mean by that?"

"Well, there were large profits."

"Did you believe them honest . . . ?"

"So considered."

"So considered by you?"

"By everybody that gets government contracts."

"Why, then, did you believe that it was necessary that you, a member of this firm, should never see a contract?"

Fish paused, stared at the ceiling. "I had implicit faith that these contracts existed."

"And you considered that there was nothing to prevent you from telling other people that the firm of Grant & Ward had government contracts, but nevertheless the interests of General Grant as a candidate for the presidency forbade that you, a member of that firm—raising millions of dollars to be used in filling the contracts, and lending hundreds of thousands of dollars of the money of your bank to be used in filling them—should not see them?"

Fish's voice shook. "I was always very reserved in speaking about government contracts, and always as confidential as I could."

But hadn't he ever inquired about them? After all, he was urging others to invest in them.

"I did not desire to know about them personally."

"Why not?"

"Nothing. Only I had no curiosity."[52]

Fish's attorneys said they planned to call some twenty witnesses willing to testify to their client's lifelong reputation for honesty. The judge allowed only one to take the stand, former New York governor John T. Hoffman: the issue was not whether Mr. Fish had been honest before he formed his partnership with Ferdinand Ward, the judge ruled; what mattered was what he had helped Ward do once they had begun to work together.

Fish's attorney called his client back to the witness chair to explain that he had at least once consulted Grant about the business of the firm. Fish said,

> In the latter part of 1883, I called at the office of our firm to see Mr. Ward. I met General Grant in the outside office and after some general conversation, I asked him how business was. He answered that it was first-rate; that the success of Grant & Ward was phenomenal. "I think we have made more money than any other house in Wall Street, perhaps in the city." He said that Ward was the ablest young businessman he ever saw. I asked him whether he ever examined the books of the firm. He said, no; he had only looked over the monthly statements which were satisfactory to him.

Fish's return to the stand did not help his case.

"*Why* did you ask General Grant if he had examined the books?" Root demanded.

"Because I had a perfect right to do so!"

"You testified that you had never examined them yourself."

"I did so testify."

"Then, why did you want to know whether General Grant had examined them or not?"

"Well, I had the curiosity to ask him."

"Is that the best reason you can give?"

"That is all."[53]

Wasn't it at about that time, Root asked, that Fish had conveyed $100,000 worth of real estate to his children?

"It might have been."

"What connection was there between the conveyances and your conversation with General Grant?"

"None in the world."

And hadn't Grant & Ward also changed its way of doing business around then, using city deposits to provide money to the bank for the firm to use?

"I never thought of it."

The defense rested on April 10. In his summation, Edwin Smith did what he could for his badly damaged client. His errors had all been committed in good conscience, he argued. Ward, not Fish, was the villain. "It is absurd," he concluded, "to argue that Mr. Fish deliberately went to work to defraud the bank which he considered the apple of his eye, and which he loved as the children of his loins."[54]

Elihu Root's response was devastating, its impact enhanced by a severe cold that had reduced his voice to a hoarse rasp so that everyone in the courtroom had to strain to hear him. Nearly everything to which Fish had testified in court led inexorably to a finding of fraud, he said. Fish had admitted that he'd made fictitious loans for which no securities had ever been deposited with the bank; he'd known all along that Grant & Ward, to which he was lending these enormous sums, had no firm basis and no credit beyond what the use of the Marine Bank's funds gave it; he had allowed his partner to overdraw his account by $750,000 and also to borrow $1.5 million without having to put up any collateral; and as bank president and business partner he had made deals between the bank and himself that had betrayed his depositors.

"That man," Root said, pointing to Fish, "that man is ready to testify to anything which he thinks will save him from the Penitentiary."

> To the crime of defalcation he has added that of perjury. . . . Either he knew he was putting the money of the bank

into the hands of a confederate to defraud the bank, or else he tried to cheat the United States government by helping his confederate to carry out his fraudulent contracts. His defense reduces itself into this—that he knew the bank's money was used in corrupt practices unequalled since the days of the Tweed ring.

Mr. Smith said that the bank was wrecked because James D. Fish believed Ward. I say it was wrecked because James D. Fish entered into a conspiracy with Ferdinand Ward to rob the bank, to lend its money to carry out contracts which he knew were fraudulent. He deliberately allowed the firm of which he was a partner to honeycomb the bank; he deliberately embarked the funds intrusted to his charge on a fraudulent scheme. Whether he was deceived by Ferdinand Ward or not, James D. Fish deceived the directors of the bank, he deceived the stockholders and the depositors. If this man cannot be convicted upon the evidence furnished, there is no use of talking about the integrity and probity of our financial institutions. We might as well acknowledge that only the poor may be punished.[55]

General Grant's increasing frailty was still on everyone's mind. Fish's effort to justify his own actions by implicating Grant in the contract business now seemed especially cruel. Root took full advantage of this, his voice now a mere whisper.

These conspirators knew that great heart could not stoop to the pettiness of their greed. His one weakness was that singular truthfulness and steadfastness which gave him, in his firmness of attachment and unwillingness to suspect wrong, the simplicity of a child. . . . . I do not know in the records of business treachery any story that can parallel this treatment of a simple and great soldier by these two conspirators. Forever be sunk into infamy the ignoble soul that would seek to besmirch that great reputation which is the glory of our country, for the sake of gain by petty treacheries, faithlessness to trust and lying devices.[56]

The jury agreed. It took less than six hours to find Fish guilty on twelve of the twenty-five original counts. (The verdicts on five would later be overturned on appeal, but seven stuck.)

Despite everything, the editor of Fish's hometown paper remained sympathetic: "Expressions of sadness at this ending of the trial are general in our village, notwithstanding there are so many sufferers from the wrecking of the Marine Bank. Many elder persons of the Mystics cannot forget that Mr. Fish was their school-mate and companion in youth, and many others seem to feel that, however irregular may have been his proceedings in the bank matter, he is not worse than many others in like positions."[57]

The *New York Times* was less forgiving: "Upon Mr. Fish's own statement it appears that a person so guileless, simple and confiding as he depicts himself to be, should not be the President of a bank. Moreover, such a person, does not, in fact, become the President of a bank."[58]

THIRTEEN

A Verdict at Last

James Fish's lawyers moved immediately for a new trial. Until that issue was resolved, he was remanded to the Ludlow Street Jail, where a reporter found him the next morning in his own comfortable rooms, smoking a cigar and reading the newspaper accounts of his conviction. He was philosophical at first. "Well, it can't be helped," he said, putting down the paper. He continued to maintain his complete innocence, but "I suppose . . . if a man steals—and perjures himself and does all they say I have—he must take the consequences. . . . There is one thing certain, however, and that is that badly off as I may appear today"—here, his face reddened and his fists clenched—"there is one who is in a much worse position in the eyes of all honest men." He pointed toward Ferd's rooms on the other side of the wall. "There is a man whom I took by the hand as a boy and loaded with favors, and how has he repaid me? Why, I should as soon have thought of one of my own children stabbing me." Fish said that he had reached an age when rest and quiet mattered most to him; those could be found even in the penitentiary. But "wherever I go . . . I shall feel happy in the thought that this scoundrel will follow me. I will do all I can to further that end; and although I generally do not harbor malice. I feel that assisting to bring this man to justice will be a public duty."[1]

U.S. Attorney Root felt the same way. But nearly a year after the crash, no grand jury had issued a criminal indictment against Ferdinand Ward. Rival jurisdictions were part of the problem. "This office would only be too glad to bring Mr. Ward to trial," one of Root's assistants said, "but as long as he is protected by a civil process from the state courts we can't do it."[2]

But the real problem lay deeper. In order to convict Ferd of a crime, prosecutors needed reliable witnesses to testify against him, and those with whom he had done business, winners and losers alike, were proving reluctant to talk about it. Ferd's assignee, George Holt, put it best. "There is no doubt that Ward's contracts were shams and he could be indicted for the offences if witnesses could be procured who would swear that he had pretended that he actually had contracts. Those men who made money by him are, naturally, not anxious to come forward, and those who were summoned before the Grand Jury could not remember the circumstances or pretended not to. The truth is that most of those who invested did so without asking any questions."[3] To testify honestly about Ferd's promises, then, was publicly to admit either venality or an embarrassing willingness to suspend disbelief. Either admission would badly undercut a man's reputation on Wall Street.*

---

* At least one investor's lawyer sought to explain to a judge Ward's power over such a large host of men who, in hindsight, should have known better than to do business with him.

> I do not believe there was any man ever brought into personal contact with Ferdinand Ward without feeling . . . his wonderful arithmetical power and glibness in the statement of facts and results, the amazing honesty of tone which he adopted, the skill with which he surrounded himself with everything which indicated the man of education, refinement and taste, as well as the man of prosperity—a rising man. Anyone who saw him with the prestige thrown around him by his relation to the bank president and the Grants and by his former success, and with all his peculiar surroundings, must have believed that he was in contact with an extraordinary man. This is a fascination which we all recognize in the case of politicians and also in the case of women. He had the power of fixing his eyes on a man and willing the dollars out of his pocket, such as no man ever had since the world was. I am thankful that while I may have been exposed to other fascinations, I never, never was brought in contact with Mr. Ferdinand Ward before his failure.

Argument of Charles B. Alexander, representing George C. Holt as Assignee, &c.; against William S. Warner before Supreme Court, City and County of New York, Grant & Ward Bankruptcy Collection, Morris Library, Southern Illinois University, Carbondale.

. . .

On May 3, Dr. Phelps, the New Jersey doctor who had attended Sallie Reber during her final days, came to see Fish at Ludlow Street. He was worried. Reporters from the *New York Times* had been poking around Carlstadt. They had already talked with the woman in whose house Sallie had died and the station agent who had helped arrange for her body to be shipped into the city. It seemed only a matter of a day or two before the story of the relationship between the banker and the stage star turned up in the newspapers. That evening, the doctor sent Sallie's brother-in-law the coded message they'd agreed upon.

> To Frank A. Layman, Sandusky
> Look Out for Breakers; Letter on the Way.
> Phelps

On May 7, a year and a day since Fish's world had collapsed, the front page of the morning *New York Times* carried a long, lurid story headlined "SALLIE REBER'S SAD DEATH; A MYSTERY IN WHICH JAMES D. FISH IS CONCERNED; SUSPICIOUS CIRCUMSTANCES CONNECTING WITH THE AFFAIR." That same day, Frank Layman assured a Sandusky reporter that there was no mystery, no scandal: Fish and his sister-in-law had secretly been married in May 1884, at about the time of the crash, he said. "In order to escape the notoriety that might ensue," he continued, "Sallie stipulated that the marriage should be kept secret until such time as he was free again" and had insisted on maintaining this silence until the day she died. "In justice to Mr. Fish," he added, "he has been anxious from the first to make known the marriage and [now that he's been] absolved by the family from secrecy will do so today."[4]

But Fish didn't. When a reporter somehow got into the jail the following morning, asking for a comment, he was evasive. He had been acquainted with Mrs. Laing, of course: "She was as pure and noble a soul as ever I knew. Any suggestion of impropriety on her part is a foul calumny." But, when asked if he had married her, he confirmed only that he had been her "benefactor." The reporter pointed out that on the day Dr. Phelps signed the baby's birth certificate naming Sallie's late husband as the baby's father, Franklin Laing had been dead for a year and a half; Fish said only that it did seem "somewhat singular."[5]

As soon as his jailhouse interview moved on the wires, an anxious telegram arrived from Layman: "*Daily News* wires me you deny marriage with Sallie. Is it true? Answer immediately."

"I do not deny it and shall not do so," Fish wired back.

Eventually, he summoned his old friend George Alfred Townsend, the financial reporter for the *Philadelphia Inquirer*, to help him coordinate his story with the one Layman was telling. He had begun calling on Sallie after her husband's death, he said, and, "being a widower and without any home of my own, I thought I was rich enough to take a wife and spend some of my remaining life with a companion." But Sallie had initially been reluctant: married actresses had a hard time finding work, she'd said, and her mother had not approved of widows remarrying for at least a year. But in the spring of 1884, when Fish still thought himself worth at least a million dollars, he had pressed his suit and she had agreed. No date was set, but, "finding myself loved by this young lady, I was anxious to marry her as soon as possible. Suddenly came my failure. I then felt all the more lonesome and in need of domestic life. She, perhaps, took an additional interest in me from my misfortune. . . . It was like her to prove her attachment to me in marrying me in the midst of these reverses."[6]

The marriage had taken place almost precisely nine months before their daughter was born, Fish asserted, though no one in either her family or his had been told about it at the time. He was oddly vague about the details, too. Sometimes he said the marriage had taken place on May 20, sometimes on May 28. There was no church wedding; no civil ceremony, either.[*] Instead, Fish said, on the advice of an old friend, New York Supreme Court Justice Charles Donohue, he and Sallie had been "married according to the laws of New York in a perfectly regular way. We signed a written contract of marriage which is now in the possession of [Sallie's] mother in Sandusky."[7]

Judge Benedict rejected Fish's request for a new trial and summoned him back to his courtroom for sentencing. He had been convicted on seven counts, each of which carried a ten-year term in prison. "A more shameful or more lawless abuse of the powers of the president of a National Bank can scarcely be imagined,"[8] the judge said. Fish bowed his head. But because of the defendant's age, he would be allowed to serve them concurrently at Auburn Prison in Auburn, New York.

---

[*] No document attesting to their marriage at any time in 1884 survives in the municipal archives of any of New York's five boroughs.

Before he left, Fish arranged for his baby—now named Alice Reber Fish, after Sallie's younger sister—to be cared for by his unmarried daughter, Annie, who moved with the infant to a boardinghouse in Auburn to be near him. "We can't believe it is his," she said, "but as he says it is we have taken it in and will give it a home."[9]

At some point, the Reber family had a headstone placed above Sallie Reber's grave at the Oakland cemetery in Sandusky, formally identifying her as "The wife of James D. Fish." But evidently even her daughter remained unsure whether that was true. Alice inherited her mother's theatrical trunk and kept it with her all of her long life. But one member of the family remembered that she never dared open it, perhaps because she was afraid of what its contents might reveal about the relationship between the father she knew and loved and her mother, the actress who died after giving her birth.

On July 1, three days after James Fish entered Auburn Prison, Mark Twain visited General Grant again, this time at a friend's cottage at Mount McGregor in the hills above Saratoga Springs, New York. The dying man had gone there with his family in the hope that the clear, dry mountain air would make him more comfortable. The manuscript of his memoir—now planned for two volumes—was finished, and he was hard at work on revising the galleys. His visitor sat with him on the porch. Buck and Jesse Grant were there, too. Grant was a shrunken figure now, wearing a winter coat and top hat and swathed in blankets despite the summer sun. His voice mostly gone, he communicated by writing on little slips of paper. The subject of Fish's imprisonment came up. Jesse said ten years was far too light a sentence for a man like him. Buck agreed, cursing his name. Twain cursed him, too. Grant listened, then scrawled a note: "He was not as bad as the other."[10]

Fred Grant preferred not to talk about the disaster. "Father is letting you see that the Grant family are a pack of fools, Mr. Clemens," he said.

The general disagreed, Twain remembered. "He said in substance that . . . when Ward laid siege to a man that man would turn out to be a fool, too—as much of a fool as any Grant." Was Hugh J. Jewett, president of the Erie Railroad, a fool? He lost tens of thousands when the Marine Bank failed. He named other prominent businessmen whom Ferd had gulled, including one who had paid him $300,000 for a share in a mine that was not for sale, and another whom he had robbed of $300,000 "without giving him a scrap of anything to show that the transaction had taken place and today that man is not among the prosecutors of Ward at all for the reason . . . that he would rather lose all that money than have the fact get out that he was deceived in so childish a way."[11]

Twain was unconvinced at first. But then he put himself in the embarrassed investors' place "and confessed . . . it was a hundred to one that I would have done the very thing that [they] had done, and I was thoroughly well aware that . . . there was not a preacher nor a widow in Christendom who would not have done it; for these people are always seeking investments that pay illegitimately large sums; and they never, or seldom, stop to inquire into the nature of the business."[12]

Three weeks later, General Grant declared that he had done all he could do to finish his memoirs: he had revised the galleys of the first volume; the manuscript of the second was ready for the printer. "Do *not*," he wrote in a note he handed to Fred, "let the memory of me interfere with the progress of the book."*

Without work to do, what Twain called the general's "tedious weariness" rapidly increased. "I do not sleep though I sometimes doze a little," he wrote to one of his physicians. "If up I am talked to and in my effort to answer cause pain. The fact is I think I am a verb instead of a personal pronoun. A verb is anything that signifies to be; to do; or to suffer. I signify all three."[13] Word spread that he was sinking. The newspapers resumed their lugubrious drumbeat: "General Grant's Death Imminent"; "The End Near"; "General Grant not Expected to Survive the Night."[14]

He died on the morning of July 23. Two weeks of national mourning followed. Messages of condolence arrived from North and South alike. The climax was a vast slow-moving Manhattan procession up Broadway to the hastily constructed vault at 122nd Street that was to hold the general's body until a suitably grand tomb could be completed.

Ferd paid his way out of jail that afternoon to watch it pass. Smoked glasses kept him from being recognized; they also made it impossible

---

* Grant's book, *Personal Memoirs*, was published that winter. In February 1886, Twain presented Julia Grant with her first royalty check, for $200,000, the largest in publishing history up to that time. With it, she was able to pay off many of her husband's creditors. Eventually, 300,000 two-volume sets were sold and she would earn more than $420,000—almost $10 million today.

for anyone to know how he really felt at Grant's passing. He always claimed that he genuinely grieved for his former partner, but he also knew that the public reaction to the general's death would make his efforts at least to share the blame for all that had happened immeasurably more difficult.

His mother felt no ambivalence. She had not forgotten that the general and his sons had said terrible things about her boy. She told Sarah how much she deplored "this furor over Gen'l Grant. . . . It must indeed seem, as you say, a grand farce in the eyes of a God who 'will not give His glory to another' and before whom such 'hero worship' is wicked idolatry. It is 2 o'clock and Father has just left to attend the services to be held in the courthouse yard from 2 till 5 this PM. He, as chaplain of the G.A.R., had to be present but he will take no part in the services. How disgusting the papers have been about [the general]. I am glad I am not his wife nor any connexion of his."[15]

Ferdinand Ward was not merely "the plunderer of Grant," said the *Washington Post*, but also "in the estimate of many his murderer."[16] Threatening letters flooded the Ludlow Street Jail. Some were anonymous; others were signed by Union veterans eager to avenge their old commander. Ferd was now, as he himself said, "the best-hated man in the United States," his name a nationwide byword for swindling and chicanery.

A Reno dry goods merchant used Ferd in a newspaper advertisement:

> Ferdinand Ward is said to be an expert
> in "robbing Peter to pay Paul;"
> not so with
> Gallatin & Folsom,
> for they give their customers a fair shake on every proposition.[17]

A New York songwriter named M. H. Rosenfeld rushed out a tune called "I've Just Been Down to the Bank," dedicated to "Ferdinand Ward, Esq., Hotel du Ludlow, N.Y." The authors of a new manual of phrenology published that fall included a portrait of "Ferdinand Ward, False Financier," with a caption helpfully explaining that his "low-top head, very broad from side to side," revealed "Secretiveness, Cunning, Acquisitiveness, Destructiveness."[18]

Public anger was exacerbated by the fact that nearly sixteen months after Ferd's arrest he had yet to face a single charge in court. Elihu Root had helped to get six indictments handed down against him before leaving office in July. Ferd had pled not guilty to all of them, and his lawyers had prepared his defense against each. But the trials had all been postponed at the last minute, largely because prosecutors weren't sure they had enough witnesses on hand willing to admit to their own folly or venality while implicating Ferd.

Now, the editors of the *National Police Gazette* suggested that if the "Arch Thief" weren't formally tried and convicted soon, there was another remedy: "Unless Ferdinand Ward be brought to the bar shortly, and the penalty of his fatal theft be visited upon him, the rude justice of revenge will break into his comfortable cell and swing him in the pitiless air as other thieves and villains have, ere this, been less justly swung. See if it doesn't."[19]

Talk like that enraged Ferd. "I consider it extraordinary—I might say outrageous," he told a newspaperman. "I am hammered at by the press day in and day out as leading a luxurious life in Ludlow Street Jail and yet I am always ready for trial, brought into court time and time again . . . simply to be utilized as a pretext for new abuse. . . . My counsel are ready. The people are not. It is mysterious."[20]

He lashed out in all directions. Will leaked a letter outlining what Ferd claimed he was prepared to prove when he finally got a chance to defend himself in court. "The Grant family had drawn out more money from the firm than they'd put in"; Grant's sons had engaged in the contract business even though they said they had known nothing about it; "a number of prominent men, including bank presidents, etc.," had also pocketed exorbitant gains on those so-called contracts but had been allowed to remain anonymous.[21]

Ferd threatened to reveal their names, then said he could not do so, on advice of counsel. But he also issued a warning: he had copies of all his correspondence; those who attacked him unfairly could expect to be embarrassed. "I am not dead," he said. "Other people have had their day and I have suffered, but there is an end to everything, and Ferdinand Ward will soon be heard from on his behalf."[22]

Finally, he granted a lengthy interview to a reporter for the *New York Herald*, providing a detailed history of Grant & Ward, ten densely printed newspaper columns carefully skewed to put the blame for everything that had happened where he always insisted it belonged: on others. If it hadn't been for foolish investments insisted upon by Fish and the Grants and a sudden downturn on the stock market in early 1882 he would never have had to begin the borrowing that brought about disaster. Fred and Buck Grant had encouraged him to deal in the supposed government contracts, though they denied it. William S. Warner and the anonymous members of his blind pool had victimized him and his firm. The directors of the Marine Bank had approved each and every loan made to Grant & Ward; if they hadn't understood that there was no collateral supporting some of them, he and Fish alone should not be blamed.

Ferd made no mention of the chronic deceit that characterized everything he'd done from his days as the Sunday school treasurer at the Church of the Pilgrims through his wholesale looting of the treasury of New York City. Individual investors may or may not have thought the government contracts Ferd described were improper; only he had known that they had never existed at all.

The *Herald's* man had a final question. Ferd had been in jail for months, time enough to have discovered who his real friends were. Had he anything to say about that?

He had been waiting for the question. He rose dramatically from his chair, strode to the fireplace and gazed out the window for a moment, then returned to his chair. "Well," he said, tapping his teeth with his tortoise-shell spectacles.

> It seems to me that these men, several of them old enough to be my father, some of whom had made conspicuous fortunes in life before I was born, having utilized me and my endeavors to the tune of millions of dollars of profit, having patted me on the back in the noonday of prosperity, have now turned away and slipped so far to the background that the public look to me alone for explanation, for restitution. I have accepted my position, and, in order that I might do what a man ought, have stripped myself. As to the position occupied by these others who have not been stripped, and who have not stripped themselves, I leave the public to ponder and the courts to determine.[23]

In the face of all the damage he'd done, his self-pity and stubborn self-righteousness were breathtaking, but there was something in what he said, nonetheless. A grand jury had charged J. Nelson Tappan with actions "incompatible with the trustworthy and satisfactory discharge of the duties of his office," but he had been allowed to resign because of ill health and died before any court could move against him. S. Hastings Grant blamed everything on his late co-conspirator—"[Mr. Tappan] was the custodian of the city's money and I knew very little about banks," he said—and managed to remain in office until the election of a new mayor.

The Erie Railroad dismissed Bird W. Spencer, the treasurer and heavy investor who had arranged the train trip to see the Kinzua Viaduct, but he, too, escaped prosecution and would one day retire as president of the People's Bank and Trust Company of Passaic, New Jersey.

Former mayor Grace always denied that he had invested in Grant & Ward's government contracts. When Joseph Pulitzer's garish *New York World* charged that Grace had known all along that Ferd was dishonest and that he and his confidential secretary, E. H. Tobey, had "shared the profits of Ward's rascality," Grace sued Pulitzer for libel. Five days later, however, Tobey was accused of larceny and brought before a grand jury. Called to testify, Grace claimed that if Tobey had done wrong he had "done it all alone." The case never reached court. Neither did Tobey. When his case was called he did not appear; Mr. Grace had sent him out of the country, all the way to Peru, to work for him in the guano business.[24]

Ferd hurried up the broad marble steps of the New York County Courthouse on Chambers Street on Monday morning, October 19. He was escorted by Warden Kiernan, two lawyers, and Will Ward, whom one newspaper described as a "sturdy, stubby figure . . . the faithful friend who sticks by his brother like a brother."[25]

This was Ferd's first public appearance since the death of General Grant had intensified the public's interest in finally seeing him tried for his crimes. Bootblacks and newspaper boys shouted his name. Reporters hurried from their offices on Park Row. Curiosity seekers so clogged the corridors that lawyers had to elbow their way up the stairs and into the court of oyer and terminer—the criminal trial branch of the New York Supreme Court—where more than a hundred spectators were already seated and fifty more stood at the back.

Ferd took his seat at the defense table. Four times since June, he and his attorneys had been summoned to court to answer a criminal indictment. Four times he had pled not guilty. And four times, the prosecution had pigeonholed the indictment rather than chance a trial in a case undercut by reluctant or uncooperative witnesses. "Anxious to be tried," one reporter noted, "Ward had begged and implored and beseeched his counsel to be prepared. . . . Always thin and attenuated, always placid exteriorly, always self-contained and self-poised, Ward bore the scrutiny of a thousand eyes with the easy nonchalance of a man of the world."[26] Others who knew him better noted that he'd lost weight at Ludlow Street, and that he drummed his fingers on the rim of the derby in his lap and nibbled nervously at the fringe of his thin blond moustache.

The two lawyers seated at his side were among the best in the business. The chief counsel, General Benjamin Franklin Tracy, was a grave, gray-bearded veteran of the Civil War from an old upstate family, a former U.S. attorney, prominent in Republican politics, and widely admired for the cool but relentless skill he brought to cross-examination. His assistant counsel was his mirror opposite: W. Bourke Cockran, clean-shaven, red-faced, Irish born, a Democratic Party orator whose florid style of speechmaking Winston Churchill would one day credit with having helped shape his own. Neither had much confidence that anything but a guilty verdict was possible, given the public mood and the number of accusations that continued to be made against their client, but they were prepared to do their best to get him off—or at least minimize his punishment.

But once again, the prosecutors startled everyone. District Attorney Randolph B. Martine told the judge he was unable to proceed on the original indictment charging Ferd and Fish with defrauding the Marine Bank, because of a dearth of witnesses: Nathan Daboli, the Marine Bank cashier who had spent weeks testifying at Fish's trial, was now too ill to come to court; E. H. Tobey, Mayor Grace's man, had vanished altogether; William Warner, just hit with an unexpected federal indictment charging him with conspiring with Ferd to defraud the Marine Bank, was unlikely to testify against his co-defendant for fear of incriminating himself.

Martine proposed therefore to try Ferd on a brand-new indictment for grand larceny. He waved a fresh bundle of papers. This indictment alleged that on the morning of May 5, the day before the crash, Ward, already overdrawn at the Marine Bank, deposited a check for $75,000 drawn on the First National Bank, where he had less than $2,500 in his account. Then he wrote an individual check to William S. Warner for $71,800 on the Marine Bank and had it certified on the strength of his earlier deposit, knowing all the time that that check had been worthless. This constituted a crime under Section 529 of the Penal Code, punishable by ten years in prison.

"My object was to present the clearest and simplest of all the complaints against him," Martine later explained to a reporter who asked why he'd decided to proceed with this indictment rather than any of its predecessors, "so that I could make the trial short and effective and call few witnesses. In plain English, I want to convict Ward and I have no doubt that I will, and by choosing the plainest and briefest one I hope to avoid even the possibility of any such mischances as are likely to occur in . . . long trials."[27]

Under normal circumstances, it might have been risky. James Fish, the principal prosecution witness, was a convicted felon, after all, whose loathing of his former partner was well known and who had nothing to lose by lying. But further delay was politically unacceptable: the district attorney hoped that the public's anger would help make a jury overlook its suspicion of Fish in the interest of putting Ward permanently behind bars.

Fish was at first reluctant to reemerge before the public; he said he hated being "made a Jumbo." But in the end he could not resist the opportunity to testify against Ferd, whose "punishment is about the only thing I care to live to see."[28]

Ferd again pled not guilty. Justice George C. Barrett, a Tammany jurist with exaggerated sideburns and a reputation for moving his cases right along, gave the defense just three days to prepare for trial on the new charges. When General Tracy argued that he needed more time, the judge said it shouldn't take long to find out whether or not his client had had money in his account when he wrote his check. He would see everyone Thursday morning at ten o'clock.

A thick oak bar blocked the door of the courthouse when Ferd and his team arrived that morning. The officer who let them pass was stationed there to make sure the crowds were more carefully controlled than they had been for Ferd's first appearance. Shortly after the *voir dire* began, the district attorney moved that since Ferd was now a criminal defendant he should be moved from his comfortable lodgings at Ludlow Street to the big, noisome, Egyptian-style city jail called the Tombs. Judge Barrett agreed.

Warden Kiernan walked him there that evening, stopping for a last drink along the way for old times' sake. The Tombs was not a pleasant place: it stank of sewage, rats scurried along the corridors, and prisoners were packed three and four at a time into narrow cells built for one. Ferd somehow got a cell to himself on the second tier. He refused to speak to the common criminals on either side of him and saw to it that dinner was brought in to him from outside every evening.

It took four wearying days for the lawyers to work their way through nearly seven hundred potential jurors, trying to find a dozen men who had not already made up their minds about the guilt of Ferdinand Ward. The last man seated had him confused with the Brooklyn pastor Henry Ward Beecher. The jurors picked as their foreman an ice cream manufacturer named Moses Huntoon.

Shortly after noon on Monday the 26th, the twelve men took their seats in the jury box and District Attorney Martine finally began outlining the state's case. "You are to try the defendant upon this charge and upon no other," he said when he was finished. Then, he added helpfully, "You are *not* to try him on the charge of having, by fraud and deceit, obtained from General Grant and his family all the money they ever had and sending the great soldier down to the grave heartbroken. Neither are you to try him upon having by fraud and deceit sent an old man to the penitentiary who had treated him like a son."[29]

General Tracy was on his feet. "I emphatically object," he said. The district attorney was seeking to prejudice the jury against his client even before the testimony began.[30]

Martine said he was merely making it clear what the jurors were to consider and what they were to ignore. Judge Barrett overruled the defense.

Fish was called to the stand. He had been staying under guard for several days at the Murray Hill Hotel waiting for this moment. Assistant District Attorney Ambrose H. Purdy had escorted him to the Casino one evening, where the two men watched the chorus from the same box Fish had once shared with Ferd. Fish's daughter brought his eight-month-old infant to his room so that he could see her. Former associates dropped by too, and Purdy suggested to some that they begin the process of applying for a presidential pardon for their old friend. It would be a fitting reward for the contribution he was about to make to the cause of justice, he said.

Now, Fish settled into the witness chair, he looked younger and more vigorous than he'd seemed when he himself had been on trial.

He wore a crisply pressed dark suit and a blindingly white shirt with an old-fashioned upstanding collar. He crossed his legs and, staring down at Ferd, began polishing his spectacles with a silk handkerchief, eager to reveal to the world what he called "the true inwardness of Ward's villainy."[31]

Before he could begin doing so, General Tracy was on his feet again. He moved that because of the district attorney's improper opening statement, the jury should be discharged and a new one empaneled.

"I can hardly suppose you are making that motion seriously," Judge Barrett said.

"I am making it most seriously."

"Then I will most seriously decline to entertain it."

Purdy asked the witness to identify himself.

"My name is James D. Fish. I am sixty-six years old. I am an inmate of Auburn penitentiary, having been sent there under a sentence of ten years at hard labor. And by occupation I am a convict."[32]

Purdy showed him Ferd's check for $71,800, made out to William S. Warner. He had personally certified it, Fish said, after Ferd told him over the telephone that there was money to cover it in his account at the First National Bank. He'd spoken with Ward hundreds of times on that telephone, Fish said. His voice had been unmistakable; so was his reassuring message.

"Did you trust in that statement?"

"Most implicitly," he answered, almost shouting. "I believed him to be an honorable and truthful man—a man with whom I would have trusted everything I had in God's world."[33]

"Do you know the defendant? Do you recognize him here in the court?"

Fish leaned down, peering over the heads of the attorneys sitting between him and the defense table, and glared at Ferd. "Yes," he said, "that—is—the man."

Ferd glared back.

General Tracy handled the cross-examination. If his client were to have any chance at all, he needed to destroy Fish's credibility. Ferd always contended that it was Fish's troubled bank, not Grant & Ward's demands, that had brought on the crash: how else to explain Fish's pressure on him in the preceding days to raise money to shore it up?

Ferd had armed his lawyers with nineteen letters from his former partner showing that Fish had been anxious about the health of his bank for more than two years. The most damaging was written a little over a month before the crash.

> (Private)   March 29, 1884
> My dear Mr. Ward: "Life is short" as we often have it quoted to us. . . . We carry an immense burden, that no other bank would, for the company and for many of their employees, and on collateral that no other bank would recognize. If the bank cannot be relieved of some of it I shall leave as sure as anything in the world. I see no prospects of things getting better with them.
>
>   Yours.
>   J. D. Fish[34]

What had he meant? Tracy asked. He had merely been "annoyed," not really worried, when he wrote it, Fish said. Business hadn't been as bad as all that. By saying he would "leave,"[35] he had merely meant that he would one day retire.

The letters showed that Fish was an unreliable chronicler of his bank's history, just as Ferd knew they would. Fish had been fully aware that the loans he had approved to Grant & Ward and its employees were questionable, at best; he'd known also that Ferd and the firm were frequently overdrawn; he had always been afraid that everything might end in disaster.

But the same documents also presented serious problems for the defense because they showed that at the heart of all of Fish's anxieties were Ferd's business practices: he repeatedly asked his young partner to replenish his overdrawn accounts, explain what was going on, bring securities back to the bank to satisfy the National Bank examiner. "Grant & Ward were at the bottom of it all," Fish said several times. "I had constant trouble with Ward. The promises that he did not keep and the heavy loans to his firm kept us always in a state of annoyance and uncertainty."[36]

Tracy pushed on, nonetheless. Had Fish believed all the money loaned to Ferd and to the firm had been amply secured? He had. He had thought his bank was "well secured and solid as a rock"—and he hadn't known on May 5 that Ferd had taken away his satchel filled with securities.

Tracy asked that the reference to the satchel be stricken as irrelevant. Barrett sustained him.

But hadn't Fish actually believed on May 5th that if he didn't certify Ferd's check, his bank as well as his firm would have been ruined?

Fish struggled to explain. His actions had been dictated by who had signed the check, he said. If the bank had refused to certify a check written by a comparative stranger like William Warner, it would have had no serious impact. But if a large check to an outsider had been rejected—a check written and signed by Ward, who was both a director of the bank and a partner of its president—the news would have spread fast and cast serious doubt on the bank's health.

Tracy pounced: then Fish *had* certified the check because failure to do so would have brought ruin?

"I did not say that."

"Well, did you not believe that?"

"I believed the bank and Mr. Ward were perfectly sound. If we had possessed all those millions of dollars of government contracts that Ward said we had, there would have been no trouble. With such securities in hand we could have got aid from other banks. I did not know until the morning of May 6, 1884, that those government contracts were myths."

Tracy interrupted. "I object to that. What I want is information concerning the condition of the Marine Bank."

"I am prepared to tell you, General," Fish said, leaning forward, his voice shaking. "Don't you see the effect of my having been deceived about those contracts? If we had what I supposed we had, there would have been no such collapse as occurred."[37]

Tracy moved that any mention of the supposed contracts be stricken as irrelevant to the simple question at hand. Barrett denied the motion.

The contracts swindle now seemed fair game. Assistant District Attorney De Lancey Nicoll eagerly pursued the subject on redirect, prompting Fish to describe the promises Ferd had made to him in February 1882: huge profits harvested from secret government contracts secured with behind-the-scenes help from former senator Chaffee, Stephen Elkins, and General Grant himself.

Tracy was back on his feet. Out of respect for the late general's memory, he said, the part he and his name had played in the affairs of Grant & Ward should be declared out of bounds. "If the prosecution desires to open this avenue of detraction and drag in the mire the great name of the dead for whom the nation mourns, then upon their head must rest the responsibility. If they desire—"

Judge Barrett cut in. "General Tracy, I have had enough of this. There is no call for any such remarks. This is merely a matter of law."[38]

Fish was allowed to go on about the contracts for a time before Barrett stopped Nicoll to ask what he was driving at. The assistant district attorney said he hoped to show that it had been Grant & Ward's constant demands for unsecured cash that had threatened the bank.

Barrett told him to stop; intriguing as that line of questioning might be, it had no bearing on the question of Ferd's fraudulent check.

As a final question for his chief witness, Nicoll asked Fish to describe the evening Ferd had come to his apartment after the crash to apologize. The old man erupted at the question. His face turned red. His voice rose. He raised his arm high above his head to show how he had threatened to crush his visitor with a chair. "I told him he was a black-hearted, treacherous scoundrel, and that if he were not such a contemptible crawling little villain I would kill him in his tracks." He was shouting now. The defense tried to interrupt; so did Justice Barrett. Fish could not be stopped. He had urged Ferd to "drown himself, hang himself, *anything* to rid the world of his presence," while the defendant had cowered on the ground, groveling, whimpering.[39]

Ferd sat through it all smiling slightly, one reporter noted, "as though he rather enjoyed seeing the helpless old gentleman in rage and fume."

Fish was excused. His brother, Benjamin, the bank's former paying teller, swore he had been present when his brother and Ward spoke over the telephone about Ward's worthless checks. Even though his brother had held the receiver close to his ear, Benjamin claimed, he had clearly heard every word Ward had said. Jurors spoke up, expressing skepticism. The court crier was dragooned into holding an imaginary receiver to his ear while the younger Fish showed how close he had been. At first, he said he'd been only six inches away from the mouthpiece; later, he admitted it had been more like eighteen.

The prosecution rested.

Justice Barrett invited the defense to present its case.

Bourke Cockran rose to his feet. His huge voice filled the courtroom and could be distinctly heard in the corridors beyond. He asserted that no one in New York history had ever endured such calumny as his client had suffered over the past eighteen months. He'd been accused of every kind of crime and hounded by the press, by shadowy businessmen, by the members of a "prominent family." Now, he was the innocent target of the largely uncorroborated testimony of a vengeful felon.

> James D. Fish comes here and, animated by venom, swears to anything that comes into his head, and being utterly irresponsible knows that he cannot be punished. . . . He is probably working for a pardon and to make Ward a scape-goat. It is an outrage that the liberty of a citizen should be sworn away upon the testimony of a convict, who cannot be punished for perjury because he is already under a sentence which will exceed the small margin that remains to him before he attains his allotted three-score years and ten. It is infamous that the penitentiaries should pour out their vomit for such a purpose as this. This man Fish has been brought from State Prison for a holiday to swear away the life and liberty of Ferdinand Ward.

There had been no fraud on Ward's part, in any case. Fish had needed no assurances from Ferd before certifying the check in question; he had known the bank's condition was dire and simply wanted to try to save himself as well as his institution. Testimony based on telephone conversations had never been used in court before, and Benjamin Fish's inability to say how far he'd been from the earpiece when he claimed to have heard and recognized Ferd's voice showed how utterly unreliable his testimony had been.

The district attorney had hoped Ferd himself would testify on his own behalf so that he could establish a record on which other indictments might be based. But Ferd's lawyers would not him let him anywhere near the witness stand. Instead, General Tracy called just three witnesses. None did their client much good.

William Warner, who had changed his mind about testifying, said that it had been he, not Ferd, who'd had his check certified; Ward had handed it to him in his office as payment for one of many obligations coming due that week. But he became agitated and nervous when asked by Nicoll to explain the nature of his transactions with Ward.

William C. Smith, the broker who'd handled Grant & Ward's transactions on Wall Street, claimed he had had no sense of impending crisis in the spring of 1885; it was the bank, not his part of the business, that had been in trouble, he said. But then he admitted he couldn't recall how things actually stood on May 5th or how much money he'd helped to raise or anything at all about the firm's relations with the city of New York.

Finally, General Tracy asked Julian Davies, the firm's receiver, to read off an impressive-sounding list of securities he'd found in its vault after the crash—but on redirect the prosecutor showed that none of them had actually belonged to Grant & Ward.

"Perhaps you would like to know how much money I found in the assets?" Davies asked.

"I would."

"There were $700 in the office and the bank accounts were all overdrawn."

During all of this disastrous testimony, a reporter noted, "Fish seemed to take delight in observing the nervous manifestations of his former friend and partner. Like a cat watching a mouse, Fish sat for more than two hours a few feet from Ward, with his eyes fixed on the prisoner's face."

At 7:20 in the evening on October 28, after closing statements from both sides, Justice Barrett sent the jury off to deliberate. Buck Grant had joined the crowd now, wearing a mourning band in honor of his father and eager to see Ward punished at last. Ferd and his counsel waited an hour or so. Then, escorted by Warden Kiernan and the Ludlow Street janitor, Billy Smith, he strolled to a saloon for a ham sandwich and a glass of beer.

On the way back to court he lit up a cigar and talked with a reporter for the *Sun*. As they walked along, he did his best to seem cheerful. "You newspapermen, instead of abusing me, should be my warmest friends, for have I not kept you pretty busy for over a year?" He thought his chances for acquittal were poor, and wanted to know the worst just as soon as possible. "If I am convicted I shall go up the river at once. I would rather be anywhere than in the Tombs." But he wasn't through, he warned. He was being railroaded to halt further investigations, but the powerful, faceless figures behind the prosecution should not take too much comfort in its success: "I have a great many letters . . . that will prove interesting to a great many persons and I know a great deal that has not yet been made public."

The jury filed back into the courtroom at 12:40 in the morning. Despite the lateness of the hour, most of the spectators' seats were still filled.

At the defendant's table, Ferd gnawed at his moustache and passed a hand over his eyes.

He was asked to stand. He rose, and then stared at the floor.

"Gentlemen of the jury, have you reached a verdict?" the clerk asked.

"We have agreed," foreman Huntoon answered.

"And do you find the prisoner at the bar guilty or not guilty?"

Ferd lifted his head. His hands shook.

"Guilty."[40]

Before sentencing Ferd, Judge Barrett paid tribute to the members of the jury. The trial had been truly impartial, he said; most men would not have needed even to leave their seats to come to a guilty verdict. Then, he addressed the defendant.

> I have nothing to say further to affect you. Probably it would be useless. You have remained throughout the trial apparently insensible of your condition and unrepentant. . . . You have done more than any other man ever did for undermining commercial honor and affecting injuriously financial confidence. Yet your demeanor shows no repentance whatever. I simply content myself with passing judgment upon you that you be confined in the State Prison at hard labor for ten years.[41]

Shortly after two that afternoon, a closed carriage stopped in front of the Forty-second Street entrance to Grand Central Depot. Four men got down and hurried inside. Two were lawmen—Sheriff Alexander Davidson of New York County, and Warden Kiernan. Ed Doty, carrying a black box tied with twine that contained a change of underwear for his boyhood friend and former boss, struggled to keep up as the group crossed the waiting room beneath the vast glass-and-iron ceiling.

It was the fourth man—small and slender with a blond moustache, wearing an elegantly tailored suit and smoking a cigar—who quickly drew a crowd. Ferd Ward had first passed through Grand Central a dozen years before. He had been penniless then, anxious but eager and anonymous. He had no more money now than he'd had when he arrived—was hundreds of thousands of dollars in debt, in fact—and was almost universally reviled. The 2:30 train that would carry him north along the Hudson to Sing Sing was about to pull out. As Ward and his escorts hurried across the waiting room and down the long stone platform between hissing trains old acquaintances nodded to him. Ferd nodded back, but when one stepped forward and tried to speak to him, he moved past without replying.

The little party filed into the smoking car and settled into the dusty velvet-covered swivel seats. Several reporters got on too, and just as the train started to move, newsboys appeared on the platform, shouting, "Evening papers! Evening papers! Sentence of Ferdinand Ward!"

Ferd kept his composure for a time, chatting quietly with his escorts. But when the train reached Spuyten Duyvil in the Bronx and the broad Hudson swept into view, he fell silent and let the hand that held his cigar fall to his side.

FOURTEEN

The Model Prisoner

At first glance, Sing Sing looked more like an oddly compacted industrial city than a traditional prison. A cluster of tall redbrick factory chimneys streamed black smoke into the sky above the Hudson. White clouds of steam rose from a warren of workshops. New York's largest prison was also the largest source of involuntary labor in the United States. When Ferd arrived, virtually all of the 1,500 inmates who lived in the sixty-year-old, six-story stone cellblock that dominated the complex spent six days a week performing contract labor. As many as 900 men were marched to the Perry & Company stove works each morning; some 200 more labored in the Bay State Shoe Factory; another 160 toiled in a vast laundry, washing, drying, and starching 2,400 shirts a day. Scores more made cabinets and furniture, forged chains, fashioned harnesses, and hacked away at the marble and limestone quarries that honeycombed the nearby hillside. Freight trains rattled through the prison grounds on a special spur that led down to two riverfront quays where sailing ships and steamboats came and went all day, their decks piled high with prison-made stoves and shoes, bookcases and coiled lengths of chain for distribution up and down the river. "The steam screeched through factory whistles," a visitor reported, "pigeons cooed on the gutters, lines of convicts tramped to and fro, adjacent mill wheels flew around like lightning, . . . ceaseless activity dominated all the place."[1]

Incarceration was meant to punish, according to New York's superintendent of prisons; rehabilitation was a "senseless notion" dreamed up by "morbid sentimentalists."[2] Prisoners were to pay for their upkeep with their hard work—and were to be kept at it by a combination of strict discipline and unapologetic brutality.

When Ferd ducked beneath the ivy that overhung the main entrance to the prison and disappeared inside, he was entering a world unlike any he had ever known. Newspapermen were barred from following him very far, but Jimmy Connaughton, the big, beefy, red-faced principal keeper, later came out to tell them what had gone on. Ferd was escorted to the chaplain's office and asked to wait, facing the wall, arms folded, forbidden to speak, until the prison clerk appeared.

Name?

Ferdinand Ward.

Age?

Thirty-three.

Occupation?

Banker.

Religion?

Protestant.

Had he attended Sunday school? He had.

He stood five feet nine and a half inches; weighed 130 pounds; had blue, deep-set eyes; "a long rather large and crooked nose," and "a long neck and large Adam's apple."[3]

He affirmed that he could read and write, drank alcohol, used tobacco moderately, and had never been in prison before. He agreed to sign the form authorizing prison officials to read all his mail, coming in and going out: he could receive an unlimited number of letters but was permitted to mail just one envelope a month. Contact with his family was severely limited, too: they could send him a box of eatables every sixty days, and he was permitted a single visitor for only half an hour every other month.

He was issued a striped uniform and told to bathe. He turned over the contents of his pockets, including an alligator-skin wallet and $185.77 in cash, to be held until his release. The doctor pronounced him able-bodied enough to start work in the stove factory on Monday morning.

Then he was escorted to cell number 927, on the fourth tier on the northern side of the prison, facing away from the river. His neighbor on one side was a burglar; on the other side was a lifer in for first-degree manslaughter.

"We shall have no difficulty with Ward," Connaughton assured the reporters as they started back toward the city. "He has come here in the right spirit, and intends to do his duty. He will be shown no favors. We are favorably impressed with his conduct, and I predict that he will get through without even a reprimand."[4]

Throughout the process, Ferd had been polite, deferential, and eager to please, as he almost always was. But things weren't quite as they seemed. During his first hour or so in prison, Ferd had almost surely been asked another question Connaughton had not told the newspapermen about, a question asked of every newcomer: Could he be counted on to "put up?"[5]—that is, to come up with enough money to pay off guards and keepers for the soft jobs and special privileges most prisoners could not afford.

Sing Sing was every bit as corrupt as the Ludlow Street Jail had been. "The world of 'touch' does not end for the convicted prisoner when he leaves the county prison," one of Ferd's fellow prisoners wrote. "In fact, he really is only entering it when he gets to Sing Sing and the value of money is nowhere more assured than within the prison walls themselves."[6]

Ferd understood the uses of money better than most, and he quickly sized up the officials he would need to please. Warden Augustus A. Brush was technically in charge. A corpulent gray-bearded martinet, he was also the Republican boss of the 1st Assembly District of Dutchess County. Once, when a prisoner threatened to reveal that thousands of dollars were missing from the accounts of just one of the contract businesses under the warden's supervision, Brush saw to it that the potential whistleblower was shunted off to an asylum to assure his silence.

But the man who really ran things was Principal Keeper Connaughton. "Wardens come and go, the administrations change," a veteran convict remembered, "but Jimmy remains always smiling, always on duty, alert, vigilant, capable and dominant."[7] Connaughton was a Tammany man who counted among his close friends Ferd's lawyer, Bourke Cockran, and Henry Jaehne, a New York alderman locked up for massive theft, whose paid-for prison privileges included being allowed to keep two pet dogs and to wander anywhere he liked. Johnny Hope, a cigar-smoking bank burglar, acted as Connaughton's unofficial assistant and deal maker, selling easy posts for handsome prices and keeping his boss abreast of what other prisoners were up to.

Poorly trained, poorly paid, and vastly outnumbered, the keepers and guards Connaughton supervised gambled and drank and routinely pilfered state property. "After a man has been a prison officer for a little time, he loses his perception of ownership," a long time prisoner remembered.

> There are old officers in Sing Sing prison living in rented houses in the village, which they have furnished with tables, chairs, bedsteads, cutlery and tin-ware from the prison; the soap with which their weekly washing is done is similarly obtained, and the oil which they burn is supplied in the same way. It doesn't make any difference what it is, they will and do take it: bread from the prison bakery; meat for their dogs from the convict if it isn't good enough to eat themselves, pens, paper, pencils, anything and everything. . . . The convict who gets along best is he who aids them.[8]

Even with time off for good behavior, Ferd's ten-year sentence was sure to keep him behind bars for six and a half years. For all of that time, he was determined to be among those who got along best.

Sing Sing was rugged, frightening. There were twelve hundred tiny cells, each just seven feet deep by three feet wide, arranged back to back in six tiers. Each cell contained a bucket, a wash-basin, a filthy straw mattress, and a narrow iron bed frame hooked to the thick stone wall so it could be folded up during daylight hours. Fetid air and fingers of light entered through the iron grate that topped each thick steel door. Cells were icy in winter, stifling in summer, and far too small for exercise—just three steps from front to back. Bedbugs infested the tiers. Men were allowed one bath and a single pair of fresh underwear a week.

Punishment for infractions, real or imagined, were brutal and severe. Any convict who talked back, one veteran guard recalled, ran the risk of being hustled into his cell and beaten into a "pudding." More serious offenders were thrown into one of ten special "dark" cells, to subsist in pitch blackness on nothing but bread and water, sometimes for ten days at a time. Men thought to be shirking work were subjected to what Principal Keeper Connaughton called the "weighing machine"—they were handcuffed behind their backs and hung by their wrists with their feet off the floor until they begged to be allowed to return to their jobs. Connaughton claimed that no man ever stood it more than thirty seconds; in fact, he sometimes suspended men for up to thirty minutes, until they passed out. The prison chaplain, Rev. Silas W. Edgerton—whom Ferd's father considered a friend as well as a colleague—often asked to be present at the weighings, not to offer spiritual solace but because he liked seeing men writhe in pain and plead for mercy. Perhaps not surprisingly, his Sunday sermons were often punctuated by hisses.

The daily schedule was monotonous and unchanging. Everyone was awakened at 6:15. There were fifteen minutes for washing. Then, inmates were ordered into the corridor to dump out their night buckets and fall into line for breakfast. They marched to the huge, low-ceilinged dining hall in lockstep. Each man held the sides of the man in front of him with both hands while the leader folded his arms and gave the step, accenting it sharply with his left foot, the rest of the men marking time with him, moving down the corridor in perfect cadence like some giant, striped, many-legged insect. A keeper with a club ensured that not a word was spoken. Breakfast, served in silence at long tables, never changed: hash, hunks of bread, and tin cups of "bootleg"—fake coffee brewed from dried peas and charred bread.

At 7:30, a whistle blew and the men were marched off to work. When Ferd arrived at the stove factory on his first morning, its assistant superintendent recalled, ashes were heaped waist high around the boilers. He asked his boss if he could have a convict to shovel it all up and cart it away. Yes, the boss said—but "don't take Ward."

The fix was evidently already in, but over the factory's din the assistant misunderstood his boss and thought he'd said, "*Take* Ward."

He turned to the keeper and asked him if he could put Ferd to work.

"Take the devil," the keeper said. "It serves the son of a bitch right."[9]

Ferd was handed a shovel and did his best, carrying ashes till his hands blistered. But he couldn't understand how this could be happening to him. He'd already paid to be excused from this sort of thing. He wondered aloud if former mayor Grace, whom he had publicly accused of profiting from the fictional contract business, might somehow be responsible. "Has he got pull enough here to hound me . . . and make me do a piece of work like this?"[10] he asked. He was assured it had been a simple mistake, but he was kept at it long enough for the newspapers to headline their stories: "Shoveling Ashes in Sing Sing; Ward Does His Bit."[11] Then he was shifted to the job he had been meant to have all along: keeping accounts for the shoe contractor.

Within a day or two, he realized that the single basket of foodstuffs Ella and his mother were allowed to send him every two months would be insufficient for his rarefied tastes. Prison fare was appalling—salt pork, watery stew, codfish on Fridays. He tentatively approached a lifer and asked if, for a price, he'd be willing to accept delivery of another basket and then quietly turn it over to him. The older man told him to go to hell: "You come around here trying to get me into more trouble and I'll brain you."[12] Ferd backed off.

It would take time to learn the ropes. A few evenings later, he was lying in his darkened cell when he heard a hoarse whisper coming through the ventilator in the wall behind him. It was a convict named Morgan, locked up on the other side of the wall for grand larceny. He had a proposal to make. As a Sing Sing veteran he knew how lonely prison could be for a newcomer, how difficult it was to confine one's communication with the outside world to a single letter a month. He could help. He had a way of smuggling mail out undetected, but it would cost Ferd some money. Ferd agreed to pay, though he said it would take him a day or two to get the cash together. He wrote three letters, folded them as small as possible, and poked them through the ventilator.

All were addressed to the same woman. The *New York Tribune* identified her only as "a lady in Brooklyn . . . not his wife." It's impossible now to know for certain who she was. But the most likely candidate seems to have been a striking, dark-haired twenty-seven-year-old woman named Isabelle Augusta Storer. We know very little about her other than that she was born at Kreischerville in the township of Westfield on Staten Island, where her father, John W. Storer, was in the clay and brick-making business with his brothers. She was the seventh of ten children born to her mother, Rachel Shea Storer, and seems to have lived with relatives in Brooklyn. She knew both Wards well, and attended Wells College in Aurora, New York, for a single term in 1885—her tuition had possibly been paid by Ferd. Beyond that, she remains a mystery, relevant only because she would reappear in his life nearly a decade later.

The *Tribune* reporter, who evidently got a look at one of Ferd's first letters to the mysterious woman, pronounced it "not emotional. It simply gave a history of Ward in Sing-Sing prison, how he liked black coffee, bacon and a [tiny] cell, with no poker parties and no margins for profits."

But for Ella, abandoned with her infant son, newspaper stories about her husband trying to smuggle letters out to an unmarried woman must have been deeply humiliating. Her disappointment and anger may account for the fact that while Ferd kept in his cell nearly all the almost-weekly letters his wife wrote to him in prison, only three brief notes survive from 1886. At about this time, too, she changed her son's name from Ferdinand to Clarence.

In the end, Ferd's first letters to the mysterious woman were never mailed. Morgan turned them over to Jimmy Connaughton, perhaps because Ferd was slow to pay, possibly to curry favor with the principal keeper. Ferd claimed he hadn't known he was doing anything wrong. "From that moment to this, Ward has obeyed the rules implicitly," Connaughton told a reporter several months later. "He has never been subjected to punishment, and would not be if he were here a hundred years. He is a model prisoner."[13]

Connaughton knew firsthand that that was only partly true, that Ferd would always be willing to put up, to pay heavily for special privileges. Among the papers Ferd kept in his cell was a tiny folded slip of lined paper he had addressed to the principal keeper himself.

> Sir:
> There is a man named Harry Johnson locked in cell 56 in the extension. Can't he be moved to cell 83 and then put me in 56? Please do this for me and I will be *very grateful to you.*
>   Respectfully,
>   Ferdinand Ward

Ferd's note did the trick. Convict Johnson stayed where he was, but someone—presumably Connaughton himself—scrawled "51" on the back of the note and Ferd was moved to that cell. Ella—who had supplied her husband with the means with which to express his gratitude to the warden—wrote to Ferd that she was pleased to hear that he liked his new cell and was now living with "so few of the other prisoners."[14]

In letters to his parents and his siblings, Ferd always maintained the air of aggrieved innocence he had affected since boarding school days.

His mother summarized for Sarah one of the letters he wrote home to Geneseo in the summer of 1886: "It presents a sad account of the unfavorable influences around him and yet a determination to avoid contamination if possible.* Let this be the theme of our prayers that God will keep him from degenerating and help him to follow the best of his instincts as a gentleman and become only more refined as he sees the want of it in others. Pray, too, that he may find favor with the guards and *all* who are over him."[15]

He did find favor with them. A number were already on his payroll. With cash from friends and family members funneled in to him through compliant guards and keepers, Ferd bought himself a series of easy jobs: he left the shoe factory to become a messenger for Connaughton and was permitted the run of the prison; then he counted shirts washed and ironed by others in the laundry. Finally, he took over an old printing press that ran off letterheads and bills for Perry & Company, using the skills he'd learned as a teenager in Geneseo turning out his *Valley Gem*.

His accommodations steadily improved. An oriental rug materialized to warm the stone floor of his cell. A hair mattress replaced the standard-issue heap of straw. Ella embroidered a handsome silk cover with which to hide his bed when it was hooked up to the wall. She sent him a comfortable easy chair, too, a reading lamp, and a steady supply of the especially fragrant tobacco he liked to smoke in an old Dutch

---

* Ferd's avoidance of "contamination" did not include steering clear of dirty jokes. This one, carefully written out in pencil in his own hand so that he wouldn't forget it, was among the items he kept in his prison trunk.

Two brothers named Moss had a misfortune on the same day. One lost his wife, the other his boat. A lady Scripture-reader sympathized with the one who lost his boat, thinking it was the same who lost his wife.

Lady: "Oh. Mr. Moss, I am sorry for your loss."

Moss: "Oh, man, it was a loss, but she was rotten the first time I got into her."

Lady (Horrified): Pray, don't say that Mr. Moss."

Moss: "Why the first time I got into her she made water."

Lady (Trying to find somewhere to run away to): "Horrible!"

Moss: "Why, she had such a crack I had to screw her up and do her bottom over!"

Lady (Almost paralyzed): "Horrible, horrible!"

Moss: "Why, when me and George and John and Bill Blair got into her together, she busted."

Lady faints.

Author's collection.

pipe. His walls were hung with pictures and memorabilia, including a hand-painted menu bound in red velvet, a souvenir of a dinner given by General Grant in honor of the president of Mexico at which he had been a guest. A reporter for the *National Police Gazette* who toured Sing Sing in the summer of 1886 pronounced Ferd's cell "the nicest in the prison."[16]

Despite the privileges he enjoyed, most of the other inmates seem to have liked Ferd, in part because, as always, he was happy to share the wealth other people provided him with. A pickpocket recalled that Ferdinand Ward was "one of the best liked of the convicts I met [in Sing Sing]. He did many a kindness in stir to those who were tough and had few friends."[17] Ferd kept a bottle of whiskey in the print shop so that he could pour a drink for any thirsty keeper or privileged prisoner who happened to drop by. (The alcohol was made and sold to convicts for fifty cents a pint by the prison physician, Dr. Hiram Barber, known as "Butcher Barber" to his patients.)

On Thanksgiving Day in 1886, when most prisoners were locked in their cells all day, one ex-convict remembered, a keeper named Gale escorted Ferd and four other prisoners to Perry & Company's stove-fitting shop. Ferd's companions included two embezzlers, "Allen the Dude" and "Sanctimonious Morse," a con man called "Hungry Joe," and James Jameson, identified only as "a negro burglar." The official story was that the company clerk needed them to help overhaul the company books. But "instead of looking over ledgers . . . the four white convicts spent the day playing draw-poker, smoking cigars, drinking wine and liquor, and enjoying a delicious collation which had been sent to them by friends in New York. Convict Jameson acted as waiter and Keeper Gale watched the games and took out [40] percent of every pot. The cards, wines and delicacies had been sent by the American Express in four boxes to Perry & Company, but were in reality for the poker players, and were opened by them." The games went on all day. Ferd ended up winning $7.50 and gave $3 of it to the keeper. "At five o'clock," the prisoner remembered, Ferd and his friends "were led in a very merry condition back to their cells. They couldn't walk straight."[18]

Ferd's chronic conviction that he was suffering for sins of which others were at least equally guilty deepened when federal indictments against William S. Warner and his brother-in-law, J. Henry Work, for stealing from the Marine Bank were dropped on a technicality. Referee Hamilton Cole, appointed to decide to whom Ferd's assets should be assigned, did finally overturn the midnight conveyances Ferd and Ella had been forced to make: Warner was ordered to give up the titles to all the property he'd taken from them and to pay to Ferd's creditors $1,401,908.79 (all of the supposed profits he had made on his investments in phantom contracts, plus interest accrued since the crash).* Ferd was pleased to hear that Warner was now nearly as penniless as he was. Ella was pleased as well, even though he'd run out on a $500 bill at the Champion House: "He has no money now, they say," she told her husband.[19] When the State of New York belatedly moved against Warner for violating its banking laws, he managed to escape arrest and flee the country with his wife and children.[†]

Ferd found at least some consolation in the fact that James Fish was still behind bars. And so when word reached him that Fish's sons, John, Irving, and Dean, had begun circulating a petition among the banker's old associates aimed at securing a presidential pardon for their father, he wrote right away to Grover Cleveland to protest. He had no desire to stand in the way of Mr. Fish's freedom, he said; after all, his former partner was an old man and hadn't long to live. But he did not wish to be left alone to shoulder the blame for the failures of Grant & Ward and the Marine Bank, either, and so asked "most respectfully" that before the president acted he acquaint himself with "certain facts and letters" he would be happy to provide.[20]

Colonel Daniel S. Lamont, private and military secretary to the president, wrote back to say that, while no such petition had yet arrived, if one did Ferd would be informed.

Word of Ferd's letter somehow reached Auburn Prison. Fish imme-

---

* Referee Cole did not claim that Warner had been aware that the firm's dealings were fraudulent (though he did not "make a finding of positive good faith" on Warner's part, either). Nor did he believe Warner had used duress to force Ferd and Ella to transfer their property to him. It would have been perfectly legitimate for him to obtain the transfer if he had been a valid creditor of the firm. But he was not a valid creditor. Since the contracts in which he had invested never existed, the $578,500 worth of obligations Warner claimed the firm owed to him were "mere waste paper and [therefore] could not be enforced against anyone." Furthermore, when he had taken the Wards' property he knew the firm was insolvent. *New York Herald*, March 18, 1886.

† He bought himself a handsome country home near Turbridge Wells in England, where he lived until he suffered a fatal heart attack in 1890.

diately agreed to speak at length with two reporters for the *New York World,* eager to drum up public sympathy for himself and further blacken his ex-partner's name. He professed no interest in going free: "Were it not for my children," he claimed, "I would rather end my days here. . . . All I want to show is that I have never been anything but an honest man." Ward was to blame for everything. He was a toady, a liar, an ingrate, a thief. Fish went on for two hours. His "dignity and refinement" impressed his visitors, whose story appeared beneath a sympathetic headline: "It Was a Great Tragedy in Which the Old Man Was an Actor."[21]

When the published interview was shown to Ferd at Sing Sing a few days later, he responded in kind. Fish was every bit as guilty as he was. The Marine Bank had been "rotten" for years before it collapsed. He now claimed the phony checks for which he'd been sent to prison had actually been written at Fish's suggestion; they had been "dummies," never meant to go through. With his former partner's connivance he had written similar checks "hundreds of times" to improve appearances at the bank. "Fish pretends he was ignorant about what this contract business was," he continued. "Well, perhaps he was: but if so, it was because he wanted to be. . . . Fish didn't care where the money came from so long as he got his monthly dividends."[22]

As soon as the pardon petition, signed by scores of businessmen, reached the White House, Ferd wrote the president again, demanding to know what it said: "If [Fish] in his application seeks to make me the sole instigator & prosecutor of the troubles which wrecked the firm of Grant & Ward & the Marine Bank, I do *most earnestly* desire to defend myself by presenting certain facts & letters which have not met the public eye & which, I feel Sir, will convince you that he stands equally guilty with myself."[23]

Nothing angered Ferd more than the widespread notion that he had somehow squirreled away a fortune. "There are people right here in this prison who think I have got a lot of money—a million or so stowed away," he told the *World.* "But I am poor; I haven't anything, although I don't suppose you could make the public think so. They tell all sorts of stories about my family. . . . My wife is living on $1,500 a year."[24]

When the skeptical editor of the *Baltimore American* read those words he asked a reporter traveling to Stamford on other business to see what he could find out about Ella's finances. She and Clarence were now living in the house she owned at 18 South Street. The newspaper-man spent an afternoon across the road with his notepad.

> From what I heard and saw I was convinced that if Mrs. Ward really does live on less than $1,500 per annum she is as pecu-liarly talented in financial management as her enterprising hus-band. Her house is a large three-story dwelling. A sweeping carriage drive leads past the portico on the side, and in the rear is a well-appointed stable sheltering three horses.
>
> The big shade-trees on the grounds, from one of which depends a hammock filled with satin-covered cushions; a group of cozy easy-chairs on the portico; vases and hanging baskets filled with flowers and trailing plants—all this gave an appear-ance of wealth which seemed entirely incompatible with the small income which Mrs. Ward says she enjoys.
>
> While I stood eyeing the house with the curiosity and free-dom of a stranger, Mrs. Ward came out the front door and commenced to water and arrange the plants in the swinging baskets on the portico. She wore a dainty morning wrapper of foulard silk, which, despite its flowing proportions, could not conceal the beautiful contour of her graceful figure.
>
> There was a cold, indifferent look on her face and a certain mechanism about her movements which showed that her mind was not on her work. Could she have been thinking of her dash-ing young husband, . . . within the gray stone walls up among the Hudson hills? It seemed more than possible, as once she paused, and, seating herself slowly in one of the chairs, turned her face wearily skyward. She sat like a statue for nearly three minutes, when she caught a glimpse of the motionless spec-tator near the street, then she got up and disappeared. Mrs. Ward's home is small, but it is handsomely furnished, and she keeps three servants. If she lives on less than $3,000 or $4,000 per annum she certainly has acquired the faculty of making a dollar go twice as far as the average mortal.[25]

The *Tribune* correspondent had heavily embellished his story. Ella's house was modest. Her husband had no hidden fortune. Whatever she was spending came from the interest on her share of what was left of her father's estate. Months of anxiety and loneliness and disil-lusionment had taken their toll; she now looked far older than she was, matronly and heavyset, unsmiling, peering out at the world through pince-nez.

Despite everything, she had remained committed to her husband, dutifully writing to him at least once a week, packing and shipping his box of foodstuffs every two months, trying somehow to keep alive a marriage that she must have known by now had been built largely on lies. Ferd's letters to her are lost, but her letters to him survive and suggest what his must have been like. He constantly asked for things—new shoes, silk handkerchiefs, a lampshade, a tobacco pouch, a sachet, a new razor, the latest novel by H. Rider Haggard. And he never stopped demanding cash—from friends, from family members, from her own bank account. She was "greatly mortified" when he tried to wheedle money out of Dr. Vail, their Stamford minister,[26] and angered when he somehow managed to persuade Brentano's to send him a sheaf of expensive sheet music and then present her with the bill: "This will have to come out of the money which I have set aside for your box," she told him. "You must remember, Ferd, that my income is smaller than ever."[27]

When he told her he was sending someone to see her on a "business matter," she saw it for what it was: a scheme to funnel illicit cash to him through an intermediary. "I feel that I would rather not see anyone on business," she told him. "There is nothing that I care to talk about in regard to my affairs excepting [with] Mr. [James] McKeen [her friend and attorney]."[28] And when Ferd spoke of publishing an autobiography intended to bolster his case against a pardon for Fish, she was adamantly opposed: "I would not have you do it for anything. You know how I feel about any more publicity."[29]

The details of her own life did not seem to interest him. She'd had a bleak Christmas, she reported one year, helped decorate the Stamford church for Easter with daisies, buttercups, and ferns, went yachting with old friends off Shippan Point in the summer, and suffered from sick headaches that often kept her housebound. Even the baby's activities prompted little response from Ferd's cell. "Bunnie"—Ella's pet name for Clarence—was "very bright and has a most remarkable memory," she wrote; at two and a half he could "repeat nearly all the stories in Mother Goose" and sang "a great deal and has such a funny deep voice."[30] When she finally had the boy's long yellow curls cut and sent a handful of clippings to Sing Sing, Ferd didn't thank her. He didn't bother to acknowledge the photographs of Clarence she sent him, either.

She felt deserted. Her brothers and sister visited only rarely; none of them could understand why she remained so loyal to the man who had done so much damage to their family. Her mother, in Brooklyn, was sinking into severe dementia that at least one newspaper attributed to the shock of her son-in-law's betrayal. Ella took Clarence to the Champion House, where she and Ferd had once entertained their New York friends, but left quickly, feeling "rather lonesome as there is no one here I care for."[31]

When Ferd suggested that she and the boy move in with his parents—in order to keep her inheritance intact and available to him on his release—Ella rejected the idea outright. "Do not let my future trouble you," she told him. "I could not go to Geneseo and I feel that it would not be best, either for your mother or myself."[32] She was right about that. Her mother-in-law, who had always disapproved of Ella's "worldly" family, was also scornful and dismissive of her personally. "I hope Ella has been to see you—Poor thing," Jane Shaw Ward wrote to her daughter in the summer of 1886. "She has not been well and I suppose is troubled about many things. She insisted on sending Ferd a box though I begged her not to. It was to be sent tomorrow to arrive with mine, or about the same time. I wish she might not send every time for I can do it a great deal better than she. She does not say a word about coming here, but I will not urge it. Perhaps bye and bye she will come."[33] She never did.

To numb her headaches and perhaps also to blunt the increasing loneliness she felt, Ella began to rely more and more on alcohol-laced "female tonics" prescribed by her family physician. In mid-September of 1887, she failed to appear in the visitors' room at Sing Sing as promised. "I suppose you are wondering why you do not hear from me," she told her husband a few days later. "I had a very severe fall last week. I was just stepping down the stairs when I turned my foot and down I went the whole length. The girls picked me up as I was insensible. After I recovered I sent for the doctor and found no bones broken, but I am very much bruised and have a fearful-looking eye. I am better although not able to leave my door today but in a few days I shall be all right."[34]

Three photographs—now tea-colored and faded—were taken in Ferdinand De Wilton Ward's tiny second-floor study in Geneseo sometime in the late 1880s. The room is a dark, claustrophobic place. Books are shelved in double rows—leather-bound sets with titles in gilt, massive reference volumes, miniature prayer books. There are heaps of manuscript, too, and piles of journals and stacks of small notes impaled on spikes. Newspaper clippings are pinned to the edges of the bookshelves, along with maps, lists, and two large photographs of a mummy's desiccated face, meant to remind visitors of man's mortality. The old man himself sits at the heart of these defenses, wearing a high clerical collar and self-consciously holding a pen above a blank sheet of paper. His long, pouchy face is composed, unreadable, as if he were determined to withhold from the intrusive photographer any hint of the impact of the disgrace his son had brought to him and to his family.

Publicly, he stood steadfastly at Ferd's side. When a Boston columnist argued that his son and Fish were equally guilty and that the banker therefore deserved no pardon, he sent him a letter of thanks.

> Most heartily do I thank you for your true and manly utterances that cannot but tell for justice regarding my son. For nearly three years Mr. Fish took two meals a day at his table and was treated [as] a parent. My child did wrong. He himself admits it. But he was a country lad. In Wall Street he met those who were old enough to be his father; temptations were presented, and he was not old enough to see the result; nor strong enough to resist. He has no desire to have Mr. Fish kept in prison, but he does not wish to bear all the burden of his evil doing. My boy is not chargeable with immorality, but is gentlemanly, generous, moral and an idol in a large domestic circle among whom are my brother-in-law, Hon. Freeman Clark, late Hon. Samuel G. Selden, etc., etc., etc.[35]

But privately, he could not bear to see his boy locked up. In September 1887, he told Sarah he planned a trip to meetings of clergymen in Auburn, New York City, Princeton, and Stamford. "Here is a question—to be seriously pondered—don't answer hastily—ask your good husband's opinion. Is it needful or desirable for me to stop at *Sing Sing*? My strong feeling is *against* it. I *don't* think that F [would] like to have me. . . . If I must see F, I shall. Don't say ought [about the] above in letters to Mother."[36]

Jane Shaw Ward was photographed separately at about the same time. Small and shrunken, she sits dwarfed by a cane rocker she and her husband had managed to bring home with them from India forty years before. On the wall behind her hangs a Seneca mask, a relic of her husband's boyhood in the Bergen woods. She wears an old-fashioned lace cap to cover her thinning white hair. Her eyes stare mournfully away, and she keeps her clasped hands partly hidden in her skirt because she continued to think they were too large to look well. She seems utterly alone, cut off from the world by deafness and old age and the unimaginable things her son has been convicted of doing.

She took what she called "melancholy pleasure in packing poor Ferdie's box"[37] and agonized over his ceaseless requests for cash. "This brings me to the oft-repeated subject of money," she told him in one letter. "I do not know how to get it to you without acting underhanded. If you will only tell me just how I can honestly send it, you shall have $6 or $8 every month and I would not consider it wasted at all."[38]

Then, on December 30, 1887, she received from Ferd the letter she had hoped for all her life. He said he had at last become a committed Christian: "I feel Mother dear that, hard as this imprisonment is, it is going to be the best thing for me, for it has brought before me the evil of my ways and I feel from day to day a growing rest in God's promises & mercy. I never felt so before, but now it seems at times as if He was right here in my cell and I talk to Him and tell Him all I feel and it brings comfort & hope & new courage."[39]

Jane reported her joy at his conversion to Sarah.

Ferd's father was not so easily persuaded by his son's newfound piety. For one thing, his profession of faith was accompanied by yet another request for money to be sent to him by way of an errant keeper. "Oh, that he may not be *deceiving himself* & *is* respecting his religious feelings," he wrote.[40] "Doesn't he know the consequences to us & to him to be perilous should we send it? He cannot need it for lawful purposes. Doesn't he know that many are watching to see him do wrong & thus keep him where he is through the full term of his sentence? We must not send him a dime. Our motive is right, though he may not see it."[41]

Ferd did not see it, and continued to shower his mother with bitter complaints. His tone had not changed since he'd been a homesick schoolboy. He complained again about his eyes, about the hard work he was forced to do. Will was being cruel to him. Ella was seeking to punish him by failing to visit frequently enough. No one would send him any cash, even though other prisoners had plenty of it.

His mother wrote him three times a week—"Letter writing is the great relief of her burdened heart," her husband said[42]—but her letters showed as little understanding of her son's true nature as they ever had. He was not to dwell on "the sad and discouraging features" of life in prison, she told him.

Try, dear, to find a little joy in turning your thoughts upon those who love you outside of your sin and sorrow, who when they think of you rejoice to know that once you did all you could to make them happy and who find a great deal of enjoyment in what you have done. Think of me in my carriage driving friends about to see the country and taking great pleasure in the many improvements of the place and the furniture your kindness provided for the home. Think of Will, too, with his wife and children and Sallie with all her hopes and comforts with her family. I know you think of these things but I want you to have *joy* in our happiness and comforts and don't compare and contrast your own condition with ours. It is a true saying that there is no happiness so great in this life as in knowing of the happiness of those we love and rejoicing in it. It will lessen one's despondency and keep the mind from giving way. So, let your imagination picture all the comfort and happiness that those whom you love are enjoying even though you cannot partake in the same.[43]

Ferd was incapable of partaking in such joy. In his own eyes he remained a perpetual sufferer; the happiness of others was only a reminder of his own unhappiness, evidence of how unfairly the world continued to treat him.

"Above all, dear," his mother told him on August 17, 1888, "don't dwell on the fear that you may die in prison."

God will take care of that as he has done in thousands of cases before and if He should be allowed would not the freedom from sin and sorrow be joyful to you . . . ? If you cannot live to redeem your own character, Christ will redeem it for you. Leave it all with Him, dear, and don't be afraid.

You have many loving friends and you must not dwell on the sad features of your life or the unjust charges that may be brought against you. It is not God's fault that men are unjust or unkind, and as to the terrible life of a prison, remember dear, that you would never have been brought to it if you had been faithful to God. Try then to serve your time with courage and hope and don't fear dying in prison, for Christ will be just as near you there as anywhere, and the world is a dangerous place to live in. Just make up your mind that you are better off in

prison than you would be in Wall Street with your old disposition to be rich.[44]

A month or so after she wrote that letter, Jane Shaw Ward fell ill with
"catarrhal fever"—acute influenza. She died early on the morning of
October 6, 1888, at the age of seventy-six.

Her funeral was held in the Central Presbyterian Church two days
later. Sarah was unable to attend. But William hurried east to help his
grieving father get through the ceremony. Ella and four-year-old Clarence were there, too.

Cousin George K. Ward of Danville was one of the four clergymen
of different faiths who officiated. Reverend Joseph Kitteridge delivered the sermon. Jane Shaw Ward, he said, had been "a modest, retiring woman, almost morbidly sensitive to publicity" but a tireless and
effective worker in the cause of Christianity—altogether "a woman
worth emulating." The congregation joined in the words of her favorite hymn:

> *My hope is built on nothing less*
> *Than Jesus' blood and righteousness.*
> *I dare not trust the sweetest frame,*
> *But wholly lean on Jesus' name.*
>
> *On Christ the solid rock I stand,*
> *All other ground is sinking sand.*
> *All other ground is sinking sand.*

Friends and former parishioners bore the body to Edge Hill Cemetery.
Clergymen of all denominations filed along behind, accompanied by
scores of townspeople. Many downtown businesses closed. Jane's fellow members of the Women's Christian Temperance Union passed a
resolution in praise of her "blameless life." The Young Ladies' Missionary Society had the grave lined with evergreen boughs. There were
banked floral tributes, as well—including a crown and cross of carna-
tions and white roses and a pillow of mixed blossoms with "REST"
picked out in heliotrope.

Six weeks later, Ferdinand's mother-in-law died at 37 Monroe Place,
her children at her side. Ella was shattered: "How sad it is to feel that

you are in your old home for the last time," she wrote Ferd. "I am sitting in the backroom upstairs and looking at papa's pictures and my thoughts go back to when he was with me."[45] Ferdinand was unmoved: he knew Mrs. Green's offspring blamed him for her decline; it had begun, they believed, when it became clear that her son-in-law had stolen her fortune and most of theirs. He was convinced that Ella's siblings would somehow now cheat her out of her legacy, a legacy in which he had hoped one day to share. Ella tried to reassure him. Her brothers and sister would never take advantage of her, she said, and in any case her lawyer, James McKeen, was there to protect her interests. This was of little comfort to Ferd: her interests concerned him only as far as they coincided with his own, and he knew that McKeen—who had attended his trial, had listened to his testimony before Referee Cole, and knew how he had plundered the Green family fortune—was hostile to him.

Ferd hoped that Will might intervene on his behalf, but in January 1889, he and Kate and their family set sail for Europe. Will was to represent Colorado at the upcoming Paris Exposition. It was an honor to have been asked. It was also a way to get out from under the pressure of his imprisoned brother's inexhaustible demands. On New Year's Day, he wrote a farewell letter to Ferd.

> My first letter of the New Year will be to you my dear brother and with it the wish that the year may not be more sad or heavy than you can bear.
>
> I sail on Saturday and shall not see you till my return. I wish to send you a word of love—of brother love, constant and sincere—although I know that you do not think I love you as I do. Words are vain at times and I will not write them but all I can say is that you have never had nor will you have in life a truer heart near you than mine.
>
> Your loving brother,
Will[46]

A few weeks later, more bad news: on January 29, President Grover Cleveland commuted James Fish's sentence. He was to be released on May 11.

Ferd was livid. Bourke Cockran begged him to keep his anger to

himself; it would not advance his cause. "I hope you will be very careful in the 'Fish' matter," Ella wrote, "and say *nothing* to the papers."[47]
She was too late. Ferd had already told a visiting reporter that he was
"pleased" by the news, so long as the commutation was "based on the
grounds of [Fish's] age, failing health and that he has suffered enough
for the crime. My opinion would be different if it has come through
further vilification of me."[48]

His worst fears were quickly confirmed. In his official memoran-
dum, Cleveland took note of the "great respectability and business
standing" of those who had signed the pardon petition, and then went
on to say that, while he did not wish to comment upon the evidence
against Fish, the banker's "actual and willful intent to defraud depends
upon inferences somewhat uncertain."

Ferd fired off two letters to the White House. "That the public
should, for one moment, think that Fish had no 'criminal intent' to
defraud," he told the president, "is so unjust and cruel that I cannot sit
still and quietly submit to the injustice of it."[49] Writing to the president's secretary, he was considerably more shrill. Cleveland had been
wickedly misled, he said.

> Surrounded as he doubtless was by men who, *from interests bet-*
> *ter known to me than to you*, were strong for [Fish's] release in
> any way possible & who knew that I was so situated that my
> word would stand a poor showing against theirs. They have
> doubtless persuaded the President that I & I alone am the
> guilty one & that Fish was but a duped tool subject to my call.
> I do not believe, Sir, that you will fail to see the injustice of
> such a one-sided attack. If I could but for an hour have a free &
> earnest talk with you I could soon convince you who the parties
> were who, though not appearing on the surface, still from the
> background worked this matter through. . . .
>
> As I look on the names of the signers of that petition I find
> many whose motive for signing the same appear as clear to me
> as they do not to you.
>
> My trial & conviction on the evidence of Fish & his [broth-
> ers], one of whom swore to an alleged conversation with me
> through a telephone & the other that he heard what I said,
> though he stood 8 feet from the telephone & in an office where
> the noises of the street were incessant, must on the face of it

seem absurd to you. If you will but try it you will see how impossible it is. Just call up someone through your telephone & then stand 8 feet from the mouth-piece and see if you can hear the answer. Yet this is what I was convicted on, & although I felt deeply the injustice of it all, what could I do against public clamor, which was bound to convict me no matter on what basis. I bore this patiently . . . & what I have suffered, no man knows. The loss of my dear Mother some months ago seemed to take all heart out of me & I have often longed to see what the end might be, still I have a wife & child, dear to me, & whose love I cherish as much as any man. My family are beyond reproach & though they carry but little weight politically, still I feel that any inquiries you might make would convince you that though I have committed a wrong still I have the instincts of a gentleman & that those instincts suffer most severely from such unjust & cruel attacks.[*]

Colonel Lamont did not bother to reply.

---

[*] Ferd also wrote to New York governor David B. Hill, begging him for a pardon. His tone was just as self-pitying as it had been when writing to President Cleveland.

> Dear as liberty would be to me, & severe as my punishment has been for the past three years & three months, neither will compare with the pain inflicted by those who, to cover up their own faults, have sought to blacken me before the eyes of the world as the sole offender & wrecker of the lives & wealth of so many. I am, & always have been ready to take my share of the punishment . . . , but when a man like James D. Fish, whose career doing our business I know, as no one else does, should endeavor to whitewash himself by [spreading] on me the blackness of his own covering, is more than I can bear. I beg sir, that in reading this letter you will not [treat it] as the outcome of malicious spite, but simply as coming from one who, though in sore trouble, has as deep a feeling of shame & remorse for the ignominy brought by him on his name & family, as ever did any man likewise situated.

Ferd felt no actual shame or remorse, of course, and Governor Hill took no action. Ferdinand Ward to President Grover Cleveland, February 6, 1889; Ferdinand Ward to New York governor David B. Hill, February 6, 1889, author's collection.

FIFTEEN

All That Loved Me Are in Heaven

A crowd of newspapermen and townspeople was waiting as James D. Fish emerged from Auburn Prison on the morning of May 11, 1889. He seemed "transformed" by his time behind bars, one reporter wrote. "His face looked fresh and pink with health. His rather small and furtive black eyes snapped with excitement. His step was firm, his movements vigorous."[1] He looked neither right nor left, and spoke to no one as he climbed into a waiting carriage. "In an instant the phaeton was whirring up State Street at a spanking trot, leaving the crowd of curiosity-seekers staring stupidly at its wake of eddying dust."[2] The carriage zigzagged through town for a time, trying to lose the reporters who pursued it, then clattered to a stop at the corner of Park Avenue and Nelson Street.

There, another newspaperman continued, "a beautiful sight met [Fish's] view. Just where the road crests the hill . . . stood another phaeton with a beautiful team attached and in the carriage, with smiling faces, his two children, Anna, his heroic daughter, who had planned this little scheme for his escaping the rude curiosity of the crowd and his little daughter, [Alice], poor dead Sallie Reber's child, in a red frock and with one of those wide-brimmed expanses of straw wreathed with blossoms which all the tots wear these days."[3] The little girl handed her father a bunch of lilacs, then climbed onto his knee for the ride to the depot. "The old man held [the bouquet] proudly . . . during the drive, sniffing its fragrance now and then, and now and then stopping to hug young Miss Fish. A happier, more contented trio seldom set out on a rare May morning for a lovely country drive. . . . Oh, how sweet freedom must have been to the worried, prison-worn old man. To think of that dark cavern of misery . . . and then to think of plunging from that free as the air and into such a laughing, foliage-waving, flower-bedecked, madcap May morning as was that of yesterday!"*

Newspaper stories like that, describing his old partner walking free and being reunited with his family while he himself remained in prison, set Ferd off again. Ella again begged him to say nothing to the press. His father told him not to take Fish's release "too much to heart."[4] But Ferd demanded that Bourke Cockran go to the newspapers and protest on his behalf. Cockran refused. Ferd accused him of betrayal, of abandonment, of believing him guilty when he was innocent. Cockran wrote to correct the record.

I have never entertained the slightest doubt of the guilt of James D. Fish, nor the falsity of the testimony which he gave against you. But I can conceive no advantage to you which can flow from my expression of dissatisfaction on the course of the late president in commuting his sentence. The hardship of imprisonment to a man of your character and association is painfully evident to me and is never without my warmest sympathy. If I could befriend you in any way, I would not hesitate to extend to you some practical proof of the warmth of my sympathy, but I am helpless either to shorten the term of your punishment or to mitigate its severity. When I advised you to bear your captivity with patience, I gave you the only advice which I knew would be useful to you. It is of course easy for one who is free to exhort a captive to patience, but . . . to encourage you to entertain hopes of liberation would be to subject you to bitter

* Fish refused ever again to speak to the press. He returned to his old house on Henry Street in Brooklyn, where his sister Prudence and his son-in-law Uriah H. Dudley now lived. He wrote a pamphlet about his early business career in which the Marine Bank was never mentioned, collected books and prints, and stayed away from Wall Street. He died in Brooklyn in 1912 at the age of ninety-three. *New York Herald*, May 12, 1889.

disappointment and I sincerely trust you will do me the justice
to believe that nobody regrets more than I do, the hopelessness
of any attempt to secure a commutation of your sentence.[5]

Ferd would have to serve at least three and a half more years in Sing
Sing. To maintain the status he had enjoyed so far would require access
to more cash. His malleable mother was gone. His father was adamantly opposed to sending him money, as were his brother and sister
and most of his old friends. His only potential source of funds was his
weary wife.

Relations between the two had not improved. Ella continued to re-
sent his lack of interest in the lonely life his imprisonment forced her
to live. When she found the love letters Ferd had written to her during
their courtship while cleaning out her parents' house, she asked what
he would like done with them—hoping he would think them precious
and ask that they be saved. He did not bother to respond. "As my letters do not seem to interest you very much," she told him the following
week, "I will not write today."[6]

Not even Clarence could cheer her. The normal noises of a boy at
play caused her head to throb. She did not dare take him to church
for fear he would cause a "row."[7] She was, she said, "depressed and
sad . . . as blue as indigo."[8]

James McKeen had convinced her to stop spending down the principal of her estate to finance her husband's comforts, but Ferd knew
she still had a drawer full of jewelry as well as a few trinkets given to
her by General Grant. (What little remained of the jewelry she had
smuggled to Ferd at Ludlow Street had been smuggled out again just
before he went on trial.) He wanted the immediate use of all of it.

In July, he sent her another message through a shadowy intermediary. He had already had to sell off a gold watch General Grant had
given him, he said, now he needed her to sell more valuables and
somehow get the proceeds to him right away. She refused.

> Dear Ferd,
>
> I shall send this letter by way of Tarrytown but after this
> shall only write through the regular means. As regards the
> watch, of course as it is sold there is not much that I can say.
> I feel very badly about it. I think after taking about 25 or 30
> thousand dollars of my jewels and 6 thousand dollars of my

money after the failure [respectively $610,000, $722,000, and $144,000 in modern terms] you might at least leave me what little I have left. I would not care if it was going to do you the *least* good, but it will only be taken by those you employ for their own purse.

However, as the watch is gone, I need say no more! I, of course, would never take you any more money. I felt very badly about it. I would try always to get it to you in some way as you seem to want that more than anything else, but I never could take it again to you.[9]

His demands only accelerated. He insisted she sell a silver pitcher and send him the proceeds, then suggested she pry the diamond from a favorite brooch and see what she could get for it. "I have the little gold bird but would not care to take the diamond out of it," she answered, "but if you wish I will send you the one in my wedding ring."[10]

Even those bitter words did not deter her husband. On the morning of October 3, a stranger knocked on Ella's front door. He would not give his name, but he had a letter from Mr. Ward, he said. He would return later in the day for her answer.

Ella closed the door and tore open the envelope. It was a list of items Ferd wanted sold or smuggled in to him. She answered right away.

At first I thought that I would send you back no reply, but as I presume your messenger would think that rather strange I will send a few words. 1st as to the [diamond] clips, I have already sent them. 2nd I have no piece of silver to give you and this you know for I told you so. As to the pen-knife, paper cutter, pencils [all items valuable because they had been gifts from General Grant]—those I will send to you in the proper way. . . .

As to the diamond I will not take that out of the bird but you can have the one that I wrote about [from her wedding ring], as I do not care for that.

This letter I will leave for the man that you send, but I do not care to see him, as I told you last time you sent one that I should not see another. I also will probably not write you again for some time as I have nothing of interest to write . . . but will send you word if any of us are sick.

I feel very much discouraged over you and feel that unless

you can get something out of me that you care for little else. You need not feel badly about this letter, but I have felt that I must take a stand or I should have nothing left.

Yours,
Ella[11]

For the first time in all her letters to Sing Sing she failed to add the word "love."

Ferd remained eerily oblivious of her feelings. In early November, the Green house on Monroe Place was sold for $23,000. He determined to get his hands on at least a portion of that sum. From Ludlow Street—and then from Sing Sing—he had been forced to watch, helpless, as, one by one, all the possessions in which he had taken such pride were auctioned off to others. His books and paintings had gone first: his prize canvas, *Christ Raising Jairus's Daughter*, garnered just $1,300, less than a third of what he'd paid for it. The furnishings of the Pierrepont Street house followed, 400 lots of curtain rods and cooking pots, clocks and oriental carpets, tables and chairs, thirteen bottles of whiskey, 150 bottles of sherry, half a case of Apollinaire water, a buggy, and a sleigh. A billiard table valued at $800 and complete with cues, racks, bridges, and three sets of ivory balls fetched only $115. Ferd's own carved ash bedstead, billed by the auctioneer as a precious "souvenir of one of the greatest men of the age—of his kind,"[12] brought just $47.

Rosemount, the Ward's sprawling Stamford estate, was thought to be worth $60,000 at the time of the crash, but a New York financier snapped it up for just over half that sum. The furnishings also went for a fraction of what they had cost, except for one leather-covered chair prized by the buyer because General Grant was said once to have occupied it.

Each sale had increased Ferd's anger and resentment: others continued to benefit from his misfortune; not one cent was coming to him. He would not now willingly let the sale of the Greens' house go by without somehow participating in the profits. He demanded that Ella send her share of the proceeds from this latest sale to him immediately, so that he could invest them.

Again, she said no.

I am very sorry that anything of a business nature should come between us, for there can be but one thing for me to do, and that is to refuse to engage in anything connected to your work. I feel that the little that I have I *must* have invested very safely and also in something I know about. I care very little about money now, beyond what will keep me and Clarence in comfort. I think you need not fear for the future for with what I have we can live when you get out and you will be able I assume to find something to do. I am sorry to disappoint you.[13]

On Friday, November 22, 1889, Ella made her way once more to Sing Sing. She took with her a Thanksgiving box: a turkey, celery, crackers, and a jar of preserves made by his late mother. Ferdinand's thirty-seventh birthday had fallen on the previous day. It was an especially stormy visit. He wept and denounced her for denying him the comforts he needed, for robbing him of money he was convinced was his.

After she got home she wrote him a brief note: "I was *very* sorry to leave you on Friday feeling so badly. . . . I hope you feel differently about some matters before I see you again."[14]

Influenza swept through the mid-Atlantic states in early January 1890. It hit Philadelphia especially hard. Everyone in the Brinton household except Sarah, the doctor, and the servants who waited on them fell ill. Caring for them all, Sarah told her father, "leaves one very inert."[15] On the twelfth, her oldest son, George, came home from the Bethlehem Steel Works in Bethlehem, Pennsylvania, with a raging fever. He had been working there as a supervisor since his graduation from the University of Pennsylvania two years earlier. George was twenty-one years old, six feet four inches tall, a star athlete who had excelled in every college sport from tug-of-war to tennis and set records at the standing long jump and the hammer throw.* He was worshiped by his younger brothers and adored by his mother, who often leaned upon him when the demands of her large brood momentarily grew too great.

All the beds at 1423 Spruce Street were taken. She gave him her own, the bed in which he'd been born. The rest of the household

---

* He was so well muscled and athletically skilled that the photographer Eadweard Muybridge had him pose for his camera in the nude, throwing a hammer and heaving a twenty-pound rock, as part of his pioneering study of human and animal locomotion.

slowly returned to health. George did not. He developed pneumonia. His father and his uncle, Dr. Da Costa, administered every remedy they knew: cocaine, opium, quinine, codeine. Nothing helped. At 5:39 a.m. on January 24, George slipped away.

His mother seemed inconsolable.

> Dear Father,
>   We bury our boy tomorrow at eleven. Will I ever be reconciled? I cannot see God. Where is he? I am crushed and broken. Pray for me and for John. Thank you for your sympathy. I would not have you here. Just write.
> Your own daughter.[16]

A day or two later, she wrote to her father again. The faith he believed had been his greatest gift to her was failing: "I see no light. I cannot pray. I cannot work. I cannot do anything. . . . I am quiet and cool just as you would have me be, but my heart is nearly broken. . . . So far, I see nothing but life without my boy. . . . I know there is a God but I am too stunned to seek Him and He does not come unbidden. . . . Pray for us dear Father that light may shine out of darkness."[17]

From Sing Sing, Ferdinand dutifully expressed sorrow at his nephew's death. But, as always, his own circumstances and struggles remained uppermost in his mind. He was angry that Ella now seemed to be skipping every opportunity to visit him in prison: one week she said she had twisted her foot; later, she said she was simply too tired to come; looking after Clarence—whose nurse she'd had to let go to save money—had worn her out. Ferd expressed no sympathy. To him it was all abandonment; he and he alone remained the victim of his crimes.

In early March, the *New York Herald* ran a gaudy series exposing corruption at the Ludlow Street Jail, where Ferd had spent seventeen expensive months before he was sent to Sing Sing. The headlines caused a sensation: "Money Laughs at Both Jail and Jailers"; "Ludlow Street Jail a Pleasure Resort"; "A Man Who Will Pay Exorbitantly Can Live Like a Lord and Walk Abroad When Ever He Takes the Notion"; "Caged Financiers in Clover."[18] Hoping to keep selling papers, the editor sent a reporter up to Sing Sing to see if Ferdinand Ward, perhaps the jail's most famously pampered prisoner, would be willing to comment. He feigned reluctance at first. "I have had all the notoriety I want," he said. But he hadn't. He welcomed the chance to be back in the newspapers, to complain again about his victimization, to get back at the officials who had fleeced him. Yes, indeed, he said, he'd spent thousands of dollars for special privileges while locked up in Ludlow Street, "because I had it and knew I would have to pay for everything I got." He described in detail his after-dinner cigars, his strolls along Grand Street, carriage rides through Central Park, evenings out at the Casino, all paid for in cash. And he carefully named the officials whom he had bribed—warden Phil Kiernan, sheriff Alexander Davidson, and deputy sheriff David McGonigal.

Money could buy you everything you wanted, he said.

"Everything but escape from jail?"

"Oh, bosh!" Ferd answered. He could have escaped easily, and "so could anybody who had the privileges I paid for."

"Well, why didn't you?"

"Simply because I made up my mind to face the music, that is all."[19]

Having spoken so freely to the *Herald*, Ferd panicked. Fearing that the Sing Sing officials whom he was now paying off might do away with him rather than run the risk of his someday naming them, too, he wrote a letter to the editor of the rival *New York World* claiming he had been misquoted.

He was still uneasy several weeks later. A reporter friend reassured him that his old friends in Manhattan had been bolstered by his denial: "I have heard many people say that they would have despised you had you left them to think that you had accepted favors at the jail and then betrayed those who took you into their confidence. I have assured all such that you are no traitor."[20] Then the newspaperman went on to offer the same counsel Ferd had ignored so many times before: "Let me advise you in the future not to see or talk to a reporter or in fact to anyone else in whom you have not the most implicit confidence."[21]

Ferdinand was incapable of following that kind of guidance. Newspaper interviews kept him at the center of things, where he was always sure he belonged. Fame and notoriety were interchangeable for him. He had loved being the "Young Napoleon of Finance," and, despite all that had befallen him, part of him relished being America's best-hated man, too. Now he wanted the world to see him as he saw himself, as the victim of the unreasonable avarice of others.

.   .   .

Rev. Ferdinand De Wilton Ward was alone now in the old Geneseo parsonage. Ellen, the Irish housekeeper who had worked for Jane, saw to the cooking and tidying up. But the old man spent most of every day in his dark study hard at work on what would be his last book, *Suggestive Scripture Questions: Sixty Questions with Expository and Practical Answers*. Nonetheless, the plight of his youngest child continued to torment him. He told Sarah of his anguish in a letter on April 6, 1890.

> I was awakened at one o'clock this morning with thoughts of F.
> & could not go to sleep. I said to myself "Are Sarah & William
> to suffer in their children what your mother & I have in *him?*"
> *Why* not? Was not F. brought up well? It won't do to cast him
> off. He has done wrong, but he is *my son* and *your* & William's
> *brother.* He has been generous to us. You see it in your *parlor*—I
> in my house, without & within. But you say, "It was not his
> money." Much of it *was* & we are benefited. He has done noth-
> ing low & beastly. Your friend, Mrs. Bradley Martin, has a son
> who when intoxicated married a lewd actress; General Wad-
> sworth had a son who died of delirium tremens in an insane
> asylum. . . .* *F. is none such.* His morals are sure.[22]

---

* Mrs. Bradley Martin was a leader of New York society. In London in the autumn of 1889, her alcoholic nineteen-year-old son, Sherman, married Annie Munn, a woman who was eleven years older than he and said to have been a concert-hall entertainer. His father—fresh from a hunting vacation in Scotland during which he and his guests bagged seventy stags and two thousand pheasants—announced that he would have nothing more to do with his son unless he stopped drinking and ended the marriage. The young Martin was persuaded to take a "world tour" with his tutor and without his wife—who refused repeated offers of large sums of money to agree to a divorce and ran advertisements charging her husband's parents with abduction. Newspapers on both sides of the Atlantic delighted in the story. Back in Manhattan in 1894, the young man collapsed after spending several weeks undergoing treatment for alcoholism. He was carried to his family's home on West Twentieth Street—where he fell dead of what the family physician called "apoplexy of the brain."

Charles F. Wadsworth, who had served as his father's aide during the Civil War, never recovered from it. He spent nearly every evening of his postwar life drinking himself senseless in the bar of the American Hotel in Geneseo. Whatever the weather, a carriage and driver waited outside to take him home at closing time. *The New York Times*, December 3, 1889, December 23, 1894; Alden Hatch, *The Wadsworths of the Genesee*, p. 100.

On the morning of April 9, 1890, three days after his father paid tribute to his morals, Ferd was at work in his print shop. By then, the convict labor system had been done away with. The stove works for which he had printed letterheads had closed down, and most convicts remained locked in their cells most of the day. But Ferd's skill at printing had caught the attention of the prison authorities and he had been put to work knocking out copies of the exacting prison rules he routinely flouted, printing hymns for the chaplains at Auburn and Clinton as well as Sing Sing, and producing elaborate visiting cards for Warden Brush and other prison officials, featuring a view of the prison yard engraved by an incarcerated forger. Ferd enjoyed the proximity to power his shop afforded—Principal Keeper Connaughton's office was right next door—as well as the privileges for which his wife's money had paid: he now enjoyed special evening meals served to him in the hospital; was allowed to wear a straw hat rather than the standard-issue striped cap his fellow prisoners wore; and got to play with a resident spaniel and the two puppies she had chosen to give birth to beneath his press. Even Ferd seemed at least momentarily pleased at how things were going. "I am very glad to learn from your letter that you are so comfortable," Ella wrote him. "You seem to have the idea that I do not want you to have any comforts. You are mistaken in this. I am certainly very glad to have you have all the comforts that it is possible for you to have."

Then, everything changed. A guard handed him a telegram. Ella had died suddenly in Stamford.

"Peritonitis" was the official cause, but the physician who signed the death certificate was also a family friend, and years later Clarence would be told that his mother's ever-growing reliance on patent medicines laced with alcohol had been at least partly responsible for her death. In the end, he would retain only a single vivid memory of her: sitting next to his mother on the stairs of the Stamford house during a thunderstorm and wondering if the crashing sounds outside would ever stop.

Prison rules forbade Warden Brush from allowing Ferd out to attend the funeral. His sister, still in mourning for her own son, came to see him and took with her to Stamford a rose from the Sing Sing greenhouse with instructions to place it in Ella's hand before her burial. Clarence remembered his nurse handing him pieces of candy to keep him quiet during the funeral. Ella was buried at Green-Wood Cemetery in Brooklyn, next to her parents and the infant she and Ferd had lost.

Ferd made the most of Ella's death. He saw to it that the newspapers were notified that he had cruelly been kept from his wife's graveside, and he carefully kept all the letters of sympathy he received from strangers, responding especially warmly to those whose writers seemed most likely to have access to cash. But for him, the real tragedy was that he now had no immediate prospect of any money of his own. Back in June 1887, Ferdinand's late father and mother had signed more or less identical wills, dividing their modest estates into three parts. Sarah and Will each received a third. The remaining third was to be invested and the "interest, dividends and income" paid to Ferdinand by his siblings "from time to time" for his "comfort, maintenance and support" and for no other purpose. Will and their cousin Levi F. Ward were the executors.

No ready cash there.

Now, Ella's will, drawn up with James McKeen's help and quietly signed by her in the spring of 1889, proved still more disappointing. Her estate—amounting to some $30,000 ($730,000 today)—was to be devoted entirely to "the use, support, education and maintenance" of Clarence until he became twenty-five, when "the principal, together with any income remaining unapplied shall be conveyed, set over and paid to him."*

Ferd—who had been banking on inheriting everything himself and was now entitled to nothing—vowed to fight. He would argue always that his wife's estate had come from him. It had not.

In 1881, he had talked his mother-in-law into selling Ella several Chicago house lots for the nominal consideration of $20,000 ($433,000 today). Ferd had then supposedly invested all of that cash in Tonawanda Valley and Cuba Railroad bonds on Mrs. Green's behalf; over the next four years, he had given her periodic reports showing how splendidly they were doing. When Grant & Ward collapsed, a Brooklyn lawyer named Hiland G. Batcheller, who had lost heavily with the firm, went to court in Chicago and had Ella's real estate holdings attached. He argued that they had really belonged to Ferd all along, and that he had

---

* Even if Clarence were to die before the age of twenty-five, Ferdinand was to receive only the interest on half of Ella's estate; the principal was to go to her sister, Mary. Last Will and Testament of Mrs. Ella C. Ward, April 19, 1889, author's collection.

actually paid his mother-in-law on his wife's behalf in order to shield him from creditors like himself. Batcheller might have had a case had Ferd ever actually purchased the bonds. But it turned out that he had never done so—and had been insolvent at the time of the supposed purchase, in any case. James McKeen successfully had the attachment lifted and the property reassigned to Mrs. Green. The lots were afterward sold for some $60,000, and the bulk of Ella's estate was her third of the proceeds from this sale.[23]

Questions about the disposition of Ella's property and what to do about her six-year-old son did not bring out the best in either the Green or the Ward families. Ferd had done too much damage to them all. Ella's younger brother, Sidney, fled to the South rather than get involved. Her older sister, Mary, seemed concerned only that her imprisoned brother-in-law get nothing that was not his: "I can't endure to think of Mama's property going to Ferdinand Ward who was actually the cause of her death," she wrote.[24]

Ella had named Will and Levi Ward as her executors, rather than her own siblings. She knew that Ferd would object to the terms she had set and told McKeen that members of her own family had suffered so grievously in their dealings with her husband that it seemed only fair that his relatives should bear the responsibility of countering his demands. But Levi Ward immediately relinquished his rights as executor. As a banker and insurance executive with a reputation to uphold in Rochester, he did not wish to bring further embarrassment to his family by mixing in Ferd's affairs. Will Ward hurried home from Europe but then did the same; he had had enough of his brother's dealings. Nor was he willing to take Clarence back to Europe with him; his excuse was that Kate was ill (in fact, she was simply pregnant with their fourth and last child).[25]

Despite the recent loss of her eldest son, Sarah Ward Brinton wanted to care for Clarence, but Dr. Brinton would not hear of it. If the boy came to live in his house it would inevitably mean renewed contact with Ferd, and he wanted nothing more to do with the brother-in-law who had bankrupted his old commander and brought scandal to his family. "It has been a great grief to me that I could not take him," Sarah told Ferd. "Had I been able to have my own way, there would have been no question as to who was to have Clarence. I want the boy and I know Ella would have preferred me to have him, and . . . the responsibility I would not have minded. But I am helpless to do what I would in the matter. John is the head and in all questions of our home life I have yielded to him. . . . I want you to understand this and never think I refused to help you in your need."[26]

Instead, it was decided that at least for the immediate future Fred Green and his wife, Ellen Chaffee Green, known as "Nellie," would take Clarence to live with them and their two little girls on their chicken farm in Thompson, Connecticut. A weekly stipend from the Franklin Trust would pay for his upkeep. "I am sure [Fred] will do well by Clarence," Sarah assured Ferd. "[He] impressed me as being a very kind and gentle man. He loves Clarence but of course he is not going to keep him unless you wish it."[27]

Ferd was not reassured. The flurry of letters he wrote denouncing everyone involved have been lost, but the surviving replies from those he wounded hint at how he was thinking. When he denounced Will for abandoning him, Kate Ward assured him that while "at first, of course, [her husband's decision to relinquish his executorship] looked hard, I am sure it must be for the best. They all think so and at any rate whatever has been done has been done with the best intentions and judgment possible. How I wish there was more we could do to comfort you."[28] Sarah, too, told him he was being unjust to Will. "He does feel very much for you . . . dear Ferd, never again let a reproachful thought come into your heart toward this, the best and truest of brothers."[29]

As always, it was money that mattered most to Ferd. As Ella's widower, he demanded the right to administer her trust, even though state law expressly forbade prisoners from playing that role. "I appreciate the trying helplessness of your position," wrote James McKeen, Ella's friend and attorney, "and [would] certainly not willingly be a party to any scheme which took wrongful advantage to thwart your just desires. Not the least claim of your wife to the esteem of all who have had occasion to know her during these trying years was her adherence to you and the promotion of your welfare in good and ill repute."[30]

Nothing could calm Ferd down. He offered objection after objection to having the Greens care for his son, tried to block weekly payments to them, threatened to join his own creditors in a suit against Clarence and Ella's estate rather than see any of it fall into Fred Green's hands. And he repeatedly accused McKeen of poisoning the minds of members of his own family against him. "Your brother and cousin [gave] reasons for not accepting the trust which are such that it would be ungracious for me to press them further," McKeen replied.

"You again write as if I had used some influence or advice to 'persuade' your 'brother not to act.' You must know that I did all in my power to persuade him or your cousin to act. . . . [Mrs. Ward's] sufferings have won from your creditors a kindly feeling towards her and I do not think they would applaud your appearance as their champion and against your boy."[31]

Ferd did not get around to writing to his boy until July 13, nearly three months after Ella's death. Though his letter is painstakingly written in block capitals—in the apparent hope that Clarence himself might read it—it includes not a word about how his son might be feeling at the loss of his mother. It is, as always, all about Ferd.

> MY DEAR SON:
> THIS LETTER IS FROM YOUR FATHER WHOM YOU HAVE NEVER SEEN TO KNOW, BUT WHO THINKS OF YOU ALL THE TIME AND WHO LOVES YOU DEARLY. YOU MAY NEVER SEE ME CLARENCE, BUT WHEN YOU GROW UP YOU WILL LEARN OF ME, AND I WANT YOU TO TRY AND LOVE ME, FOR YOU ARE ALL I HAVE ON EARTH TO LOVE NOW. YOUR DEAR MOTHER LOVED ME TO THE END IN SPITE OF ALL THE CRUEL WRONGS DONE TO ME FOR SHE KNEW ME TO BE TRUE TO HER, AND WHEN SHE DIED I LOST THE LAST AND ONLY FRIEND I HAD, BUT MY BOY WHEN OTHERS SPEAK TO YOU OF ME, TRY TO BELIEVE THAT I LOVE YOU AND WOULD COME TO YOU IF I COULD.
> I MAY SOMEDAY COME AND SEE YOU, AND WILL MAKE YOU HAPPY IN SPITE OF MY ENEMIES, BUT IF I DIE, CLARENCE, YOU MUST TRY AND LIVE A GOOD LIFE. YOU MUST TRUST NO ONE, FOR PEOPLE WILL PRETEND TO BE YOUR FRIENDS TILL YOU GET INTO TROUBLE, AND THEN THEY WILL BELIEVE ANYTHING OF YOU.
> GOODBYE MY DEAR BOY. GOD BLESS YOU AND MAKE YOU AS TRUE A MAN AS YOUR DEAR MOTHER WAS A WOMAN.
>   YOUR LOVING FATHER
>   FERDINAND WARD
>   WON'T YOU PLEASE
>   WRITE TO ME?[32]

Fred Green was a reticent man who mostly kept his anger at the damage Ferd had done to his family to himself; Clarence would be almost fully grown before his uncle told him what he really thought of the boy's father. But he could not bring himself to answer Ferd's letters. That duty would always fall to his patient wife, Nellie.

> Dear Mr. Ward,
> Clarence was very happy to receive your letter a few days ago and wishes me to send his love and to say that he will be very glad to see you when you come home. I hope you do not think Fred and I are not friends of yours. We will always be glad to do whatever we can for you. What you may have done or may not have done we do not know, but we *do* know that we are not perfect enough ourselves to condemn another too hastily. And Clarence will never be taught by us anything but love and respect for you. He is very well and happy and good and we grow [more] fond of him every day. . . .
> There is to be a private school started in Thompson this fall which [their older daughter] Helen and Clarence will attend.
> We had a little kitten which died not long since. Clarence made a coffin from bits of boards which he covered with glass and trimmed beautifully with myrtle and daisies. We were all called out in turn to admire it. Then Florence [their younger daughter] and Clarence put it in a little express cart and asked our minister if he would preach at the funeral. They were so earnest about it and so sure that they were doing just the right thing that our minister did not even smile but excused himself because he had a previous engagement. So back they came and Clarence preached and they both sang and had a lovely time. But when the time came for the burial they both decided that the coffin was far too pretty to be covered up, so they dumped the kitty into the ground and saved the coffin for future service. . . . And so they play, as busy as can be all day long.[33]

More letters from Ferd to Nellie Green would follow over the coming months, by turns cloying, vengeful, self-pitying, and riddled with self-serving lies. He accused everyone else of neglecting Ella's grave: "There are large granite works here in this prison and I am going to have a plain but handsome cross made. . . . Would that I were buried beside her."[34] (He never ordered up a cross; her grave at Green-Wood remains undifferentiated to this day.) He begged Nellie to send him $50 in an unmarked envelope, in care of a certain prison clerk, assuring her that "this is allowed here."[35] (It was not allowed, of course, as his own postscript made clear: "If you can't send the money, then simply write me a letter saying you can't do as I ask, nothing more.")[36] He repeated over and over again that Clarence was all that stood between him and suicide, but he couldn't remember the date of his son's birth. And he boasted of how loyal he had been to Ella and how glad he was that she had never doubted his single-minded devotion to her. (He may or may not have been faithful; she certainly knew that he had been caught writing to another woman.)

He made his son dreamy promises: "When I come, Clarence, we will go off and travel and see all the nice things and sail in a ship and ride in the cars and you shall learn to drive horses and we will have dogs and go fishing and swimming together and we will go down by the big ocean and dig up the sand and catch the crabs and hear the band play."[37]

And he offered the Greens child-raising counsel that had little to do with his boy and everything to do with his continual reflections about himself. Clarence was not to be forced to attend church or Sunday school against his will: "Don't be too strict in religious matters, for to this I lay much of my misfortune. . . . You must not think of me as an infidel, for I am not. . . . [But] I have seen so much deceit and lying among professed Christians that I can't bring myself to unite with them in worship and be of Christian fellowship."[38] He had ideas about his son's education, too, strangely like those that had turned out so badly for him. He did not want Clarence to "come into intimate association with that class of boys who are so low-born as to influence him the wrong way. . . . [Therefore] I believe in Boarding School. . . . The school I have in mind is conducted by a Presbyterian minister and will be a good, homelike place for him."[39] Ferd also wanted his son to have spending money whenever he liked: "Wealth is only worth what good it can do. Let him feel this. He will be a rich man some day."[40] He saw his son, like everything and everyone else, as an extension of himself: "I mean . . . that some day Clarence shall help me, or I shall help him, to redeem my name in Wall Street. . . ."[41]

Nellie Green urged Ferd not to dwell on his misfortune but instead to concentrate on those who loved him. His brother and sister no longer mattered to him, he answered; they had left him to his enemies. Without money from them, he was sure to lose his "privileges," and might even be transferred to Clinton Prison, where he knew no one. "Do not speak to me of others, for I have lost all love for those who in my time of sorest need, leave me to my enemies. That is not love—at least not what I call love. All that loved me are in Heaven."[42]

Ferd's father was evidently not among those whom he believed loved him. But twice a month the old man set aside the time to write his younger son. His letters were stiff and old-fashioned, filled with the same admonitions Ferd had been ignoring all his life: "Do not *despair.* Do not be *hardened.* . . . Look *above* for help."[43]

> Fancy, on pleasantly hopeful wing, bears me onward a few years when I shall see you a free man, having fully paid the debt to justice. You take up some business not financial in Wall Street. . . . But in a pleasant village. . . . Dear Clarence near you at school. Yourself fully fixed in all that is good. Identified with Christ and His church as you *once were.* Having on you the eyes of your glorified wife and Mother, oft visited by your many stalwart friends, rejoicing to see that the clouds are all dispersed and you are happy again. Why not all these things. With God's help (which He never refuses) they can be, will be. God grant it.[44]

In early 1891, Will arranged for his father to travel to Oxford, where Will was a visiting lecturer in geology. Ferdinand wrote long letters home to the *Livingston Republican*, just as he had done during the Civil War: hometown readers would be happy, he knew, to hear that every Oxford student attended chapel daily and that only "a limited number of theatrical performances are allowed each year, expurgated of all gross and vicious scenes and words."[45]

That summer, the Wards moved to the Villa Clarenzia, an inn overlooking Lake Geneva at Clarens, Switzerland. At first, Ferdinand was still vigorous enough at seventy-nine to bicycle along the country roads. But as the summer wore on, he sometimes got confused: once, when a maid knocked on his door, he was unable to understand why she didn't enter when he repeatedly told her to do so in Tamil, the language he hadn't spoken since leaving India forty-five years earlier.

On August 11, Kate Ward reported to Nellie Green, "he passed away in perfect peace."

We have buried his remains for the time being in the little cemetery here, one of the most lovely places you could imagine. Some day we shall remove his remains to Temple Hill to rest by the side of his life-long companion.

Poor Ferd, it does seem as tho' fortune is determined to spare him nothing. With his hard life within those granite walls comes death after death of those he loves best till he will face the world when he comes out with half his world gone![46]

If Ferd grieved for his father, there is no record of it.

In late 1891, as his release day grew near, Ferd finally got some good news. The U.S. district attorney had dropped the two remaining federal indictments against him, on the grounds that he had already been found guilty of his most serious crimes, had served his time, and had not appealed his sentence. Six state charges against him remained, however, and he wrote Bourke Cockran, now a New York congressman, begging him to help have them dismissed them as well.

If you would now aid me in getting the indictments *quashed*, it would be a still greater relief for then I could start out anew, unhampered by fear of future trouble.

To tell you the truth, Sir, I want to marry again. I have secured the affections of one of the sweetest girls living, whose family stands high in the community & one with whose help I feel sure I may regain my good name, but I feel that it would be unjust to her for me to take such a step before I was beyond doubt, a free man.

I know you will agree with me in this & will help me in my effort to make a home for my boy as well as an honest living for myself.

No one but my immediate family know of this, & I beg that you will keep it entirely secret for the present, as I wish to avoid any public notoriety for her.[47]

It's hard to know how much truth there was to Ferd's giddy secret. He had actually told his family nothing about wedding plans and may, in fact, have had none; during his first weeks of freedom he would not act like even a secretly engaged man. But if there really was a "sweetest girl" with whom he had at least discussed marriage, she was most likely Isabelle Storer, the Brooklyn woman with whom he had been caught communicating early in his term.

In any case, he told the Greens nothing at all about his future plans except that he was determined to have his son: "As to the future [I] will send for Clarence as soon as I go out. Please either see that his wardrobe is sufficient for a long trip or let me know what he needs and I will get it."[48] Fred Green was sufficiently alarmed by what this might mean for the little boy that he sent Ferd's letter on to James McKeen and asked him how to deal with Ferd if he really did turn up and demand his son. McKeen urged him to hold the line.

> If Clarence's father should appear on his release, as he will probably do, you will have to be governed by circumstances. I cannot suppose he would seek to take the child away forcibly or otherwise than with the latter's free volition and after an agreement with the Trust Company as to any new agreement.
>
> In the imagined case of his seeking to take the child away . . . , in your place, as his Uncle, and having his care by arrangement with the Trustee, you should keep the child. The father's only proper remedy would be a writ of *habeas corpus*, requiring you to produce the child before a court or judge whose disposition of the matter would be your full protection. I write this, of course, with no anticipation of any trouble of the kind. But [the best] course [is to] not hesitate a moment to take a firm stand in behalf of the child's protection, having no fear that any parental rights of his father go [to] the length of warranting any despotic conduct.[49]

Ferdinand Ward rose early on his last day in prison, Saturday, April 30, 1892. He shuffled in silence to breakfast with his fellow prisoners, just as he had each morning since he'd arrived at Sing Sing. But when the other prisoners were marched off to work, he was escorted to the warden's office instead.

Augustus Brush was gone, replaced just a few weeks earlier by William F. Brown, a Democratic boss from Newburgh. At first, Ferd had worried that the new warden might withdraw the privileges he had bought and paid for during the Brush regime, and he'd worked overtime to win Brown's favor. He turned out reams of calendars and balance sheets and "fancy printing," which Brown declared "almost marvelous,"[50] and he turned on all the charm he had once used to persuade veteran financiers to trust him. He told such compelling stories of Wall Street that the new warden once took him home to dinner to hear more, and he made such a plaintive case against his in-laws that Brown put him in touch with a lawyer friend in Newburgh who specialized in estate and custody cases.

Brown was completely won over. "Ward, like all the rest who come to us from the educated and cultivated ranks of life, was a good prisoner," Brown assured the *Brooklyn Eagle* the morning of Ferd's release.

> He was always a gentleman . . . perfectly tractable and obedient . . . a man that we all liked and thoroughly appreciated. I hope he will find some of his old friends who will gather around him. No one knows what a man of his sensitive nature suffers in six long years of imprisonment. He is not like a common criminal; take for instance the man that [will be] discharged with him this morning, who is a horse thief, and has been in nearly every prison in the country. He cannot stay away from here six weeks to save his life. . . . I expect him back any time inside of two months. Ward is however made of different stuff.[51]

Brown handed back to Ferd everything he had had with him when he entered Sing Sing—his gold watch, the gold matchbox given to him by General Grant, two automatic pencils, his alligator wallet, and $185.77 in cash. With them went the standard $10 given to all freed prisoners, an additional $20.45 he had earned working as the prison printer, a new prison-made suit, and a railroad ticket marked "Convict—Half-Fare."

The prison-issue suit was evidently not to Ferd's liking. When he emerged from the prison gate at eight fifty he was wearing a finely tailored tan outfit and patent-leather shoes from the old days, with a matching topcoat and derby. He carried a folded pair of tan gloves. To the clutch of New York newspapermen waiting in hopes of an interview, he looked pale but jaunty. Jimmy Connaughton and half a dozen jailers walked him to a waiting carriage. After he had swung himself up into the seat, they took turns shaking his hand and wishing him luck.

For once, he had nothing to say to the press; everything depended on getting possession of the eight-year-old son who did not know him. Instead, as the team started off toward the railroad station, he waved and shouted, "I'm off to see my boy!"[52]

PART FIVE

THE LOVING FATHER

SIXTEEN

Driven to Desperation

Randolph H. Chandler was a successful lawyer, sometime state legislator, and one of Thompson, Connecticut's, most prosperous citizens—prosperous enough to travel in Europe, where a stranger once asked him where he came from.

"Thompson, Connecticut," he answered.

Where's that?

"Well," he said, "it's one mile from Quaddick and a mile and a half from Brandy Hill."[1]

To outsiders, Thompson was just an especially handsome New England village in the northeastern corner of Connecticut: forty-odd houses arranged around a triangular common and along the three dusty elm-shaded tracks that formed it; two churches—Congregational and Baptist; a one-room schoolhouse; an old inn; a general store; a town hall; and a sturdy little Greek Revival bank.

But for eight-year-old Clarence Ward, brought to Thompson to live two years earlier, in 1890, it had become the world. Its center was the big white Early Republican house behind the Congregational church to which his uncle Fred Green and his aunt Nellie and their two daughters had moved in the summer of 1885.* Green was gruff and taciturn, short and stubby with a black beard grown to mask a receding chin. Clarence would remember that he was "a kindly man of mediocre accomplishments."[2] He had loved his late sister, but the collapse of Grant & Ward had wiped out his savings, and he remained embittered by what her husband had done to him and his family. He had been forced to give up his job as manager of the Champion House and now found himself rising at four each morning, trying to make ends meet selling eggs and milk, apples and peaches and vegetables produced on eight nearby acres. "He wasn't really a farmer," Clarence recalled. "He tried but he'd had no training for it. He called his enterprise the 'Thompson Fruit and Poultry Farm,' but I doubt if he ever earned any money."[3] The monthly stipend for Clarence's food and clothing formed a sizable portion of the family income.

Aunt Nellie Green was warmer, abler, better read than her husband, an affectionate and caring surrogate mother for the boy. And Clarence had quickly become accustomed to the regular rhythm of the Green household. Each school day began with oatmeal for breakfast, followed by a half-mile walk to the one-room schoolhouse next door to Rand Chandler's house in which children in all eight grades learned their lessons from a single teacher, Miss Fanny Mills. Clarence was "usually quiet," his teacher reported, "or at least sufficiently so as to make little or no disturbance."[4] At recess, he and the other children played a single-base variation of baseball called "Old Cat." After school, he wandered home with his two cousins, Helen, four years older than he, and Florence, one year younger, dawdling along the tops of the old stone walls that ran in and out of the neighbors' yards, and stopping at the big rock outcropping behind their house that they called the "post office" to see if some schoolmate had left a message for them slipped between the stones. Supper was at six. Bed followed promptly at half past seven.

Sundays were filled by services at the Congregational church. Fred Green was superintendent of the Sunday school. His wife sang in the choir and taught the girls' class. Clarence was so impressed by the

---

* The house and farm cost $4,000 and were purchased in Ellen Chaffee Green's name. No one knows whether she bought them with a small legacy of her own because his funds were entirely wiped out by the failure or because he wanted her to hold title in order to thwart Grant & Ward's creditors, who might have laid claim to property owned by him. Dr. Karl P. Stofko to the author, October 22, 2010.

attention the congregation paid to the minister, Rev. George H. Cummings, that he began delivering his own sermons from the landing in
his uncle's house while his worshipful cousin Florence listened down
below.

By April 1892, Clarence had spent one-quarter of his life in
Thompson. His memories of his mother and the lonely life they had
led together in Stamford had begun to blur. He had never known his
father, had never even been told where he was or why he could not
come to see him. That was all about to change.

As the train slowed, chuffing its way into Putnam—the depot nearest
to Thompson—Ferdinand Ward was waiting impatiently between the
cars, his blue eyes bright and expectant. It was a beautiful spring day,
and things seemed at last to be turning his way. He leaped down onto
the platform, a porter puffing along behind with his valise, hurried into
the adjacent livery stable, and ordered up the fastest horse and carriage
in town to take him to Thompson.

But as the horse was being harnessed, Fred Green appeared in the
doorway and extended his hand. Ferdinand grandly tipped the porter
and the stable boy a dollar each for their trouble and hurried off after
his brother-in-law toward Perry & Brown's Dry Goods Store.

There, Clarence and Florence stood together on the wooden sidewalk, holding hands and ringed by reporters and passersby gathered to
see the boy reunited with his notorious father.

"Suddenly," one newspapermen wrote, "Clarence spied Mr. Green
walking toward him with [a] strange pallid man and said, 'There is
Uncle now.'"

"Yes," answered Florence, "and that other man must be your Papa."[5]

Ignoring the crowd, refusing to answer questions from reporters,
Ferdinand knelt and embraced his son. Together, they climbed into
Fred's buggy. Ferd's arm was around Clarence's shoulder, and as his
brother-in-law whipped his horse into action and they started toward
Thompson, a reporter noted, he was "gazing fondly into his [son's]
face, the sweetest sight his eyes had seen for six-and-a-half long years."[6]
Several carriages followed along behind, hired by newspapermen still
hoping for a few words from Ferd. But when the buggy reached the
Green home, he, Fred, and the children hurried inside. Ferd said nothing to anyone.

The reporters were back the next morning, gathered around the door of the Congregational church. It was Sunday, and they all hoped for a chance to talk with Ferd. When he failed to appear, they still had column inches to fill, so they wrote about Clarence and Florence Green instead.

> A little man of [eight] years walked down the main street of the old-fashioned town of Thompson yesterday. He was rosy-cheeked, blue-eyed and fair-haired, and the cheerful expression on his face was infectious and caused many a smile to spread.
>
> He wore a derby hat, a dark blue pea jacket, knee breeches and kid gloves, and so sturdy was his small figure that no one could readily imagine circumstances under which the tiny maid of six whom he led by the hand would need a more valiant protector.
>
> The little girl was dark-eyed and smiling. She went with the lad up the stone steps of the white-steepled Congregational Church and walked with him sedately to pew No. 23 on the right hand side of the middle aisle, which they both entered. With a pretty expression she took from his hand the old-time, much-thumbed hymnal which he had politely handed to her.
>
> The lad was happier than he had ever been before, because he had at last found his father whom he could not recall ever having seen, and had been clasped to his bosom. But he did not know that that father had just left a prison where he had served six years and a half for as sensational financial frauds as ever were known in this country. He did not know what it will mean to him in time to come when he has to say: "I am the son of Ferdinand Ward."[7]

When the service finally ended and the Greens emerged from the church with the other worshippers, the disappointed newspapermen crowded around Fred.

"Why did Ward not go to church today?"

"I don't suppose he wanted to face a crowd of strangers who would look at him and make remarks. . . . He ought to keep himself quiet until he is ready to go to work."

Had he said what he planned to do, now that he was free?

He had not, and the stories that he had a fortune hidden away somewhere were false. "He has not any money. He did not save anything."

How long did Ward plan to stay in Thompson?

"I do not know. I do not like to ask him a question like that on the first day. He might think I wanted him to go."[8]

He did want him to go, of course—and the next day he did. Ferd's interest in getting to know his son had lasted just a little over twenty-four hours. He began weeks of restless travel in search of some way to reestablish himself as a rich man. He had a number of schemes in mind. None involved working for a living.

His first stop was Newburgh, New York, where he consulted with John M. Gardner, the attorney who specialized in breaking wills and rewriting estate agreements whom Warden Brown of Sing Sing had recommended to him.[*]

Together, he and Gardner traveled to New York to confront Ella's lawyer, James McKeen. They insisted on being shown every item of property being held as part of Ella's estate; Ferd made it clear he believed virtually all of it was rightfully his and that he was prepared to prove it in court. But before he could even begin to do so, the six state indictments still outstanding against him had to be dismissed. Meanwhile, he thought it best to feign cordial feelings toward the Greens. "How is my dear little fellow?" he asked his sister-in-law. "Oh how my heart goes out to him & how grateful I am to you all for caring for him as you have. God will bless you for it. Kiss him for me & tell him how I love him. Gratefully yours, F. Ward."[9]

Ferd hurried on alone to Geneseo to have a look at the old parsonage, boarded up since his father's death. An old family friend, Mrs. E. Fred Youngs, gave a dinner party to welcome him back to town. Everyone agreed in advance that out of respect for the memory of his late parents, it would be best not to make any mention of where he had been the past few years. Everything went well enough until the guests strolled into the dining room, and Ferd noticed that each table setting included a tiny plate, just large enough to hold a single butter pat. He

---

[*] His earlier attorneys no longer represented him: General Benjamin F. Tracy was now secretary of war; Bourke Cockran had long since concluded that his former client was "unbalanced."

hadn't seen a table so elegantly set since he'd left Brooklyn Heights, and he said how impressed he was that his old hometown seemed so fashionably up to date.

"Why, Ferd Ward," his hostess said, "where *have* you been!"[*]

He moved on to the Champion House in East Haddam, where the manager who was now leasing it from the Franklin Trust Company kindly allowed him to stay for a time without charge. He spent his afternoons on the piazza overlooking the Connecticut River, chatting up wealthy vacationers and paying court to Miss Francis Pelton, a twenty-three-year-old woman from Middletown who was the potential heir to the tidy fortune her father made from packaging headache powders. Ferd spent so much time with her, spinning along the country roads in a hired carriage, that local newspapers got wind of it in early August and reported that the couple was about to be married. Miss Pelton's father denied the story—and whisked his daughter off to a friend's home in Massachusetts until she came to her senses.

Ferd was already looking elsewhere. He returned to Thompson several times that summer. As an old man, Clarence could remember nothing of those visits other than his father's insistence that he come along on a terrifying series of long, plunging buggy rides through the countryside. But around the corner from the Greens lived Mrs. Robert Tallman, the widow of a Congregational minister, and her nineteen-year-old daughter, Frances. Sometime during one of his visits Ferdinand began to call at the Tallman home. Seventeen years earlier, when he had first stepped into his in-laws' Brooklyn parlor, he had presented himself as an innocent newcomer in need of help adjusting to life in the big city. Now he was just as courtly and soft-spoken, apparently pious and eager to please as he had been then, but he also portrayed himself as a grieving widower, a fond father unfairly denied custody of his son, the victim of others' greed who had bravely shouldered guilt that should have been far more widely shared.

Frances believed it all. Before long Ferd was calling her "Fannie." By the end of August, the *New Haven Register* was sure she and Ferd were engaged. They were "inseparable," the newspaper reported.

---

[*] There are several variations of this story, evidently once a favorite in Geneseo; this one was told to the author by the hostess's niece, Mrs. Esther Page Campbell, August 23, 1971. Another version had the hostess say, "Shall we go into the dining room? Let's all go together in lock-step." (Mrs. Irene Beale to the author, May 15, 1981.) Still another version appears in Carl Carmer's *Dark Trees to the Wind*, p. 354.

"They are constantly together when not driving behind Ward's trotters or enjoying long walks about Thompson."[10] She gave Ferd photographs of herself and wrote him fond, encouraging letters whenever they were apart.

Then, he overplayed his hand. A few days after the *Register* story, he hurriedly left town, saying he had to attend to important business and promising to return soon to spend the winter with the Greens. The next morning, the owner of the Putnam livery stable turned up at Fred Green's front door; Ferd had run up a bill for $66 ($1,740 today) for the hire of fast horses and a fashionable carriage he had insisted on having specially imported from New York. Then he had refused to pay for it, claiming he'd been overcharged. Local shopkeepers who had sold him armsful of flowers and box after box of candy with which he'd courted Frances Tallman had also not been paid. Neither had the dentist. Just as he had as a fifteen-year-old boy in Geneseo, Ferd had spent lavishly and expected someone else to foot the bills. His mother had paid them then; now, Fred Green, who had introduced his brother-in-law to all his latest creditors, was left to come up with the money.

Green was so angry he did not trust himself to write to Ferd. His wife again did it for him.

> I feel very sorry about it but Fred does not feel willing to [have you] come here to spend the winter for he has lost confidence in you and says he would worry about you all the time. Of course you can come to see Clarence whenever you wish to do so.
>
> I am sorry and disappointed about you, Ferd. I hoped your bitter experience might be a lesson and in less than a year to start in the same way seems dreadful to me. You say you will be "driven to desperation and do something that will send you back to Sing Sing." Do you ever think that you obtain money from other people by false representations that they have got to work and work hard for?
>
> Please, Ferd, act as you should. You will be happier than you ever can be in this way you are doing now. . . . So now do start to be a man. You do not want to be dependent upon your brother for your board and you can get something to do if you do not ask for a position of too great responsibility. Do something for yourself and show people what you can do and then come back to your boy and us and you will find a welcome always.[11]

Ferd responded in fury.

> Mrs. Green,
> Your letter just received, it is but what I expected. Did it ever occur to you that the treatment of my own family & friends has *caused* this trouble? Had you done by me, as was my right to be done by, this trouble [would] never [have] occurred.
>
> But God *will* punish you for it, as He is now punishing Will [whose wife was ill]. If Kate dies it will be but a judgment on him for this inhuman treatment, & so, too, I fear your punishment will come for keeping my boy from me. I suffer now, but mark my words, as long as you keep my boy from me, you will never be happy. God will punish you some way.
>
> I have begged for work. I have offered to do *anything* but can find nothing. You enjoy happiness & a home out of the income of my boy's estate, while, I, his father, must choose between starvation & prison. Mark my words you & Fred will never prosper while you keep him from me.
> F. Ward[12]

Things were about to grow still worse. A few days after leaving Thompson for Newburgh, Ferd had written Fannie's mother a letter carefully marked "Private."

> My dear Mrs. Tallman,
> I want to make a little investment of $75 for Frances [nearly $1,930 today], & I know if I do it myself she will be angry. I shan't tell you what it is but if you wish me to I will do it & you can send the money & then can say you paid for it, & I will return the money to you when I come. It will please her greatly & be of profit besides. You can send the money to me care of James W. Graff Esq., 2325 Seventh Avenue, N.Y. City & I will get it, & don't say a word to her or to anyone about it. . . . * If she was not so particular about such things, I would do it myself. I will be in New York till next Tuesday, so you

---

* James W. "Pop" Graff was a longtime reporter for the City News Association who had befriended Ferd after his arrest, offered him advice on how to deal with the press while in Sing Sing, and stuck with him for a time after his release.

must send it *at once* or I will not get it. You can send a check or get a draft at the bank.

This is a secret between you & I—so if you do it or not, say nothing to anyone. I am crowded with business but will be all through soon & then will come up for a nice time. Don't let Fannie get blue. . . .

Fondly,
Ferdinand Ward[13]

Mrs. Tallman evidently did send him the money, for in a hasty note on September 20, Ferd acknowledged that he had received it and that he would be up shortly "for a day or so. . . . Give Fannie my love & tell her I shall soon be there."[14]

When neither Ferdinand nor her money had turned up by the first week of October, Mrs. Tallman (who had likely heard of Ferd's unpaid bills by then), wrote to Ferdinand, now hinting at legal action if her money—along with her daughter's letters and photographs—were not returned to her immediately.

Ferdinand did his best to head her off. He claimed to be "looking hourly for a remittance due me and the moment it comes I will see that [your] money is mailed to you."[15] Enclosed in the letter was a note from his lawyer, John Gardner, claiming that Ferd should have had the interest due to him from his share of the income from his parents' estates "long before this."[16] Nothing was said about her daughter's pictures or love letters.

Mrs. Tallman now explicitly threatened to sue.

Ferd responded from Stamford, where he was trying to talk one or another of his and Ella's old friends into providing him with cash.

What can I say that will convince you of how utterly I suffer from want of funds? Since leaving Newburgh I have had but $30 in all to pay my expenses & am now working on a farm for my board. [He was in fact living off the charity of the couple who had once grown the roses in his greenhouse.]

You little know, Madame, how cruelly I have been treated by those who should stand by me in this trying time. I am legally entitled to certain moneys but being without funds to press my claim, & being hampered by those who should help me, I am left simply to write. That I will succeed in the end there is *no doubt*, but at present I am left utterly devoid of the necessities of life. Could you know how I suffer, I feel that your maternal heart would sympathize with me, for I have always found in you a friend. I have at times felt strongly tempted to end it all but for the sake of that boy I have waited & will try my best to pull through. I beg that you will deal leniently with me for it's so hard. You little know how I suffer and God grant that it may soon come to an end. I beg that you will be patient a little longer for I am *sure* all will come in time. I have no one to go to for the money. But . . . I will soon have it & will send it. For the sake of my boy, if not for mine, I beg that you will bear with me a little longer. With a heart full of gratitude & a hope for a soon change in my troubles I remain

Fondly,
F. Ward

Your daughter's letters & pictures are not here & I have no money left to get where they are, but you may rest assured they will be sent [to] you just as soon as I can get there. No one shall see them. . . . As to those reports [of unpaid bills], please . . . remember how many there always are to kick a man when he is down.[17]

Mrs. Tallman showed Ferd's letters to the Greens. Fred was understandably outraged. His brother-in-law's unpaid bills had been bad enough. Now it was clear that Ferdinand had abused the hospitality of his friends in Thompson, just as he had ruined his family in Brooklyn.

Meanwhile, Sarah Ward Brinton—unaware that Ferd was in trouble again but wary—had innocently written the Greens to ask if her brother couldn't stay with them over the winter. Her own husband would not have him in his house.

> I have just received a letter from my brother. In it he says, "I can't get work nor can I starve." He sends his address "Care of J.M. Gardner, Newburgh, NY." Now, I know this man to be one who had some dealings with Ferd while he was at Sing Sing and I thought him at the time a doubtful acquaintance, and I am not willing to pass any money through him to Ferd. At the same time I do not wish to feel that, as his sister, I have left him to "starve. . . ."

I begged him—the week before his release—to apply for some job *away* from New York where he could earn a living by the labor of his hands until he earned the confidence of the public. This he has not done, evidently.[18]

She and her brother would be happy, she continued, to pay for his board if that would help. "I want to keep Ferd in the proper way but I do not wish to be black-mailed by his bad associates."

Nellie Green told her what had happened. Under the circumstances, it was simply impossible to have him stay in Thompson. Saddened but not surprised, Sarah responded right away.

I thank you very much for writing me just as you have done for, hard as it may be, it is always best to know the truth and my only regret is that you should have carried the trouble for so long without my sharing it. I knew nothing of Ferd or his ways, nor had I reason for suspicion until his letter to me this week. From the look and tone of it I knew he was deceiving me and yet I felt that I should not condemn him until I did know something. I do not wonder Mr. Green feels as he does and if Ferd goes on as he has begun there is but one end. I cannot influence him. I have tried hard enough but nothing seems to appeal to him. I fear that he has no reluctance to bring disgrace upon others. The small income which will be due him from his father's estate will not bring him any luxuries and the principal is in trust, so fixed that there is not the smallest possibility of its ever being broken.

Your letter to him was most kind and gentle and I feel deeply grateful to you for your patience with him.

My sorrow for my brother is too great for me to speak much of it. He has always been gentle and kind to me but if he continues his transgressions what avails all that he has done?[19]

Sarah sent Nellie Green's letter on to her brother Will. He, too, wrote to reassure the Greens.

I wish I knew what to say. Alas! I can say nothing. You have been kind and gentle to Clarence and I thank you and beg that you and Mr. Green will simply go on in the same old way.

I note in one of your letters that you say that you fear you may have been unjust to me in your thoughts [presumably for failing to take more responsibility for his brother]. I had not known it but I do know that those whose opinion I prized did not understand me and that I could not make them. I have been more kind and gentle to F. than others think, but I have had to act in ways which no doubt seemed harsh. No matter. Some day all will be all right. And now I only wish that so far as you and Mr. Green can do so, you cease to worry. There are enough sad hearts without yours. When you write me again just tell me about Clarence and your home, etc. In fact we will try and forget what is sad from now on.[20]

It would not be that easy. Nothing was working out for Ferd. It was not surprising that his time in Stamford yielded no one willing to provide him with a stake. "The Connecticut Valley in the vicinity of Stamford is full of his victims," an investigator who had helped work up the case that put him behind bars recalled. "Whenever he heard of anyone with a little money he would cultivate that person until he got the money."[21] Stamford citizens were not inclined to let him rob them a second time.

Ferd kept writing to Thompson. His letters to Clarence were saccharine and filled with self-pity.

> My own dear boy,
>   Your papa sends you love, *all the love of his heart*, and a sweet goodbye kiss. We will never see each other again, my dear son, but when you grow up you will know the reason why through a friend of papa's. Try and think kindly of me, my dear son, and remember that while we lived your mama and papa loved you more than anything in the world. May god bless you and keep you happy.
>
>   Your heart-broken papa,
>   F. Ward
>   (*a sweet kiss*)[22]

To Nellie Green, his tone was very different. As always when caught doing wrong, he blamed it all on others. His brother and sister had looted his parents' home in Geneseo, he said, leaving him nothing but battered furnishings as his share of their inheritance. (In fact, Sarah had not been in Geneseo since her father's funeral three years earlier; Will had been there for just half a day; nothing was missing.) If the Greens had not wanted him to do wrong while he was in Thompson, he continued, they should not have put temptations in his path.

As to my *behavior* since I left Sing Sing I don't care if the whole world knows it. I noticed you did not hesitate to encourage my getting cookies, flowers & c. & horses, too. As to my being *trusted* by *anyone* on *your account*, that is *utterly false.* . . .

You say you *"Know what I did & what I intended doing,"* as to the former I do not care, but as to your knowledge of what I *intended doing, you talk foolishly.* In your letter you refer to *a widow.* I suppose you mean Mrs. Tallman. As to my relations with *that* family, I guess they will say nothing. Perhaps were I to show you some letters you would better know the truth but I am not one to attack unless I am attacked, but *if I am attacked* you may rest assured I won't come out the worst. . . .

You say I may go back to prison. Do you know that if I looked out the window now and saw a sheriff coming for me I would hail him gladly? What do I care for life or liberty? I am robbed of my father's estate. I have applied to over 50 people for work. I have answered over 30 advertisements to get work. I have written to Will my exact position but get no answer. I even asked you to keep me till I could get help but this you refused. I am sitting here today, living on the charity of an Irishman, with not a stitch of winter clothes to my name. Old and hungry. [He was forty-one.] I have been for work to everyone I know and many I do not. You talk about getting work, why your own husband can't earn enough to support his family but has to take my money to do it. You live in comfort. Why? Because you get $600 a year more than you spend from the trust company on Clarence. But your day of sorrow will come.

I can't live on nothing, so must borrow money till I get work. If my boy had been given to me, as Ella wished, then I would never have had trouble, but now I will go back to prison and on the shoulders of those who have borne me down shall rest the blame. Life is *nothing* to me without that boy. I have no home, no money, am cold for want of clothes, can get no work. My own brother keeps me from even the small income left me by my dear mother. What care I for life? If this is your *Christian* spirit, then I want none of it. Sooner a life and death in prison, than to be free and robbed of my own. That boy some day will right these wrongs. I have written a full history of everything since I left prison and it will be published just as soon as I am arrested or if I die it will come out and when Clarence grows older he will know it all and you may rest assured he will revenge it.

Here, where dear Ella died, I hope to die, but if I am again put in prison and die there, I have no fear but that a just God will reward me for this cruelly unjust suffering. . . . When I die from starvation and hunger, then will begin your suffering, if you have a heart beyond greed to get my money for your own use.

Were it not for my love for my boy, you know that I could have every dollar of his money to myself except what came from the [Greens'] Monroe Place house. . . . I'll die willingly for his sake but God will punish you for it all.

As I told you before if I am left alone. I'll have that boy if I have to take him.[23]

The Greens were alarmed by Ferd's threats. They sent copies of his letters to Sarah Ward Brinton and asked her how seriously she thought they should take them. She responded with the care and consideration that characterized her throughout her life.

Let me talk to you a bit about my brother. I understand the whole position and am no stranger to the kind of letters which you received from him. Your duty and obligations begin and end with Clarence. I believe you have done your very best to make the boy happy, honest and true. I feel glad whenever I think of him that he has found so good a home and where he is watched so carefully and loved so tenderly. . . . You are not only doing what is right in keeping Clarence, but you are doing kindly to the child.

Ask yourself what could his father do for and with him. What a miserable existence the boy would have without care. I beg you not to allow yourself to be worried or distressed by communications from his father. When a letter comes from him, let Mr. Green, if he pleases, glance over it and then throw it into the fire and do not give it another thought or attempt to reply.

When my brother . . . puts himself industriously to work in some place far from his former life and makes a home where he can provide for his boy it will be time enough to think of giving him up—not before. I see that this thing is worrying you and I want you to put it out of your thoughts and become stoical. If you worry, it will distress your husband and you both have had trouble enough.[24]

Will was less willing to take sides. "If F. has any legal claims on the boy and his income it is natural that he should advance them," he wrote. "As to his claims I have *no knowledge whatever* but it seems to me that Mr. McKeen, who had so much to do with the matter could tell you at once what claims F. has. As to having any influence over F., I never had any and have not now. Nor was I aware till your letter that any such an attempt was to be made. If I were you I should not worry but would endeavor to obtain some legal opinion on the subject."[25]

Ferd's threats to the Greens fell off for a time, though Clarence received a brief doleful note from his father every month: "Papa is so lonely without you, but God will give you to me some day I know."[26] "Try and study hard and grow up a smart boy then you can help papa in his work some day."[27] "Cruel people keep you away from me."[28]

His name cropped up in the newspapers now and again. One reporter spotted him in the gallery at the Produce Exchange where he had gotten his start; another heard he planned to get back into the mining business. In February, the New York County district attorney dropped all six of the remaining indictments against him. He found a job, clerking in the office of E. Scott & Company, a religious publisher located on West Twenty-third Street. Will paid for his room and board in Brooklyn, sending checks directly to the landlord so that Ferd would have no access to cash.

Then, in April, the stock market collapsed, setting off a depression that would last for nearly five years. Within six months 156 railroads would go bankrupt. Four hundred banks collapsed. So did eight thousand businesses. By August, all of Will Ward's investments had gone bad. His savings were wiped out. The Wards were forced to sell their ranch and big Denver home.

At first, Ferd was delighted. "Your Uncle Will has failed in business," he told Clarence, "and all those who treat us cruelly will suffer in [the] same way, I know."[29] It was a sign that God was on his side. But his exultation was quickly tempered when he realized that Will would no longer be paying his living expenses, that he would now have to survive on his salary alone. "May you . . . never know what it is to suffer for food for I know it now," he told Clarence in October. "Would that I might take you in my arms and kiss you and then go to Mama, for I am tired of life."[30]

That same month, he told the press he was finishing a book that would vindicate him. He had begun *The Founding, Life, and Financial Death of the House of Grant & Ward*, he claimed, only because of his son: "The oft-repeated argument that 'it is all over now and the least said the better' would be true and would be observed did not the welfare of one in whom I have a greater interest than in anything else, even life itself, demand the clearing up of everything possible in connection with the unfortunate past of the old banking house." Most of the case he made was all too familiar: his real crime had been his failure, not his methods; those who had profited most from his transactions had gotten away scot-free; had New York Chamberlain Nelson Tappan not fallen ill, city funds would never have been withdrawn from the Marine Bank, whose directors had been fully aware of everything that had gone on and then lied about it under oath.

In hopes of landing a publisher's advance, he did add one sensational new charge: "That General Grant supposed he was speculating in government contracts I most emphatically assert. I can, and if necessary, will produce and publish correspondence over autographs that will give undisputed proof of my correctness."[31] But he actually had no proof of Grant's complicity other than the already-published letter that he—with or without James Fish's connivance—had talked the general into signing without reading. No publisher was interested. Ferd was falling behind in his rent. Bills were piling up. He needed to do something.

SEVENTEEN

The Kidnapping

In January 1894, Fred Green got another alarming letter from his brother-in-law: if he did not surrender Clarence within one week, Ferd would come to Thompson and take his boy away. No one should try to stop him.

James McKeen advised the Greens not to respond to this new threat, but instead to consult Charles E. Searls, a local attorney who happened to live right across the street from them, with an eye toward applying to the Thompson probate court to have Fred Green formally named as Clarence's guardian. Fred was reluctant; a court battle would be costly and prolonged and by no means certain of success. McKeen agreed that the "application might better and more forcibly come from someone in the *father's* family. I should suppose William Ward would make it though [the Wards] have all shown rather a disposition to shirk responsibility in these affairs, for which one can hardly blame them."[1] Will, living in far-off Denver, with four children of his own to support and most of his fortune gone, declined to do battle with his younger brother.

The deadline passed. Ferd did not turn up in Thompson. Then, on March 18, the Greens got startling news from a Geneseo attorney, Lockwood R. Doty: his client, Clarence's father, was about to remarry and move back to Geneseo to provide his son with a real home of his own, he said; it was therefore now time to give the boy up.

Then began a skirmish between attorneys, Ferd's lawyer threatening court action unless the boy was surrendered to his father, and the Greens' attorneys warning Ferd not to try it. Before the Greens could even consider turning Clarence over to his father, Charles Searls wrote, both they and the Franklin Trust needed to know how Ferd was financially fixed and whom he was going to marry. Under Connecticut law, he added, a child's relatives or the selectmen of the town where the child lived could ask the court to appoint a guardian when the natural parent was deemed an "unfit person."

> We sincerely hope that circumstances may not arise which will remedy it necessary for the courts to pass upon the question of Mr. Ward's fitness, moral or in other respects, to assume the custody of this child and the oversight of his intellectual and moral training. We trust that no such investigation of Mr. Ward's past or present, as must be involved in any such hearing, may become necessary, for the sake of the father as well as the son.[2]

Four days later, the newspapers answered at least one of the Greens' questions.

WILL MARRY MISS STORER

FERDINAND WARD TO BE MARRIED TODAY IN HIS BOYHOOD
HOME TO A RESIDENT OF BROOKLYN

GENESEO, N.Y. MARCH 20, 1894—Ferdinand Ward reached this village two weeks ago and put up at the Big Tree Inn. Geneseo was Mr. Ward's boyhood home, and he has frequently made visits here of two or three day's duration. A little more importance was attached to this visit, however, from the fact that it was longer than usual.

A young woman stopped at the Big Tree Inn about a week ago and registered as Miss Belle Storer of Brooklyn, N.Y., and immediately afterward Mr. Ward changed his residence to the home of Dr. J. A. West.

Miss Storer and Ward were frequently seen in the streets together, and it was rumored that they were about to be married. I learned that the rumor is true and that they will be married at the home of Dr. West tomorrow.[3]

More details appeared the following day.

Only the most intimate friends of the parties were present, among them being John Storer of New York City, the uncle of the bride, with whom she lived and with whom Mr. Ward boarded when in the city. The groom has been here about two weeks and the bride about ten days. The bride is a comely brunette of majestic appearance and looks like one who cared nothing for what the world might say about her husband and the vicissitudes of life through which he had passed.

In an interview, Mr. Ward said he had formulated no plans for the future further than to go to New York to conclude some business, then to return to Geneseo, occupy the old homestead and bring his . . . son here to live and educate him.

The bride is not reputed be wealthy, but is said to have good prospects.[4]

A few days later, Lockwood Doty responded to Charles Searls on Ferd's behalf. Since Clarence's legal residence was really with his father in New York State, Connecticut law was irrelevant, he argued, and the issue of his alleged fitness or unfitness therefore out of bounds. His financial condition was no one's business but his own, either; the Franklin Trust had no legitimate say as to whom it made its payments on Clarence's behalf.

"Mr. Ward was married Thursday of last week and is preparing to occupy his old home with his wife and boy," Doty continued.

The lady whom he married appears to be in every way estimable. . . . Geneseo has one of the best Normal schools in the State, the climate is unsurpassed, and the surroundings altogether are of a character to make it most desirable for the health and proper development of Clarence, and I am satisfied that every attention will be paid to his welfare. . . .

There is but little left to Mr. Ward save his family to yield any satisfaction in his life, and I think it would be extremely ungracious on the part of Mr. Green to thwart him in so natural and humane a purpose as securing possession of his boy. I have advised the course which has been taken to the end that Mr. Ward may be absolved from any imputation of hasty or improvident action, although most men in a similar situation would be tempted to act impetuously.[5]

Searls conferred with McKeen, then wrote a long, careful response on behalf of them both. The Connecticut courts were sure to assert jurisdiction; Clarence and his late mother had been residents of that state ever since Ferd had been sent to Sing Sing. Then he issued a blunt warning in the most courtly possible terms.

We beg to emphasize . . . that we have not the least doubt of your good faith and the honest belief entertained by you concerning these matters, but the writer is confident that there are facts in the case unknown to you. His residence being in Thompson, he saw something of Mr. Ward during his stay there, and while entertaining personally none but the most kindly feelings towards him, does not believe that the happiness or welfare of Clarence will be enhanced by a change at present in his surroundings. It is not necessary at this time, as bearing on the question of "fitness," to refer to any details of Mr. Ward's life in Thompson or to certain correspondence [with the Tallmans] which has passed under the writer's observation as indicative of one of its phases; with regard to which correspondence, its cause and consequences, Mr. Ward has doubtless advised you. [If he had not done so, Searls knew, he would have to do it now.]

As to Mr. Ward's affection for his son; it was not conspicuously manifested while in Thompson, and, upon his sudden departure, he indicated no wish to have Clarence accompany him. No affection was developed on the part of the boy towards his father, and a change from his present home would be extremely repugnant to him. . . . Whether Mr. Ward's treatment of Mr. and Mrs. Green, the only persons of all his kith and kin who gave him a welcome when he came out of prison, is such as their great kindness toward him [deserves] we need not discuss now.

It seems to Mr. Green and to others interested in the boy's welfare that he should not be turned over to Mr. Ward without more ample assurances from him as to the stability of his expressed purposes and plans than he is at present able to give. If that time ever comes, we feel assured that Clarence will be returned to his father with the hearty consent of all those who are interested in him and in the development, during the transition period of his life, of a manly and noble character.[6]

James McKeen complimented Searls on how well he had spelled out the Greens' case. Now that Ferd had been forced to tell his legal advisers about his attempt to extort money from the Tallmans, he was sure they would "admonish him to let well enough alone. I do not believe they will countenance any kidnap methods."[7] Five months went by without another word from Ferdinand.

At eight thirty on the morning of September 12, 1894, Clarence—now ten years old—finished his morning oatmeal, threw his book bag over his shoulder, said good-bye to his aunt and uncle, and began the half-mile walk to school with his two cousins. Soon after turning left onto Main Street they were joined by Clarence's friend Dunbar Ives, son of the Baptist minister. The great arching elms that made the unpaved street into a leafy tunnel were showing the first red and orange signs of autumn.

Just as the four children reached the front of Rand Chandler's big house, next door to the schoolhouse, Clarence turned and saw a sleek little runabout of the kind people then called a democrat coming up fast behind them. The horse, a handsome sorrel, slowed, then stopped. Two men were on the seat. Clarence had never seen either of them before. One held the reins. The other leaned down and asked Dunbar Ives if he was Clarence Ward.

No, he said, and pointed to his companion.

"Good morning, Clarence," the stranger said. "Your father wants to see you. You're to come along with us to Putnam."

Clarence was puzzled. He had only seen his father a few times two summers earlier, and he'd been taught to be polite to adults. "I had no reason to think it wasn't a perfectly *bona fide* thing," he remembered many years later. Still, he hesitated. His aunt had warned him that if his father ever turned up he should run home, and if anyone tried to take him away he should start shouting and keep it up until Uncle Fred could get there.

The stranger jumped down, seized the boy beneath the arms, swung him up onto the seat, and climbed up behind him. The driver whipped up the sorrel, and the democrat clattered southward down Main Street toward Putnam.

Clarence, squeezed beneath the two strange men, began to shout, "I won't go! I won't go!"

Men and women ran out of their houses, set just a few feet back from the road, to see what was causing the commotion. Some ran after the buggy. "I yelled my best," Clarence remembered. "The man saw that the people heard me . . . , so he grabbed me by the throat. Then, he found that I got black in the face—I heard the driver say I did—and he put his hand over my mouth."[8]

Meanwhile, fourteen-year-old Helen Green raced toward home, screaming that her cousin was being kidnapped. Other children on the way to school started shouting too.

Mrs. Rand Chandler gathered up her skirts and ran to E. S. Backus's grocery and dry goods store, where there was a telephone station. With the help of Mr. Backus, she reached the authorities in Putnam, alerting them that Clarence and his kidnappers were on their way there, presumably to catch the fast train to New York.

But as he was speaking, a woman's voice broke in on the line. Mrs. George Nichols, wife of the president of the Dime Savings Bank of Thompson, was calling from her home on the Putnam road about two miles southwest of town. A fast-moving buggy carrying Clarence Ward and two strangers had just turned off the road in front of her house, she said. They were no longer headed for Putnam but were already trotting along a narrow, meandering dirt track that led north through the village of Grosvenordale to the main road to Webster, just over the Massachusetts border, ten miles away. She could still hear the boy screaming.

By then, Fred Green had harnessed his own carriage and started toward Main Street. Pastor Cummings climbed up next to him. E. S. Van Arsdale, a summer resident from New York, ran out of his house with a revolver and handed it up to Fred. He lashed his horses. Other Thompson citizens followed as quickly as they could, some in carriages, some on horseback. If they failed to catch the kidnappers before they crossed the state line and Ferd managed to get his hands on the boy beyond the reach of Connecticut law, they would lose him forever.

Just as James McKeen had predicted, once Ferd's attorney learned that his client had been caught trying to steal money from the widow Tallman after leaving Sing Sing, he had advised him to delay his attempt to get legal custody of his son until he and his new wife were reestablished in his hometown and he had proved himself willing to earn a legitimate living. But neither attorney understood the depth of Ferd's anger or the obsessive nature of his sense of grievance. For nine years, the world had conspired to deny him those things he deemed rightfully his. Now, his own lawyer wouldn't help him, and the courts offered no remedy, so he had resolved at last to seize his son.

Despite all the threats he had made over the past two years, he did not dare do the job himself. Confrontation was not his style. Instead, with the help of Massachusetts state senator Charles Haggerty, a Webster attorney with political connections in Boston, he had devised a brutally simple plan: a paid agent would snatch the boy from in front of his school. First he would pretend to be taking him south to Putnam, where his father would presumably be waiting to put him on the New York train. Then he would head north instead, to Webster, where Ferd would smuggle him aboard the noon train to Boston before anyone knew what had happened.*

With Haggerty's help, he had hired a former police detective from Boston named Frank J. Ryder, who was willing to act on his behalf. The two men had arrived in Webster on the previous afternoon's train and made their way to the best hotel in town, the sprawling two-story Joslin House. Ferd signed the register as "Frank Ward" and picked a room on the second floor where he was to wait for his boy to be delivered to him. Then they had hired a buggy and headed off toward Thompson so that Ryder could get a sense of the lay of the land. Ferd knew the back roads well from his summer visits two years earlier, and he wanted to show his hireling the street that ran past the Thompson schoolhouse where he was to kidnap Clarence the next morning.

Ryder and J. Duggan, the local liveryman whose horse and runabout he'd hired, had followed Ferd's plan to the letter. But Clarence's screams had given away their true destination, and by feinting toward Putnam and then taking a winding country track that linked with the

* There would be no federal law against interstate kidnapping until after the death of Charles Lindbergh's infant son, thirty-eight years later.

main road to Webster, they had gone well out of their way. Fred Green and his Thompson posse headed straight for Grosvenordale, hoping to cut them off. When they reached the junction, he stopped to ask a small boy picking apples if he had seen a carriage with two men and a boy. Yes, he said. They had just trotted out of sight. They, too, had stopped by the orchard, to ask him if they were on the right road to Webster.

Fred lashed his team. About four miles from town, he spotted the kidnappers trotting along ahead of him.

He urged his team into a full-out gallop.

The gap between them began to close. Clarence saw his uncle's carriage coming.

"Come and take me, Uncle! Come and take me!"[9]

Duggan whipped his horse. Ryder again tried to muffle the boy's screams.

Green drew closer. He dared not fire his borrowed revolver for fear of hitting the boy. The road was too narrow for one buggy to pass another. The race went on for two miles, three miles, four.

As they reached the outskirts of Webster, Fred's weary team began to slow, then fall back.

A carriage was coming the other way. Webster Constable Joseph C. Love happened to be out for a morning drive. Seeing the runabout hurtling toward him with a stranger holding his hand over a small boy's mouth, he assumed the child had been hurt in an accident and pulled off the road to let them pass. But Fred Green, coming right behind, stood in the carriage, waving his free arm and shouting that the boy was being kidnapped. Love wheeled his buggy around, made room on the seat for Fred and Pastor Cummings, and started into town after the retreating carriage.

The Joslin House had been established half a century earlier as a temperance establishment, but its new owners had thoughtfully installed a barroom between the attached livery stable and the hotel lobby so that every visitor had a chance at a drink before checking in.

Duggan drove his lathered horse into the stable. Ryder jumped down and carried the boy into the barroom. The bartender looked startled. Ryder told him some men were following him, and tossed him a $5 gold piece for his promise to tell them he hadn't seen him or the boy.

He raced up the stairs with Clarence over his shoulder, carried him down the corridor, and opened the door to the room where Ferd had promised to be waiting. He wasn't there. Ryder put the boy down and warned him not to make a sound.

That morning was meant to mark Ferd's greatest triumph, the end of almost a decade of failure and frustration. He had defied his lawyer, outwitted the courts, outmaneuvered the Greens, and was about to gain control of his boy—and with it immediate access to the interest from his wife's estate and potential command of the principal, as well. Everything seemed to be going as planned, but he had still been anxious, agitated, unable to sit still. He paced the room, repeatedly consulted his father's gold watch, peered out the window, then suddenly decided to step down the street for a quick shave. It had taken him and Ryder about an hour and a half to cover the back roads from Thompson to Webster the previous evening, and so when he left his hotel room at about nine thirty and headed for the barber shop, he thought he still had roughly half an hour to wait before the boy was finally in his hands.

But he had miscalculated. He and Ryder had been trotting when they'd timed their travel. His agents were now at the end of a galloping, headlong race. Ferd was seated in the barber's chair, feet up, towel around his shoulders, chin lathered, when the runabout carrying Clarence and the kidnappers flashed past the shop window. By the time he'd wiped off the lather, paid the barber, and stepped outside, Fred Green and Constable Love were already in sight, followed by a stream of carriages and mounted men from Thompson, some waving pistols. Ferd shrank back into the doorway, then slipped down the street in search of his lawyer, Senator Haggerty.

A minute or two after Clarence and his kidnapper climbed the stairs to Ferd's room, Fred Green burst through the door of the bar. He asked if anyone had seen a man and a small boy.

The bartender Ryder had bribed shook his head. But a customer nursing a midmorning beer in the back of the room silently pointed upstairs.

Green took the steps two at a time. He banged on the door of Ferd's room. Ryder opened it, thinking it must be the boy's father.

Green pushed his way in. Clarence tried to run to his uncle. The kidnapper held on to him.

"What right have you with that boy?" Green shouted.

"His father is here."

"Where?"

"He'll be here in a minute."

"I demand that you give me the child."

"By what authority?"

"By this authority," said Constable Love, stepping into the room and throwing open his coat to display his badge. "And if you don't turn over the child, I'll put you under arrest."[10]

The Boston detective backed down. He hadn't bargained for jail time.

Fred Green and the constable led Clarence down the stairs, anxious to get him back across the Connecticut line before his missing father could be found. By now, a crowd of townspeople had gathered in front of the hotel. Buggies from Thompson filled the street. The crowd was angry. When someone cursed Frank Ryder, he displayed his Boston detective's badge—"as large as a soup plate," one reporter wrote—and tried to "overawe the country folks." "I was taking the boy home to his loving father," he said.

"Yes and half-strangled him on the way," an angry farmer answered.[11]

As Green and Love lifted Clarence up onto the seat of the constable's carriage, the red marks left by Ryder's fingers could be seen on the boy's neck.

Haggerty thought it best to pretend he had known nothing of the kidnap plan in advance. "I had been in court trying a case and was on the street looking at the fun," he told a newspaperman, "when somebody told me that Ward wanted to see me. I made my way through the crowd and spoke to Ward and he said he wanted to see me at my office."

Haggerty told Ferd there was no time to talk. "There is your boy," he said, "and if you want to keep that boy in Massachusetts you must act quickly." Ferd held back.

Constable Love's buggy started down the street toward Thompson. Love held the reins. Clarence sat safely between him and his uncle Fred. The little army from Thompson fell in behind them.

"If Ferdinand Ward had told me to act as his counsel instead of telling me he wanted to consult," Haggerty continued, "I would have put my hands on young Ward, 'This boy is ours.' Neither Frederick D. Green nor any constable or Connecticut farmer would have taken the boy out of Massachusetts unless by due process of law."[12]

In the end, no one was arrested: since the boy had been taken in Connecticut it was unclear whether a case against his kidnappers could be made to stick in Massachusetts. Ferd paid the hotel bill. Then he and Ryder hurried to the depot and stepped onto the northbound train, without the boy they had come to steal.

The *New York Herald* summarized the day's events: "Ferdinand Ward, late of Wall Street, but more lately of Sing Sing, must have lost much of his cunning, for his attempt to kidnap his own son was a dramatic fiasco."

The failure was bad enough from Ferd's point of view, but ridicule was intolerable. He bought space for a personal reply the following day.

A CARD FROM FERDINAND WARD

To The Editor Of The *Herald*:—

Your story in this morning's paper is in every respect most cruelly unjust and not true in nearly every point.

The boy came willingly and no force was used of any kind. I can't believe that you could knowingly have let such falsehoods appear. I have but one desire, and that is to gain the custody of my child, and were you similarly situated, I feel sure you would feel as I do.

I do not ask or expect any of the income of his estate, although every dollar of it came from me. I have a home for my boy and I want him with me, and he will gladly come.

The Greens have poisoned his mind against me, for the income they get from the estate is all they have to live on, and hence their lies and slanders. I thought the HERALD meant to be just, but it seems that I can't expect that even from it.

I will prove before the courts soon that I am in the right in this matter, and so convince you of how cruel this article is.

FERDINAND WARD
GENESEO, N.Y. Sept. 14, 1894.[13]

It is impossible to know how much or how little of what Ferd wrote he had actually come to believe, but every assertion he made was untrue.

The boy had been terrified. Force was used. Ferd desperately wanted access to his son's income. Ella's estate had not come from him. Until the kidnapping, the Greens had been scrupulous in keeping their opinion of Ferd from his son.

But now, they petitioned the probate court in Thompson to have Fred Green appointed as Clarence's legal guardian. A hearing was scheduled for October 8.

James McKeen and Charles Searls believed that the kidnapping alone would go a long way toward demonstrating Ferd's "unfitness" for having his son restored to him. But they wanted as much additional evidence as they could gather. Nellie Green remembered that at one point during a shrill exchange with Ferd, he had threatened that if the Greens and his brother and sister were not more generous with him, he would have no choice but to marry what he called a "dissolute woman."[14] Five days after Ferd's notice appeared, Fred Green received an anonymous letter that seemed to suggest that he had done just that.

> New York
> September 18, 1894
> Dear Sir,
>
> If you want to keep the boy and beat Ward, why don't you attack the character of Belle Storer the woman he married, and show she is not a proper person, or he either for that matter, to have control of the boy, you can do it safely as she was for years the mistress of a certain man and Ward knew it when he married her.
>
> She is the woman Ward sent to Wells College and paid one term's tuition for just before he was sent to Sing-Sing. She is the woman who constantly visited him all the time he was in prison. She is the woman your sister, Mrs. Ward, knew he was infatuated with, and intended to take up with again when he came out as he has done, for the scheme was cut and dried long before your sister died and she knew or suspected it.
>
> The Storer woman never married Ward because she cared anything about him, but she thought as he did that he was going to get the money that was left to the boy and she would do anything for money, and marrying anyone that had it. Ward don't want the boy but he does want the money that was left to the boy. The boy's mother was smart enough to keep him from

getting control of it, for the money would come in very nicely to support himself and the woman who was your sister's and is your son's worst enemy.

If Ward cared anything about his son or had that son's welfare at heart, he would at least have brought in a respectable woman to take his mother's place, and not one who was another man's mistress.

A personal inserted in the NY *Herald* worded something like the following—"Quid Pro Quo. Any information relating to F. Ward and B. Storer thankfully received. Green"—will be most likely to bring a little more knowledge to you. In case you need it at any time.

Yours truly,
Quid Pro Quo[15]

Perhaps fearing further publicity, the Greens did not place an ad in the paper, but James McKeen asked Sidney Green, Fred's younger brother, to see what he could dig up about Belle Storer in Brooklyn. The results were mixed. The "uncle" who was supposed to have attended her wedding turned out to have been a "myth" invented by Ferd. "She went [to Geneseo], alone, to be married," McKeen reported, clear evidence that she was estranged from her family. And it seemed at least possible that she and Ferd had lived together in Brooklyn; one reporter said they had roomed in the same boardinghouse before coming to Geneseo. But, McKeen admitted on the eve of the hearing, "thus far nothing has been found which will warrant any attack on the present Mrs. Ward, though there seems little doubt that her antecedents are disreputable."*

---

* It is impossible to know now how many of *Quid Quo Pro*'s charges were true. Isabelle Storer did attend Wells College. Whether she had ever been anyone's mistress or visited Ferd in prison is probably unknowable. She was most likely the woman to whom Ferd tried to smuggle letters early in his imprisonment and may have been the one about whom he wrote to Bourke Cockran just before his release. But if they had always planned to marry, it is hard to understand how he could have been courting at least two other women in the weeks after his release—unless he'd simply hoped to find a bride with a fortune of her own. In any case, no matter how colorful Storer's past may have been, once she and Ferd were married she would stick by her turbulent husband until the end of his life. James McKeen to Charles Searls, October 4, 1894, author's collection.

.   .   .

The hearing was set to begin in the battered old Thompson town hall at one o'clock in the afternoon on Monday, October 8. The town was so enthralled by the drama about to unfold in its midst that school was canceled for the afternoon. Most of Clarence's schoolmates filed inside the town hall, as did a large number of men and nearly every woman in the village, until every seat was filled. A sizable crowd was left outside hoping to overhear what was being said.

But by one thirty, no judges or lawyers had appeared. A reporter walked down the street to the office of probate judge George Flint and discovered that he and the lawyers had already begun the hearing there, hoping to avoid what they knew would be a very large crowd. It didn't work. Word spread, the town hall emptied, and the judge's small office was quickly filled so completely that he and consulting judge M. A. Shumway of the superior court were forced to lead the lawyers, the witnesses, and the whole crowd back to the town hall and start over again.

As soon as Flint called for silence, Senator Haggerty of Webster moved that the case be dismissed outright: since Clarence was being unlawfully held in Connecticut, its courts had no jurisdiction; any proceeding affecting the child had to be brought in New York State, the home of his father and therefore Clarence's real home as well.

Charles Searls, the Greens' attorney, and Charles Perkins, a New York lawyer appearing on behalf of the Franklin Trust Company, each argued that section 453 of the Connecticut code empowered the court to appoint a guardian for any child residing within its jurisdiction if the parent was found to be unfit.

Judge Flint agreed.

Haggerty then refused to defend against the Greens' petition. He would neither call nor cross-examine witnesses. His client would not appear, either. There was a murmur of disappointment at this news; everyone in Thompson had hoped to get at least a glimpse of Ferd, whom some in the crowd had threatened to tar and feather if he ever returned to town.

Searls asked for a judgment by default in the Greens' favor.

The judge was sympathetic but thought it important that the petitioners offer enough evidence to make a *prima facie* case that Ferd was unfit to be his son's guardian.

They were happy to oblige. James McKeen began with a litany of Ferd's dishonest dealings with his late wife and her family. Sidney Green corroborated everything to which the family's lawyer had testified. Fred Green read out the bills Ferd had left unpaid after visiting Thompson. The female onlookers murmured when they learned he had run up an $11 tab for "bon-bons"[16] ($283 today). They murmured again when Ferd's damning correspondence with Mrs. Tallman was introduced into evidence. Nellie Green read from his menacing letters to her, told of his threat to marry a loose woman, and testified that he had never shown any genuine affection for Clarence when he was in town and had never bothered to send his son so much as a birthday present since his release from prison.

At the end of the day, the court appointed Frederick D. Green the legal guardian of Clarence Ward. When the boy started toward home with his aunt and uncle their neighbors stood and applauded on the Thompson common.

Ferd moved back to Geneseo, to the old parsonage at the corner of Second Street and Ward Place, surrounded by the books and well-worn furnishings of his boyhood. He opened a small-scale carpentry shop in the house, offering to do the same sort of minor repairs he had done at seventeen. Two old friends, surrogate judge Edward Coyne and the county clerk, William E. Humphrey, jointly hired him as their clerk, at $6 a week, and he was soon walking up Main Street each morning to his office and back again each evening, just as he had when he'd worked for Strang & Adams before leaving for Manhattan twenty-one years before. Except for the absence of his parents and the presence of his new wife, it was as if the fifteen years he'd spent in New York and Stamford—the country houses and blooded horses and evenings on the town—as well as the six and a half years in Sing Sing had all been simply an interruption, a sort of dream.

Some seventy years later, a woman who grew up just across the street remembered the Wards well. Belle was "vivacious and very blonde [by then]—almost platinum," she said, a wonderful cook who always kept a crock of freshly baked cookies ready for small visitors. Ferdinand was charming, too, but "queer-looking—like a plucked chicken—with a drooping moustache, an impossibly thin face and a prominent adam's apple that bobbed up and down when he talked."[17]

His favorite topic continued to be himself, his favorite theme the constant sorrow he claimed to feel at being kept apart from his boy. He told his story so often and with such straight-faced skill that even after the kidnapping most of his fellow citizens sided with him in his efforts to get custody of Clarence. "Those who have known Ferdinand Ward since his return to this village are with him in this matter and interested that he shall succeed in his purpose," a Rochester reporter wrote after canvassing his neighbors. "His every act since his discharge from prison has been calculated to win back the confidence and esteem which he enjoyed in early life and he finds every citizen of Geneseo as the result his friend and . . . has the good will of them all."[18]

So long as there was even a remote chance that he might still gain custody of his son—and his son's income—he kept up his monthly letters to Clarence, writing as if the kidnapping had never occurred. Each letter was addressed to "my dear son" and signed "Your loving father, F. Ward." Sometimes he spelled out Geneseo attractions he thought might appeal to a boy—a snowy mile-long slope lit by strings of electric lights for nighttime sledding; a dog and a cage full of canaries; the semiprofessional baseball team that rented out the second floor of the parsonage; a minstrel show, organized to raise funds for the Livingston County Historical Society, in which Ferd had played a featured role.

But more often, his letters were meant merely to make his son and those who were caring for him feel guilty for the misery he himself felt. When the used pair of ice skates he sent his son for Christmas failed to fit—the only gift of which there's any record—he used the occasion to bemoan his fate: "Papa and Mama did not get anything for Christmas. . . . Papa used to try to make everybody happy on Xmas and now those that he made happy seem to try to make him unhappy."[19] He also continued to attack the Greens and the care they were providing: "I know you have a poor school and get associated with many boys unfit for you, but try and live above them and be a gentleman."[20] He outdid himself on the anniversary of Ella's death.

> These are hard days for your papa, for it is just five years ago that your dear mama died and went to Heaven. I know you are young yet and cannot realize what a loss came to us both then, but some day you *will* know and I will tell you all about her. It seems as if I *must* have you near me, my boy. Papa is getting old [he was now forty-three] and feels each year more lonely and

needs his boy to cheer and comfort him. I sat last night here in the old house and read over many of your mother's letters and in almost every one she spoke of you and how happy we might be together. But now she is dead and you, our boy, whom she left me and whom we both loved, are kept from me by your cruel Aunt and Uncle and all because they can't earn money for themselves but must have that which I earned.[21]

Ferd had not been reading Ella's letters. He had none: he'd left them all behind in Thompson when he fled to avoid the bill collectors.

Again and again in his letters to Thompson, Ferd made it clear that he remained determined to have his son. Fred Green had won the guardianship battle in probate (and its judgment had subsequently been upheld by a higher court), but no one could be sure what Ferd might still do. For months after the kidnapping, whenever a strange horse and carriage was spotted on the road that led past the Greens' house, Clarence was told to run to the attic or the woodshed and lock the door from the inside until it was gone. When he went out after dark to collect eggs from the henhouse, he sang hymns to keep up his courage.

In the summer of 1895, Ferd persuaded Judge Coyne, his boss at the surrogate court, to appoint as his son's guardian a local attorney and former assemblyman named Otto Kelsey. (Presumably, Kelsey had been promised a share of the proceeds once Ferd had control of his late wife's estate.) The former assemblyman then applied to the Connecticut courts to compel Clarence's immediate surrender.

On January 12, 1896, all the parties converged on the superior court in Hartford. Ferd was in a hurry; under New York law, when a minor reached the age of fourteen he or she could choose between guardians. Clarence was now just eight weeks away from his fourteenth birthday.

As the proceedings dragged on, Clarence sat between his aunt and uncle, fiddling with a Kodak camera. Ferd sat on the other side of the courtroom with Belle, his lawyers, and three sympathetic ladies from Geneseo, imported to show the town's solidarity with his cause.

His attorney charged again that Clarence was being "illegally held and imprisoned"[22] by his uncle, and that he was now and always had been a resident of New York, not Connecticut.

Attorneys for the Greens and for the Franklin Trust hit back hard. It would be an "outrage," Charles Searls said, to tear Clarence from those who loved him and "deliver him to a stranger." The boy was a "clever little fellow"[23] who ought to be allowed to say where and with whom he wanted to live. Charles Perkins went further: Mr. Kelsey was a straw man, appointed purely to fulfill Ferd's "mercenary purposes," he said. "He would not lie awake nights if the child was not delivered to him but the boy and his uncle would lie awake nights if he were removed."[24]

The presiding judge agreed. So did the Connecticut Supreme Court of Errors when the case reached it: "The child is not the father's property," the court said. "It is a human being, and has rights of its own."[25] Fred and Nellie Green took Clarence home with them to Thompson.

Epilogue

By the time my grandfather first told me the story of his kidnapping and rescue, he had been head of the art department at Oberlin College and director of its Allen Art Museum for nearly forty years.

I suppose everyone's grandfather seems special. Despite everything that had happened to him in the aftermath of his father's crimes, mine really was. Everyone who lived in Oberlin, Ohio, thought so. He was a masterful teacher but also a master promoter who began his career in charge of an assortment of dusty plaster casts and ended it presiding over one of the great college art collections in the country. A man of boundless optimism and limitless energy, he was persuaded early on, as my brother, Andrew, has written, "that if he didn't take charge, nothing at all would happen. . . . He was by nature a conspicuous man. He made his presence and absence felt, and his energy spilled off in a hundred directions. His company was by turns exhilarating and exhausting."[1]

He was a specialist in Romanesque and Gothic architecture who did not believe he fully understood a cathedral unless he had clambered all the way up to sit astride its ridgepole, and he was an eager builder who could not seem to stop adding rooms to his own house.

For him, problems were always meant to be solved. When a white barber turned away black customers downtown, he helped bankroll an African American competitor and then became one of his first and steadiest customers. When he saw that people from the farming communities surrounding Oberlin—men and women like those he had grown up with in Thompson—were reluctant to attend the loftily cerebral First Church in Oberlin, whose congregation was made up largely of professors and their students, he designed a separate house of worship on the eastern edge of town, helped raise funds to build it, and then served as its pastor for twenty years—although he had never actually been ordained.

The lectern and the pulpit suited him equally; each afforded him an audience. He seemed to be in perpetual need of the attention he'd been denied as a boy, and he could be petulant if he lost at cards or was interrupted when he thought he had the floor. But he was also a loving and attentive husband and father and grandfather; for him, holidays—marked by bravura carving of the turkey he insisted he and he alone knew how to roast—were celebrations of the kind of family closeness that meant everything to him, perhaps because he'd known so little of it when he was young.

In his spare time he built cathedrals the size of Volkswagens on his sun porch, painstakingly put together from his collection of fifty thousand stone blocks, complete with flying buttresses, soaring arches, and stained-glass windows that glowed from within, meant to dazzle his grandchildren at Christmastime.

For seven years—from 1897 to 1905—Ferdinand vanished from Clarence's life. Once it was clear that he could not immediately win legal possession of his son or access to the boy's income, he saw no need to feign further interest in him. There would be time enough for that once Clarence reached the age of twenty-one. For all Ferd's supposed suffering at being kept from his son, he made no effort whatsoever to keep track of what was actually happening to him.*

---

* Shortly after Ferd's final bid for custody was rejected, Claude Bragdon, a young architect based in Rochester, began visiting Geneseo to oversee construction of a new colonial-style county courthouse at the north end of Main Street. From time to time, he remembered, he had reason to drop into the old county clerk's office.

    There, I sometimes saw a poorly-dressed old-looking man whose face had the unnatural pallor of mushrooms grown in a cellar.

At fifteen, Clarence had been devastated when Nellie Green, the aunt who had treated him always as if he were her own child, died of cancer. We have no record of how Ferd took this news when it reached him, but, judging by the pleasure he had taken in the financial disaster suffered by his own brother a few years earlier, it must have been with something like delight.

The impact on Clarence was unmistakable. His aunt had loved him; he could never quite be sure his uncle did. Asked many years later about the man who raised him, Clarence could say only that Fred Green had "always been good" to him and "appreciative of the fact that I did a lot for him, especially after his wife . . . died, to make his life more comfortable."[2] The boy found himself splitting wood and trimming the wicks of all the oil lamps in the house; he fed the chickens, groomed the horses, shoveled out the stable, peddled milk from door to door at a nickel a quart, and learned to cook for the whole family. He never complained. By working with such energy and devotion he earned his uncle's terse gratitude, but never his open affection.

Clarence would work extra hard to win people over to the end of his life. When Ferd was still trying to persuade everyone that his boy belonged with him, he had expressed contempt for the sort of young people with whom he was supposedly being forced to consort in Thompson. In fact, those with whom Clarence spent the most time came from just the sort of families his father would have liked to cultivate: the self-styled "Summer Crowd," like the four sons and two daughters of Norman B. Ream, a Chicago steel and railroad magnate so rich that his offspring and their friends could race their big tally-ho along seven miles of macadam road without ever leaving his vast estate, and so influential that he could order express trains on the New Haven line halted at Thompson so that frequent guests like Robert Todd Lincoln could get on and off. They were "a snobbish crowd," Clarence

---

"Do you know who that man is?" Judge Coyne once asked me. "That is Ferdinand Ward."

He was as sorry a scoundrel as ever the light of publicity ever brought blinking out of his rat-hole. . . . There he was performing petty purgatorial tasks until his "foul crimes had been burnt and purged away." He could not have been more dead so far as the world was concerned, if the grass had been growing on his dishonoured grave.

He was not dead, of course; he was just biding his time. Claude Fayette Bragdon, *Secret Springs: An Autobiography*, p. 65.

admitted, but he made himself welcome among them with the energy and enthusiasm he brought to every game of euchre and croquet, every picnic and sing-along and taffy pull.[3]

He attended high school for three years in Putnam, where he won a $10 gold piece and a set of Shakespeare for his skill at debating. He then spent a year preparing for Princeton at the newly established British-style Pomfret boarding school. There, he found the odds stacked against him. He entered in the sixth and final form, while most of his classmates had been there since the school's founding. He was too small to do well in the team sports that mattered most to his fellow students. Then, too, he remembered, "my uncle knew nothing about what boys wore. I was sent up to Pomfret with a pair of trousers . . . such as you wore with a cutaway coat, and with [cologne], and with things which were not at all in accord with what the boys at Pomfret . . . were used to. They were known as 'Peck's Bad Boys' then,[*] and were supposed to have been sent there because their families couldn't handle them. They picked on me and made my life miserable." He was so homesick for Thompson that he regularly wandered a mile or so out of town to a hilltop just to have a glimpse of the far-off steeple of the Congregational church.

He did much better at Princeton, where he discovered art and architecture with one of America's first full-time art historians, Allan Marquand, and resolved to follow in his footsteps. "When I came home . . . and told my uncle . . . he was terribly shocked and taken aback," he recalled. "The word 'professor' applied to bootblacks and ordinary tradesmen and was never considered to have any standing in the community at all. The idea of this boy whom he'd nurtured and sent to college now coming back to be a college professor was very shocking to him."[4]

March 11, 1905, was Clarence's twenty-first birthday. His lawyer, James McKeen, had warned him to be prepared for fresh assaults by his father. Sure enough, a small blue envelope arrived in the morning mail. It was postmarked Geneseo, and closed with a wax seal in which

---

[*] A reference both to Pomfret's founding principal, William E. Peck, and to best-selling books by a newspaperman named George W. Peck about a mischievous child who became known as "Peck's Bad Boy."

was stamped an elaborate "W," for "Ward." The opening salvo was in his stepmother's handwriting, but she was clearly speaking for her husband.

> My dear Clarence,
>
> Best wishes and congratulations on your twenty-first birthday. We have made you a member of the Andrew Warde Association of which you are a direct descendant. The certificate of membership we sent you by today's mail.[*]
>
> Clarence, dear, your father feels now that you have gained your [majority], he hopes you will be a devoted son, and carry out your mother's interest in him, and prove yourself worthy of the trust, they both carefully planned for you. He has a copy of all legal papers, your Mother's will, and everything connected with the trust. It is on these matters he is very anxious to see you, and will meet you in New York, or elsewhere, as you wish, and is waiting for your reply. I know, Clarence, you will learn to love your father, and not *fear* him, for he loves you dearly. Think of how he has suffered. For eleven long years he has tried to have you with him and now that it rests entirely with you, to make him happy do so, my boy, and I will do everything in my power for you both. Your father feels this long separation deeply, and I have every confidence in you, Clarence, for I feel you will do your duty toward making the best of a great wrong in which you had no control.
>
> Again, sending many happy returns of the day.
>
> > With love,
> > Yours very affectionately,
> > Isabelle A. Ward[5]

Clarence responded gingerly: he was grateful for Mrs. Ward's birthday greeting, but he wanted her to know that so far as his mother's estate was concerned "I have no more power now than I had before, since it is still in trust [until he was twenty-five and would inherit the principal] and I do not see what there could be to discuss with my father about

---

[*] The Association of Descendants of Andrew Warde, the first member of the family to reach the New World, was established in 1910. Warde landed in Massachusetts Colony in 1630 and was instrumental in building up the towns of Watertown, Massachusetts, and Wethersfield, Stamford, and Fairfield in Connecticut.

it. If there is anything important that he wants to know, however, I will try to meet him at Mr. McKeen's office, as he is the only one who can give advice on such matters."[6]

Ferd wrote right back. He was "surprised and hurt," he said, at the idea that his own son would assume he wanted to talk about his mother's estate. (That was, of course, precisely what his wife's letter had said he wanted to do.) It was his *parents'* estates he wanted to discuss.

> If you are not man enough at the age of twenty-one, to meet your father as a man should, and talk over a business matter in a fair and frank way, then let me know when you will meet me at McKeen's office and I will be there, but I see no reason at your age you should deem it necessary to talk with your own father before an attorney. There are certain duties a son owes to a parent, Clarence, and one of them is to at least allow that parent opportunity to be heard before showing the want of confidence that your letter indicates.
>
> If you start in the world on this tack, my son, I fear you will come to grief.[7]

Clarence agreed to see his father. They met for lunch in a dining hall at Princeton. Ferd settled into a seat facing the door, then suddenly paled and asked his son to swap seats with him. Clarence turned around to see what the trouble was. Mark Twain was standing in the doorway, unmistakable in his ice cream suit. Ferd was evidently frightened that if Twain recognized him he would make good on his threat to avenge General Grant. Twain didn't spot him and was safely ushered to a table on the other side of the room.

They ordered lunch. Ferd spun out an elaborate story. He was staying with friends in Newark, New Jersey, now, he said. His job in Geneseo had recently been eliminated and he saw no prospect of finding another there. In his desperation he had been forced to borrow $1,000 from his own lawyer, who was now demanding payment. He needed Clarence's help.

The last part was true. Nothing else was. Ferd was not visiting friends; he was living in Newark because he had been caught stealing in Geneseo and forced to flee his hometown. His employers had foolishly allowed him to use his courthouse office after hours to do accounts for local businessmen, among them a remarkably gullible fire insurance agent named Henry B. Curtis. Somehow, Ferd had managed to siphon money from seventeen of Curtis's customers, who thought they were paying premiums to protect their property. His victims had banded together and approached his lawyer, threatening to sue if they weren't repaid right away. He needed $1,000 to buy them off so that he could move to Manhattan, where he and his wife planned to rent a brownstone on West Seventy-third Street and take in well-to-do boarders.

His parents' wills expressly barred him from using any of the income from their estates to pay his debts, but he had managed to persuade the executor, his cousin Levi, to relinquish his post to a pliant friend who planned to borrow against the principal and then share the proceeds with Ferd. Clarence, as a contingent legatee, was the only potential obstacle. His father pulled from his pocket a pen and a release relinquishing Clarence's rights to any part of his grandparents' estates, and insisted he sign it on the spot. "With all the property you have from your Mother," he said, "you might let me have the small amount left to me by *my* parents."[8]

Clarence said he would have to check with Mr. McKeen.

Ferd was furious. "I have done everything in my power to gain your affection Clarence," he wrote a few days later, "but it seems of no avail, and now I feel that the time has come when sentiment must be set aside and I must act. I have known much injustice for the sake of my affection for you, but as it brings no return, I am determined to see that my rights are protected. You will avoid all this trouble by signing that release and in doing so no later than Saturday."[9]

Clarence did not sign, but he did agree that the Franklin Trust should pay the thousand dollars needed to keep his father out of prison.

Within weeks, Ferd was making still more demands. This time even Clarence, who had remained courteous if detached when dealing with his father, was angered. "Your last letter," he told him, "was so unjust that I am induced by it to take the stand that I can do nothing for you. . . . I would be pleased if you would avoid the mockery of signing 'your loving father' in any further communications which you may have with me."[10]

Ferd paid no attention. When Clarence graduated from Princeton in June, he asked him to "accept a Father's love and congratulations"— and promptly threatened to sue for the jewels he continued to claim had belonged to him and not to Clarence's mother. Five years of lies and harangues and threatened lawsuits followed.

Clarence consulted McKeen and other attorneys, but he also seems always to have been anxious that no actual injustice be done to his father. He traveled to Geneseo and Rochester to see for himself what was going on, and conferred with his uncle Will and aunt Sarah, even though neither one had been willing to take him in after his mother died. Over and over again he said he wanted nothing to which he was not entitled.

Through it all, Clarence also did his best to lead a normal life. The summer after his graduation, his ex-roommate Charles Adams introduced him to his wife's younger sister, Miss Helen Eshbaugh. A Mount Holyoke sophomore from Montclair, New Jersey, with a personality both "witty and angular," according to one of her grandchildren, she was studying biology, intending to become a schoolteacher. She and Clarence clung to one another, perhaps in part because each had had to live with a legacy of scandal: her father, D. O. Eshbaugh, the Pennsylvania-born president of the New England Loan and Trust Company, had drowned himself after his firm went bankrupt in 1898, leaving Helen's mother with six children to raise. Clarence wrote Helen poems, took the train from Princeton up to Mount Holyoke to see her nearly every weekend, bought his mother's engagement ring from the Franklin Trust for $675, and then asked her to marry him.

The wedding took place in July 1907; throughout their lives together, she would provide him with the loving admiration he craved and the sense of equilibrium he needed.

Two weeks after Clarence was married, Ferd attacked him again, his anger evidently intensified by his son's happiness. He felt "the most violent hostility toward his son," one of his own lawyers reported to Clarence, "and wants measures taken which will deprive you of your property, even though he admits he cannot get anything for himself."[11]

When Ferd could find no lawyer willing to undertake his baseless suit against the Franklin Trust, he concocted an elaborate scheme in partnership with a New Jersey warehouseman named Thomas Morton. Morton was to sue him to collect payment on a large fictitious loan. Ferd would then declare bankruptcy so that Morton could claim the jewels Ferd falsely said were his. The co-conspirators would split the profits, if there were any. Mr. McKeen had grown so weary of Ferd's shamelessness that he told Clarence "if you were not his son, I should be inclined to advise you to hunt him up and give him a good, old-fashioned licking. He is, and has always been a physical coward."[12]

The bankruptcy hearing took place in Newark shortly after Clarence's twenty-fifth birthday in 1909, the date on which the principal of his mother's estate and the jewels should all have been turned over to him. Ferd, Clarence, and McKeen testified. All the New York papers covered it. The case came to nothing. Morton backed off. The principal of the estate and Ella Ward's jewels were finally turned over to her son. He used a sizable portion of the money to build himself a house in Montclair, New Jersey. He had a daughter now, named Helen after her mother.

Everything seemed to be over, at last, but Ferd hadn't quite given up. In December 1910, he began publishing a series of weekly articles about Grant & Ward in the Sunday supplement of the *New York Herald*. There was nothing new in any of them—in his version of the crash he remained always the victim, never the villain—but, gussied up with splashy double-page illustrations, they put him back into the news, where he always liked to be.

He had been threatening to publish an account of his career ever since he was locked up in the Ludlow Street Jail, and had once claimed he'd written it only because he wanted his boy—about whom he cared more "than life itself"[13]—to understand the great wrong that had been done him. Now, he hoped to wield it as a weapon against that same son.

"You have doubtless read my articles on Gen'l. Grant which appeared in the New York *Sunday Herald* of Dec. 19, 26, Jan 2, 9 & 16th," he wrote Clarence on January 26, 1911.

> I have been asked to write another article giving a history of my own life and that of *my immediate family*. I dislike very much to do this, but as it is absolutely necessary for me to have money enough to live on, and as you insist on keeping from me what is rightfully my own, I have no choice as I cannot starve.
>
> I have asked nothing from you but what is rightfully my own and as every dollar you now possess came from me, it seems only right that you should consider this, as well as your dear Mother's wishes and act justly with me.
>
> I write this simply that you may know my position in the matter and not censure me for not letting you know my intentions.
>
> Your Father
Ferdinand Ward[14]

James McKeen assured Clarence he needn't worry. He was quite sure no such offer had ever been made by the *Herald*. His father continued to suffer from "hallucinations in money matters."[15]

A few weeks later, Belle Ward bustled into the office of Edward Day, Clarence's New Jersey attorney. She had a "compromise" to offer, she said. Her husband now wanted $2,500 from Clarence, she said ($58,200 today), plus "the diamonds."[16] If he didn't get everything he wanted, he would publish a story about his cruel and ungrateful son and she would personally call upon the president and faculty of Rutgers University, where Clarence was now an associate professor, in order to blacken his name.

Day laughed her out of his office, but Clarence took her threat seriously enough to ask for an appointment with the president of Rutgers, the Reverend Dr. William Henry Steele Demarest. He wanted to make sure Demarest understood who his father was; if he felt the presence on the faculty of a swindler's son would embarrass the institution, he was willing to resign. President Demarest told him to go back to the classroom and not to worry; the sins of the father would not be visited on him.

Six years later, when Clarence was interviewed by the president of Oberlin College, Henry Churchill King, to see if he was the right man to head its art department, he would again make sure everyone understood that his father was Ferdinand Ward. King saw no problem, either.

Clarence and Helen Ward would spend the rest of their lives in Oberlin, where they raised their children—my aunt Helen and my father, Frederick Champion Ward. But Clarence made few concessions to the Midwest. Rural New England was evident in his unchanging, unmistakable accent; in his refusal to wear a coat or a hat during the coldest Ohio winters; in his politics—he was a lifelong Republican, just as almost everyone in Thompson had been.[*]

By the time the younger Wards got to Oberlin in 1917, Ferd and his wife had found at least a temporary home in her father's old house on Staten Island. He was too frail to look for work—or so he claimed—and Clarence began sending him $20 a month out of his professor's salary to live on.

---

[*] He liked to quote one of the town's handful of Democrats who supposedly wandered by accident into a Republican meeting and afterward said, "I felt like one grain of wheat in a whole barrel of rat turd." Interview with Clarence Ward by Andrew Ward, 1967.

One summer, when Clarence and Helen were visiting the East Coast, they took their children to Staten Island so that Ferd could see his grandchildren. My father remembered only that he was thin and pale and seemed far older than his wife: "She was his promoter," he said. "I remember her saying, 'Remember your grandfather and write to him.'"[17] They only stayed about twenty minutes.

Many years later, when one of his grandchildren asked Clarence why he had bothered to make that visit, and why he had provided Ferd financial support after all the trouble he had caused him over so many years, he seemed genuinely surprised by the question. "He was my father, after all," he said.

Ferdinand Ward outlived his son's attorney, James McKeen, who died in 1911; his own old partner James D. Fish, who passed away the following year at ninety-three; his long-suffering brother, Will, who died on his own seventy-fourth birthday in 1917; and his patient sister, Sarah Ward Brinton, who followed Will in 1924, at the age of eighty-seven.

Ferd finally died of nephritis in a boardinghouse in White Plains, New York, on March 3, 1925. He was seventy-three. Isabelle Storer Ward died the following year. Both were buried in the Green family plot at Green-Wood Cemetery in Brooklyn. It fell to Clarence to make all the arrangements.

Fifty-five years later, I was fortunate enough to speak separately with the last two people to have known Ferdinand Ward well.

Jasper Yeats Brinton, Sarah Ward Brinton's fourth son, was ninety-three then, home on a visit from Cairo, where he had been a judge on the International Court for many years. He had the same deep-set blue eyes and generous nose that Ferdinand De Wilton Ward and Ferdinand Ward and Clarence Ward had all possessed. Like his father before him, he saw himself as the guardian of the Brinton family's long and distinguished history, and ninety years after the fall of Grant & Ward he was still reluctant to discuss its impact upon his parents. He had never heard anyone so much as hint that Uncle Ferd was "anything but guilty," he said. "I'm sorry to say it, especially to *you*, but during his visits he always had a slippery air. Always full of ideas and schemes and wanting to be introduced." The judge had a hoard of family letters—more than a thousand of them—and was willing to share them with me. But when I asked if he knew what had happened to a box of documents dating from the time of the crash that Ferd was believed to have left with his sister for safekeeping, he brightened. "I burned them," he said, spreading his long fingers out toward his visitor. "*With these hands.*"

The judge's first wife, Alice Bates McFadden, then Mrs. Laurence Eyre, had a different impression. She had only recently married Jasper Brinton when Ferd came to call in 1910. No member of the family had ever so much as mentioned "Uncle Ferd" to her beforehand, she remembered. But he explained who he was, and she invited him in for tea. He told her his long sad story, and by the end of the afternoon she had taken it upon herself to make him feel welcome in her husband's family. He had also managed to borrow $500. "I knew him well and liked him immensely." She smiled. "He could charm the birds from the trees." She never got her money back.

ACKNOWLEDGMENTS

My grandfather turned over to me the contents of his father's Sing Sing trunk in 1965, so I've been thinking about this book, or reading for it, or actually writing it, for nearly fifty years, off and on. Any author whose book has a gestation period that long piles up debts to a remarkable number of people. I will do my best to thank them all here but beg forgiveness in advance if I have inadvertently left out someone's name.

It took so long to complete this book that some without whom it could never have been written did not live to see the final result: my grandparents, Helen and Clarence Ward, and my father, Champ Ward; my cousins Judge Jasper Brinton and his children, John H. and Pamela Brinton, who shared my fascination with this story and made it possible for me to read more than a thousand family letters; Mrs. Lawrence Eyre, who recounted to me her encounters with Ferdinand Ward; Harold A. and William S. Ward Jr., who talked with me about their parents, William and Kate Ward; and their cousins Allen and Alice Ward, who generously shared their original research into family history; Miss Margaret E. Gilmore, the town historian of Geneseo, who took me around the village where my forebears lived and made it seem as if they had just left town; and Professor John Y. Simon, executive director of the Ulysses S. Grant Association.

Again and again, as he has so many times in the past, Mike Hill has come through for me, finding materials I never thought I'd see; I can't imagine tackling any topic without his help and counsel. I'm also grateful to the current Jasper Brinton, Judge Brinton's grandson, for welcoming me into his lovely Pennsylvania home and providing me with a sizable cache of still more family letters; Sonny Mehta and my old friend Ashbel Green of Alfred A. Knopf, who thought this book might be a good idea, and my new friend and editor, Andrew Miller, whose suggestions made it better; Kevin Bourke, Kathy Hourigan, Amy Stackhouse, and Maggie Hinders, who helped bring coherence to the manuscript; and Dr. Jody M. Davies, who did the same for its author; my longtime agent and friend Carl Brandt, who kept me going when it seemed unlikely I would ever finish; Professors Alan Brinkley and Akeel Belgrami, who made available to me Columbia University's invaluable online resources; Amy Halstead, the great-granddaughter of James D. Fish, who shares my fascination with finding out exactly what our ancestors were up to; Edith Matthews of Geneseo's Central Presbyterian Church, who opened church records that allowed me to piece together the story of the schism that split her church and her town; Joe Lamartino, town historian of Thompson, Connecticut, who patiently answered a host of questions about the village where my grandfather grew up; Dr. Karl F. Stofko, who holds the same post in East Haddam and helped me get straight the story of the Champion House; and Richard Rubin of Florentine Films, who took time out to help me solve several vexing genealogical questions.

I'm also grateful to several readers who saved me from embarrassment of one kind or another: Martha Saxton and Enrico Ferorelli; Richard White, whose splendid book, *Railroaded,* offers enough sordid details about my ancestors' contemporaries in banking and finance to make me feel a little less defensive about his crimes; my forbearing brother, Andrew; my sister, Helen; my sharp-eyed daughter, Kelly; and my mother, Duira Ward, whose firsthand knowledge of life in a small-town Presbyterian parsonage—and aversion to adverbs and the passive voice—proved invaluable.

Here are the names of a host of men and women who also helped me along the way. I'm grateful to all of them.
   John B. Ahouse, Specialized Libraries and Archival Collections, University of Southern California, Los Angeles
   Amie Alden, historian, Livingston County
   Robert B. Allen

Elizabeth P. Andrew

Kevin Baker

Anthony and Elizabeth Bannon

Ray Barber

William R. Battey

Roland M. Baumann, archivist, Oberlin College Archives

Janet Begnoche, archivist, Princeton University

Edward Blair

Sarah Botstein

Carole M. Bowker, Mystic Seaport Museum

Robert F. Bryan

Julian Gerard Buckley

Ken Burns

Mrs. Ward C. Campbell

Scott Chase

Heather Cole, Houghton Library, Harvard University

J. Richard Collins

Helaine Dauphinais, Thompson Public Library

Carlotta DeFillo, Staten Island Historical Society

Ulysses S. Grant Dietz

Stephen Dudley

Joanne Dunn

Leigh C. Eckmair, Local History Collection, Gilbertsville
    Free Library

Paul Rogers Fish III

Ellen Fladger, head of special collections, Schaffer Library,
    Union College

Ann Gardiner

Jim Gerencser, special collections librarian, Dickinson College

Timothy J. Gilfoyle

Richard Goldhurst

Dorothy S. Grimm

Ken Grossi, archivist, Oberlin College

Helen M. Hall, Rathbun Free Memorial Library, East Haddam,
    Connecticut

Barbara Halsted

Professor Paul Harris

Rev. William O. Harris, librarian and archivist for special
    collections, Princeton Seminary Library

Catherine D. Hayes
Melissa Lewis Heim
Dorothy C. Howard
James T. Ivy
Bob and Trisha Jones
Karl Kabelac, University of Rochester Library
George Kurian
Gerald Lauderdale
Charles M. Lee
David Littlefield
Frank K. Lorenz, curator of special collections, Hamilton College
Gerald McCauley
David McCullough
Claire McCurdy, archivist, Union Theological Seminary
Blake McKelvey, Rochester City Historian
Mrs. Frances Marsh
Marie Varrelman Melchiori
Diane Melves, U. S. Grant Network
John D. Milligan
Allen P. Mills
Anne D. Moffett
Marisa Morigi, registrar, Historical Society of New Jersey
Michael Musick
Tal Nada, New York Public Library
Julian Nieman
Lynn Novick
Patricia J. Palmer, manuscript librarian, Stanford University
    Libraries
David W. Parish, town historian, Geneseo
Richard Peek, Rare Books, Special Collections and Preservation,
    University of Rochester
Thomas M. Pitkin
Robert Poole
Marie C. Preston, historian, Livingston County
Helen R. Purtle, Armed Forces Institute of Pathology
Walter Ray, political papers archivist, Morris Library, Southern
    Illinois University, Carbondale
G. P. Reuben, librarian, American College Madurai
Rev. Cally Rogers-Witte, Global Ministries

Paul R. Rugen, keeper of manuscripts, New York Public Library
Mary Ellen A. Sarbaugh
Morgan Sawn, Beinecke Rare Book and Manuscript Library,
    Yale University
Mrs. R. Meyer de Schauensee
Sylvan Schendler
Georgiana M. Searles
Martha Slotten, archivist, Dickinson College
Christine Hill Smith
Richard F. Snow
Wallace Stegner
Karl P. Stofko, DDS, municipal historian, East Haddam
Gary E. Swinson
Mattie Taormina, Green Library, Stanford University
Anne Thacher Tate, library director, Stonington Historical Society
Rick Teller, archivist, Williston Northampton School
Gabriele Tenebaum
Henry Thiagaraj
Professor Elizabeth Tooker
Mrs. O. Leslie Van Camp
Cynthia Van Ness, Buffalo and Erie County Historical Society
Jennifer Vega
John G. Wait
Mary Walker
Jasper Ward
Mike Ward
Judith Wastcott, East Haddam Free Public Library
John W. Watson, Long Island Historical Society
Pastor C. F. Yoos, Central Presbyterian Church, Geneseo,
    New York

Finally, I want to thank my wife, Diane, who has endured life with the family sociopath for thirty years without complaint, and who makes all things—including books—possible.

Khem Villas
Sherpur Village
Rajasthan, 2011

NOTES

A Note on Sources

Ferdinand Ward, his crimes, and their aftermath made sporadic headlines for some twenty-five years. The reporting style of the period was vivid, prolix, and richly detailed. Thus, everything in this book, from the artwork hanging on the walls of Ferdinand Ward's house on Brooklyn Heights to the color of the gloves he carried as he left Sing Sing, was described by at least one reporter and often by several. When newspapers differed as to precisely what was said by one character or another I have tried to use the least gaudy, most plausible version. But nothing is invented.

To calculate the current value of nineteenth-century dollars, I used the consumer price index provided by the Web site www.measuringworth.com.

PROLOGUE
1. Richard Goldhurst, *Many Are the Hearts*, p. 241.
2. Ferdinand Ward, "General Grant as I Knew Him."
3. Jane Shaw Ward to Ferdinand Ward, August 17, 1888, author's collection.

CHAPTER ONE
1. Geoffrey C. Ward, "Two Missionaries' Ordeal by Faith in a Distant Clime."
2. Ferdinand De Wilton Ward, "Letter from Mr. Ward: The Wants of Madras" to the ABCFM Board, January 22, 1845, American Board of Commissioners for Foreign Missions Archive, Houghton Library, Harvard University.
3. Ferdinand De Wilton Ward, *India and the Hindoos*, p. 107.
4. Ibid.
5. George K. Ward, ed., *Andrew Warde and His Descendants 1597–1910*, p. 86. The laudatory profile of Deacon Ward was written by his son, Ferdinand.
6. Ibid., p. 87.
7. Ibid., p. 2.
8. Anonymous, *Home Volume Dedicated to the Bergen Wards and Their Descendants* (Rochester, 1886), p. 36.

9. Austin Warren, *The Elder Henry James*, p. 21.
10. *Religious Intelligencer,* April 5, 1828.
11. Ferdinand De Wilton Ward, *Diary—No. 1*, p. 2, Brinton Collection.
12. Ferdinand De Wilton Ward, typed manuscript of *Diary—No. 1, Extending from January 9th, 1831, to September 20th, 1831*, pp. 2–3, Brinton Collection.
13. Ferdinand De Wilton Ward to Henrietta Ward, November 27, 1829, Freeman Clarke Family Papers, Department of Rare Books, Special Collections and Preservation, University of Rochester.
14. Ferdinand De Wilton Ward to Henrietta Ward, n.d. 1830, Freeman Clarke Family Papers.
15. Ferdinand De Wilton Ward to Henrietta Ward, June 16, 1831, Freeman Clarke Family Papers.
16. Ferdinand De Wilton Ward to Henrietta Ward, June 25, 1831, Freeman Clarke Family Papers.
17. Paul E. Johnson, *A Shopkeeper's Millennium*, p. 94.
18. Ibid., p. 95.
19. Ferdinand De Wilton Ward to Henrietta Ward, March 31, 1831, Freeman Clarke Family Papers.
20. Ferdinand De Wilton Ward to Henrietta Ward, July 6, 1831, Freeman Clarke Family Papers.
21. Ferdinand De Wilton Ward, *Auto-Biography*, p. 4, Brinton Collection.
22. Ferdinand De Wilton Ward to Henrietta Ward, July 7, 1832, Freeman Clarke Family Papers.
23. Ferdinand De Wilton Ward to Henrietta Ward, July 7, 1832, Freeman Clarke Family Papers.
24. Ferdinand De Wilton Ward to Henrietta Ward, January 1, 1833, Freeman Clarke Family Papers.
25. Charles E. Rosenberg, *The Cholera Years*, p. 50.
26. Ferdinand De Wilton Ward to Henrietta Ward, July 7, 1832, Freeman Clarke Family Papers.
27. Reverend Doctors Archibald Alexander and Samuel Miller to Rev. Rufus Anderson, Corresponding Secretary of the American Board of Commissioners for Foreign Missions (ABCFM), March 15, 1836, American Board of Commissioners for Foreign Missions Archive.
28. Ferdinand De Wilton Ward, typed manuscript of *Auto-Biography*, p. 4, Brinton Collection.
29. Ferdinand De Wilton Ward to Henrietta Ward Clarke, October 8, 1834, Freeman Clarke Family Papers.
30. Ferdinand De Wilton Ward to Rev. Rufus Anderson, November 4, 1835, American Board of Commissioners for Foreign Missions Archive.
31. Mary Zwiep, *Pilgrim Path*, p. 16.
32. Ibid.
33. Ibid., p. 5.
34. Ibid., p. 6.
35. Ferdinand De Wilton Ward, typed manuscript of *Auto-Biography No. 2*, p. 7, Brinton Collection.
36. Ibid.
37. Jane Shaw Ward to Sarah Ward Brinton, October 1, 1875, Brinton Collection.
38. Rev. Charles Hall to Rev. Rufus Anderson, August 5, 1836, American Board of Commissioners for Foreign Missions Archive.

39. Rev. Asa D. Smith to Rev. Rufus Anderson, August 5, 1836, American Board of Commissioners for Foreign Missions Archive.

40. Jane Shaw to Ferdinand De Wilton Ward, August 29, 1836, Brinton Collection.

41. Ward, "Two Missionaries' Ordeal by Faith in a Distant Clime."

42. Brinton Collection.

43. Henrietta Schuck, pioneer missionary to China, quoted in Dana L. Robert, *American Women in Mission*, p. 49.

44. Ferdinand to Dr. and Mrs. Levi Ward, September 18, 1836, Brinton Collection.

45. *New-York Evangelist*, December 3, 1836.

46. Ibid.

47. Ferdinand De Wilton Ward to Dr. and Mrs. Levi Ward, November 20, 1836, Brinton Collection.

48. Ferdinand De Wilton Ward to Dr. Levi Ward, November 23, 1863, Brinton Collection.

49. Ferdinand De Wilton Ward (on behalf of the ship's company) to Rufus Anderson, March 21, 1837, American Board of Commissioners for Foreign Missions Archive.

50. Clifton J. Phillips, *Protestant America and the Pagan World*, p. 52.

51. Ferdinand De Wilton Ward (on behalf of the ship's company) to Rufus Anderson, March 21, 1837, American Board of Commissioners for Foreign Missions Archive.

52. Ferdinand De Wilton Ward to Dr. and Mrs. Levi Ward, n.d., but written aboard the *Saracen*, Brinton Collection.

53. Ferdinand De Wilton Ward (on behalf of the ship's company) to Rufus Anderson, March 21, 1837, American Board of Commissioners for Foreign Missions Archive.

CHAPTER TWO

1. Ferdinand De Wilton Ward Journal, March 27, 1837, Ferdinand De Wilton Ward Collection, Waidner-Spahr Library, Dickinson College.

2. Ibid., March 26, 1837.

3. Ibid., April 22, 1837.

4. Geoffrey C. Ward, "Two Missionaries' Ordeal by Faith in a Distant Clime."

5. Ibid.

6. "A Lady" (Mrs. Julia Charlotte Maitland), *Letters from Madras During the Years 1836–1839*, p. 28.

7. Ferdinand De Wilton Ward to Dr. and Mrs. Levi Ward, n.d., 1837, Brinton Collection.

8. Ferdinand De Wilton Ward Journal, April 30, 1837, Ferdinand De Wilton Ward Collection.

9. Ibid., August 26, 1839.

10. Ferdinand De Wilton Ward, *India and the Hindoos*, p. 120.

11. Ferdinand De Wilton Ward to Rufus Anderson, October n.d., 1839, American Board of Commissioners for Foreign Missions Archive.

12. Ferdinand De Wilton Ward, "Madras-Madura Travel Diary," October 1837, Brinton Collection.

13. Ibid.

14. Ibid.

15. Ward, "Two Missionaries' Ordeal by Faith in a Distant Clime."

16. Ibid.

17. John S. Chandler, *Seventy-five Years in the Madura Mission*, p. 35.
18. Ward, "Two Missionaries' Ordeal by Faith in a Distant Clime."
19. Ferdinand Ward to Henrietta Ward, n.d., Freeman Clarke Family Papers.
20. Ward, "Two Missionaries' Ordeal by Faith in a Distant Clime."
21. Ferdinand De Wilton Ward Journal, Ferdinand De Wilton Ward Collection.
22. Jane Shaw Ward to Ferdinand De Wilton Ward, n.d. 1838, Brinton Collection.
23. Miron Winslow, quoted in Ferdinand De Wilton's notes on a discussion held at the Jaffna mission on "The Question of What Are the Limits of the Duties of the Wives of Missionaries?" February 13, 1840, American Board of Commissioners for Foreign Missions Archive.
24. Mary Zwiep, *Pilgrim Path*, p. 17.
25. Ibid., p. 16.
26. Quoted in Ferdinand De Wilton's notes on a discussion held at the Jaffna mission on "The Question of What Are the Limits of the Duties of the Wives of Missionaries?" February 13, 1840. American Board of Commissioners for Foreign Missions Archive.
27. Ferdinand De Wilton Ward to Rev. Rufus Anderson, n.d. 1837, American Board of Commissioners for Foreign Missions Archive.
28. Ward, *India and the Hindoos*, p. 74.
29. Ibid., p. 212.
30. Ibid., p. 225.
31. Ward, "Two Missionaries' Ordeal by Faith in a Distant Clime."
32. Ibid.
33. "A Lady," *Letters from Madras During the Years 1836–1839*, p. 30.
34. Ferdinand De Wilton and Jane Shaw Ward to Henrietta Ward Clarke, n.d., Freeman Clarke Family Papers.
35. Ferdinand De Wilton Ward to Dr. and Mrs. Levi Ward, July 1841, Brinton Collection.
36. Ward, "Two Missionaries' Ordeal by Faith in a Distant Clime."
37. Ferdinand De Wilton to Dr. and Mrs. Levi Ward, April 18, 1842, Brinton Collection.
38. Paul William Harris, *Nothing but Christ*, p. 62.
39. Ferdinand De Wilton Ward to Henrietta Ward Clarke, September 25, 1842, Freeman Clarke Family Papers.
40. Ward, *India and the Hindoos*, p. 23.
41. Ferdinand De Wilton Ward to the brethren of the Madura Mission, February 2, 1843, American Board of Commissioners for Foreign Missions Archive.
42. Ward, "Two Missionaries' Ordeal by Faith in a Distant Clime."
43. Rev. Nathan Crane to unknown, December 1844, American Board of Commissioners for Foreign Missions Archive.
44. Ferdinand De Wilton Ward to Henrietta Ward Clarke, December 8, 1844, Freeman Clarke Family Papers.
45. Ferdinand De Wilton Ward to Rufus Anderson, January 22, 1845, American Board of Commissioners for Foreign Missions Archive.
46. Madras Mission's Annual Report to the American Board, January 1, 1845, American Board of Commissioners for Foreign Missions Archive.
47. Ferdinand De Wilton Ward to Rufus Anderson, October 22, 1845, Madras Mission's Annual Report to the ABCFM, January 1, 1845, American Board of Commissioners for Foreign Missions Archive.

48. Report by Dr. I. W. Sherman, included in a letter from Ferdinand De Wilton Ward to Rufus Anderson, January 11, 1845, American Board of Commissioners for Foreign Missions Archive.

CHAPTER THREE

1. George K. Ward, "Grove Place and Its People in the Early Days," Bob Jones Collection, Geneseo, N.Y.
2. Henry Cherry to Rufus Anderson, November 30, 1846, American Board of Commissioners for Foreign Missions Archive.
3. Henry Cherry to Rufus Anderson, n.d. 1849, American Board of Commissioners for Foreign Missions Archive.
4. Ferdinand De Wilton Ward to Rufus Anderson, December 11, 1846, American Board of Commissioners for Foreign Missions Archive.
5. Ferdinand De Wilton Ward to Rufus Anderson, November 4, 1846, American Board of Commissioners for Foreign Missions Archive.
6. Alfred North to Rufus Anderson, September 20, 1846, American Board of Commissioners for Foreign Missions Archive.
7. Alfred North to Rufus Anderson, n.d. 1847, American Board of Commissioners for Foreign Missions Archive.
8. Ferdinand De Wilton Ward to Rufus Anderson, January 1, 1848, American Board of Commissioners for Foreign Missions Archive.
9. Ferdinand De Wilton Ward to Rufus Anderson, February 17, 1848, American Board of Commissioners for Foreign Missions Archive.
10. Ibid.
11. Ferdinand De Wilton Ward, *Village Memories of Twenty Years*, p. 3.
12. Ferdinand De Wilton Ward, *Geneseo, Livingston County N.Y., 1848–1888*, p. 4.
13. Ferdinand De Wilton Ward to Levi A. Ward, April 19, 1849, Ward Collection, Local History Division, Rochester Public Library.
14. Ferdinand De Wilton Ward to Levi A. Ward, December 20, 1848, Ward Collection.
15. Ferdinand De Wilton Ward to Levi A. Ward, June 27, 1849, Ward Collection.
16. Ferdinand De Wilton Ward to Rufus Anderson, November 5, 1849, American Board of Commissioners for Foreign Missions Archive.
17. Ibid.
18. Ferdinand De Wilton Ward to William Shaw Ward, October 9, 1875, Brinton Collection.
19. Ward, *India and the Hindoos*, p. 39.
20. Ibid., p. 36.
21. Robert Hastings Nichols, *Presbyterianism in New York State*, p. 116.
22. James H. Moorhead "The 'Restless Spirit of Radicalism.'"
23. *New-York Evangelist*, June 7, 1848.
24. Ferdinand De Wilton Ward to Levi A. Ward, April 28, 1851, Ward Collection.
25. Anonymous, "View of the Livingston County High-School, on Temple Hill, Geneseo: Under the Care of Seth Sweetser, C. C. Felton, and H. R. Cleveland."
26. Ferdinand De Wilton Ward to Levi A. Ward, November 10, 1849, Ward Collection.
27. Ferdinand De Wilton Ward to Levi A. Ward, October 11, 1850, Ward Collection.
28. Ferdinand De Wilton Ward to Levi A. Ward, n.d. 1850, Ward Collection.

29. Ferdinand De Wilton Ward, *A Christian Gift, or Pastoral Letters.*
30. Ferdinand De Wilton Ward to Levi A. Ward, April 14, 1851, Ward Collection.
31. Ibid.
32. Ferdinand De Wilton Ward to Levi A. Ward, June 5, 1851, Ward Collection.
33. Ferdinand De Wilton Ward to Levi A. Ward, July 9, 1851, Ward Collection.
34. Ibid.
35. Quoted in Ferdinand De Wilton Ward to Levi A. Ward, May 15, 1851, Ward Collection.
36. Ibid.
37. Jane Shaw Ward to William Shaw Ward, February 11, 1865, Brinton Collection.

CHAPTER FOUR

1. Ferdinand Ward to Nellie Green, October 19, 1890, and March 20, 1891, author's collection.
2. Ferdinand De Wilton Ward to Sarah Ward Brinton, n.d., autumn 1875, Brinton Collection.
3. Ferdinand De Wilton Journal, January 30 and June 2, 1856, Central Church Collection, Geneseo, N.Y.
4. Ferdinand De Wilton Ward to Levi A. Ward, January 19, 1851, Ward Collection, Local History Division, Rochester Public Library.
5. Ferdinand De Wilton Ward to Levi A. Ward, n.d., Ward Collection.
6. Ferdinand De Wilton Ward to Levi A. Ward, April 30, 1852, Ward Collection.
7. *New-York Evangelist*, May 13, 1852.
8. Ferdinand De Wilton Ward to Levi A. Ward, April 30, 1852, Ward Collection.
9. Dr. Walter E. Lauderdale to John Vance Lauderdale, January 14, 1859, John Vance Lauderdale Papers, Collection of Western Americana, Beinecke Rare Book and Manuscript Library, Yale University.
10. Ferdinand De Wilton Ward to Levi A. Ward, September 20, 1853, Ward Collection.
11. Ferdinand De Wilton Ward to Levi A. Ward, May 6, 1852, Ward Collection.
12. Ibid.
13. *New-York Evangelist*, December 23, 1858.
14. Peter Josyph, ed., *The Wounded River: The Civil War Letters of John Vance Lauderdale*, p. 17.
15. Levi Parsons, *History of Rochester Presbytery*, p. 52.
16. Session Book, Central Presbyterian Church, Geneseo, N.Y.
17. Ferdinand Ward to Sarah Ward Brinton, July 8, 1887, Brinton Collection.
18. Jane Shaw Ward to Sarah Ward, December 18, 1857, Brinton Collection.
19. Jane Shaw Ward to Sarah Ward Brinton, December 11, 1857, Brinton Collection.
20. Jane Shaw Ward to Sarah Ward, December 18, 1857, Brinton Collection.
21. Jane Shaw Ward to William Shaw Ward, December 25, 1857, Brinton Collection.
22. Jane Shaw Ward to Ferdinand Ward, December 25, 1857, Brinton Collection.
23. Jane Shaw Ward to Sarah Ward, March n.d., 1858, Brinton Collection.
24. Jane Shaw Ward to Sarah Ward, April 3, 1858, Brinton Collection.
25. Jane Shaw Ward to Sarah Ward, March n.d., 1858, Brinton Collection.
26. Jane Shaw Ward to Sarah Ward Brinton, December 11, 1857, Brinton Collection.

27. *New-York Evangelist*, December 23, 1858.
28. Jane Shaw Ward to Sarah Ward Brinton, March 9, 1858, Brinton Collection.
29. Jane Shaw Ward to Sarah Ward Brinton, March 4, 1858, Brinton Collection.
30. August 11, 1858, Session Book, Central Presbyterian Church, Geneseo, N.Y.
31. Ferdinand De Wilton Ward to Levi A. Ward, April 1858, Ward Collection.
32. August 11, 1858, Session Book.
33. Ibid.
34. August 25, 1858, Session Book.
35. Ferdinand Ward, fragment of farewell sermon, Ferdinand De Wilton Ward Collection, Waidner-Spahr Library, Dickinson College.
36. *Geneseo Democrat*, October 14, 1858.
37. October 18, 1858, Session Book.
38. Dr. Walter E. Lauderdale to John Vance Lauderdale, November 7, 1858, John Vance Lauderdale Papers.
39. October 25, 1858, Session Book.
40. Dr. Walter E. Lauderdale to John Vance Lauderdale, January 14, 1859, John Vance Lauderdale Papers.
41. Walter Lauderdale Jr. to Frances Lauderdale, January 1, 1859, John Vance Lauderdale Papers.
42. *New-York Evangelist*, January 4, 1859.
43. Ibid., January 13, 1859.
44. Ferdinand De Wilton Ward, *Why I Am an Old-School Presbyterian*.
45. William Shaw Ward, "The Cloud and the Silver Lining," Brinton Collection.
46. Jane Shaw Ward to William Shaw Ward, February 24, 1860, Brinton Collection.

CHAPTER FIVE
1. *Livingston Republican*, September 10, 1862.
2. Sarah Ward to Ferdinand De Wilton Ward, September n.d., 1862, Brinton Collection.
3. Jane Shaw Ward to William Shaw Ward, October 21, 1862, Brinton Collection.
4. Ferdinand De Wilton Ward to Sarah Ward, November 20, 1862, Brinton Collection.
5. *Livingston Republican*, January 18, 1863.
6. Ferdinand De Wilton Ward to William Shaw Ward, January 27, 1863, Brinton Collection.
7. W. S. (William Shaw) Ward, "How We Ran the Vicksburg Batteries," p. 604.
8. *Livingston Republican*, May 10, 1863.
9. Stephen W. Sears, *Chancellorsville*, p. 186.
10. Sarah Ward to Ferdinand De Wilton Ward, May 27, 1863, Brinton Collection.
11. *Livingston Republican*, April 28, 1880.
12. *Livingston Republican*, July 9 and August 12, 1863.
13. Ferdinand De Wilton Ward to Sarah Ward, August 24, 1863, Brinton Collection.
14. Jane Shaw Ward to William Shaw Ward, October 7, 1863, Brinton Collection.
15. Jane Shaw Ward to William Shaw Ward, October 22, 1863, Brinton Collection.
16. Jane Shaw Ward to Sarah Ward, October 17, 1863, Brinton Collection.
17. Jane Shaw Ward to Sarah Ward, November 17, 1863, Brinton Collection.
18. Daniel F. Kemp, Civil War Letters, A64–97, Buffalo and Erie County Historical Society Archives.

19. *Livingston Republican*, November 12, 1863.
20. Jane Shaw to Henrietta Ward Clarke, November n.d., 1863, Freeman Clarke Family Papers, Freeman Clarke Family Papers.
21. Ferdinand De Wilton Ward to Sarah Ward, January 15, 1864, Brinton Collection.
22. Sarah Ward to Jane Shaw Ward, March 1, 1864, Brinton Collection.
23. Sarah Ward to Jane Shaw Ward, January 1, 1866, Brinton Collection.
24. Sarah Ward to Jane Shaw Ward, March 1, 1864, Brinton Collection.
25. Sarah Ward to Jane Shaw Ward, August 20, 1864, Brinton Collection.
26. Ibid.
27. John H. Brinton, *Personal Memoirs of John H. Brinton*, p. 67.
28. U. S. Grant to John H. Brinton, June 11, 1873; John Y. Simon et al., eds., *The Papers of U. S. Grant*, vol. 24: *1873*, p. 143.
29. Sarah Ward to Jane Shaw Ward, December 17, 1866, Brinton Collection.
30. Jane Shaw Ward to Sarah Ward, February 16, 1865, Brinton Papers, Historical Society of Pennsylvania.
31. Jane Shaw Ward to Sarah Ward Brinton, n.d., Brinton Papers, Historical Society of Pennsylvania.
32. Sarah Ward to Jane Shaw Ward, January 17 or 18, 1866, Brinton Collection.
33. Ferdinand De Wilton Ward to Sarah Ward, September 22, 1865, Brinton Collection.
34. Sarah Ward to Jane Shaw Ward, January 26, 1866, Brinton Collection.
35. Mary M. Brinton to Sarah Ward, January 25, 1866, Brinton Collection.
36. Ferdinand De Wilton Ward to Sarah Ward Brinton, February 7, 1868, Brinton Collection.
37. Sarah Ward to William Shaw Ward, February 6, 1865, Brinton Collection.
38. Ferdinand De Wilton Ward to Sarah Ward, December 6, 1866, Brinton Collection.
39. Ferdinand De Wilton Ward to Sarah Ward Brinton, June 8, 1867, Brinton Collection.
40. Jane Shaw Ward to Sarah Ward Brinton, January 19, 1873, Brinton Collection.
41. Jane Shaw Ward to William Shaw Ward, March 27, 1867, Brinton Collection.
42. Ibid.
43. Jane Shaw Ward to William Shaw Ward, March 15, 1867, Brinton Collection.

CHAPTER SIX
1. Jane Shaw Ward to William Shaw Ward, March 15, 1867, Brinton Collection.
2. "Ferd Ward's Boyhood," *St. Louis Globe-Democrat*, June 24, 1884.
3. Jane Shaw Ward to Sarah Ward Brinton, January 25, 1865, Brinton Collection.
4. Jane Shaw Ward to William Shaw Ward, April 10, 1867, Brinton Collection.
5. Ferdinand De Wilton Ward to Sara Ward Brinton, November 27, 1875, Brinton Collection.
6. Author's interview with Harold Ward, October 22, 1969.
7. Jane Shaw Ward to William Shaw Ward, April 25, 1868, Brinton Collection.
8. Ferdinand De Wilton Ward to William Shaw Ward, undated fragment, Brinton Collection.
9. Ferdinand De Wilton Ward to William Shaw Ward, undated fragment, Brinton Collection.
10. Ferdinand Ward to William Shaw Ward, September 7, 1868, Brinton Collection.

11. *St. Louis Globe-Democrat*, May 14, 1884.
12. Jane Shaw Ward to Sarah Ward Brinton, January 25, 1869, Brinton Collection.
13. Jane Shaw Ward to Sarah Ward Brinton, January 25, 1869, Brinton Collection.
14. Jane Shaw Ward to Sarah Ward Brinton, February 14, 1869, Brinton Collection.
15. Jane Shaw Ward to Sarah Ward Brinton, January 14, 1869, Brinton Collection.
16. Jane Shaw Ward to Sarah Ward Brinton, February 27, 1869, Brinton Collection.
17. *St. Louis Globe-Democrat*, June 24, 1884.
18. Ferdinand De Wilton Ward to Sarah Ward Brinton, January 13, 1870. Brinton Collection.
19. Ibid.
20. Jane Shaw Ward to Sarah Ward Brinton, January 18, 1870, Brinton Collection.
21. Jane Shaw Ward to William Shaw Ward, February 13, 1870, Brinton Collection.
22. Jane Shaw Ward to Sarah Ward Brinton, January 20, 1870, Brinton Collection.
23. Jane Shaw Ward to Sarah Ward Brinton, January 22, 1879, Brinton Collection.
24. Jane Shaw Ward to William Shaw Ward, February 9, 1870, Brinton Collection.
25. Jane Shaw Ward to Sarah Ward Brinton, February 13, 1870, Brinton Collection.
26. Ibid.
27. Jane Shaw Ward to Sarah Ward Brinton, March 3, 1870, Brinton Collection.
28. Jane Shaw Ward to Sarah Ward Brinton, March 9, 1870, Brinton Collection.
29. Ferdinand De Wilton Ward to Sarah Ward Brinton, November 25, 1871, Brinton Collection.
30. *Macon* (Georgia) *Weekly Telegraph*, June 7, 1884.
31. Jane Shaw Ward to Sarah Ward Brinton, October 10, 1872, Brinton Collection.
32. Jane Shaw Ward to Sarah Ward Brinton, November 22, 1872, Brinton Collection.
33. Ibid.
34. Ibid.
35. Jane Shaw Ward to Sarah Ward Brinton, December 19, 1872, Brinton Collection.
36. Jane Shaw Ward to Sarah Ward Brinton, December 26, 1873, Brinton Collection.
37. Jane Shaw Ward to Sarah Ward Brinton, January 19, 1873, Brinton Collection.
38. Jane Shaw Ward to Sarah Ward Brinton, January 22, 1873, Brinton Collection.
39. Jane Shaw Ward to Sarah Ward Brinton, February 17, 1873, Brinton Collection.
40. Ferdinand De Wilton Ward to Ferdinand Ward, September 2, 1873, author's collection.

CHAPTER SEVEN
1. *New York Times*, October 30, 1882.
2. Jane Shaw Ward to Sarah Ward Brinton, November 17, 1873, Brinton Collection.
3. Jane Shaw Ward to Sarah Ward Brinton, July 7, 1874, Brinton Collection.
4. Jane Shaw Ward to William Shaw Ward, July 17, 1874, Brinton Collection.
5. Ibid.
6. *New York Tribune*, May 11, 1884.
7. Ferdinand Ward to Jane Shaw Ward, September 26, 1874, Brinton Collection.
8. Jane Shaw Ward to William Shaw Ward, n.d. 1874, Brinton Collection.
9. James H. Callender, *Yesterdays on Brooklyn Heights*, pp. 103–04.
10. Stephen Fiske, *Off-hand Portraits of Prominent New Yorkers*, p. 303.
11. Ferdinand Ward to Sarah Ward Brinton, July 21, 1875, Brinton Collection.

12. Jane Shaw Ward to Sarah Ward Brinton, March 28, 1874, Brinton Collection.
13. Ferdinand Ward to William Shaw Ward, March 18, 1875, Brinton Collection.
14. Ferdinand Ward to Sarah Ward Brinton, July 21, 1875, Brinton Collection.
15. Interview with James D. Fish, *Philadelphia Inquirer*, November 17, 1883.
16. Ibid.
17. Ferdinand Ward to Jane Shaw Ward, August 13, 1873, Brinton Collection.
18. Jane Shaw Ward to William Shaw Ward, August n.d., 1873, Brinton Collection.
19. Ibid.
20. Ferdinand De Wilton Ward to Sidney Green, August 4, 1875, Brinton Collection.
21. Ferdinand De Wilton Ward to Sarah Ward Brinton, November 27, 1875, Brinton Collection.
22 Ferdinand De Wilton Ward to William Shaw Ward, March 10, 1876, Brinton Collection.
23. Ferdinand De Wilton Ward to William Shaw Ward, February 11, 1876, Brinton Collection.
24. Ibid.
25. *Brooklyn Eagle*, March 27, 1868.
26. Ferdinand De Wilton Ward to William Shaw Ward, November 23, 1875, Brinton Collection.
27. Jane Shaw Ward to William Shaw Ward, June 11, 1875, Brinton Collection.
28. Jane Shaw Ward to William Shaw Ward, March 13, 1877, Brinton Collection.
29. *New York Tribune*, November 7, 1885.
30. Jane Shaw Ward to William Shaw Ward, September 3, 1877, Brinton Collection.
31. Ferdinand Ward to Jane Shaw Ward, October 25, 1877, Brinton Collection.
32. Jane Shaw Ward to William Shaw Ward, October 12, 1877, Brinton Collection.
33. Ibid.
34. Jane Shaw Ward to William Shaw Ward, November 9, 1877, Brinton Collection.
35. Jane Shaw Ward to William Shaw Ward, April 10, 1878, Brinton Collection.

CHAPTER EIGHT
1. *New York World*, July 7, 1886.
2. *New York World*, July 2, 1886.
3. *Philadelphia Inquirer*, November 27, 1883.
4. David L. Rinear, *The Temple of Momus: Mitchell's Olympic Theatre*, p. 75.
5. Ibid., p. 125.
6. *Philadelphia Inquirer*, November 27, 1883.
7. Ibid.
8. *New York Tribune*, May 11, 1884.
9. *Philadelphia Inquirer*, May 7, 1884.
10. *New York Times*, May 7, 1884.
11. *New York Tribune*, March 28, 1884.
12. Ibid.
13. *Wall Street Journal*, February 16, 1931.
14. Jane Shaw Ward to William Shaw Ward, April 20, 1878, Brinton Collection.
15. Ferdinand De Wilton Ward to William Shaw Ward, May 22, 1877, Brinton Collection.
16. *Chicago Tribune*, November 9, 1880.
17. Joseph J. Perling, *Presidents' Sons*, p. 171.

18. George W. Bishop Jr., *Charles H. Dow and the Dow Theory*, p. 354.

19. John Y. Simon et al., eds., *The Papers of Ulysses S. Grant*, vol. 28, p. 6.

20. Jane Shaw Ward to William Shaw Ward, January 22, 1879, Brinton Collection.

21. Don L. Griswold and Jean Harvey Griswold, *The Carbonate Camp Called Leadville*, p. 207.

22. Rodman W. Paul, ed., *A Victorian Gentlewoman in the Far West*, p. 177.

23. Ibid., p. 183.

24. Mary Hallock Foote to Helena Gilder, July l8, 1879, courtesy of Department of Special Collections and University Archives, Stanford University Libraries.

25. Mary Hallock Foote to Helena Gilder, September 8, 1879, courtesy of Department of Special Collections and University Archives, Stanford University Libraries.

26. Mary Hallock Foote to Helena Gilder, "Friday before Christmas," 1879, courtesy of Department of Special Collections and University Archives, Stanford University Libraries.

27. *Chicago Tribune*, April 29, 1880.

28. *New York World*, July 2, 1886.

29. Ibid.

30. *Philadelphia Inquirer*, November 27, 1883.

31. *Atlanta Constitution*, May 15, 1884.

32. *New York World*, July 11, 1886.

33. Ibid.

34. *New York Times*, March 28, 1885.

35. *New York Times*, December 28, 1884.

36. *New York Herald*, May 10, 1884.

37. Ferdinand De Wilton Ward to Sarah Ward Brinton, April 24, 1880, Brinton Collection.

38. *Chicago Daily Inter-Ocean*, August 7, 1887.

39. *Brooklyn Daily Eagle*, May 11, 1884.

40. Ibid.

41. *New York Herald*, October 10, 1885.

42. *New York Tribune*, January 4, 1885.

43. Ibid.

CHAPTER NINE

1. Jean Edward Smith, *Grant*, p. 618.

2. Julia Dent Grant, *The Personal Memoirs of Julia Dent Grant*, p. 208.

3. Smith, *Grant*, p. 15.

4. Ibid., p. 610.

5. Josiah Bunting III, *Ulysses S. Grant*, pp. 115-16.

6. Smith, *Grant*, p. 18.

7. Henry Clews, *Twenty-eight Years on Wall Street*, p. 37.

8. *New York World*, July 21, 1886.

9. Hamlin Garland, "A Romance of Wall Street."

10. *Wall Street Journal*, February 16, 1931.

11. Jane Shaw Ward to Sarah Ward Brinton, March n.d., 1881, Brinton Collection.

12. Jane Shaw Ward to Sarah Ward Brinton, August n.d., 1882, Brinton Collection.

13. *New York Times*, December 1, 1883.

14. *Wall Street Journal*, February 16, 1931.

15. *Livingston Republican*, August 25, 1881.
16. Ferdinand De Wilton Ward to Sarah Ward Brinton, August 27, 1881, Brinton Collection.
17. Ferdinand De Wilton Ward to Sarah Ward Brinton, January 15, 1880, Brinton Collection.
18. Ferdinand De Wilton Ward to Sarah Ward Brinton, December 13, 1881.
19. *New York Times*, December 21, 1881.
20. Jasper Yeates Brinton, *Fourteen Twenty-three Spruce Street*, p. 25, Brinton Collection.
21. Ibid., p. 28.
22. Jane Shaw Ward to Sarah Ward Brinton, n.d., Historical Society of Pennsylvania.
23. Jane Shaw Ward to Sarah Ward Brinton, February n.d., 1882, Brinton Collection.
24. Ibid.
25. *New York Tribune*, May 11, 1884.
26. *New York Herald*, October 8, 1885.
27. Ibid.
28. Ibid.
29. In fact, he had begun it long before, but not on the breathtaking scale that followed. *New York Tribune*, October 8, 1885.
30. *New York Herald*, March 28, 1885.
31. Ibid.
32. *Boston Globe*, September 21, 1885.
33. *New York Times*, October 9, 1885.
34. *New York Herald*, March 28, 1885.
35. Ibid.
36. Ibid.
37. Ibid.
38. *New York Herald*, October 27, 1885.
39. *New York Tribune*, May 27, 1884.
40. Ibid.
41. Ibid.
42. *New York Herald*, March 31, 1885.
43. Ibid.
44. *Atlanta Constitution*, December 11, 1885.
45. Ferdinand Ward, "General Grant as I Knew Him," *New York Herald*, December 19, 1909.
46. *New York World*, July 11, 1886.

CHAPTER TEN
1. *Philadelphia Inquirer*, November 27, 1883.
2. Ibid.
3. *New York Herald*, May 8, 1884.
4. New Orleans *Times-Picayune*, May 12, 1885.
5. Parker Morell, *Lillian Russell: The Era of Plush*, p. 62.
6. David Stone, "Secrets and Lies," p. 18.
7. *Wilkes-Barre Leader*, November 29, 1877.
8. *Galveston Daily News*, June 14, 1885.

9. Richard Lockridge, *Darling of Misfortune: Edwin Booth, 1833–1893*, p. 85.
10. Ferdinand Ward, "General Grant's Dinner to President Diaz."
11. Ferdinand De Wilton Ward to Sarah Ward Brinton, July 13, 1882, Brinton Collection.
12. *New York World*, July 2, 1886.
13. Jane Shaw Ward to Sarah Ward Brinton, July 10, 1882, Brinton Collection.
14. *New York World*, July 2, 1886.
15. Henry Clews, *Twenty-eight Years on Wall Street*, p. 216.
16. *New York Herald*, October 8, 1885.
17. Ibid.
18. *Mystic Press*, April 18, 1885.
19. Author's collection.
20. *New York Times*, October 15, 1885.
21. Ferdinand Ward, "General Grant an Easy Prey for the Wolves of Finance."
22. Reprinted in *Rocky Mountain News*, December 16, 1883.
23. Reprinted in *Cincinnati Inquirer*, November 27, 1883.
24. Ibid.
25. Reprinted in *Cincinnati Enquirer*, November 30, 1883.
26. *New York Times*, April 9, 1885.
27. Julia Dent Grant, *The Personal Memoirs of Julia Dent Grant*, pp. 327–28.
28. John Y. Simon et al., eds., *The Papers of Ulysses S. Grant*, vol. 31, p. xvii.
29. Jane Shaw Ward to Sarah Ward Brinton, December 26, 1883, Brinton Collection.

CHAPTER ELEVEN
1. Jane Shaw Ward to Ferdinand Ward, August 17, 1888, author's collection.
2. *Boston Globe*, April 18, 1884.
3. *New York Evening Post*, October 27, 1885.
4. *New York Tribune*, March 20, 1885.
5. *New York World*, July 21, 1886.
6. *New York Tribune*, October 18, 1885.
7. *New York Times*, October 27, 1885.
8. Ibid.
9. *New York Times*, October 15, 1885.
10. *New York Herald*, December 26, 1909.
11. Ibid.
12. *New York Sun*, October 28, 1885.
13. *New York Times*, March 18, 1885.
14. *Chicago Tribune*, October 27, 1885.
15. *New York Times*, May 17, 1884.
16. Jean Edward Smith, *Grant*, p. 620.
17. Ibid.
18. Smith, *Grant*, p. 620.
19. *New York Herald*, December 17, 1884.
20. *New York Times*, November 28, 1885.
21. *New York Times*, March 19, 1885.
22. *New York Times*, September 9, 1885.
23. *New York Times*, May 17, 1884.
24. Ibid.

25. *New York Herald*, December 17, 1884.
26. Hamlin Garland, "A Romance of Wall Street."
27. Ibid.
28. *New York Times*, May 7, 1884.
29. Ibid.
30. James Grant, *Money of the Mind*, p. 61.
31. Alexander Dana Noyes, *The Market Place: Reminiscences of a Financial Editor*, pp. 44–45.
32. Smith, *Grant*, p. 620.
33. Richard Goldhurst, *Many Are the Hearts*, pp. 7–8.
34. *New York Times*, September 18, 1885.
35. *New York Tribune*, November 1, 1885.
36. *New York Sun*, May 10, 1884.
37. Jane Shaw Ward to Sarah Ward Brinton, April 11, 1885, Brinton Collection.
38. *Brooklyn Eagle*, May 8, 1884.
39. *Brooklyn Eagle*, May 11, 1884.
40. Ibid.
41. *New York Herald*, October 28, 1885.
42. *New York Tribune*, May 29, 1884.
43. *New York Herald*, October 28, 1885.

CHAPTER TWELVE
1. *New York Times*, May 11, 1884.
2. *New York Times*, May 12, 1884.
3. Ibid.
4. *Boston Daily Advertiser*, May 20, 1884.
5. *New York Times*, May 15, 1884.
6. Ibid.
7. Ibid.
8. *New York Times*, May 17, 1884.
9. Ibid.
10. Ibid.
11. *New York Times*, May 21, 1884.
12. *New York Sun*, May 22, 1884.
13. Ibid.
14. *New York Herald*, March 7, 1890.
15. *Washington Post*, November 30, 1884.
16. A. R. Macdonald, *Prison Secrets*, p. 10.
17. *New York Times*, May 23, 1884.
18. Anonymous, "The Romance and Reality of American Railroads."
19. Ibid.
20. *New York Herald*, March 7, 1890.
21. Ibid.
22. John Y. Simon et al., eds., *The Papers of Ulysses S. Grant*, vol. 29, p. 162.
23. Robert Underwood Johnson to Richard Watson Gilder, July 1, 1884, Richard Watson Gilder Papers, Manuscripts and Archives Division, New York Public Library, Astor, Lenox and Tilden Foundations.
24. *Rocky Mountain News*, May 18, 1884.
25. Thomas M. Pitkin, *The Captain Departs*, p. 6.

26. Simon et al., eds., *The Papers of Ulysses S. Grant*, p. 148.
27. Ibid., p. 154.
28. Ibid., p. 142.
29. David Stone, "Secrets and Lies."
30. *Hartford Courant*, May 10, 1885.
31. Pitkin, *The Captain Departs*, p. 24.
32. Ibid., p. 20.
33. Richard Goldhurst, *Many Are the Hearts*, p. 150.
34. Pitkin, *The Captain Departs*, p. 22.
35. Harriet Elinor Smith, ed., *Autobiography of Mark Twain*, vol. 1, p. 83.
36. *New York World*, November 3, 1885.
37. *New York Times*, May 8, 1885.
38. Robert A. M. Stern, *New York 1880*, p. 136.
39. Phillip C. Jessup, *Elihu Root*, p. 142.
40. Ibid., p. 141.
41. *New York Times*, March 24, 1885.
42. Ibid.
43. *New York Times*, March 17, 1885.
44. *New York Times*, March 28, 1885.
45. Ibid.
46. Ibid.
47. *Brooklyn Eagle*, April 2 and 3, 1885.
48. Ferdinand Ward to Thomas H. Hubbard, March 31, 1885, Ford Autograph Collection, Manuscript and Archives Division, New York Public Library, Astor, Lenox and Tilden Foundations.
49. *New York Times*, April 7, 1885.
50. *New York Times*, April 1, 1885.
51. *New York Times*, April 3, 1885.
52. *New York Times*, April 7, 1885.
53. *New York Times*, April 10, 1885.
54. *New York Times*, April 11, 1885.
55. Ibid.
56. *New York Herald*, April 12, 1885.
57. *Mystic Press*, July 1, 1885.
58. *New York Times*, March 28, 1885.

CHAPTER THIRTEEN
1. *New York Herald*, April 14, 1885.
2. *Boston Daily Globe*, June 4, 1885.
3. *New York Tribune*, September 26, 1885.
4. *New York Times*, May 8, 1885.
5. *Cincinnati Enquirer*, May 29, 1885.
6. *Cincinnati Enquirer*, May 30, 1885.
7. *Philadelphia Inquirer*, May 8, 1885.
8. *New York Times*, June 28, 1885.
9. *New York Times*, October 31, 1885.
10. Richard Goldhurst, *Many Are the Hearts*, p. 220.
11. Harriet Elinor Smith, ed., *Autobiography of Mark Twain*, p. 84.
12. Ibid.

13. William McFeely, *Grant: A Biography*, p. 517.
14. *Brooklyn Daily Eagle*, July 22, 1885.
15. Jane Shaw Ward to Sarah Ward Brinton, August 7, 1885, Brinton Collection.
16. *Washington Post*, August 9, 1885.
17. *Reno Evening Gazette*, October 19, 1885.
18. Nelson Sizer and Henry Shipton Drayton, *Heads and Faces and How to Study Them*, p. 73.
19. *National Police Gazette*, August 8, 1885.
20. *New York Herald*, October 20, 1885.
21. *Boston Daily Globe*, September 29, 1885.
22. *Chicago Tribune*, September 29, 1885.
23. *New York Herald*, October 8, 1885.
24. Marquis James, *Merchant Adventurer*, pp. 206–07.
25. *New York Herald*, October 20, 1885.
26. Ibid.
27. *Frederick* (Maryland) *News*, October 22, 1885.
28. *New York Times*, October 30, 1885.
29. *New York Sun*, October 27, 1885.
30. Ibid.
31. *New York Times*, October 31, 1885.
32. *New York Sun*, October 27, 1885.
33. *New York Times*, October 27, 1885.
34. *New York Sun*, October 27, 1885.
35. Ibid.
36. *New York Times*, October 28, 2010.
37. Ibid.
38. Ibid.
39. *New York Sun*, October 28, 1885.
40. *New York Times*, October 29, 1885.
41. *New York Tribune*, November 1, 1885.

CHAPTER FOURTEEN
1. *New York World*, November 3, 1885.
2. Timothy J. Gilfoyle, *A Pickpocket's Tale*, p. 53.
3. Sing Sing Admission Register, Series B00143–80, vol. 7, p. 555, New York State Archives.
4. *New York World*, November 3, 1885.
5. Gilfoyle, *A Pickpocket's Tale*, p. 160.
6. "Number 1500," *Life in Sing Sing*, p. 38.
7. Ibid., p. 228.
8. Ibid., p. 47.
9. *New York Times*, July 3, 1910.
10. Ibid.
11. Ibid.
12. Ibid.
13. *New York Herald*, May 12, 1889.
14. Ella Ward to Ferdinand Ward, June n.d., 1888, author's collection.
15. Jane Shaw Ward to Sarah Ward Brinton, n.d., summer, 1888, Brinton Collection.
16. *National Police Gazette*, July 10, 1886.

17. Hutchins Hapgood, *The Autobiography of a Thief*, pp. 175–76.
18. *Atlanta Constitution*, February 6, 1887.
19. Ella Ward to Ferdinand Ward, February 13, 1887, author's collection.
20. Ferdinand Wilton to President Grover Cleveland, May 8, 1886, Grover Cleveland Papers, Library of Congress.
21. *New York World*, July 2, 1886.
22. *New York World*, July 11, 1886.
23. Ferdinand Ward to Hon. Daniel S. Lamont, August 3, 1887, author's collection, Grover Cleveland Papers, Library of Congress.
24. *New York World*, July 11, 1886.
25. *Chicago Tribune*, August 12, 1886.
26. Ella Ward to Ferdinand Ward, May 10, 1886, author's collection.
27. Ella Ward to Ferdinand Ward, February 19, 1887, author's collection.
28. Ella Ward to Ferdinand Ward, March 13, 1887, author's collection.
29. Ella Ward to Ferdinand Ward, June 5, 1887, author's collection.
30. Ella Ward to Ferdinand Ward, September 4, 1887, author's collection.
31. Ella Ward to Ferdinand Ward, August 13, 1887, author's collection.
32. Ella Ward to Ferdinand Ward, January 30, 1887, author's collection.
33. Jane Shaw Ward to Sarah Ward Brinton, June 28, 1886, Ferdinand De Wilton Ward Collection, Waidner-Spahr Library, Dickinson College.
34. Ella Ward to Ferdinand Ward, September 13, 1887, author's collection.
35. *Boston Globe*, February 7, 1887.
36. Ferdinand De Wilton Ward to Sarah Ward Brinton, September n.d., 1887, Brinton Collection.
37. Jane Shaw Ward to Sarah Ward Brinton, June 28, 1886, Brinton Collection.
38. Jane Shaw Ward to Sarah Ward Brinton, August 17, 1886, Brinton Collection.
39. Ferdinand Ward to Jane Shaw Ward, December 29, 1887, Brinton Collection.
40. Ferdinand De Wilton Ward to Sarah Ward Brinton, January 4, 1888, Brinton Collection.
41. Ibid.
42. Ibid.
43. Jane Shaw Ward to Ferdinand Ward, August 19, 1888, author's collection.
44. Jane Shaw Ward to Ferdinand Ward, August 17, 1888, author's collection.
45. Ella Ward to Ferdinand Ward, November 22, 1888, author's collection.
46. William Shaw Ward to Ferdinand Ward, January 1, 1889, author's collection.
47. Ella Ward to Ferdinand Ward, February 2, 1889, author's collection.
48. *New York Herald*, January 29, 1889.
49. Ferdinand Ward to President Grover Cleveland, February 6, 1889, Grover Cleveland Papers.

CHAPTER FIFTEEN

1. *New York Herald*, May 12, 1889.
2. Ibid.
3. *New York World*, May 12, 1889.
4. Ferdinand De Wilton Ward to Ella Ward, June 17, 1889, author's collection.
5. W. Bourke Cockran to Ferdinand Ward, June 14, 1889, author's collection.
6. Ella Ward to Ferdinand Ward, January 28, 1889, author's collection.
7. Ella Ward to Ferdinand Ward, May 5, 1889, author's collection.
8. Ibid.
9. Author's collection.

10. Ella Ward to Ferdinand Ward, September 30, 1889, author's collection.

11. Ella Ward to Ferdinand Ward, October 3, 1889, author's collection.

12. *Brooklyn Eagle*, April 24, 1885.

13. Ella Ward to Ferdinand Ward, November 9, 1889, author's collection.

14. Ella Ward to Ferdinand Ward, November 24, 1889, author's collection.

15. Sarah Ward Brinton to Ferdinand De Wilton Ward, January 12, 1890, Brinton Collection.

16. Sarah Ward Brinton to Ferdinand De Wilton Ward, January 26, 1890, Brinton Collection.

17. Sarah Ward Brinton to Ferdinand De Wilton Ward, January 30, 1890, Brinton Collection.

18. *New York Herald*, March 3, 1890.

19. *New York Herald*, March 7, 1890.

20. James W. Graff to Ferdinand Ward, April 2, 1890, author's collection.

21. Ibid.

22. Ferdinand De Wilton Ward to Sarah Ward Brinton, April 7, 1891, Brinton Collection.

23. James McKeen to Clarence Ward, October 11, 1905, author's collection.

24. Mary D. Green to Fred Green, May 1, 1890, author's collection.

25. Harold Ward would be born in Oxford, England, September 19, 1890.

26. Sarah Ward Brinton to Ferdinand Ward, May 20, 1890, author's collection.

27. Sarah Ward Brinton to Ferdinand Ward, April 18, 1890, author's collection.

28. Emma Jane Ward to Ferdinand Ward, May 31, 1890, author's collection.

29. Sarah Ward Brinton to Ferdinand Ward, May 8, 1890, author's collection.

30. James McKeen to Ferdinand Ward, May 26, 1890, author's collection.

31. James McKeen to Ferdinand Ward, May 26 and June 30, 1890, author's collection.

32. Ferdinand Ward to Clarence Ward, July 13, 1890, author's collection.

33. Nellie Green to Ferdinand Ward, July 20, 1890,

34. Ferdinand Ward to Nellie Green, November 4, 1890, author's collection.

35. Ferdinand Ward to Nellie Green, June 9 and August 21, 1891, author's collection.

36. Ferdinand Ward to Nellie Green, August 21, 1891, author's collection.

37. Ferdinand Ward to Clarence Ward, July 20, 1891, author's collection.

38. Ferdinand Ward to Nellie Green, February 3, 1891, author's collection.

39. Ferdinand Ward to Nellie Green, April 19, 1891, author's collection.

40. Ferdinand Ward to Nellie Green, July 21, 1891, author's collection.

41. Ibid.

42. Ferdinand Ward to Nellie Green, July 5, 1891, author's collection.

43. Ferdinand De Wilton Ward to Ferdinand Ward, April 9, 1890, author's collection.

44. Ferdinand De Wilton Ward to Ferdinand Ward, April 22, 1890, author's collection.

45. *Livingston Republican*, May 7, 1891.

46. Emma Jane "Kate" Ward to Nellie Green, September 17, 1891, author's collection.

47. Ferdinand Ward to W. Bourke Cockran, April 26, 1892, William Bourke Cockran Papers, Manuscripts and Archives Division, New York Public Library, Astor, Lenox and Tilden Foundations.

48. Ferdinand Ward to Nellie Green, February 18, 1892, author's collection.

49. James McKeen to Fred Green, April 11, 1892, author's collection.
50. *Brooklyn Eagle*, April 30, 1892.
51. Ibid.
52. *New York Times*, May 1, 1892.

CHAPTER SIXTEEN

1. Author's interview with Clarence Ward, 1967.
2. Clarence Ward interview with Andrew Ward, summer 1967.
3. Ibid.
4. Clarence Ward report card, December 17, 1890, author's collection.
5. *New York Herald*, April 2, 1892.
6. *New York Times*, April 2, 1892.
7. *New York Herald*, April 2, 1892.
8. Ibid.
9. Ferdinand Ward to Nellie Green, May 4, 1892, author's collection.
10. *New Haven Register*, August 30, 1892.
11. Nellie Green to Ferdinand Ward, September 28, 1892, author's collection.
12. Ferdinand Ward to Nellie Green, September 28, 1892, author's collection.
13. Ferdinand Ward to Mrs. Robert Tallman, September 9, 1892, author's collection.
14. Ferdinand Ward to Mrs. Robert Tallman, September 20, 1892, author's collection.
15. Ferdinand Ward to Mrs. Robert Tallman, October 11, 1892, author's collection.
16. John Gardner to Ferdinand Ward, October 11, 1892, author's collection.
17. Ferdinand Ward to Mrs. Robert Tallman, October 22, 1892, author's collection.
18. Sarah Ward Brinton to Nellie Green, September 27, 1892, author's collection.
19. Sarah Ward Brinton to Nellie Green, September 30, 1892, author's collection.
20. William Shaw Ward to Nellie Green, October 5, 1892, author's collection.
21. *New York Times*, October 31, 1885.
22. Ferdinand Ward to Clarence Ward, October 23, 1892, author's collection.
23. Ferdinand Ward to Nellie Green, November 12, 1892, author's collection.
24. Sarah Ward Brinton to Nellie Green, December 30, 1893, author's collection.
25. William Shaw Ward to Fred Green, January 18, 1894, author's collection.
26. Ferdinand Ward to Clarence Ward, January 18, 1893, author's collection.
27. Ferdinand Ward to Clarence Ward, February 21, 1893, author's collection.
28. Ferdinand Ward to Clarence Ward, February 26, 1893, author's collection.
29. Ferdinand Ward to Clarence Ward, August 20, 1893, author's collection.
30. Ferdinand Ward to Clarence Ward, October 15, 1893, author's collection.
31. *Dallas Morning News*, October 14, 1893.

CHAPTER SEVENTEEN

1. James McKeen to Charles E. Searls, January 17, 1894, author's collection.
2. Charles E. Searls to Lockwood R. Doty, March 17, 1894, author's collection.
3. *New York Herald*, March 21, 1894.
4. *Washington Post*, March 22, 1894.
5. Lockwood R. Doty, March 26, 1894, author's collection.
6. Charles Searls to Lockwood R. Doty, April 5, 1894, author's collection.
7. James McKeen to Charles E. Searls, April 10, 1894, author's collection.
8. *New York Herald*, September 14, 1894.
9. Ibid.

10. *Hartford Courant,* September 14, 1894.
11. *New York Herald,* September 14, 1894.
12. *Putnam Patriot,* September 21, 1894.
13. *New York Herald,* September 17, 1894.
14. *New York Herald,* October 9, 1894.
15. "Quid Pro Quo" to Fred Green, September 18, 1894, author's collection.
16. Ibid.
17. Author's interview with Mrs. George Teall, August 24, 1971.
18. *Rochester Democrat and Chronicle,* October 10, 1894.
19. Ferdinand Ward to Clarence Ward, December 29, 1894, author's collection.
20. Ferdinand Ward to Clarence Ward, March 9, 1895, author's collection.
21. Ferdinand Ward to Clarence Ward, April 9, 1895, author's collection.
22. *Hartford Courant,* January 13, 1897.
23. Ibid.
24. Ibid.
25. *Central Law Journal* (1874–1927), September 17, 1897.

EPILOGUE
1. Interview with Clarence Ward conducted by Andrew Ward, 1967.
2. Ibid.
3. Ibid.
4. Draft of letter from Clarence to Isabelle Ward, n.d. 1905, author's collection.
5. Isabella A. Ward to Clarence Ward, March 10, 1905, author's collection.
6. Ferdinand Ward to Clarence Ward, May 2, 1905, author's collection.
7. Ferdinand Ward to Clarence Ward, May 11, 1905, author's collection.
8. Ibid.
9. Clarence Ward to Ferdinand Ward, January 9, 1906, author's collection.
10. James McKeen to Clarence Ward, September 18, 1906, author's collection.
11. Ibid.
12. *Dallas Morning News,* October 14, 1893.
13. Ferdinand Ward to Clarence Ward, January 26, 1910, author's collection.
14. James McKeen to Clarence Ward, February 11, 1910, author's collection.
15. Edward A. Day to Clarence Ward, May 19, 1910, author's collection.
16. Author's interview with F. C. Ward.
17. Interview with F. C. Ward by Andrew Ward, 1967.

BIBLIOGRAPHY

BOOKS

Ackerman, Kenneth D. *Boss Tweed: The Rise and Fall of the Corrupt Pol Who Conceived the Soul of Modern New York*. New York, 2005.

Adams, Samuel Hawley. *Life of Henry Foster, M.D., Founder Clifton Springs Sanitarium, Clifton Springs, New York*. Clifton Springs, N.Y., 1921.

Ahlstrom, Sidney E. *A Religious History of the American People*. New Haven, Conn., 1972.

"A Lady" (Mrs. Julia Charlotte Maitland). *Letters from Madras, During the Years 1836–1839*. London, 1846.

Allison, Rev. Charles Elemer. *A Historical Sketch of Hamilton College, Clinton, New York*. Yonkers, N.Y., 1870.

American Madura Mission Jubilee Volume 1834–1884. Madras, 1884.

Ames, Nathaniel. *A Mariner's Sketches*. Providence, R.I., 1830.

Anderson, Rufus. *History of the Missions of the American Board of Commissioners for Foreign Missions in India*. Boston, 1974.

Auerbach, Joseph Smith. *Julian T. Davies: Memorial of a Leader of the Bar*. New York, 1921.

Austin, Warren. *The Elder Henry James*. New York, 1934.

Badeau, Adam. *Grant in Peace, from Appomattox to Mt. McGregor, and Personal Memoir*. New York, 1887.

Balmer, Randall, and John R. Fitzmier. *The Presbyterians*. Westport, Conn., 1993.

Barber, Raymond G., and Gary E. Swinson, eds. *The Civil War Letters of Charles Barber, Private, 104th New York Volunteer Infantry*. Torrance, Calif., 1991.

Barrows, Samuel June. *The Doom of the Majority of Mankind*. New York, 1883.

Bartlett, Samuel Colcord. *Historical Sketch of the Missions of the American Board in India and Ceylon*. Boston, 1880.

Bayles, Richard M. *History of Windham County, Connecticut*. New York, 1889.

Beadie, Nancy, ed. *Chartered Schools: Two Hundred Years of Independent Academies in the United States, 1727–1925*. London, 2002.

Bean, Susan. *Yankee India: American Commercial and Cultural Encounters with India in the Age of Sail, 1784–1860*. Salem, Mass., 2001.

Bishop, George W. Jr. *Charles H. Dow and the Dow Theory.* New York, 1960.

Blair, Edward. *Leadville: Colorado's Magic City.* Boulder, Colo., 1980.

Blaufuss, Mary Schaller. *Changing Goals of the American Madura Mission in India, 1830–1916.* Frankfurt, 2003.

Bodry-Sanders. *Carl Akeley: Africa's Collector, Africa's Savior.* New York, 1991.

Bragdon, Claude Fayette. *Secret Springs: An Autobiography.* New York, 1917.

Brinton, Jasper Yeates. *Fourteen Twenty-three Spruce Street: Memories of a Philadelphia Boyhood.* Privately printed. Beirut, 1973.

Brinton, John H. *Personal Memoirs of John H. Brinton, Civil War Surgeon, 1861–1865.* New York, 1914.

Buckley, Julian Gerard. *Thirty Years at Bleak House, 1905–1935.* Privately printed. New York, 1979.

Bull, Bonnie K. *Stamford.* Charleston, S.C., 1997.

Bunting, Josiah III. *Ulysses S. Grant.* New York, 2004.

Burke, John. *Duet in Diamonds.* New York, 1972.

Callender, James H. *Yesterdays on Brooklyn Heights.* New York, 1927.

Carmer, Carl. *Dark Trees to the Wind.* New York, 1949.

Cayleff, Susan E. *Wash and Be Healed: The Water-Cure Movement and Women's Health.* Philadelphia, 1987.

Central Presbyterian Church. *Through the Years: Central Presbyterian Church of Geneseo, New York: 150th Anniversary, 1810–1960.* Geneseo, N.Y., 1960.

Chancellor, Edward. *Devil Take the Hindmost: A History of Financial Speculation.* New York, 1997.

Chandler, Alfred D. Jr. *The Visible Hand: The Managerial Revolution in American Business.* Cambridge, Mass., 1977.

Chandler, John S. *The Madura Mission: A Condensed Sketch, 1834–1886.* Boston, 1886.

———. *Seventy-five Years in the Madura Mission.* Madras, 1909.

Chanler, Mrs. Winthrop. *Autumn in the Valley.* Boston, 1936.

Chidsey, Donald Barr. *The Gentleman from New York: A Life of Roscoe Conkling.* New Haven, Conn., 1935.

Church of the Pilgrims. *The Fiftieth Anniversary of the Installation of Richard Salter Storrs as Pastor of the Church of the Pilgrims, Brooklyn, New York.* Brooklyn, N.Y., 1897.

Clews, Henry. *Twenty-eight Years on Wall Street.* New York, 1888.

———. *Fifty Years on Wall Street.* New York, 1908.

Coit, John T. *Death of an Aged Christian: A Discourse Delivered at the Funeral of Dr. Levi Ward, in St. Peter's Church, Rochester, January 7, 1861.* Rochester, N.Y., 1861.

Conover, Ted. *Newjack: Guarding Sing Sing.* New York, 2000.

Cross, Whitney R. *The Burned-Over District: The Social and Intellectual History of Enthusiastic Religion in Western New York, 1800–1850.* New York, 1950.

Crossette, Barbara. *The Great Hill Stations of Asia.* Boulder, Colo., 1998.

Dalrymple, William. *At the Court of the Fish-Eyed Goddess: Travels in the Indian Subcontinent.* Delhi, 1998.

David, Immanuel. *Reformed Church in American Missionaries in South India, 1839–1938: An Analytical Study.* Bangalore, 1986.

Davis, Henry. *A Narrative of the Embarrassments and Decline of Hamilton College.* Clinton, N.Y., 1833.

Dayton, Abram C. *Last Days of Knickerbocker Life in New York.* New York, 1882.

Dickerman, Edward Dwight, and George Sherwood Dickerman. *Families of Dickerman Ancestry: Descendants of Thomas Dickerman, an Early Settler of Dorchester, Massachusetts.* New Haven, Conn., 1892.

Dodge, Melvin G., comp. *Fifty Years Ago: The Half-Century Annalists' Letters to the Hamilton College Alumni Association, 1865 to 1900*. Kirkland, N.Y., 1900.

Donegan, Jane B. *Hydropathic Highway to Health: Women and Water-Cure in Antebellum America*. New York, 1986.

Doty, Lockwood R. *History of Livingston County, New York*. Geneseo, N.Y., 1876.

Dupree, A. Hunter. *Asa Gray: American Botanist, Friend of Darwin*. Baltimore, Md., 1988.

Edel, Leon. *Henry James, 1843–1870: The Untried Years*. Philadelphia, 1953.

Ely, Elisha, pub. *A Directory for the Village of Rochester Containing the Names, Residence and Occupations of All Male Inhabitants over Fifteen Years, in Said Village, on the First of January, 1827. To Which Is Added a Sketch of the History of the Village from 1812 to 1827*. Rochester, N.Y., 1827.

Fausold, Martin L. *James W. Wadsworth: The Gentleman from New York*. Syracuse, N.Y., 1975.

Feinstein, Estelle F. *Stamford in the Gilded Age: The Political Life of a Connecticut Town, 1868–1893*. Stamford, Conn., 1973.

Feinstein, Estelle F., Joyce S. Pendery, and Robert Lockwood Mills. *Stamford: An Illustrated History*. Sun Valley, Calif., 2002.

Fischer, Victor, and Michael B. Frank, eds. *Mark Twain's Letters*, vol. 3: *1869*. Berkeley, Calif., 1992.

Fish, James Dean. *Memories of Early Business Life and Associates*. Privately printed. Mystic, Conn., n.d.

Fisher, Gordon McRea. *Three Paths to Gettysburg*. E-book, 2004.

Fiske, Stephen. *Off-Hand Portraits of Prominent New Yorkers*. New York, 1884.

Fitch, Charles Elliott. *Encyclopedia of Biography of New York*. New York, 1916.

Flexner, James T. *George Washington in the American Revolution, 1775–1783*. New York, 1968.

Flick, Alexander C. *Samuel J. Tilden: A Study in Sagacity*. New York, 1939.

Folsom, G. P. *History of the Second Presbyterian Church: A Discourse Delivered January 5, 1868, on the Fiftieth Anniversary of the Dedication of the 2nd Presbyterian Church of Geneseo, New York*. Geneseo, N.Y., 1868.

Fowler, William Worthington. *Ten Years in Wall Street; or, Revelations of Inside Life and Experience on the 'Change*. New York, 1870.

Furgurson, Ernest B. *Chancellorsville 1863: The Souls of the Brave*. New York, 1992.

Gardner, James. *Memoirs of Christian Females with an Essay on the Influences of Female Piety*. New York, 1852.

Garland, Hamlin. *Ulysses S. Grant: His Life and Character*. New York, 1898.

Geisst, Charles R. *Wall Street: A History*. New York, 1997.

Gifford, Frederick L. *The Early History of the Village of Clifton Springs*. Canandaigua, N.Y., 1984.

Gilfoyle, Timothy J. *A Pickpocket's Tale: The Underworld of Nineteenth-Century New York*. New York, 2006.

Gillespie, Edward T. W. *1641–1892: Picturesque Stamford—A Souvenir of the Two Hundred and Fiftieth Anniversary of the Settlement of the Town of Stamford, Containing an Historical Sketch Covering Salient Points of Stamford's History from 1641 to 1892*. Stamford, Conn., 1892.

Goldhurst, Richard. *Many Are the Hearts: The Agony and the Triumph of Ulysses S. Grant*. New York, 1975.

Gradie, Charlotte and Jan Sweet. *Haddam, 1870–1930*. Charlotte, S.C., 2005.

Grant, James. *Money of the Mind: Borrowing and Lending in America from the Civil War to Michael Milken*. New York, 1992.

Grant, Jesse R. *In the Days of My Father, General Grant.* New York, 1925.

Grant, Julia Dent. *The Personal Memoirs of Julia Dent Grant (Mrs. Ulysses S. Grant).* Carbondale, Ill., 1975.

Grant, Ulysses S. III. *Ulysses S. Grant: Warrior and Statesman.* New York, 1969.

Green, Horace. *General Grant's Last Stand.* New York, 1936.

Greene, Richard Henry. *Greene (Green) Family of Plymouth Colony.* New York, 1909.

Griffith, Elisabeth. *In Her Own Right: The Life of Elizabeth Cady Stanton.* New York, 1984.

Griswold, Don L., and Jean Harvey Griswold. *The Carbonate Camp Called Leadville.* Denver, Colo., 1951.

Gronowicz, Antoni. *Modjeska: Her Life and Loves.* New York, 1956.

Hall, Basil. *Travels in North America,* vol. 1. Graz, Austria, 1965.

Hambrick-Stowe, Charles E. *Charles G. Finney and the Spirit of American Evangelicalism.* Grand Rapids, Mich., 1996.

Hapgood, Hutchins. *The Autobiography of a Thief.* New York, 1903.

Harris, Paul William. *Nothing but Christ: Rufus Anderson and the Ideology of Protestant Foreign Missions.* New York, 1999.

Hatch, Alden. *The Wadsworths of the Genesee.* New York, 1959.

Hesseltine, William B. *Ulysses S. Grant: Politician.* New York, 1935.

Howland, William W., and Rev. James Herrick. *Historical Sketch of the Ceylon Mission, by Rev. William W. Howland, and of the Madura and Madras Missions, by Rev. James Herrick.* New York, 1865.

Hutchinson, William R. *Errand to the World: American Protestant Thought and Foreign Missions.* Chicago, 1987.

James, Marquis. *Merchant Adventurer: The Story of W. R. Grace.* Wilmington, Dela., 1993.

Jayawardena, Kumari. *The White Woman's Other Burden: Western Women and South Asia During British Rule.* New York, 1995.

Jeffrey, Mary Pauline. *Ida S. Scudder of Vellore.* Mysore City, 1939.

Jessup, Philip C. *Elihu Root.* 2 vols. New York, 1938.

Johnson, Paul E. *A Shopkeeper's Millennium: Society and Revivals in Rochester, New York, 1815–1837.* New York, 1978.

———. *Sam Patch, the Famous Jumper.* New York, 2003.

Jordan, David M. *Roscoe Conkling: Voice in the Senate.* Ithaca, N.Y., 1971.

Joseph, Peter, ed. *The Wounded River: The Civil War Letters of John Vance Lauderdale, M.D.,* East Lansing, Mich., 1993.

Kelsey, John. *Lives and Reminiscences of the Pioneers of Rochester and Western New York.* Rochester, N.Y., 1854.

King, Moses. *King's Handbook of New York City, 1892.* Boston, 1892.

———. *Notable New Yorkers of 1896–1899.* New York, 1899.

Koustam, Angus and Tony Bryan. *Union River Ironclads, 1861–1865.* New York, 2002.

Laas, Virginia Jeans, ed. *Wartime Washington: The Civil War Letters of Elizabeth Blair Lee.* Urbana, Ill., 1991.

Lawes, Lewis E. *Twenty Thousand Years in Sing Sing.* New York, 1932.

Levinson, Leonard Louis. *Wall Street: A Pictorial History.* New York, 1961.

Lewis, Tayler. *Memoirs of Eliphalet Nott, D.D., L.L.D., for Sixty-two Years President of Union College.* New York, 1876.

Lockridge, Richard. *Darling of Misfortune. Edwin Booth, 1833–1893.* London, 1932.

MacAbe, James B. *Lights and Shadows of New York Life.* Philadelphia, 1872.

Macdonald, A. R. *Prison Secrets: Things Seen, Suffered, and Recorded during Seven Years in Ludlow Street Jail.* New York, 1893.

Maitland, Mrs. Julia Charlotte. *Letters from Madras, During the Years 1836–1839.* London, 1846.

Malo, Paul. *Landmarks of Rochester and Monroe County: A Guide to Neighborhoods and Villages.* Syracuse, N.Y., 1974.

Marsden, George M. *The Evangelical Mind and the New School Presbyterian Experience: A Case Study of Thought and Theology in Nineteenth-Century America.* Eugene, Ore., 1970.

Martin, J. R., FRS. *The Influences of Tropical Climates on European Constitutions. Including Practical Observations on the Nature and Treatment of the Diseases of Europeans on Their Return from Tropical Climates.* London, 1856.

Marty, Martin E. *Pilgrims in Their Own Land: 500 Years of Religion in America.* Boston, 1984.

Martyn, Charles. *The Life of Artemus Ward.* New York, 1921.

Masur, Louis P. *1831: Year of Eclipse.* New York, 2001.

McFeely, William S. *Grant: A Biography.* New York, 1982.

McKelvey, Blake. *Rochester on the Genesee: The Growth of a City.* Syracuse, N.Y., 1993.

McKivigam, John R. *The War Against Proslavery Religion: Abolitionism and the Northern Churches.* Ithaca, N.Y., 1984.

Miller, Darlis A. *Mary Hallock Foote: Author-Illustrator of the American West.* Norman, Okla., 2002.

Mitchell, Nora. *The Indian Hill Station: Kodaikanal.* Chicago, 1972.

Mitchell, Mrs. Murray. *In Southern India: A Visit to Some of the Chief Mission Stations in the Madras Presidency.* London, 1885.

Morell, Parker. *Lillian Russell: The Era of Plush.* New York, 1940.

Mott, Edward Harold. *Between the Ocean and the Lakes: The Story of Erie.* New York, 1899.

Murray, John, pub. *A Handbook for Travellers in India, Burma and Ceylon, Including the Provinces of Bengal, Bombay, Madras, the United Provinces of Agra and Lucknow, the Panjab, Eastern Bengal and Assam, the Northwest Frontier Province, Baluchistan, and the Central Provinces, and the Native States of Rajputana, Central India, Kashmir, Hyderabad. Mysore, etc.* London, 1909.

Musicant, Ivan. *Divided Waters: The Naval History of the Civil War.* New York, 1995.

Neill, Stephen. *A History of Christianity in India, 1707–1858.* Cambridge, Mass., 1985.

Nichols, Hastings. *Presbyterianism in New York State.* Philadelphia, 1965.

Noyes, Alexander Dana. *Forty Years of American Finance.* New York, 1909.

———. *The Market Place. Reminiscences of a Financial Editor.* New York, 1938.

"Number 1500." *Life in Sing Sing.* Indianapolis, Ind., 1904.

Oppel, Frank, ed. *Gaslight New York Revisited.* Secaucus, N.Y., 1989.

O'Reilly, Henry. *Sketches of Rochester with Incidental Notices of Western New-York.* Rochester, N.Y., 1838.

Paine, Albert Bigelow. *Th. Nast: His Period and His Pictures.* Princeton, N.J., 1904.

Parker, Jenny Marsh. *Rochester: A Story Historical.* Rochester, N.Y., 1884.

Parsons, Levi. *History of Rochester Presbytery.* Rochester, N.Y., 1889.

Pathak, Sushil Madhava. *American Missionaries and Hinduism: A Study of Their Contacts from 1813–1910.* New Delhi, 1967.

Patton, Jacob Harris. *A Popular History of the Presbyterian Church in the United States of America.* New York, 1900.

Paul, Rodman W., ed. *A Victorian Gentlewoman in the Far West: The Reminiscences of Mary Hallock Foote*. San Marino, Calif., 1972.

Paul, Rodman Wilson. *Mining Frontiers of the Far West, 1848–1880*. Albuquerque, N.M., 1963.

Peck, William Farley. *History of Rochester and Monroe County, New York*. Rochester, N.Y., 1908.

Penney, Joseph. *Claims of the Missionary Enterprise: A Discourse at the Ordination of the Rev. F. D.W. Ward and the Rev. Henry Cherry, as Missionaries to Southern India*. New York, 1836.

Perret, Geoffrey. *Ulysses S. Grant: Soldier and President*. New York, 1997.

Phillips, Clifton J. *Protestant America and the Pagan World: American Board of Commissioners for Foreign Missions, 1810–1860*. Cambridge, Mass., 1969.

Phisterer, Frederick. *New York in the War of Rebellion, 1861 to 1865*. Albany, N.Y., 1890.

Pierson, Hamilton Wilcox, ed. *American Missionary Memorial*. Boston, 1853.

Pilkington, Walter. *Hamilton College, 1812–1862*. Clinton, N.Y., 1962.

Pitkin, Thomas M. *The Captain Departs: Ulysses S. Grant's Last Campaign*. Carbondale, Ill., 1973.

Plazak, Dan. *A Hole in the Ground with a Liar at the Top: Fraud and Deceit in the Golden Age of American Mining*. Salt Lake City, Utah, 2006.

Pratt, Sereno S. *The Work of Wall Street*. New York, 1912.

Putnam, George Haven. *Memories of a Publisher*. New York, 1915.

Reeves, Thomas C. *Gentleman Boss: The Life of Chester Arthur*. New York, 1975.

Rinear, David L. *The Temple of Momus: Mitchell's Olympic Theatre*. Metuchen, N.J., 1987.

Robert, Dana L. *American Women in Mission: A Social History of Their Thought and Practice*. Macon, Ga., 1997.

Rodgers, Andrew Denny II. *John Torrey: A Story of North American Botany*. London, 1942.

Rosenberg, Charles E. *The Cholera Years: The United States in 1832, 1849, and 1866*. Chicago, 1987.

Ross, Ishbel. *The General's Wife: The Life of Mrs. Ulysses S. Grant*. New York, 1959.

Sackett, William Edgar, et al., eds. *Scannell's New Jersey's First Citizens and State Guide*. New York, 1919.

Scudder, Dorothy Jealous. *A Thousand Years in Thy Sight: The Story of the Scudder Missionaries of India*. New York, 1984.

Scudder, Horace E. *The Life and Letters of David Coit Scudder, Missionary in Southern India*. New York, 1864.

Seaburg, Carl, and Stanley Paterson. *The Ice King: Frederic Tudor and His Circle*. Ed. Alan Seaburg. Mystic, Conn., 2003.

Sears, Stephen W. *Chancellorsville*. New York, 1996.

Sherring, Rev. M. A., *The History of Protestant Missions in India from Their Commencement in 1706 to 1881*. London, 1884.

Simon, John Y., et al., eds. *The Papers of Ulysses S. Grant*, vols. 24–31. Carbondale, Ill., 2005–2009.

Sizer, Nelson, and Henry Shipton Drayton. *Heads and Faces and How to Study Them: A Manual of Phrenology and Physiognomy for the People*. New York, 1885.

Smith, Duane A. *Horace Tabor: His Life and Legend*. Denver, Colo., 1989.

Smith, Harriet Elinor, ed. *Autobiography of Mark Twain*, vol. 1. Berkeley, Calif., 2010.

Smith, James H. *History of Livingston County, New York.* Syracuse, N.Y., 1881.

Smith, Jean Edward. *Grant.* New York, 2001.

Smith, Matthew Hale Jr. *Twenty Years Among the Bulls and Bears of Wall Street.* New York, 1871.

———. *Wonders of a Great City, or the Sights, Secrets and Sins of New York: Being a Wonderful Portrayal of the Varied Phases of Life in the Greatest City of America.* Chicago, 1887.

Sobel, Robert. *Panic on Wall Street: A History of America's Financial Disasters.* New York, 1968.

Squire, Newton. *The New York Clearing House: Its Methods and Systems and a Description of the London Clearing House with Valuable Statistics and Other Information.* New York, 1888.

Stanton, Elizabeth Cady. *Eighty Years and More: Reminiscences, 1815–1897.* New York, 1898.

Stanton, Henry B. *Random Collections.* New York, 1887.

Stern, Robert A. M., Thomas Mellins, and David Fishman. *New York, 1880: Architecture and Urbanism in the Gilded Age.* New York, 1999.

Strong, Samuel Meredith, MD. *The Great Blizzard of 1888.* New York, 1938.

Thomas, Dana L. *The Plungers and the Peacocks.* New York, 1967.

Walling, George W. *Recollections of a New York Chief of Police.* New York, 1887.

Ward, Ferdinand De Wilton. *"On Missionary Encouragement in Southern India": The Historical and Statistical Parts of a Missionary Address, Delivered in the Scotch Kirk on the Evening of October 3, 1843.* Madras, 1843.

———. *Practical Expositions of the Parables of Christ and of the Briefer Similes, Employed by the Divine Teacher in Illustrating and Enforcing the Doctrines and Duties of Christianity.* Madras, 1844.

———. *Questions Proposed to and Answers Returned by the Great Teacher.* Madras, 1844.

———. *Appeal for the Hindu: Addressed to British and Other Christian Foreigners Residing in India.* Madras, 1845.

———. *The Elements of Geography for Little Children.* Madras, 1845.

———. *India and the Hindoos: Being a Popular View of the Geography, History, Government, Manners, Customs, Literature and Religion of That Ancient People; with an Account of Christian Missions Among Them.* New York, 1851.

———. *A Christian Gift: Or, Pastoral Letters.* Rochester, N.Y., 1853.

———. *Do Thyself No Harm: A Sermon Delivered Before the Students of Geneseo Academy in the Presbyterian Church, Geneseo, March 30, 1856.* Geneseo, N.Y., 1856.

———. *A Summer Vacation Abroad; or, Notes of a Visit to England, Scotland, Ireland, France, Italy, and Belgium.* Rochester, N.Y., 1856.

———. *An Address Before the Association at Its Annual Gathering and Festival, October 26, 1859.* Rochester, N.Y., 1859.

———. *An Address Delivered before the Junior Pioneer Association, October 25, 1859; Re-delivered Before Association and Citizens of Rochester at Corinthian Hall, December 12, 1859.* Rochester, N.Y., 1860.

———. *Geneseo Academy: Historical Sketch of Geneseo Academy.* Geneseo, N.Y., 1866.

———. *Why I Am an Old School Presbyterian.* Geneseo, N.Y., 1867.

———. *An Earnest Protest, Against the Sale and Use of Alcoholic Liquors, Except for Purely Medicinal Purposes: The Substance of a Funeral Address, Delivered in the Central Presbyterian Church, in Geneseo, March 21st, 1869.* Geneseo, N.Y., 1869.

———. *Village Memories of Twenty Years; or Geneseo Between 1848 and 1868: An Address*

Delivered in the Central Presbyterian Church, Geneseo, November 8, 1868. Geneseo, N.Y., 1869.

———. *Churches of Rochester: Ecclesiastical History of Rochester, New York, August 1815 to July 1871.* Rochester, N.Y., 1870.

———. *Lessons of Practical Instruction Drawn from the Life and Death of President Garfield.* Rochester, N.Y., 1881.

———. *Geneseo, Livingston County, N.Y., 1848–1888: An Historical Address by F. DeW. Ward D.D., A Forty Years Resident.* Geneseo, N.Y., 1889.

———. *Suggestive Scripture Questions: Sixty Questions with Expository and Practical Answers.* New York, 1890.

Ward, George K. *Andrew Warde and His Descendants, 1597–1910.* New York, 1920.

———. *Centennial of the Presbyterian Church, Dansville, N.Y.* Dansville, N.Y., 1925.

Ward, Roswell. *Henry A. Ward: Museum Builder to America.* Rochester, N.Y., 1948.

Ward, W. S. (William Shaw). *Pine Creek Mining District, Gilpin County, Colo.; A Descriptive Account of the New Gold Mining District of Pine Creek, Together with a Topographical Map Showing Location of Leading Mines and Prospects.* Denver, Colo., 1896.

Warren, Austin. *The Elder Henry James.* New York, 1934.

Warshaw, Robert Irving. *The Story of Wall Street.* New York, 1929.

Waterbury, Rev. Jared Bell. *Memoir of the Rev. John Scudder, M.D., Thirty-six Years a Missionary in India.* New York, 1870.

Watkins, T. H. *Gold and Silver in the West: The Illustrated History of an American Dream.* Palo Alto, Calif., 1971.

Weightman, Gavin. *The Frozen-Water Trade: A True Story.* New York, 2003.

Wendt, Lloyd. *The Wall Street Journal: The Story of Dow Jones and the Nation's Business Newspaper.* Chicago, 1982.

Wheeler, Richard. *History of the Town of Stonington.* Mystic, Conn., 1996.

Wilder Harriet. *A Century in the Madura Mission, South India, 1834–1934.* New York, 1961.

Winslow, Catherine. *Remains of Mrs. Catherine Winslow: A Member of the American Mission at Madras, India, Including a Journal and Letters.* Boston, 1851.

Winslow, Miron. *A Memoir of Mrs. H. W. Winslow Combining a Sketch of the Ceylon Mission.* New York, 1835.

Wise, J. S. *Recollections of Thirteen Presidents.* New York, 2007.

Woodbridge, William C., ed. *American Annals of Education and Instruction for the Year 1831*, vol. 1. Boston, 1832.

Woodward, William E. *Meet General Grant.* New York, 1928.

Woodworth, Steven E. *While God Is Marching On: The Religious World of Civil War Soldiers.* Lawrence, Kans., 2001.

Young, John Russell. *Around the World with General Grant: A Narrative of the Visit of General U.S. Grant, Ex-President of the United States, to Various Countries in Europe, Asia, and Africa, in 1877, 1878, 1879, to Which Are Added Certain Conversations with General Grant on Questions Connected with American Politics and History.* 2 vols. New York, 1879.

Zwiep, Mary. *Pilgrim Path: The First Company of Women Missionaries to Hawaii.* Madison, Wisc., 1991.

ARTICLES

Anonymous. "View of the Livingston County High-School, on Temple Hill, Geneseo: Under the Care of Seth Sweetser, C. C. Felton, and H. R. Cleveland." *Western Monthly Reviews* (June 1828).

———. "The Romance and Reality of American Railroads." *Quarterly Review* 158, no. 315 (July and October 1884).

Arnold, Paul B. "Helen Eshbaugh Ward, 1885–1876." *Oberlin Alumni Magazine* (March/April 1977).

Ash, Martha Montague. "The Social and Domestic Scene in Rochester, 1840–1860." *Rochester History* 18 (April 1956).

Badeau, Adam. "The Last Days of General Grant." *Century Magazine* 30, no. 6 (October 1885).

Bongiorno, Andrew. "Clarence Ward March 11, 1884–January 20, 1973. *Oberlin Alumni Magazine* (May/June 1973).

Camp, William. "The New York Clearing House." *North American Review* 205, no. 324 (March 1892).

Chernow, Ron. "Madoff and His Models." *New Yorker,* March 23, 2009.

Clarke, Mary A. "Memoir of J. M. Da Costa, M.D." *American Journal of the Medical Sciences* 125, no. 2 (February 1903).

Darrow, Mark V. Jr. "The Specimen Dealer: Entrepreneurial Natural History in America's Gilded Age." *Journal of the History of Biology* 33, no. 3 (winter 2000).

Garland, Hamlin. "A Romance of Wall Street." *McClure's Magazine* 10 (April 1898).

Hardy, Osgood. "Ulysses S. Grant, President of the Mexican Southern Railroad." *Pacific Historical Review* 24 (May 1955).

Hexter, George J. "Some of Our Best People." *North American Review* 248 (autumn 1939).

"H.H." (Helen Hunt Jackson). "To Leadville." *Atlantic Monthly* 43, no. 259 (May 1879).

Ingersoll, Ernest. "The Camp of the Carbonates." *Scribner's Monthly* 18, no. 6 (October 1879).

Judkins, Gabriel LaMar. "The Salt of the Earth: Warsaw, New York and Its Nineteenth Century Salt Industry." *Middle State Geographer* 34 (2001).

Julian, Ralph. "The City of Brooklyn." *Harper's New Monthly Magazine* 86 (April 1863).

Lanius, Judith H., and Sharon C. Park. "Martha Wadsworth's Mansion: The Gilded Age Comes to Dupont Circle." *Washington Monthly* 7, no. 1 (spring/summer 1995).

McKelvey, Blake. "Old and New Landmarks and Historic Houses." *Rochester History* 12 (April 1950).

———. "The Physical Growth of Rochester." *Rochester History* 13 (October 1951).

———. "The Historic Origins of Rochester's Museums." *Rochester History* 18 (October 1956).

———. "East Avenue's Turbulent History." *Rochester History* 28 (April and July 1966).

———. "Sesquicentennial of Rochester." *Rochester History* 29 (June 1967).

Mechen, Edgar C. "Brinton Terrace." *Colorado Magazine* 24, no. 3 (May 1947).

Moorhead, James H. "The 'Restless Spirit of Radicalism': Old School Fears and the Schism of 1837." *Journal of Presbyterian History* 78, no. 1 (spring 2000).

Naylor, Harriett Julia, ed. "And This Was Rochester! Excerpts from the Old Citizen Letters of Edwin Scranton." *Rochester History* 4 (January 1952).

Putnam, George Haven. "The Grand Jury of the County of New York: A Personal Experience." *Annals of the American Academy of Political and Social Science* 52 (March 1914).

Remsen, Jane. "Russell Sage: Yankee." *New England Quarterly* 11, no. 1 (March 1938).

Reynolds, Marc M. "Famous American Financiers and Contemporaneous Stock Exchange History." *Moody's Magazine* 8 (December 1909).

Robbins, Christine Chapman. "John Torrey (1796–1873), His Life and Times." *Bulletin of the Torrey Botanical Club* 95, no. 6 (November/December 1968).

Rohrbach, Col. John. "History of the Geneseo State Normal School." *Proceedings of the Twenty-first Annual Meeting of the Livingston County Historical Society Held at Geneseo, NY, January 19, 1897.* Nunda, 1897.

Rosenberg-Naparseck, Ruth. "Rochester's Pioneer Builders: Relinquishing the Reigns of Power." *Rochester History* 47 (July and October 1985).

Smith, Virginia Jeffrey. "Reminiscences of the Third Ward." *Rochester History* 8 (April 1956).

Stone, David. "Secrets and Lies: The Tragic Life and Mysterious Death of D'Oyly Carte Soprano Sallie Reber." *Sir Arthur Sullivan Magazine* 60 (spring 2005).

Ward, Andrew. "A Family Memoir by the Grandchildren of Helen E. Ward.". *Oberlin Alumni Magazine* (March/April 1977).

Ward, Ferdinand. "General Grant as I Knew Him." *New York Herald,* December 19, 1909.

———. "General Grant an Easy Prey for the Wolves of Finance." *New York Herald,* December 26, 1909.

———. "Marine Bank Cause of Crash." *New York Herald,* January 2, 1910.

———. "Grant Was the Only One to Give Aid." *New York Herald,* January 9, 1910.

———. "General Grant's Dinner to President Diaz." *New York Herald,* January 16, 1910.

Ward, Geoffrey C. "Two Missionaries' Ordeal by Faith in a Distant Clime." *Smithsonian* (August 1990).

Ward, W. S. (William Shaw). "The Koh-i-noor Diamond." *Appleton's Journal,* July 20, 1872.

———. "The New York Aquarium." *Appleton's Journal,* June 24, 1874.

———. "The Brighton Aquarium." *Appleton's Journal,* January 3, 1874.

———. "The Council-House of Canaeadea." *Appleton's Journal,* February 27, 1875.

———. "The New York Aquarium." *Scribner's Monthly,* 13, no. 5 (March 1877).

———. "How We Ran the Vicksburg Batteries." *Magazine of American History with Notes and Queries* 14 (July-December 1885), pp. 600–5.

Wheatly, Richard. "The New York Produce Exchange." *Harper's New Monthly Magazine* 73 (July 1886), pp. 189–218.

Woodward, C. Vann. "The Lowest Ebb." *American Heritage* 8, no. 3 (April 1957).

UNPUBLISHED MATERIALS

Audenreid, Sarah Brinton Wentz. *A Day at Fourteen-Twenty-Three (March 17th, 1888).* Jasper Yeates Brinton Collection.

Heim, Melisa Lewis. *Making a Life in India: American Missionary Households in Nineteenth-Century Madurai.* PhD dissertation. Ann Arbor, Mich., 1994.

Howard, Dorothy C. *Copies of Material on Missionaries to India in the 1830's—Especially Those Who Sailed Together from Boston to Madras in 1836 on the 'Saracen.'* Letters from Edward and Emily Cope, 1838–1840.

Raitt, James D. *The Champion House.* 1975.

Stewart, Elizabeth Hoisington. *Nancy Lyman, 1804–1878, Portrait of a Missionary.* 1985.

Stofko, Karl P. *Ella Champion Green and Her Beloved Champion House Hotel, or East Haddam and the Wall Street Panic of 1884.* 2007.

Wagner, Frederick B. Jr. *John Hill Brinton, M.D., Reconsidered.*

Ward, Andrew, ed. *So to Speak: Conversations with Frederick Champion Ward and Duira Baldinger Ward.* 1990.

Ward, Ferdinand De Wilton. *Diary—No. 1, Extending from January 9th, 1831 to September 20th, 1831.*
———. *Auto-Biography.*
———. *Auto-Biography No. 2.*
———. *Narrative Etc.*

INDEX

30–31
Livingston County Historical Society fundraiser: Livingston County
    Historical Society

32
Clarence Ward with children: Andrew Ward Collection

All other illustrations, including the frontispiece, are from the author's collection.

A NOTE ABOUT THE AUTHOR

Geoffrey C. Ward, former editor of *American Heritage* and writer of documentary films, is the author of fifteen books, including *The Civil War* (with Ken Burns and Ric Burns) and *A First Class Temperament: The Emergence of Franklin Roosevelt*, which won the 1989 National Book Critics Circle Award for biography and the 1990 Francis Parkman Prize and was a finalist for the Pulitzer Prize. He lives in New York City.

A NOTE ON THE TYPE

This book was set in Janson, a typeface thought to have been made by the Dutchman Anton Janson. It has been conclusively demonstrated that these types are actually the work of Nicholas Kis (1650–1702).

Composed by North Market Street Graphics, Lancaster, Pennsylvania

Printed and bound by Berryville Graphics, Berryville, Virginia

Designed by Maggie Hinders